Novel Strategies

Novel Strategies

A Guide to Effective College Reading

Chae Sweet
Passaic County Community College

PEARSON

Boston   Columbus   Indianapolis   New York   San Francisco   Upper Saddle River
Amsterdam   Cape Town   Dubai   London   Madrid   Milan   Munich   Paris   Montréal   Toronto
Delhi   Mexico City   São Paulo   Sydney   Hong Kong   Seoul   Singapore   Taipei   Tokyo

Editor-in-Chief, English: Eric Stano
Acquisition Editor: Nancy Blaine
Editorial Assistant: Jamie L. Fortner
Associate Managing Editor: Bayani Mendoza de Leon
Development Editor: Paul Sarkis
Marketing Manager: Kurt Massey
Senior Supplements Editor: Donna Campion
Executive Digital Producer: Stefanie Snajder
Digital Project Manager: Janell Lantana
Senior Digital Editor: Robert St. Laurent
Project Coordination, Text Design, and Electronic Page Makeup: Integra
Manufacturing Buyer: Mary Ann Gloriande
Senior Cover Design Manager/Cover Designer: Nancy Danahy
Cover Image: "Got Bookworms?" Oil Painting by Camille Engel (www.Camille-Engel.com)
Posters available upon request.

Lexile®, Lexile Framework®, Lexile Analyzer® and Lexile® logo are trademarks of
MetaMetriocs, Inc., and are registered in the United States and abroad. The trademarks
And names of other companies and productions mentioned herein are the property of their
Respective owners. Copyright © 2010 MetaMetrics, Inc. All rights reserved.

Library of Congress Cataloging-in-Publication Data on file

6 7 8 9   10 V092 16 15

www.pearsonhighered.com

ISBN-13: 978-0-205-77384-8
ISBN-10: 0-205-77384-2

Contents

PART 1 The Strategies   1

Chapter 1 Starting Strategies   2

Chapter 2 Active Reading Strategies   18

Chapter 5 Comprehension Strategies: Supporting Details 136

Chapter 6 Writing About Reading 171

PART 2 Short Readings   261

PART 3 The Reading Guide   397

Preface

The world of words is nothing like it used to be. Today, you can read a textbook or novel on your smartphone, on an e-reader, on your laptop, and in an old-fashioned book. Students of today are well versed in the many ways of encountering words and they are reading regularly – but in non-traditional mediums. Students read text messages, web pages, blogs, Facebook pages, and emails, to name a few. Basically, students read what directly relates to them and their interests. Their focus is highly localized. Necessarily then, more than ever, what students are taught in the classroom must be perceived as relevant – relevant to their lives in general and their academic lives specifically. *Novel Strategies: A Guide to Effective College Reading* addresses the issue of relevance by using a diverse mix of academic readings and literature, both fiction and non-fiction, with timely and relevant social and cultural themes to engage students, and thus create the context for discussions that foster deeper learning experiences. In other words, this textbook provides reading opportunities that nurture precisely the type of growth that is fundamental to effective critical reading and thinking – and the reading material is geared toward student engagement.

In some classrooms, instructors are already using literature to garner the interest of developmental readers. For the most part, book-length literature is often paired with one of the general-purpose developmental reading textbooks. This strategy can be successful. However, it also creates other problems: students struggle to stay engaged with a book-length work when they don't grasp the relevance; students struggle to decipher the ideas in literature using the strategies discussed in the textbook; and instructors scramble to collect innovative strategies for using literature that both engage the students and develop their critical reading abilities. *Novel Strategies: A Guide to Effective College Reading* addresses the needs of both groups – students and instructors – with a completely unique reading guide created for the college classroom. No other textbook offers both a guide to effective reading strategies and a reading guide for book-length texts of classic literature, current fiction, and engaging non-fiction.

DEVELOPING EFFECTIVE READERS

Developmental courses in reading are offered at both 2-year institutions and 4-year institutions. Within that group of institutions, more than 90% of 2-year public institutions offer a developmental reading course and over 45% of 4-year public institutions offer a developmental reading course. The teaching methods and curriculum mandates of the institutions vary; however, what is consistent across developmental education is the research that supports what is actually effective in the classroom. Some of the effective techniques, models, or structures that support effective learning are:

- having clearly specified goals and objectives;
- using mastery learning techniques;
- having a high degree of structure in the developmental classroom;
- employing varied approaches and methods in instruction of material;
- applying sound cognitive theory in the design and delivery of developmental courses;
- integrating critical thinking into the curriculum;
- having instructors who are supported by professional development.

The needs articulated by this list can be classified into two categories:

1. to provide students with sound strategies for reading and structured materials with which to do so; and
2. to provide instructors with the support needed to deliver the strategies and materials using the approaches and methods that work best in developmental courses.

DESIGN OF NOVEL STRATEGIES

Novel Strategies is intended to address the two aforementioned categorical needs. To do this, the textbook is divided into three sections:

Part One: The Strategies
Part Two: Short Readings
Part Three: The Reading Guide

Part One: The Strategies. Part One consists of eight chapters that provide students with sound strategies for reading and stimulating material with which to practice. *Novel Strategies* is intended for readers who are able to comprehend some of what they read, but they struggle to go beyond comprehension to higher level thinking and reading. These students often lack the experience of engaging with subjects for extended periods of time and especially resist doing so when the goal is not apparent. In response, Part One of *Novel Strategies* addresses students' desire for clear explanations and obtainable outcomes from the start. By first introducing reading strategies, such as activating prior knowledge and active reading which have proven success, and then broadening the application of those strategies to different reading contexts, students are always aware of the purpose and goal of the instruction.

At each phase of the reading process, students are challenged with insightful multiple choice and open-ended questions that require them to thoughtfully consider the subject. Additionally, since a majority of the questions in *Novel Strategies* are open-ended, (an annotated instructor's edition provides instructors with plenty of support) students begin to understand that knowledge is self-generated. Students will be encouraged by their ability to successfully engage the strategies as they progress through the chapters. Each of the chapters contains readings of varied length and type — textbook selections, short stories, personal essays, and articles — which are used to gauge students' comprehension and mastery of the strategies being discussed in the chapter.

Each chapter in Part One includes:

- **Strategy Quiz** – a reading selection (fiction or non-fiction) followed by a mix of multiple choice and open-ended questions that require application of the strategies from the chapter.
- **Key Term Review** – a review of important strategies and terms.
- **Strategies in Action** – two complete readings that allow students another opportunity to apply all the strategies that have been taught up to that point in the textbook.

Strategies in Action, the end-of-chapter reading selections, will appeal to diverse student populations, and it offers yet another chance for students to apply their newly acquired strategies. Having many opportunities to apply new strategies is especially important with students in developmental courses. Research has shown that these students are more likely to be visual learners or hands-on learners – meaning they need to both see how the strategies work and practice the strategies before real learning can take place.

A mixture of multiple choice questions, short answer questions, and other exercises that evaluate students on comprehensive, inferential, and interpretative levels will follow the *Strategies in Action* reading selections. Students will also have the opportunity, with each reading selection, to make connections and write about some aspect of the selection from their experience. These connective writing exercises will increase students' engagement, while broadening their comprehension of the material.

Part Two: Short Readings. Part Two will continue supporting students as they develop proficiency with the strategies and techniques they learned in Part One. In Part Two, students will read more complex, and longer selections from periodicals, story collections, newspapers, and textbooks than they encountered in Part One. After each reading, students will be challenged to respond to a variety of questions that require application of the strategies learned throughout Part One. To further maintain a connection with the ideas and themes already addressed, each of the selections in Part Two will have a thematic link to readings from Part One and the book-length works discussed in Part Three.

Part Three: The Reading Guide. Continuing on to the Reading Guide for book-length works, students will expand the scope of their engagement and continue using the strategies. The progression from excerpts and brief selections to complete short selections to book-length works will effectively create a bridge for students who are unsure about whether they will be able to "get" a "whole book." Not only will they be able to get it, they are likely to be riveted by the high interest book-length works selected.

As suggested earlier, *Novel Strategies* addresses the need for instructors to have the support needed to deliver strategies and materials, using the approaches and methods that work best in developmental courses. The Reading Guide for five book-length works is a completely unique element in the reading textbook arena. The intention is not that all five books be taught; rather, instructors will have the option to select the text(s) that best fits their course. The Reading Guide will offer practical methods and tools to progress through the selected books. As students read the longer works, themes and concepts that connect to other readings included in the textbook will create a sense of continuity. This continuity is created with the help of the readings in *Strategies in Action* in Part One and the short selections in Part Two. In essence, the readings in Part One and Two create the scaffolding that bridges to the longer works in the Reading Guide. This is an important strategy: today's students are more accustomed to short, purposeful reading (i.e. blogs, websites and emails), so transitioning to book-length texts can be a challenge without the proper structure.

With the *Novel Strategies'* Reading Guide, instructors will be able to refer students back to the strategies in Part One where direct instruction on, say, finding a main idea, can be referenced and used as they begin reading the longer works. Additionally, the Reading Guide has its own cadre of open-ended questions and topics for instructors to use as discussion topics, homework assignments, in-class writing, or as assessments of students' comprehension of the books. Opportunities for collaborative work are also integrated into the Reading Guide.

A NOVEL APPROACH

Students who use *Novel Strategies* have a textbook that offers them the practical, strategic guidance they need to become effective readers, and instructors have a textbook that offers classroom-tested tools and exercises to teach reading strategies and literature in a way that enhances and informs students' mastery of reading. *Novel Strategies: A Guide to Effective College Reading* is unique in the field. Not only will students receive the strategic instruction they need to become effective readers of academic and literary texts, but they will also be introduced to the wide-ranging utility and pleasure of reading the *world* through the *word*.

Book Specific Ancillary Materials

Annotated Instructor's Edition (0205774164). The AIE is an exact replica of the student text with answers provided on the write-in lines. The AIE also includes Lexile® measures—the most widely used reading metric in U.S. schools—providing valuable information about a student's reading ability and the complexity of text. It helps match students with reading resources and activities that are targeted to their ability level. Lexile measures indicate the reading levels of content in MyReadingLab and the longer selections in the Annotated Instructor's Editions of all Pearson's reading books. See the Annotated Instructor's Edition of *Novel Strategies* and the Instructor's Manual for more details.

Instructor's Manual and Test Bank (ISBN 0205774156). The manual features in-class activities, handouts, and exercises to accompany each chapter, as well as sample course outlines and other helpful resources for structuring and managing a developmental reading course. Available both in print and for download from the Instructor Resource Center.

MyTest Test Bank (ISBN 0205173136). Pearson MyTest is a powerful assessment generation program that helps instructors easily create and print quizzes, study guides, and exams. Select questions from the test bank to accompany *Novel Strategies* or from other developmental reading test banks; supplement them with your own questions. Save the finished test as a Word document or PDF or export it to WebCT or Blackboard. Available at www.pearsonmytest.com.

Answer Key (ISBN 020511654X). The Answer Key contains the solutions to the exercises in the student edition of the text. Available for download from the Instructor Resource Center.

MyReadingLab (www.myreadinglab.com). MyReadingLab is the first and only online learning system to diagnose both students' reading skills and reading levels. This remarkable program uses diagnostic testing, personalized practice and gradebook reports to allow instructors to measure student performance and help students gain control over their reading.

Penguin Titles. The five Penguin titles highlighted in Part Three of *Novel Strategies* can be purchased along with the text at a deep discount. Contact your local Pearson sales representative for details:

The Color of Water, by James McBride (ISBN 159448192X)

Narrative of the Life of Frederick Douglass, by Frederick Douglass (ISBN 013094484X)

Three Cups of Tea, by Greg Mortenson and David Oliver Relin (ISBN 0143038257)

The Kite Runner, by Khaled Hosseini (ISBN 0321477200)

Listening is an Act of Love, by Dave Isay (editor) (ISBN 0143114344)

Acknowledgments

The conception and completion of *Novel Strategies* is a story of collaboration. Without the insight, support, and wonderful ideas of so many, this text would not be what it is today. I am so thankful to everyone who has contributed in some way, but especially the students of Hudson County Community College in New Jersey. My students have always been the engine behind the work that I do, and this was unfailingly true in the crafting of this textbook.

My colleagues, near and far, are also due a big thank you. Many of you worked closely with me to refine the strategies and activities presented here. I am indebted to:

Christine Barrilleaux, Tallahassee Community College

Essie Childers, Blinn College-Bryan

Jan Eveler, El Paso Community college

Sharon R. D'Agastino, Hudson County Community College

Kathy Daily, Tulsa Community College

Allison DeVaney, El Camino College

Barbara S. Doyle, Arkansas State University

Margot Edlin, Queensborough Community College

Rachel Evans, St. Charles Community College

Maureen Gibson, Jefferson Community and Technical College

Dawn Graziani, Santa Fe College

Judy Harris, Lone Star College-Tomball

Angela Hebert, Hudson County Community College

Gina Henderson, Tallahassee Community College

Cathy Hunsicker, Dalton State College

Leah Jones, College of the Albemarle

Teresa Kozek, Housatonic Community College

Alison Kuehner, Ohlone College

Susan Booth Larson, Portland Community College

Ann Marshall, Weatherford College

Diane Masline, Santa Barbara City College

Karen O'Donnell, Finger Lakes Community College

Ann Palmer, Austin Community College

Dan Putscher, Pike's Peak Community College

Janaya Ross-Shaw, South Suburban College

Kari Schamberger, Wor-Wic Community College

Sheila Wiley, Santa Barbara City College

I'd also like to acknowledge the support and guidance of the Pearson team who have shepherded me from proposal to published manuscript: Craig Campanella, Kate Edwards, Eric Stano, Editor-in-Chief, Developmental Reading and Writing, Nancy Blaine, Senior Acquisitions Editor, and Jamie Fortner, Editorial Assistant. Each one of you has made this process just a little bit easier through your professionalism and wisdom.

Finally, I'd like to thank my personal cheerleaders. First and foremost is my dad, Warren Sweet, who sparked the flame that burns still. My sister, Summer Sweet-Jones, who has always been my staunchest supporter. My grandmother who has never let me forget who I am, and my friends who have always been there to celebrate with me – thank you all. And to my partner, Pol Keeley, who has been with me through everything that matters; for your support and love, I am eternally thankful.

About the Author

Chae Sweet (center) with her students (from left): Angela Lopez; Maylen Garcia; Megan Sanchez; Monique Porras; Jose Moreno; Anthony Mayer; Mehrukh Chachar; Francisco Rosario; Hannah Redwood; Qualyn Smith.

Chae Sweet is the Assistant Dean of Developmental Education at Passaic County Community College in Paterson, New Jersey. Prior to becoming an administrator, she was an Assistant Professor of English at Hudson County Community College where she taught for 10 years. She received her B.A. in English and Journalism from Rutgers University, her M.F.A. in Fiction from New School University, and is pursuing a doctorate in Developmental Education - Curriculum and Instructional Design at Grambling State University. An educator for over 12 years, Chae Sweet began her career teaching poetry and spoken word to New York City high school students and soon transferred her love of reading and writing to teaching essay writing at various colleges in the New York metro area.

Chae Sweet's career as an instructor of freshman composition and developmental reading and writing really took shape in the community college classrooms she taught in for the past decade. During that time, she helped hundreds of students learn successful reading strategies, and she shared the joy of reading to a multitude of new recruits. As a faculty leader at her college, Chae Sweet led workshops, coordinated the reading program, and developed and created curriculum. As well, she has been a writer for numerous Pearson Education publications over the past five years, and this year she is publishing her first reading textbook with Pearson Education, *Novel Strategies: A Guide to Effective College Reading*. Chae Sweet's passion for education and her belief in the power of the written word have fueled the writing of *Novel Strategies* and will hopefully be communicated to students and instructors alike.

Novel Strategies

PART 1 The Strategies

1 Starting Strategies

Learning Objectives

In this chapter you will:

- Understand reading history.
- Understand reading context.
- Identify external and internal motivations.

Language is the amber in which a thousand precious thoughts have been embedded and preserved.

—Trench

D o you remember the first time you traveled to a new world? I do. It all began when my dad came home one evening with a small bag tucked under his arm. As my brother and I danced around him, saying hello and spilling details from our school day, my dad knelt down to face us. I was eleven and thought my dad was the best thing since Saturday-morning cartoons. He smiled at us and reached into the bag. "Look at this," he said, pulling out two thin books. And so my journey began that evening when I read the first pages of Madeleine L'Engle's book *A Wind in the Door*. It was my first journey with a book, but certainly not my last.

Do you remember the first book you read on your own? Was it a comic book or a story of fantasy? Was it a mystery? Maybe you remember your first experience as vividly as I do, maybe not. Either way, something probably came to mind for you. And this is exactly the point. Whether you remember listening sleepily to your mom as she read you a bedtime story, lying on your stomach and paging through the Sunday comics, or staying up beyond your bedtime as you devoured the latest Harry Potter book, reading often has an amber-preserved place in our minds. Words on a page have an amazing ability to transport the reader to worlds previously unknown. As we grow older and begin to read for academic success, we sometimes forget the minor miracle of books, of language. Imagine what could be possible if you kept in mind the idea of reading as a journey when you open a textbook.

Thinking of reading as a journey could mean that even a textbook has a final destination, an objective more exciting than just a good grade in a class—although a good grade isn't a bad objective at all. Viewing reading as a journey means remembering how worlds are created by language. Both known and unknown worlds are created by language. Consider this: your daily experience is structured by language. What you see, you describe. What you feel, you name. What you do, you announce. What you experience, you ponder. All of this is done by using words, either by thinking or by speaking. This means that the first journey you take each day always begins when you open your eyes in the morning. You read every moment of your waking day because the world is made real through words. This may

seem crazy to think about, but it also can give you some relief: reading is not a big deal; it's something you do every day. And it's also something you can do better.

Becoming a better, more effective reader gives you the chance to understand the world even more clearly than you do now. Becoming a better, more effective reader will also prepare you to understand the new world of the college classroom. And that's a great thing. So, consider how a few handy strategies can be the magnifying glass that brings the world of "a thousand precious thoughts" into closer view.

THE IMPORTANCE OF CONTEXT

The first step toward developing strategies for reading is to develop an understanding of context. **Context**, as it will be used within these pages, simply means *the situation that surrounds something*. Everything that a person does in life occurs within a context. For example: a young woman enters a clothing store looking for an outfit to wear to a dinner date. The dinner date is her context for shopping. She will select an outfit based on the needs shaped by that particular context. A million examples of context could be discussed, but the focus here is on the context that shapes, or influences, reading. This is called the **reading context**. Whenever you pick up a book, there's a purpose guiding you. That's the reading context.

The Reading Context

For many people, the reading context is generated externally, or by outside circumstances. An external reading context, or motivation, is one that is given to you or defined by someone or some situation beyond your control. For example, if your history professor assigns three chapters, that is an **external motivation** to read. When you go home or to the library, you will read those three chapters because they have been assigned. Of course, there is nothing wrong with having an assignment and doing it. But it doesn't feel very *empowering*—it doesn't feel like something you *want* to do. Understanding the importance of context means that you can take control of the experience and provide yourself with a context, an internal context, that supports you, even motivates you. An internal context is one that comes from within; you define what it is and why you want it. An internal context is also completely within your control, and no one can change it or take it away from you. Context, then, is very much like motivation, or a reason. Some motivations, like seeking knowledge, are internal; others, like winning your boss's respect, are external. Your reading context is composed of your internal and external motivations for reading as well as other factors. Figure 1.1 offers a view of how these factors interrelate.

Let's look more closely at how internally generated and externally generated contexts work. Consider again the assignment given by the history professor. The external context for reading is that your history professor assigned the three chapters. But why else could you be reading the chapters? Why are you taking a history class at all? Take a moment to think of a few reasons why you might register for a history course (examples are provided).

It's required for my major.

I'm curious about the past. I could learn something really cool.

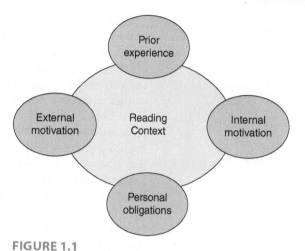

FIGURE 1.1

_____

_____

_____

Which of the reasons you gave would motivate you to do well in a history course? Were any reasons part of your longer journey, your bigger picture? If one of your reasons for taking a history course was something like, "to gain knowledge that will help me in my career," then you've got an external motivation. On the other hand, the reason that states, "I'm curious about the past" is an example of an **internal motivation.** The curiosity is generated from within and will create interest in the course that is separate from whether or not it is a requirement for a major. Internal and external contexts thus impact the way you approach a situation, and having a combination of both types is a good way to approach any circumstance.

Internal and External Motivations

Internal Motivation: a desire or drive that inspires from within and is controlled by the individual.

External Motivation: a desire or drive that occurs outside the individual or has its focus on the attainment of something external. The external motivation may function as a reward or goal but is not controlled by the individual.

Continuing with the idea of context, a major step in understanding the importance of defining your own reading context is seeing how you can view a situation in a way that fits your plans and goals. It may seem surprising that a long-term goal has something to do with reading chapters in a book. However, your long-term goals are as much a part of your reading context as the fact that you will have a quiz on the chapters during the next class. Here's why reading context is important: unless you are reading for pleasure, you are reading for a purpose. (Actually, even pleasurable reading has a purpose: enjoyment.) So, reading done in the context of the college classroom always has a purpose. Sometimes, just knowing you have a test or that the professor assigned the material is enough of a purpose to motivate you. For some students, however, that's not enough. This is when the long-term goal comes in. If you can remind yourself that this small task, reading, is one tiny step toward your ultimate destination, a night's reading assignment can take on more relevance and be accomplished with greater focus. Now, your reading context becomes not just why you are reading, but also how you motivate yourself to read.

Understanding Your Context

1. What particular challenges do you need to overcome as you seek to improve your reading effectiveness? Explain why those challenges are important to deal with now.

   _____

   _____

   _____

   _____

2. What reasons/motivations do you have to become a more effective reader? List your reasons/motivations in the chart below and divide them between internal and external reasons. *If you have listed only internal reasons or only external reasons, keep thinking about the question until you have at least one reason or motivation in each column.*

Internal Motivations	External Motivations
1.	1.
2.	2.
3.	3.
4.	4.
5.	5.

3. Based on the list you created, are you more externally or internally moti-
    vated? Do you think this type of motivation has affected how you approach
    reading and education in general?

    _____

    _____

    _____

    _____

The Reading Material

Now that we've considered your reading context, there's another context
to explore: that of the actual **reading material**. Reading material is simply whatever it is you are reading—a novel, a newspaper, a textbook, or
a bus schedule. All reading material has its own story. Just as you have
your story, and Marc who sits in the last row of the class has his story, all
reading materials have a story, too. The story is basically the context of the
reading material, *the situation that surrounds it*. For example, a novel has
a different context than a history book does. Different situations exist for
the writing and reading of a novel than exist for those of a history book.
Thus, based on the differing contexts of the reading material, you will
assume and expect different things. In a novel, you expect to read about
characters who do something. In a history book, you assume that you will
learn about important events. Considering this context will give you a position from which you can better predict what will happen after you turn
the first page.

For example, you have a book titled *Novel Strategies* open in front of
you. You may have gathered that this book's story is to share concepts or
strategies about reading. Now look at the back cover. Turn to the table
of contents. Scan the material in the opening pages of this book. Based
on your examination, what can you anticipate about this book? List your
ideas on the lines below.

1. _____

2. _____

3. _____

The actions you just took to examine this book are called previewing. Previewing will be covered in more detail in Chapter 2, but for now,
just understand that previewing reading material lets you know what to
expect. Ideally, previewing will also ease the stress or anxiety of a new

reading experience. Remember, reading is taking a journey to a new place. When people plan to travel, they look at maps, they research important stops along the way, and they try to plan the best way to enjoy their stay in the new place. If you approach reading material in that same way, you'll probably find that navigating the unique experience each new book brings is much easier. So, previewing allows you to determine the context of a book—and anything else you may read, too.

The chart below is a brief overview of different reading materials. Keeping in mind the basic contexts of certain types of reading materials can give you a head start when previewing.

Reading Material	Writing Style	Purpose
textbook	academic	instruct
short story	literary	entertain
newspaper	expository	inform
novel	literary	entertain
scholarly journal	academic/scholarly	inform/instruct
magazine	expository	entertain/inform
memoir	expository/literary	inform/entertain
blog	expository/personal	inform/entertain
online news report	expository	inform
personal web page	expository/personal	entertain/inform

KEY TERM REVIEW

Using the chapter as your reference, review the key terms noted below. The term is given to you, but you must match it with the appropriate definition.

1. Context _e_ a) the text that is being read, such as a book or magazine

2. Reading context _c_ b) the desire or drive that inspires from within and is controlled by the individual

3. Internal motivation _b_ c) the purpose guiding a person when he/she begins to read

4. External motivation _d_ d) the desire or drive that functions as a reward or goal but is not controlled by the individual

5. Reading material _a_ e) the situation that surrounds something

STRATEGIES IN ACTION

In the beginning of this chapter, you read that reading can be an opening into a new world. A young Native American boy encountered this for himself when he opened a Superman comic book at age three. Read about Sherman Alexie's encounter with the world of words, and then think about the ways in which his reading context and the reading material he chose affected his life.

Superman and Me

By Sherman Alexie

Sherman J. Alexie, Jr. (1966–) is a Spokane/Coeur d'Alene Indian. He grew up on the Spokane Indian Reservation in Wellpinit, Washington, about 50 miles northwest of Spokane, Washington. Approximately 1,100 Spokane Tribal members live there.

Born hydrocephalic, meaning with water on the brain, Alexie underwent a brain operation at the age of six months and was not expected to survive. When he did beat the odds, doctors predicted he would live with severe mental retardation. Though he showed no signs of this, he did suffer severe side effects, such as seizures, throughout his childhood. In spite of all he had to overcome, Alexie learned to read by age three, and was devouring novels, such as John Steinbeck's *The Grapes of Wrath*, by age five. All these things ostracized him from his peers, though, and he was often the brunt of other kids' jokes on the reservation.

I learned to read with a Superman comic book. Simple enough, I suppose. I cannot recall which particular Superman comic book I read, nor can I remember which villain he fought in that issue. I cannot remember the plot, nor the means by which I obtained the comic book. What I can remember is this: I was 3 years old, a Spokane Indian boy living with his family on the Spokane Indian Reservation in eastern Washington state. We were poor by most standards, but one of my parents usually managed to find some minimum-wage job or another, which made us middle-class by reservation standards. I had a brother and three sisters. We lived on a combination of irregular paychecks, hope, fear and government surplus food.

My father, who is one of the few Indians who went to Catholic school on purpose, was an avid reader of westerns, spy thrillers, murder mysteries, gangster epics, basketball player biographies and anything else he could find. He bought his books by the pound at Dutch's Pawn Shop, Goodwill, Salvation Army and Value Village. When he had extra money, he bought new novels at supermarkets, convenience stores and hospital gift shops. Our house was filled with books. They were stacked in crazy piles in the bathroom, bedrooms and living room. In a fit of unemployment-inspired creative energy, my father built a set of bookshelves and soon filled them with a random assortment of books about the Kennedy assassination, Watergate, the Vietnam War and the entire 23-book series of the Apache westerns. My father loved books, and since I loved my father with an aching devotion, I decided to love books as well.

I can remember picking up my father's books before I could read. The words themselves were mostly foreign, but I still remember the exact moment when I first understood, with a sudden clarity, the purpose of a paragraph. I didn't have the vocabulary to say "paragraph," but I realized that a paragraph was a fence that held words. The words inside a paragraph worked together for a common purpose. They had some specific reason for being inside the same fence. This knowledge delighted me. I began to think of everything in terms of paragraphs. Our reservation was a small paragraph within the United States. My family's house was a paragraph, distinct from the other paragraphs of the LeBrets to the north, the Fords to our south and the Tribal School to the west. Inside our house, each family member existed as a separate paragraph but still had genetics and common experiences to link us. Now, using this logic, I can see my changed family as an essay of seven paragraphs: mother, father, older brother, the deceased sister, my younger twin sisters and our adopted little brother.

At the same time I was seeing the world in paragraphs, I also picked up that Superman comic book. Each panel, complete with picture, dialogue and narrative was a three-dimensional paragraph. In one panel, Superman breaks through a door. His suit is red, blue and yellow. The brown door shatters into many pieces. I look at the narrative above the picture. I cannot read the words, but I assume it tells me that "Superman is breaking down the door." Aloud, I pretend to read the words and say, "Superman is breaking down the door." Words, dialogue, also float out of Superman's mouth. Because he is breaking down the door, I assume he says, "I am breaking down the door." Once again, I pretend to read the words and say aloud, "I am breaking down the door" In this way, I learned to read.

This might be an interesting story all by itself. A little Indian boy teaches himself to read at an early age and advances quickly. He reads "Grapes of Wrath" in kindergarten when other children are struggling through "Dick and Jane." If he'd been anything but an Indian boy living on the reservation, he might have been called a prodigy. But he is an Indian boy living on the reservation and is simply an oddity.

He grows into a man who often speaks of his childhood in the third-person, as if it will somehow dull the pain and make him sound more modest about his talents.

A smart Indian is a dangerous person, widely feared and ridiculed by Indians and non-Indians alike. I fought with my classmates on a daily basis. They wanted me to stay quiet when the non-Indian teacher asked for answers, for volunteers, for help. We were Indian children who were expected to be stupid. Most lived up to those expectations inside the classroom but subverted them on the outside. They struggled with basic reading in school but could remember how to sing a few dozen powwow songs. They were monosyllabic in front of their non-Indian teachers but could tell complicated stories and jokes at the dinner table. They submissively ducked their heads when confronted by a non-Indian adult but would slug it out with the Indian bully who was 10 years older. As Indian children, we were expected to fail in the non-Indian world. Those who failed were ceremonially accepted by other Indians and appropriately pitied by non-Indians.

I refused to fail. I was smart. I was arrogant. I was lucky. I read books late into the night, until I could barely keep my eyes open. I read books at recess, then during lunch, and in the few minutes left after I had finished my classroom assignments. I read books in the car when my family traveled to powwows or basketball games. In shopping malls, I ran to the bookstores and read bits and pieces of as many books as I could. I read the books my father brought home from the pawnshops and secondhand. I read the books I borrowed from the library. I read the backs of cereal boxes. I read the newspaper. I read the bulletins posted on the walls of the school, the clinic, the tribal offices, the post office. I read junk mail. I read auto-repair manuals. I read magazines. I read anything that had words and paragraphs. I read with equal parts joy and desperation. I loved those books, but I also knew that love had only one purpose. I was trying to save my life.

Despite all the books I read, I am still surprised I became a writer. I was going to be a pediatrician. These days, I write novels, short stories, and poems. I visit schools and teach creative writing to Indian kids. In all my years in the reservation school system, I was never taught how to write poetry, short stories or novels. I was certainly never taught that Indians wrote poetry, short stories and novels. Writing was something beyond Indians. I cannot recall a single time that a guest teacher visited the reservation. There must have been visiting teachers. Who were they? Where are they now? Do they exist? I visit the schools as often as possible. The Indian kids crowd the classroom. Many are writing their own poems, short stories and novels. They have read my books. They have read many other books. They look at me with bright eyes and arrogant wonder. They are trying to save their lives. Then there are the sullen and already defeated Indian kids who sit in the back rows and ignore me with theatrical precision. The pages of their notebooks are empty. They carry neither pencil nor pen. They stare out the window. They refuse and resist. "Books," I say to them. "Books," I say. I throw my weight against their locked doors. The door holds. I am smart. I am arrogant. I am lucky. I am trying to save our lives.

***

Understanding Context

1. What particular circumstances influenced Alexie to open his first "book"?

    Alexie wanted to defy the expectation of Natives.

2. Was Alexie externally or internally motivated as a young boy? How do you know? *Alexie was mostly internally motivated due to his inspirations from his father and literature that he obtained.*

3. How did Alexie's reading habit affect his social and academic life as a young boy? Use details from the essay to support your response.

    Alexie excelled at reading but was disliked by fellow Native students because of his goals to succeed.

Vocabulary in Context

Locate the numbered words used in "Superman and Me" and match the word to the appropriate definition in the second column. *Note: Some definitions will not be used.*

1. ostracize   *j*

2. villain   *d*

3. surplus   *F*

4. avid   *H*

5. clarity   *K*

6. prodigy   *l*

7. oddity   *m*

8. subvert   *C*

a) to hit with a bat

b) to fight

c) challenge

d) a wicked person; the person who fights the hero

e) cheap

f) extra

g) brief; using one-syllable words

h) eager

9. monosyllabic   *g*   i) an overweight person

10. slug it out   *b*   j) exclude

k) clearness

l) genius

m) a strange person or thing

n) a green vegetable grown in the ground

STRATEGIES IN ACTION

One of the ways to improve your achievements as a student is to understand how you learn. If you know your preferred method of learning, you can adapt various learning environments and make them work for you. This selection offers you a place to start as you determine what it will take for you to succeed in the college classroom.

Learning Styles: Different Strokes for Different Folks

by Saundra Ciccarelli and Noland White

from the textbook *Psychology: An Exploration*

Life would be so much easier, if everyone learned new information in exactly the same way. Teachers would know exactly how to present material so that all students would have an equal opportunity to learn. Unfortunately, that just is not the way it works—people are different in many ways, and one of the ways they differ is in the style of learning that works best for each person.

What exactly is a **learning style**? In general, a learning style is the particular way in which a person takes in information (Dunn et al., 1989, 2001; Felder, 1993, 1996; Felder & Spurlin, 2005). People take in information in several ways: through the eyes, by reading text or looking at charts, diagrams, and maps; through the ears, by listening, talking things out, and discussing things with others; and through the sense of touch and the movement of the body, by touching things, writing things down, drawing pictures and diagrams, and learning by doing (Barsch, 1996).

Types of Learning Styles

Learning styles are often classified based on personality theories or theories of intelligence. The number of different learning styles varies with the theory, but most theories of learning styles include **visual learners**, who learn best by seeing, reading, and looking at images; **auditory learners**, who learn best by hearing and saying things out loud; **tactile learners**, who need to touch things; **kinesthetic learners**, who prefer to learn by doing and being active; and **social learners**, who prefer to learn with other people or in groups (Dunn et al., 1989). Most people will find that they have one dominant, or most powerful, learning style along with one or two secondary styles. Notice that several of the learning styles described would work well together: Auditory learners and social learners, for example, work well together, as do tactile and kinesthetic learners, because they are both hands-on kinds of learners. Many theories simply divide people into four basic styles of learning (Barsch, 1996; Dunn et al., 1989; Jester, 2000):

- **Visual/Verbal.** These people learn best when looking at material, particularly things that are written down. Reading the textbook, using classroom notes, and having an instructor who uses overhead projections, writes on the board, or uses visual multimedia presentations are very helpful. Visual/verbal learners, because they focus on reading and taking notes, tend to learn best when studying alone rather than in a group.

- **Visual/Nonverbal.** These visual learners learn best through the use of diagrams, pictures, charts, videos, and other image-oriented material rather than printed text. This type of learner, like the visual/verbal learner, also prefers to study alone.

- **Auditory/Verbal.** Auditory/verbal learners take in information best by listening. Group discussions and a lecture format

in which the instructor talks about the subject are of the most benefit to this style of learning.

- **Tactile/Kinesthetic.** This style of learner needs a "hands-on" opportunity to learn. Lab classes are very good ways for this type of learner to absorb material. Instructors who do lots of demonstrations and use field experiences outside of the classroom are good for this style of learner. Some kinesthetic learners benefit from writing notes during a lecture or from writing a summary of their lecture notes afterward.

Notice that the social aspect of learning (studying alone or with others) is included as a part of the description of these four styles. Students who know their learning style can adapt their study habits and note-taking to methods that work best for that style.

Finding out one's style is accomplished by taking a simple test. There are a number of online assessments for learning styles, or your college's career center may have tests available. Here are a few online assessment sites:

- The Barsch Learning Style Inventory (Barsch, 1996): http://www.wou.edu/provost/aalc/learning/learning_styles.php

- The DVC Learning Style Survey for College (Jester, 2000): www.metamath.com/lsweb/dvclearn.htm

- The VARK Questionnaire (Fleming & Mills, 1992): www.vark-learn.com/English/page.asp?p=questionnaire

Learning Styles and Learning

Does knowing one's learning style really help improve learning? The research findings have produced mixed results thus far, with some finding support for the idea that matching learning styles to teaching styles produces improvement (Braio et al., 1997; Drysdale et al., 2001; Dunn et al., 1986, 1995; Ford & Chen, 2001), but a large survey of the research in this field found little consistent support (Coffield et al., 2004).

From the teacher's point of view, learning styles present a very practical problem. Instructors must teach to the most common level of understanding and may not be able to easily teach for multiple learning styles. The typical instructor may not have a lot of classroom time to do demonstrations, write things on the board, or spend time in discussions, for example. For a student, however, knowing one's learning style can have an impact on note-taking, studying, and reading the textbook.

Table 1 presents some study tips for visual, auditory, and tactile/kinesthetic learners. All of the techniques listed in this table

Table 1. Study Tips for Different Learning Styles

Visual/Verbal	Visual/Nonverbal	Auditory	Tactile/Kinesthetic
Use different colors of highlighter for different sections of information in text or notes.	Make flash cards with pictures or diagrams to aid recall of key concepts.	Join or form a study group or find a study partner so that you can discuss concepts and ideas.	Sit near the front of the classroom and take notes by jotting down key terms and making pictures or charts to help you remember what you are hearing.
Use flash cards of main points or key terms.	Make charts and diagrams and sum up information in tablets.	Talk out loud while studying or into a tape recorder that you can play back later.	When you study, read information out loud while walking back and forth.
Write out key information in whole sentences or phrases in your own words.	Use different highlighter colors for different information but do symbols and diagrams as well as key terms and ideas.	Make speeches.	Study with a friend.
When looking at diagrams, write out a description.		Tape the lectures (with permission). Take notes on the lecture sparingly, using the tape to fill in parts that you might have missed.	While exercising, listen to tapes that you have made containing important information.
Use "sticky" notes to remind yourself of key terms and information, and put them in the notebook or text or on a mirror that you use frequently.	Visualize charts, diagrams, and figures. Redraw things from memory. Study alone in a quiet place.	Read notes or text material into a tape recorder or get study materials on tape and play back while driving or doing other chores.	Write out key concepts on a large board or poster. Make flash cards, using different colors and diagrams, and lay them out on a large surface. Practice putting them in order.
Visualize spellings of words or facts to be remembered.		When learning something new, state the information in your own words out loud or to a study partner.	Make a three-dimensional model.
Rewrite things from memory. Study alone in a quiet place.			Spend extra time in the lab. Go to outside areas such as a museum or historical site to gain information. Trace letters and words to remember key facts. Use musical rhythms as memory aids, putting information to a rhyme or a tune.

are good for students who wish to improve both their understanding of a subject and their grades on tests.

Notice that all four of the learning styles make use of some similar methods but in different ways. For example, drawing graphs, charts, and diagrams is a good technique for the visual/nonverbal and the tactile/kinesthetic learners, and both types of visual learners tend to do better when studying alone to improve concentration, whereas both the auditory and the tactile/kinesthetic learners benefit from studying with others and "talking it out."

No matter what the learning style, students must read the textbook to be successful in the course.

Technology Tip

1. How do you learn best? Use one of the suggested learning style websites provided below to determine your learning style. Write your preferred learning style here.

_____

The Barsch Learning Style Inventory (Barsch, 1996): http://www.wou.edu /provost/aalc/learning/learning_styles.php

The DVC Learning Style Survey for College (Jester, 2000): www.metamath .com/lsweb/dvclearn.htm

The VARK Questionnaire (Fleming & Mills, 1992):www.vark-learn.com /English/page.asp?p=questionnaire

Understanding Context

2. Review the study tips and strategies given for the four learning styles in Table 1. Now that you know your dominant learning style, which three study tips or strategies can you apply to successfully navigate the challenges you face as a reader and a learner?

_____

_____

_____

_____

Vocabulary in Context

*Match the key terms from "Learning Styles: Different Strokes for Different Folks"
with the appropriate definition.*

1. learning style   _____

2. visual learners   _____

3. auditory learners   _____

4. tactile learners   _____

5. kinesthetic learners   _____

6. social learners   _____

a) people who prefer to learn by doing and being active

b) people who learn best by hearing and saying things aloud

c) people who need to touch objects in order to learn about them

d) the particular way in which a person takes in information

e) people who prefer to learn with other people or in groups

f) people who learn best by seeing, reading, and looking at images

Getting the Point

1. _____ Which type of learner would benefit *most* from a lecture format?
   a) visual/verbal
   b) tactile/kinesthetic
   c) auditory/verbal
   d) visual/nonverbal

2. _____ Which type of learner would benefit *most* from seeing diagrams and charts during class or while reading?
   a) visual/verbal
   b) tactile/kinesthetic
   c) auditory/verbal
   d) visual/nonverbal

3. _____ Which type of learner would benefit *most* from learning in a group or with another person?
   a) visual/verbal
   b) sensory/nonverbal
   c) tactile/kinesthetic
   d) visual/nonverbal

4. _____ Your dominant learning style is the only way you can learn effectively.
   a) True
   b) False

5. _____ It is the professor's responsibility to adjust teaching methods so that students can learn through their preferred learning style.
   a) True
   b) False

For support in meeting this chapter's objectives, go to
MyReadingLab and select **Reading Skills Diagnostic Pre-Test.**

2 Active Reading Strategies

Learning Objectives

In this chapter you will:

- Understand the purposes of active reading strategies.
- Apply textbook active reading strategies.
- Apply literature active reading strategies.
- Demonstrate appropriate use of annotation.

Reading furnishes the mind only with materials of knowledge; it is thinking that makes what we read ours.

—John Locke

Under the umbrella of active reading strategies are two sets of practices: pre-reading strategies and active reading strategies. Pre-reading strategies are actions that you take to prepare yourself for the reading experience you will have. Pre-reading is similar to what you do before you go on a vacation: you look at the city on a map, check out a few websites, think about what you will pack, and make a note about what you will do while there. All this makes sense when you are going somewhere that you've never been before. The same holds true for reading a new book—you've never read the material before, so you need to check it out. Active reading, on the other hand, involves actions you take while reading to aid and enhance your comprehension of ideas. Active reading is especially important in college because so much of the material you will learn will be shared through textbooks and other written formats.

As discussed in Chapter 1, there are many different types of reading material. You could have a psychology textbook, a novel, and a memoir of a famous actor sitting on your desk. You might think, reading is reading; however, this is not the case. You need to read each one of these books with a specific purpose in mind and using specific strategies. Also, you pre-read and read these books with a specific set of strategies. While there will be some similarities in both the reading and the pre-reading strategies you undertake for each type of book, each book will also need particular strategies based on its content. This chapter is designed to provide the strategies you will need to begin any reading material you might encounter in the college classroom and beyond.

Here's what will be covered in Chapter 2:

Textbook Active Reading Strategies
- SQ3R—Survey, Question, Read, Recite, Review

Literature Active Reading Strategies
- Previewing
- Background Check
- Making Connections
- Predicting

Universal Active Reading Strategy
- Annotation

TEXTBOOK ACTIVE READING STRATEGIES

Reading a textbook is unique in the realm of book reading. While understanding what you read is always necessary when reading a book, the methods you use to accomplish your purpose in textbook reading are unique. Unlike other books that may have a variety of reading purposes once they are sold to the public, textbooks are *written to instruct* and are *read to learn.* Given that, turning to the first page of a textbook carries different expectations than does turning to the first page of a novel. What follows is an overview of a time-honored strategy for purposeful textbook reading.

SQ3R—Survey, Question, Read, Recite, and Review

In the late 1940s, many young men and women were entering college. World War II had just ended, and higher education seemed the perfect way to prepare former soldiers for the world they needed to re-enter. It became clear very quickly that some of these new students needed assistance to succeed. Francis P. Robinson wrote a book called *Effective Study* that launched the use of a popular textbook-reading strategy called SQ3R. Today, SQ3R is still popular, and the method maintains its usefulness for students seeking strategies to aid in their college success.

A good place to begin is with an overview of the entire process. The chart that follows outlines each step; an exploration of each individual step is provided shortly after.

Survey	Preview the material by looking at elements such as the introduction, title, headings, subheadings, boldfaced and italicized items, and graphics.
Question	Develop questions based on your survey that you will answer as you read.
Read	Read the material, answering and adding questions as you proceed.
Recite	After reading each section or chapter, verify that you wrote down the key ideas and definitions.
Review	After you've completed all the previous steps, go back and review the questions and answers you wrote down. Test your recall of the key ideas and definitions.

The acronym "SQ3R" is a way to remember the Survey, Question, Read, Recite, and Review method. Most students find it helpful to think of "SQ3R" as a way to quickly refer to the five-step strategy.

Survey.   Surveying is the first step in the process and is what you do when you preview. **Surveying** is looking over, or scrutinizing, the material. Surveying includes five steps.

- **Read Introductions**—often authors will preface a chapter or a section with an introduction to the material. This introduction can be very helpful in providing the context for what you will read.

- **Read Titles**—the title of a chapter or section is a key to the central point. The title often points you toward what will be the most important information.
- **Read Headings**—reading the headings and subheadings further breaks down the material. These headings and subheadings will likely be key supporting points.
- **Find Boldfaced/Italicized Words**—these boldfaced or italicized words are generally important definitions or key ideas. Just noticing boldfaced or italicized words can help prepare your mind to understand the words when you encounter them during the actual reading. You can also use these key words in the next step, when you develop questions.
- **Review Graphics**—graphics like charts, graphs, pictures, and illustrations can also be helpful in getting a sense of the material. The old saying about a picture being worth a thousand words is just as true when the picture appears in a textbook.

Question.   Creating **questions** is the second step in the SQ3R method. **Questioning** allows you to set goals for your reading experience. Remember the discussion about setting your own context in Chapter 1? Well, developing questions before you read is one way of creating a context. When you create questions, you give your mind something to look for as you read. This creates a more focused, intentional reading experience.

The questioning process begins after you survey and continues throughout the remainder of the SQ3R process. It is helpful to write questions on a piece of paper and leave space to write in the answers as you discover them. One method for doing so is to fold a piece of paper in half, lengthwise, and write the questions on the left side and the answers on the right side. The questions you write should be focused on the information you discovered in the survey stage. One way to generate questions is by using the five Ws plus one H, which are who, what, where, when, why, and how. Creating questions with these words in mind can help you turn headings and subheadings into questions.

> **The Folded Paper Method**
>
> Fold a piece of paper in half, lengthwise, and write the questions on the left side and the answers on the right side.

Figure 2.1 is an illustration of how you might create questions using the items you surveyed (Introductions, Titles, Headings, Subheadings, Boldfaced/Italicized Words, and Graphics).

Read.   Now you've come to the fun part. Reading is the meat of the matter, the featured selection, the main character in this play. Reading is what everything else is meant to support and falls directly in the middle of the SQ3R process. What is different about reading with the SQ3R method is

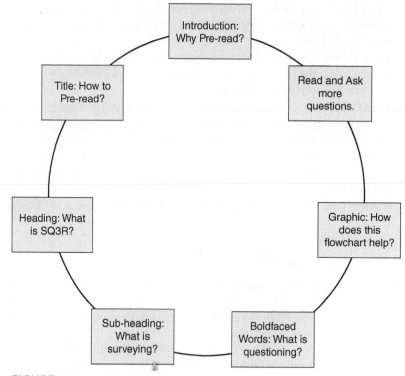

FIGURE 2.1

that you read in stages. For example, if you are reading this chapter using the SQ3R method, you would read the section on surveying, answer the question(s) you wrote about surveying, and then proceed to the next section on questioning, where you would repeat this process. When you are reading lengthy or complex material, it is helpful to read in sections or blocks. Taking short breaks or stretching between sections is also useful.

Using the SQ3R method, you read and consider what you are reading. This is a focused and intentional way to go about reading a textbook chapter. And that's exactly the reason this method is offered as a strategy.

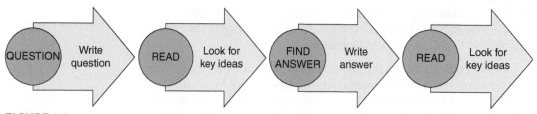

FIGURE 2.2

Recite.   Once you have finished reading the chapter or sections, you are ready to check your questions and answers. Reciting can take several shapes. You can literally recite, or speak, your questions and answers. This is helpful for learners who need to hear material. You can also reread your questions and answers silently. Whichever method you use is fine; the key is to look for accuracy and completeness in your questions and answers. Since your questions and answers are written, you can compare your notes with the text to see if you have everything you need to understand the material.

During the recite stage, ask yourself:

- Did I capture all key ideas?
- Did I exclude minor details and examples?
- Did I add questions when necessary?
- Did I answer all my questions?

Review.   The review stage is the final step of the SQ3R method. It is also where you ensure that you have learned the material. Some people confuse the Recite and the Review stages. The recite stage is really meant to be where you "check your citation." In other words, when you recite, you verify, either orally or silently, what you wrote. On the other hand, the **review** stage is when you reinforce what you read by checking your recall of key ideas and definitions. If you used the folded paper method of writing questions, you can cover the answers on the right side as you read the questions on the left. The purpose of doing so is to test your recall of the key ideas, so continue the review until you feel you have learned the material.

Use the SQ3R process to guide you through the textbook selection "Technology, Transportation, and Communication."

Exercise 2.1

Survey

Survey the reading "Technology, Transportation, and Communication." Answer these questions based on your survey.

1. Is there a **title** for the **book** this selection is in? If so, what is it?

    _____

    _____

2. Is there a **title** for this **selection**? If so, what is it?

    _____

    _____

3. Are there any **subheadings**? If so, what are they?

_____

_____

4. Are there any **boldfaced/italicized** words in this section? If so, what are they?

_____

_____

5. Are there any **graphics**? If so, what are they?

_____

_____

Technology, Transportation, and Communication

by Jean Folkerts, Stephen Lacy, & Ann Larabee

from the The Media in Your Life: An Introduction to Mass Communication

I n the beginning, communication was linked to transportation because information could travel only as fast as a horse and rider. Information traveled along trade routes along with other commodities.

The Telegraph

The link between communication and transportation was broken in 1844 when Samuel Morse opened the nation's first telegraph line with the question, "What hath God wrought?" No longer was the speed of communication dependent on how fast a horse could gallop; information could travel instantaneously by means of wires from its point of origin to a publisher's desk.

By 1846, newspapers in upstate New York were using the wires to transmit news between the state capital of Albany and other New York cities. In 1848, a group of New York newspapers, including the Courier and Enquirer, Sun, Herald, Journal of Commerce, Tribune, and Express, hired a steamer to retrieve news from the major port of Halifax, Nova Scotia. The group also negotiated a joint arrangement to use telegraph lines to transmit news from Boston to New York. Those ventures resulted in the establishment of the Associated Press, a **wire service** that dominated delivery of national and international information until the early 1900s.

Wire service: organization that collects and distributes news and information to media outlets

Radio Revolution

By the early twentieth century, the advent of radio had broken a second link between transportation and communication: Not only could news travel from its source to an editor's desk as fast as the wires could carry it, but news also could travel from the editor or commentator to the public as fast as it could travel across the air waves.

Radio technology played an important role in World War I in ship-to-shore communications and was regulated by the U.S. Navy. Amateurs also enjoyed building and using radio sets, but few had conceived of it as a broadcasting—or mass communication—tool. At the end of the war, the U.S. Navy strongly opposed returning the rights to the British-owned Marconi Company, which had a monopoly on radio parts. With what historian Christopher Sterling labeled "tacit government approval," Owen D. Young, chairman of the board for General Electric Co., organized a new corporation to hold all U.S. patents. General Electric, together with American Telephone and Telegraph, United Fruit, and Westinghouse Electric, formed the Radio Corporation of America (RCA) and bought out American Marconi for $2.5 million. The companies operated together until 1926. That arrangement set the stage for further radio development organized and controlled by big business and government.

As Westinghouse, General Electric, and RCA established stations in the early 1920s, radio became so popular that RCA sold $11 million worth of receivers in 1922 alone. By 1927, 700 U.S. stations were operating, and in 1929, $135 million worth of sets was sold. In 1923, only 7 percent of U.S. households owned a radio set; by 1930, almost 35 percent owned sets.

Motion Pictures and Television

The motion picture industry was well under way by the beginning of World War I, and experimentation with television began in the 1930s. The movies were a popular form of entertainment during the financial depression of the 1930s because people sought an escape from the harsh realities of daily life.

Television arrived after World War II in the midst of an expanding consumer society. The prosperity of the post-World War II era and the new technology together began to shape media as a basis for creating a consumer culture. The media attracted mass audiences, and the information provided by the media helped homogenize the audience, stripping it of regional characteristics, dialects, and mores.

Computers and Communication

Computers entered the mass media as typesetting machines during the late 1960s, but computer technology had a more powerful impact on mass media with the development of the home personal computer, or PC. Although traditional media such as newspapers benefit from computer-based technology, such new technologies also create forms of information exchange that were not possible with the old styles of production and distribution.

Communication by means of the computer began in the late 1960s, when the U.S. government connected four computers in Utah and California. The goal was to develop the framework for an emergency communication system by sending information across special high-speed telephone lines. After the mid-1970s, smaller networks such as that used by the National Science Foundation (NSF) decided to work together—to internetwork. Today, the Internet links millions of academic, governmental, and commercial sites. No one owns the Internet. Rather, it is a loose collection of computer networks whose users pass along information and share files. Costs are shared rather informally by a variety of institutions.

It is the Internet that allows students to e-mail their professors and allows researchers to exchange ideas worldwide. Students regularly communicate through sophisticated software programs based on the Internet and designed specifically for the classroom. Programs such as educational software allow professors to create automatic e-mail lists, to construct electronic grade books, to give students assignments, to create interchanges among students, and to provide feedback. No longer is access to a professor limited to two class periods a week and a few office hours. Messages can be sent, received, and answered in a matter of minutes.

***

Question

*Create **Questions** for this selection. Create at least six (6) questions and write them in the space provided. This format is similar to the Folded Paper Method.*

Write Questions Here	Write Answers Here
1.	

Write Questions Here	Write Answers Here
2.	
3.	
4.	
5.	
6.	

Read

***Read** the selection and write answers to your questions in the second column provided above.*

Recite

*After you have read the selection and written the answers to your questions, you are ready to **Recite**. Go over your questions and answers to evaluate your active reading work.*

1. Did you capture all the key ideas? _____
   _____

2. What would you like to add? Write it here. _____
   _____
   _____
   _____

3. What did you notice about your reading experience using the SQ3R
   method?_____
   _____
   _____

Review

As discussed previously, the purpose of the **Review** stage in SQ3R is to
learn the key ideas in the material you read. You can do this by asking

yourself the questions you posed and answering them from memory rather than by looking at the answers. Another way to review textbook material is to answer the questions presented by the textbook author. Often at the end of a section or chapter in a textbook, the author will pose questions that aid in reinforcing key concepts and ideas discussed in the section or chapter. The notes you've taken and the questions you've asked in the SQ3R process may prove helpful in answering those questions.

To practice reviewing material, answer the following questions based on the reading "Technology, Transportation, and Communication."

Technology, Transportation, and Communication

Questions for Review

_____ **1.** According to the reading, why was communication tied to transportation in the past?
   A. communication was carried by carrier pigeons that sometimes disappeared
   B. communication was delayed by ship travel from Europe and England
   C. communication was carried by a horse and rider along trade routes
   D. communication was not as important as transportation in the past?

_____ **2.** The first break in communication and transportation occurred in what year?
   A. 1846
   B. 1844
   C. 1926
   D. 1848

_____ **3.** What is a wire service?
   A. a way of connecting towns and cities to each other
   B. the name of the first telegraph company
   C. an organization that distributes news and information
   D. a company that provides telephone service to the media

_____ **4.** Samuel Morse helped promote the widespread use of radio in the early twentieth century.
   A. True
   B. False

_____ **5.** Radio played a significant role in sharing battle information during the American Civil War in the 1860s.
   A. True
   B. False

_____ **6.** After World War I, what corporation was formed to hold U.S. patents for radio?
   A. General Electric Company (GE)
   B. American Telephone and Telegraph (AT&T)
   C. Associated Press (AP)
   D. Radio Corporation of America (RCA)

_____ **7.** What did the prosperity of the post-WWII era and television help to create?
   A. consumer culture
   B. entertainment
   C. regional characteristics
   D. an escape from reality

_____ **8.** According to this reading, who owns the Internet?
   A. the U.S. government
   B. a variety of institutions
   C. the National Science Foundation (NSF)
   D. no one owns the Internet

LITERATURE ACTIVE READING STRATEGIES

Literature. Wow, that sounds serious. Sometimes it is, but sometimes it isn't. Literature is defined, quite simply, as artistic writing. Artistic writing can range from the fanciful and enjoyable writing of J.K. Rowling (*Harry Potter and the Deathly Hallows*), to the popular writing of Dan Brown (*The Da Vinci Code*), to the dramatic writing of Shakespeare (*Hamlet*). Literature can also be an autobiography by a remarkable person such as Helen Keller or Barack Obama, or an investigative account of a genocide as in Philip Gourevitch's 1998 account of Rwanda. So, yes, sometimes literature is very serious, but sometimes it is light, funny, sad, entertaining, thought provoking, illuminating, and enjoyable. Literature can fit the needs of any reader and any purpose. Given that, recommending active reading strategies for literature is trickier than recommending strategies for textbooks. Still, what follows are a few tried-and-true methods of preparing your mind for whatever journey literature has in store for you.

Previewing

Previewing comes quite naturally to most people, and most people preview all the time. Before you purchase a bag of potato chips, you preview the options on the store shelf. Before you go to a movie, you watch the trailer for a preview. Before you enter a crowded room, you preview the crowd to see who is there and to judge the mood. Basically, previewing is how you prepare yourself. Sometimes you preview to make a decision or a choice. Other times you preview to know what to expect. In the same way, previewing literature, in the context of academic success, gives you an indication of what to expect. It is not so different from the surveying you do with a textbook, but there are some differences. Here are some actions you can take to preview literature.

- **Read the title**—reading the title, subtitle, and the author's name offers you some insight into the general nature of the book.
- **Observe cover art**—the cover art of a book is meant to support the author's message and the general emotion conveyed by the book. It is helpful to notice what impressions the cover art leaves with you.
- **Read the description**—reading the book's description on the inside jacket flap for hardcover books or on the back cover of softcover or paperback books gives you a synopsis, or summary, of the book. In an anthology, you will often find a brief introduction to the author and the selection before the reading. This is a valuable source of information, too.
- **Read blurbs**—the blurbs on book covers are meant to entice you into reading the book. Usually, the blurbs, or quotations, are recommendations from notable sources. If you like or respect the source of a blurb, you will view the book and its author favorably.
- **Read the first page**—after all is said and done, reading the first page of a book drops you right into the heart of the matter. Here's where you can see for yourself how the author writes, what the book feels like emotionally, and whether or not you will be engaged with the book.

Background Check

In the twenty-first century, the Internet has made getting background information on anyone and anything as easy as turning on the computer. It has also made us quite used to the idea of researching—though we may not call it that—something or someone we are interested in knowing more about. Think of how many people use Facebook: who was that cute person your friend brought to your party? Just look him/her up on Facebook. A background check on a book or author can be just as easy.

A **background check** for literature can take many forms. Like the second step in the SQ3R method, getting background information involves some questioning. For example, you can ask yourself after previewing a book, "Was everything I read familiar? Have I ever heard of the city or country where this story takes place? Do I know anything about the time period? Does the story involve a profession or activity I am familiar with?" In many cases, the answer to at least one of these questions will be no. This is when you begin a background check. Here are a few strategies to focus your attention as you consider reading literature.

- **Author background**—author background is especially helpful if the book is nonfiction or a memoir. In these situations, the author may be featured in the text, so knowing a few things about him/her can help you gain some footing. Also, knowing some of the author's biography may be essential to establishing the context for the book. In other instances, author background may help you understand why this author wrote this particular story, and how or why he/she is qualified to do so. Note, as well, the author's years of birth and death, if they are provided.

- **Setting**—in some instances, a book may be set in a place or time period with which you are unfamiliar. The novel *The Kite Runner*, set in Afghanistan during the 1970s, is a great example. While you may know something about Afghanistan from current events, you may not be aware of its history prior to 2001. Consequently, it would be very helpful for you to research, online or in the library, some facts about both the country and that time period. Even when the book's setting is not completely unfamiliar to you, it is always helpful to check it out more thoroughly.

- **Culture**—like setting, the culture presented in a book may be unfamiliar to you for a number of reasons. The culture could be that of a foreign country, like Japan, or that of a time period, like 1845. The culture could also be that of a specific profession or group of people, like stockbrokers or the extremely wealthy. In any one of these cases, you might need to do a background check to get a few facts before you dive into the reading.

As you can see, a background check may be as easy as reading the author biography included in the book or as involved as locating photographs of a millionaire's mansion in California. Whatever research you do, its goal is to help set the stage for the action you will watch unfold when you read the first pages of the book.

Making Connections

Making connections with the book you are about to read is one of the most important pre-reading strategies you can undertake; and it takes very little time. In general, making a connection is similar to the idea of setting context. When you **make a connection,** you are considering what aspects of the book or story are familiar to you in some way. For example,

if you know that the author of the essay you are about to read was made fun of because he liked to read books, you might identify with him because you were teased for enjoying science projects—the kids in school called you a nerd because you liked creating volcano simulations. You've made a connection with the writer that leads you to wonder how his experience was similar to your experience. Not only that, but this connection also places the essay in a realm that is familiar to you—childhood experiences.

Making connections is just that simple. Understanding and learning are most effective and lasting when they occur within a realm to which we have a connection. It's the difference between climbing a tree that's a hundred years old and climbing a tree that's only ten years old. The older tree is more likely to hold your weight when you scramble onto its branches; the younger tree's limbs may bend or even break under your weight. So, when you are about to climb into the experience of a new book, you want to create a connection that is strong enough, like that of a hundred-year-old tree, to hold all that new information.

Predicting

Making predictions is another way of laying the groundwork before you begin reading. Like previewing, we make predictions every day. When you peek out your window at the sky, you are attempting to predict the weather: rain or shine? When you call your friend to find out what she's wearing to the party that evening, you are trying to predict what type of outfit will allow you to fit in (or stand out, if you are a fashionista). As humans, we are inclined to predict as often as possible. It is partly why humans have been so successful as a species (that and opposable thumbs give humans quite an edge over, say, donkeys). So, using prediction to assist you in becoming a more effective reader is a natural progression of events.

Prediction as a pre-reading strategy can take several shapes. Here are a few ways you may use prediction to prepare for a reading experience.

- **Predicting Challenges**—as you move through various pre-reading strategies for literature, you may become aware of certain challenges you will have while reading. For example, while previewing Shakespeare's *Hamlet*, you may notice that the language is a little different from what you are used to reading and speaking. You've predicted a challenge you may have and, thus, can prepare for it by giving yourself extra time to read and take notes. Other challenges might be unfamiliar time periods, new cultures, or unknown settings.

■ **Predicting Events/Plot Points**—sometimes you may be able to predict important events in a book or plot points in a story. When you find out that a young woman who has never had a boyfriend will soon meet a handsome young man, you can probably predict that a romance will bloom. Prediction does not ruin a story; rather, it creates anticipation.

■ **Predicting Motivation**—in fiction and nonfiction, it is helpful to consider what is driving the main characters or people you are reading about. If, for instance, you read in a book's description that a young boy never knew his mother, you can predict that the family members and friends of this young boy are going to be especially important because he's missing that vital bond between a mother and child. In the case of motivation, prediction can help increase the conflict and emotional depth of a story.

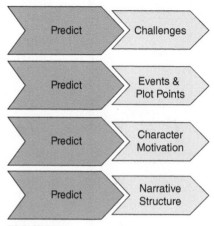

FIGURE 2.3

■ **Predicting Narrative Structure**—narrative structure is how a story is told. Authors have many options when selecting the narrative structure of their stories. They may choose a straightforward chronology or may shift between time periods. A story may have a single narrator or multiple narrators. As you read the description and first page of a book or story, try to determine what the narrative structure will be. Knowing this structure will help you keep your footing if there is a switch in setting or voice.

These are some of the ways you can use prediction as a pre-reading strategy. The funny thing about prediction, though, is that it doesn't end with pre-reading. You will continue to make predictions throughout the reading process.

Literature Active Reading Wrap-Up

Overall, there are many aspects involved in active reading for literature. While the focus in these pages has been books, the strategies of previewing, doing background checks, making connections, and making predictions are useful for all types of reading material, including essays, short stories, and even poetry. Consequently, in the exercise that follows, you will have an opportunity to practice your active reading strategies with a short story.

Exercise 2.2

For this exercise, use the story by Kate Chopin in Strategies in Action. *This short story will serve as a way for you to practice literature active reading strategies. To begin, read the introduction and first line of "The Story of an Hour." Next, answer the following questions* **before** *you read the entire story.*

Preview

1. Write a brief description of the things you discovered in your preview of "The Story of an Hour." _____

_____

_____

Background Check

2. What important information did you uncover in your background check?

_____

_____

Making Connections

3. Consider what you now know about "The Story of an Hour." Do you see any similarities to your own experiences? Is there anything regarding the author or the subject of the story that you can identify with? If so, briefly describe it. _____

_____

_____

Predicting

4. Do you foresee any challenges in reading this story? _____

_____

5. Reread the first line of the story. Does it seem to contain a clue to a future plot point? If so, what is the clue? _____

_____

_____

6. Can you determine anything about Mrs. Mallard's motivation? What about the motivations of the people around her? _____

_____

_____

7. Is there anything about the narrative structure that stands out in the first line or the introduction? _____

_____

_____

UNIVERSAL ACTIVE READING STRATEGY

A helpful and easy-to-use strategy that you can apply to any type of reading material is annotation. To **annotate** is to make comments in the margins while you are reading. As an active reader, your role is to interact with the text: you may ask questions, voice opinions, express a reaction, or wonder about an author's statements or a character's actions. Annotation is a way for you to note these thoughts as you are reading; it is also a way for you to keep track of what you find significant, confusing, or interesting about the reading. Annotation provides you, the reader, with the opportunity to engage a reading in a way that expands your connection and understanding. There are a few guidelines you can use to begin your annotation process; keep in mind, however, that as you annotate more frequently, you will likely develop a system or practice that works best for you.

What follows are tips to help you focus on appropriate material to annotate. In general, you will either write a note in the margins or highlight, circle, or underline text—or use all of these methods interchangeably.

Five Tips for Annotation

Tip 1: Ask, "What's the focus? Who is the main character?"

As soon as you encounter the author's focus or the main character, make note of it. This physical note will remind you what to pay attention to as you read.

Tip 2: Ask, "What point is the author making? What is happening to the main character or what is he/she doing?"

The author will either support an idea with various details or develop an idea through action and dialogue. When you read information that clearly relates to the focus of the text or to the main character, note this in the margins and underline or highlight it in the reading.

Tip 3: Ask questions. Answer questions.

When the author mentions a word or an idea that you are not familiar with, mark the passage somehow—by circling, underlining, or highlighting it—and write a note to yourself. What didn't you know or understand? What is the definition of the unknown word? Write it down in the margins.

Tip 4: Express agreement, surprise, or any other emotion you feel while reading.

Sometimes when you are reading, the author will include an idea that you find provocative, interesting, or surprising. Or a character may do something that you did not expect or did not like. Track your responses in the margins. When it's time to reflect further in writing or to analyze the reading on a test, your notes about various parts of the text will come in handy.

Tip 5: Make connections.

As you continue to experience life and read more, academically and otherwise, it will become increasingly likely that one text reminds you of something else you've read or experienced. When this happens, make a note of the connection. You never know how that connection could be useful for analysis or essay writing.

Exercise 2.3   Using the Five Tips for Annotation, read and annotate the short story "A Story I'll Tell You When You're Big." Some annotations have been provided to demonstrate how you might approach this reading. Continue annotating the remainder of the story.

A Story I'll Tell You When You're Big

By Jacqueline Vogtman

Who is she talking to?

You look like Snow White under glass, only your skin is red and you lie under plastic. When you are allowed to come home—just a few more pounds, to assure the doctors you will grow up an almost-normal child, a few pounds underweight, a few inches shorter, one nostril larger than the other from the tube that streams life into you now—when you begin to understand language, or maybe before that, I'll tell you this story:

Oh, it's a mom talking to her premature baby.

Your Great Aunt Maime, born between the big wars, came out early like you. No one understood why. What kind of baby would be eager to enter a world of breadlines and bitter coffee, cold fingertips and coughing neighbors? But she swam into a bedpan and thrashed around like a tadpole until the midwife scooped her out and wrapped her in old newspapers.

In the Great Depression

Mewing or crying

Maime was so tiny her cry was barely audible. Family members throughout the years have described it as the sound of a kitten keening miles away, or a wet finger rubbed along the rim of a wine glass, not that anyone could afford wine then. She was so tiny the midwife swaddled her with one article ripped out of the newspaper, a piece about the carnival coming to town, its other side too stained to read but probably a story about death, names of children who died of dysentery or polio, names of men who jumped from the top of the Macy's building because they couldn't feed their families. Maime was so tiny the midwife placed her inside a cigar box and told the child's mother, Say your goodbyes now, because she won't live through the night.

But she did live through the night, and the next and the next. Mornings, her mother picked up her cigar-smelling daughter and cradled the baby in her palm, feeding her through an eyedropper. She stripped Maime's sisters' dolls of their clothing, using it to dress Maime. On good days Maime got the princess outfit, on bad days the Raggedy Ann dress, but soon enough Maime grew out of doll clothes and wore her sisters' hand-me-downs, which she wore until joining the convent. When she told her family she was becoming a nun, they nodded, their eyes lit, finally understanding why she'd been so eager to enter this world.

She died in the convent, eighty years old. In the attic, we have a photo of Maime wearing her habit, smiling. One day, when you're asking about your ancestors, I'll dig it out and show it to you.

One day, I imagine even these trips to the NICU will become a story I'll tell you. The smell of coffee as gray light creeps through my blinds at five a.m. The cold steering wheel I grip too hard, the red lights I run to see you. The scent of bread baking in the hospital cafeteria, its yeasty rising. And you, under hot bulbs, in a tiny warmed world of your own, not yet knowing me.

KEY TERM REVIEW
Strategy Recall

Match the steps, actions, or definitions provided below with the appropriate strategy listed in the following section. Each strategy includes as many actions or steps as indicated by the numbered spaces below the strategy. Note: Some responses require a specific ordering of steps.

STEPS & ACTIONS & DEFINITIONS

A. Review	**B.** Read Description	**C.** Predict Motivation
D. Predict Plot/Events	**E.** Question	**F.** Observe Cover Art
G. To make comments in the margins while you are reading	**H.** To consider what aspects of a book or story are familiar in some way	**I.** Predict Challenges

J. Culture	**K.** Survey	**L.** Read Blurbs
M. Read the First Page	**N.** Setting	**O.** Author Background
P. Predict Narrative Structure	**Q.** Read the Title	**R.** Read
S. Recite		

STRATEGIES

Annotation (definition)

1. _G_

Textbook Reading Strategy

SQ3R (List Steps in Order)

2. _K_

3. _E_

4. _R_

5. _S_

6. _A_

Literature Reading Strategies

Previewing (List Actions)

7. _Q_

8. _F_

9. _B_

10. _L_

11. _M_

Background Check (List Actions)

12. _O_

13. _N_

14. _J_

Make Connections (definition)

15. _I-C_

Predict (List Actions)

16. _I_

17. _O_

18. _C_

19. _P_

STRATEGIES IN ACTION

The Story of an Hour

By Kate Chopin

Kate Chopin (1851–1904) was born in St. Louis, Chicago. She met and married her husband in New Orleans, where she lived until her husband's early death. She then moved back to St. Louis, where she began writing short stories. Her stories were published in popular magazines, and she enjoyed some success. Her novel *The Awakening* was published in 1899, but was not received well because it discussed the then-taboo subject of adultery, among other controversial subjects. *"The Story of an Hour"* was first published in 1894, and it is one of Kate Chopin's most widely read works.

Knowing that Mrs. Mallard was afflicted with a heart trouble, great care was taken to break to her as gently as possible the news of her husband's death.

It was her sister Josephine who told her, in broken sentences; veiled hints that revealed in half concealing. Her husband's friend Richards was there, too, near her. It was he who had been in the newspaper office when intelligence of the railroad disaster was received, with Brently Mallard's name leading the list of "killed." He had only taken the time to assure himself of its truth by a second telegram, and had hastened to forestall any less careful, less tender friend in bearing the sad message.

She did not hear the story as many women have heard the same, with a paralyzed inability to accept its significance. She wept at once, with sudden, wild abandonment, in her sister's arms. When the storm of grief had spent itself she went away to her room alone. She would have no one follow her.

There stood, facing the open window, a comfortable, roomy armchair. Into this she sank, pressed down by a physical exhaustion that haunted her body and seemed to reach into her soul.

She could see in the open square before her house the tops of trees that were all aquiver with the new spring life. The delicious breath of rain was in the air. In the street below a peddler was crying his wares. The notes of a distant song which some one was singing reached her faintly, and countless sparrows were twittering in the eaves.

There were patches of blue sky showing here and there through the clouds that had met and piled one above the other in the west facing her window.

She sat with her head thrown back upon the cushion of the chair, quite motionless, except when a sob came up into her throat and shook her, as a child who has cried itself to sleep continues to sob in its dreams.

She was young, with a fair, calm face, whose lines bespoke repression and even a certain strength. But now there was a dull stare in her eyes, whose gaze was fixed away off yonder on one of those patches of blue sky. It was not a glance of reflection, but rather indicated a suspension of intelligent thought.

There was something coming to her and she was waiting for it, fearfully. What was it? She did not know; it was too subtle and elusive to name. But she felt it, creeping out of the sky, reaching toward her through the sounds, the scents, the color that filled the air.

Now her bosom rose and fell tumultuously. She was beginning to recognize this thing that was approaching to possess her, and she was striving to beat it back with her will—as powerless as her two white slender hands would have been.

When she abandoned herself a little whispered word escaped her slightly parted lips. She said it over and over under her breath: "free, free, free!" The vacant stare and the look of terror that had followed it went from her eyes. They stayed keen and bright. Her pulses beat fast, and the coursing blood warmed and relaxed every inch of her body.

She did not stop to ask if it were or were not a monstrous joy that held her. A clear and exalted perception enabled her to dismiss the suggestion as trivial.

She knew that she would weep again when she saw the kind, tender hands folded in death; the face that had never looked save with love upon her, fixed and gray and dead. But she saw beyond that bitter moment a long procession of years to come that would belong to her absolutely. And she opened and spread her arms out to them in welcome.

There would be no one to live for during those coming years; she would live for herself. There would be no powerful will bending hers in that blind persistence with which men and women believe they have a right to impose a private will upon a fellow-creature. A kind intention or a cruel intention made the act seem no less a crime as she looked upon it in that brief moment of illumination.

And yet she had loved him—sometimes. Often she had not. What did it matter! What could love, the unsolved mystery, count for in the face of this possession of self-assertion which she suddenly recognized as the strongest impulse of her being!

"Free! Body and soul free!" she kept whispering.

Josephine was kneeling before the closed door with her lips to the keyhole, imploring for admission. "Louise, open the door! I beg; open the door—you will make yourself ill. What are you doing, Louise? For heaven's sake open the door."

"Go away. I am not making myself ill." No; she was drinking in a very elixir of life through that open window.

Her fancy was running riot along those days ahead of her. Spring days, and summer days, and all sorts of days that would be her own. She breathed a quick prayer that life might be long. It was only yesterday she had thought with a shudder that life might be long.

She arose at length and opened the door to her sister's importunities. There was a feverish triumph in her eyes, and she carried herself unwittingly like a goddess of Victory. She clasped her sister's waist, and together they descended the stairs. Richards stood waiting for them at the bottom.

Some one was opening the front door with a latchkey. It was Brently Mallard who entered, a little travel-stained, composedly carrying his grip-sack and umbrella. He had been far from the scene of the accident, and did not even know there had been one. He stood amazed at Josephine's piercing cry; at Richards' quick motion to screen him from the view of his wife.

But Richards was too late.

When the doctors came they said she had died of heart disease—of joy that kills.

***

Vocabulary Crossword: "The Story of an Hour"

Complete the crossword by matching the appropriate word with the definitions given below.

afflicted	aquiver	suspension	elixir
hasten	elusive	subtle	importune
veiled	wares	tumultuously	
forestall	bespoke	exalted	

CROSSWORD CLUES (DEFINITIONS)

ACROSS	DOWN
1. medicinal solution or liquid	2. evasive
3. tormented or bothered by	4. merchandise
5. glorified	7. to tremble

ACROSS	DOWN
6. to act quickly	9. to urge or beg persistently
8. to be suspended	10. showed or told of
12. with great agitation or excitement	11. hardly noticeable

Checking In

1. Did you uncover any background information about the author, the culture, or the setting of this story that helped you understand the story's events? If so, briefly explain.

2. Consider the predictions you made regarding challenges you might face while reading, and discuss whether or not your predictions were accurate.

3. Consider the predictions you made regarding the plot and discuss whether or not your predictions were accurate.

4. After reading "The Story of an Hour," do you have any connection to the emotions or feelings that Mrs. Mallard experienced? If so, briefly describe that connection.

Getting the Point

5. _____ Why did Josephine and Richards worry about telling Mrs. Mallard the news of her husband's death?
   a) She had an unstable mind.
   b) She had a heart condition.
   c) She was pregnant.
   d) She already knew.

6. _____ How did Richards find out about Brently Mallard's death?
   a) He received a phone call from the newspaper office.
   b) He saw Brently Mallard's body in a photograph of the train wreck.
   c) He escaped from the train wreck that had killed Brently Mallard.
   d) He saw Brently Mallard's name on the list of people killed in the wreck.

7. _____ What did Mrs. Mallard do once she was in her room?
   a) She cried loudly on her bed.
   b) She tried to jump out the window.
   c) She sat in an armchair.
   d) She looked at pictures of her husband.

8. _____ After she had been sitting quietly in her room for a while, Mrs. Mallard began to feel an emotion besides sadness.

   a) True

   b) False

9. _____ What did Mrs. Mallard realize she would be able to do now that her husband was no longer around?

   a) live for herself

   b) travel to new places

   c) marry her childhood love

   d) nothing; she was too sad

10. _____ Which word best describes Mrs. Mallard's state of mind when she left her bedroom with her sister, Josephine?

    a) depressed

    b) triumphant

    c) fragile

    d) sorrowful

11. _____ Which sentence best describes what Mrs. Mallard realized in this story?

    a) She realized that her life was empty without her husband.

    b) She realized that her husband had loved her very much.

    c) She realized that she was weak and needed her husband.

    d) She realized that she would be able to live freely without her husband.

STRATEGIES IN ACTION

Building Safe Schools for Girls in War Zones

by Anna Mulrine

Anna Mulrine, a senior editor of the Nation & World section of *U.S. News & World Report*, covers defense for the magazine and has written more than a dozen cover stories, most recently on Iraq and on Afghanistan's border wars with Pakistan. She travels frequently to the Middle East and reports on U.S. military strategy, foreign policy, the challenges of fighting the Taliban and al Qaeda, and the lives of U.S. soldiers. Prior to covering defense for *U.S. News*, Mulrine wrote about the rebuilding of New Orleans in the aftermath of Hurricane Katrina. Mulrine's work has also appeared in the *Christian Science Monitor*, *Rolling Stone*, and *National Geographic Traveler*, among other publications.

> Use the pre-reading strategies from this chapter to gain information about this reading selection.

G reg Mortenson, coauthor of the wildly successful book *Three Cups of Tea: One Man's Mission to Promote Peace ... One School at a Time*, can recall the precise moment he knew that he had created a movement.

A girls' school that Mortenson helped to open south of Kabul, Afghanistan, had been attacked by the Taliban in the summer of 2007. The insurgents had also cut down fruit trees, a valuable source of income for some of the girls' families. So, the next day the school's headmaster got on his bike and pedaled 23 miles to notify a local militia commander that the school had been shut down. That particular commander is "a little shady," Mortenson says, "but he also has daughters in school, so he sent a local posse over."

"They came in, killed two Taliban, and put a dozen guards around the school." Guards remain to this day. "Their orders are that if anybody harms any child or teacher, shoot them. While that's not how we would handle the school problems," Mortenson, 51, says of the orders, the community's concern for its school "clearly shows they are invested." It is the sort of buy-in, he adds, that has yielded payoffs in often violent places.

Published in 2006, *Three Cups of Tea* has sold more than 3 million copies in 39 countries. It is also required reading for Special Forces troops deploying to Afghanistan and has garnered praise from Pentagon heavyweights like Chairman of the Joint Chiefs Adm. Mike Mullen and Defense Secretary Robert Gates. This has made Mortenson a valued unofficial adviser to the U.S. military, a development that surprised him. "I was actually fairly critical of the military at the Pentagon after 9/11," he says. Pennies for Peace, founded by Mortenson in 1994 with schoolchildren who used their spare change to help him raise money for his first school, accepts no federal funds "and never plans to" so that it will not be "perceived as an arm of the U.S. government." Mortenson has, however, hosted commanders at his schools and visited dozens of bases to brief soldiers. "I can say the military in the last two years has gone through a huge learning curve. In many ways, I think the military is far ahead of our State Department and political leaders."

And even as the insurgency in Afghanistan has gained strength, America's growing disillusionment with the war makes Mortenson wary. "Although it may seem kind of a waste of our resources to many Americans, we made a promise," he says. When America cut funding to Afghanistan in the 1980s, "we basically abandoned the people who helped us overthrow the Soviets." He worries that history may repeat itself. "We invaded, and within a year and a half ran off to Iraq—again we abandoned the people. To me, this is our third—and final—try."

Hard climb.   There were times when Mortenson, an avid mountain climber who worked in hospital emergency rooms to fund his passion, wasn't sure he would be able to start a school in the small Pakistani village where he found himself exhausted and lost after a failed attempt to ascend the notorious K2 Himalayan summit. But he was determined to return the generosity the villagers had shown him. "I kind of had to give up everything, and sell all my possessions, until things started to change around," he says. After hearing of his efforts, American schoolchildren stepped in. Their 62,400 donated pennies helped to build his first school. The villages are supplied with masons, carpenters, and teacher training. Villages must provide free labor, wood, and land.

He now visits about 200 schools a year throughout the United States, from kindergartens to the Air Force Academy, to speak about his efforts to educate impoverished children. Pennies for Peace will be in some 20,000 schools next year, giving rise to what Mortenson hopes will become a new generation of leaders in the United States who will take up the cause of global education. "Women who have an education are not likely to condone their son getting into violence," he says. "I've seen that very vividly."

In Afghanistan in 2000, there were 800,000 children in school, nearly all boys. Today, there are 8.4 million children in school, including 2.5 million girls. "That's the greatest increase in school enrollment of any country in modern history, but very few people in America seem to be aware of it." Mortenson hopes to remedy that through his work in the years to come.

***

Vocabulary Crossword: "Building Safe Schools for Girls in War Zones"

Complete the crossword by matching the appropriate word to the definition given below.

insurgent	yield	spare	ascend
headmaster	garnered	brief	notorious
posse	deploy	wary	condone
buy-in	disillusion	avid	

CROSSWORD CLUES (DEFINITIONS)

ACROSS	DOWN
1. to support	2. to produce
4. person in charge of a private school	3. widely known
6. to excuse or pardon	5. unused
	9. accumulated

ACROSS	DOWN
7. enthusiastic in pursuit of an interest	11. disappointment
8. to tell or explain	12. to send out
10. rebel (noun)	14. to climb
13. very cautious	15. group of people

Checking In

1. Why do you think Anna Mulrine was selected to interview and write about Greg Mortenson? Be specific and refer to the author biography preceding the article.

2. If you were going to read Greg Mortenson's book, on what might you need more background information? Briefly explain how you might find this information.

3. What do you think Greg Mortenson's book is about?

Getting the Point

4. _____ What does Mortenson provide to the people of Afghanistan and Pakistan?

   a) food for families

   b) schools for girls and boys

   c) religious training

   d) combat training

5. _____ In paragraph 2, why does Mortenson relate the story of the commander who defended the girls' school?

   a) to answer the question asked by Anna Mulrine

   b) to brag about his success in Afghanistan

   c) to threaten any Taliban who might read the article

   d) to show how the local community supports the school

6. _____ How does Mortenson feel about getting federal funding for his mission to build schools?

   a) He does not want federal funding.

   b) He has tried to get federal funding several times.

   c) He can't get funding because the U.S. government doesn't support his mission.

   d) He is very angry that the federal government has offered him funding.

7. _____ Greg Mortenson used to be a mountain climber before he started his organization to build schools.

   a) True

   b) False

8. _____ Why does Mortenson feel that education will help bring peace to places like Afghanistan and Pakistan?

   a) Educated men are too worried about their studies to fight wars.

   b) He tells villagers that if they join the Taliban, he will close the school.

   c) Educated women discourage their sons from getting involved in violence.

   d) He doesn't feel that education will make any difference at all.

For support in meeting this chapter's objectives, go to MyReadingLab and select **Active Reading Strategies.**

3 Vocabulary Strategies

Learning Objectives

In this chapter you will:

- Define unfamiliar vocabulary through various types of context clues.
- Understand unfamiliar vocabulary through use of word parts.
- Select appropriate dictionary definitions for unfamiliar vocabulary.

*The difference
between the right
word and the almost
right word is like the
difference between
lightening and the
lightening bug.*
—*Mark Twain*

Words are the building blocks of language. Words are so common that we hardly think about them. But just imagine a world without words. How would anyone communicate? How would a person explain the most basic of situations? Luckily, words have been here for a long time, and they do not appear to be going anywhere. In fact, every year more and more words are added to our language. Just think: if you had said ten years ago, "Would you look at the *bling* she's wearing," no one would have known what you were talking about. Now, only the elderly and unhip, English teacher types are clueless about this word (and if you are one of the unhip: *bling* means shiny and expensive jewelry, often gold, diamonds, or platinum). The point is that the English language is constantly changing and growing. Some estimate that there are nearly a million words in the English language already.

With so many words out there, how is anybody expected to know them all? The answer is simple: no one is expected to know them all. Even a highly educated person encounters new words from time to time. The key is having strategies to decipher the meanings of these new words. This chapter will offer you those strategies.

Here's a preview of what you can expect from this chapter:

Using Context Clues

- Example
- Contrast
- Definition
- General sense
- Restatement

Using Word Parts

- Roots
- Prefixes
- Suffixes

Using Dictionary Definitions

- Parts of speech
- Multiple definitions

USING CONTEXT CLUES

Context clues are hints or indications of meaning that you will find within the very sentence or paragraph that you are reading. With context clues, you don't need to look anywhere else to understand the meaning of a word because a working definition is right there in the context that surrounds the unknown word. You only need to examine the surrounding words for the clues they offer. There are five different types of context clues: example, contrast, definition, general sense, and restatement. Each one offers a way to understand a word's meaning without having to turn to a dictionary.

Example Context Clues

Example context clues are those that provide an illustration of an unknown word. This illustration, or example, may come before or after the unknown word. Read the following sentence to see how example context clues work. In this sentence, the unknown word is *hostility*.

> The *hostility* between the two teams is really extreme. The last time they played against each other, three players from both sides were kicked out of the game for fighting.

Now, read the sentence again and look for a clue as to what *hostility* means. If you suggested that *hostility* has something to do with fighting or ill will, you are correct. Based on the example of the team players fighting each other, it seems that a working definition of *hostility* would have to include "angry feelings toward someone or something."

There's nothing like putting an idea into practice, so try your hand at the following exercise to see if you've got the idea of how to find example context clues.

Exercise 3.1 Read each of the following sentences. First, identify the <u>example context clues</u> for the *italicized* word. Then, restate the meaning of the italicized word on the line that follows the sentence(s).

Try not to look up any words in the dictionary; instead, rely only on the clues offered in the sentence(s).

1. Some friends *bicker* constantly. Just last week, Julia and Andrea ruined the evening for all of us when they disagreed about which movie to see, where to have dinner, and just about everything else. _____

   _____

2. I avoid *controversial* subjects such as religion and politics when I go to a dinner party. _____

   _____

3. Nadia required her group to take *precautions* before they set out on their hikes; they had to go with a partner, they needed to wear orange vests, and they had to have maps of the area. _____

_____

4. The suspect's case was strengthened when the defense team realized he'd been *divested* of his right to have a lawyer present and to make a phone call. _____

_____

5. Some things like speaking in front of crowds, flying on airplanes, and going to the dentist are known to cause *apprehension* in people of all ages. _____

_____

6. As a child, Larry had to deal with the school bully taking his lunch, teasing him about his glasses, and chasing him home—an overall agenda of *persecution*. _____

_____

7. Talking about life and death, the origins of the universe, and the miracle of birth are generally too *profound* to discuss on the first date. _____

_____

8. Leo's manager at the bowling alley hoped that offering *incentives* like bonus games, free soda refills, and date nights would bring in a younger crowd. _____

_____

9. During the museum trip, students ran through corridors, yelled loudly in the galleries, touched the artwork, and generally behaved in a *disgraceful* manner. _____

_____

10. Moving to a new city, the birth of a child, the loss of a parent—these are *momentous* events in the life of an adult and are likely to leave lasting impressions. _____

_____

Contrast Context Clues

Contrast context clues offer an understanding of an unknown word by showing its opposite. When you know what something is not, then what it is becomes clear.

Read the following sentence to see how contrast context clues work. In this sentence, the unknown word is *privation*.

> Louis grew up in a constant state of *privation*, but now that he's graduated from law school and found a corporate position, he will live luxuriously.

Now, read the sentence again and look for the contrast clues. This sentence has a few of them. For one, the use of the word "but" indicates that something is going to be different now that Louis has "graduated from law school and found a corporate position." We may not know what Louis's salary is, but the general understanding is that lawyers have a high income. We also find out that Louis will live "luxuriously" with his new job. All of these clues suggest that *privation* means the opposite of luxury. Thus, *privation* means without enough.

Exercise 3.2

Read each of the following sentences. First, identify the <u>contrast context clues</u> for the *italicized* word. Then, restate the meaning of the italicized word on the line that follows the sentence(s).

Try not to look up any words in the dictionary; instead, rely only on the clues offered in the sentence(s).

1. Brian rushed madly through the halls, afraid his class had *commenced*, but he was amazed to find that the teacher was waiting for him. _____
   commenced: already began.

2. Taking too many doses of certain drugs can be *lethal*, but overdosing on other drugs can lead to milder results like an upset stomach or a headache. *Lethal: dangerous to ones health.*

3. While the most vocal of the sales representatives *proposed* a number of ideas, the new hires did not offer any suggestions. *Proposed: already making a suggestion.*

4. The most sought-after players are those who play fair; on the other hand, those players who are constantly noted for *violating* the rules are generally last among the draft picks. *Violating: to harm someone or something.*

5. Aunt Nikki is a *peculiar* dresser and loves the attention she gets, but my Aunt Lisa won't wear anything that makes her stand out from the crowd. _____
   Peculiar: a liking to a odd subject.

6. The best career advice I ever received was to do what I was *compelled* to do, not what others told me I should do. _Compelled: desired and/or convinced._

7. As a social worker, Alex witnessed acts of great *depravity*, and this increased his desire to treat everyone, especially children, with respect and kindness. _Depravity: utter and destructive humiliation._

8. As children grow older, they will be better able to *perceive* the dangers of foolish actions. The young and the naïve cannot see the risks that may be very apparent to the wise. _Perceive: able to look ahead._

9. Elsie knew her mother wouldn't be able to *sustain* the household by herself, so she got a job to avoid seeing her family fall into debt. _Sustain: being able to control._

10. Marrying a man from a different religion doesn't always mean you have to *convert* to that religion; some married couples continue practicing separate faiths. _Convert: becoming someone different._

Definition Context Clues

Definition context clues can be the easiest context clues to spot because they offer a direct definition of the unknown word. Sometimes, punctuation or text formatting indicates the definition. The author may use any one of the following to set off or set apart a definition context clue:

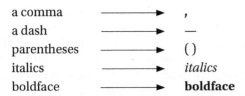

a comma ⟶ ,
a dash ⟶ —
parentheses ⟶ ( )
italics ⟶ *italics*
boldface ⟶ **boldface**

Read the following sentences to see how definition context clues work. The unknown word is underlined.

1. Danny was late to class because he needed to <u>duplicate</u>, or copy, the notes he borrowed from me last week.
2. The prosecutor was very skillful when he began to <u>refute</u>—disprove with evidence—the argument presented by the defense attorney.

3. Many people don't need to be told when they've been <u>bilked</u> (cheated).
4. People who are in love are often quite <u>jovial</u>. Sometimes to the annoyance of people not in love, their moods are *marked by good humor.*
5. Tamika hoped to be a Hollywood <u>siren</u>, **a woman capable of luring** moviegoers to her films.

Read the sentences once more and look for the definition context clues.

1. In the first sentence, *duplicate* is the unknown word, and commas are used to set off its definition: "copy."
2. In the second sentence, *refute* is the unknown word, and dashes are used to set off its definition: "disprove with evidence."
3. In the third sentence, *bilked* is the unknown word, and parentheses are used to set off its definition: "cheated."
4. In the fourth sentence, *jovial* is the unknown word, and italics are used to set off its definition: "marked by good humor."
5. In the fifth sentence, *siren* is the unknown word, and boldface type is used to set off its definition: "a woman capable of luring."

As you may have noticed from the given instances, definition context clues, when set off, can be easier to locate than other context clues. However, definition context clues are not always set off. They might be worked into the context without any special identification. Here's an example.

> A *polyglot* is a person who knows or can speak several languages.

What do you think *polyglot* means? If you said, "A person who knows or can speak several languages," you've got the right idea. The definition is given within the sentence, but is not set off by any special punctuation or text formatting.

You will most certainly encounter definition context clues in your academic studies. Definition context clues are essential in textbooks, especially those that cover specialized fields such as psychology, criminal justice, and history. In these cases, identifying the definition context clue is an even more important strategy to use for understanding new words since the definition is likely to be specific to the particular field or career being discussed. You may not even find these specific terms in a general-purpose dictionary, so context is key.

Exercise 3.3

Read each of the following sentences. First, identify the <u>definition context clues</u> for the word in boldface. Next, use the line provided to indicate which technique (punctuation, text formatting, or a word) pointed you toward the definition context clue.

Try not to look up any words in the dictionary; instead, rely only on the clues offered in the sentence(s).

1. Many people **bestow** (leave in a will) their pets to someone they know will take care of their beloved animals. _____

    _____

2. One group of investigators, chiefly sociologists such as Hunter, have been concerned with **social stratification** in the political system—how politics is affected by divisions among socioeconomic groups or classes in a community (Burns, 2004). _____

    _____

3. The most effective instrument in this process was the **parlements,** or courts dominated by the nobility (Kagan, 2004). _____

    _____

4. The **opposition** to the new law proved to be more than momentary resistance. _____

    _____

5. **Redistributive policies** are programs to shift wealth or benefits from one segment of the population to another, usually from the rich to the poor (Burns, 2004). _____

    _____

6. **Prudence** is the careful and proper use of action in conditions of extreme unrest. _____

    _____

7. Goffman described **total institutions** as places where the same people work, recreate, worship, eat, and sleep together daily (Schmalleger, 2004). _____

    _____

8. Most psychologists define **learning** as a relatively permanent change in behavior or the potential to make a response that occurs as a result of some experience (Davis, 2004). _____

    _____

9. Classical conditioning is a form of learning that occurs when two stimuli—a neutral stimulus and an unconditioned stimulus—that are **"paired"** (presented together) become associated with each (Davis, 2004). _____

    _____

10. A **phobia** is an irrational fear of an activity, object, or situation that is out of proportion to the actual danger it poses (Davis, 2004). _____

_____

Exercise 3.4   Read the following excerpt from a textbook. First, locate in the passage the words indicated below the passage, and then write the <u>definition</u> for each word on the line provided, and indicate which technique (punctuation, text formatting, or a word) pointed you toward the definition.

Increased Life Expectancy

by Barbara Hansen Lemme

from *Development In Adulthood*

Average life expectancy (generally referred to as life expectancy) refers to the number of years an individual born in a particular year can expect to live, given the conditions present at that time. The average life expectancy for an infant born in Massachusetts in 1785 was 28 years. In 1900, it was about 45. And now it is about 77, though it varies depending on race and gender. These 20th-century gains in life expectancy were equivalent to gains made in all of the preceding 5,000 years....

Thus, the nature of adulthood and aging is changing. Not only are there more older adults today, they are healthier and more active than ever due to better medical care and improvements in diet, exercise, and other lifestyle factors. These changes prompted distinctions between **chronological age**—actual age in years—and **functional age** (Birren, 1969)—actual competence and performance—as people began to behave less and less in accordance with age stereotypes. For many, functional age became younger than chronological age. For example, people in their 60s and beyond began to behave more like what was thought to be typical of people in their 50s—healthy, active, youthful-looking. Neugarten (1974) proposed the terms *young-old* and *old-old* to reflect these changes. **Young-old** "refers not to a particular age but to health and social characteristics. A young-old person may be 55 or 85. The term represents the social reality that the line between middle age and old age is no longer clear" (Neugarten & Neugarten, 1987, p. 30). **Old-old** refers to the frail elderly, the minority of older people who often need special support and care. Baltes (1997) has proposed the term *fourth age* to refer to the period from age 80 on, which he sees as the major new frontier for developmental research and theory.

Word	Definition	Context Clue Hint (punctuation, text formatting, or a word)
1. average life expectancy		
2. chronological age		
3. functional age		
4. young-old		
5. old-old		
6. fourth age		

General Sense Context Clues

General sense context clues involve the entire sentence to generate clues about a word's meaning. Basically, you can understand the meaning of an unknown word by understanding the general sense of the rest of the sentence or sentences that surround the unknown word. Read the following sentence to see how general sense context clues work. In this sentence, the unknown word is *hypersensitive.*

I'm not allergic to anything, but my sister Lisa has *hypersensitive* allergies to seafood and anything citrus—she can't even stand the smell of oranges.

Now, read the sentence again and look for the general sense context clues. If you noticed that Lisa has "hypersensitive allergies" but her sister is "not allergic to anything," then you found one of the general sense context clues. This clue tells us that "not allergic to anything" is the extreme opposite of what Lisa has. Reviewing the sentence further, we see that not only is Lisa allergic to seafood and citrus, but she also has "hypersensitive allergies" to things: Lisa can't even breathe in the smell of citrus without reacting. So, *hypersensitive* seems to mean "overly sensitive." Lisa is overly or very sensitive to seafood and citrus. Thus, using clues from the general context, you can often decipher meaning for an unknown word—without using a dictionary. Practice this new strategy in the following exercise.

Exercise 3.5 Read each of the following sentences. First, identify the <u>general sense context clues</u> for the *italicized* word. Next, restate the meaning of the italicized word on the line that follows the sentence(s).

Try not to look up any words in the dictionary; instead, rely only on the clues offered in the sentence(s).

1. They would express for me the liveliest sympathy, and *console* me with the hope that something would occur by which I might be free (Douglass, 1845). _____

   _____

2. The dialogue *represented* the conversation which took place between them (Douglass, 1845). _____

   _____

3. I knew that once we had practiced surfing the web together, he would be *enabled* to do it anytime he wanted whether I was there or not. _____

   _____

4. I *loathed* them as being the meanest as well as the most wicked of men (Douglass, 1845). _____

   _____

5. After reading and *contemplating* the letter Drew left for me, I decided to forgive him. _____

   _____

6. It had given me a view of my *wretched* condition, without the remedy (Douglass, 1845). _____

   _____

7. No matter what Alicia did, the images from that horror movie continued to *torment* her for days after she'd seen it. _____

   _____

8. After trying for hours to put together the desk she'd bought from the furniture store, Shakira finally admitted that she was completely *perplexed* by the instructions. _____

    _____

9. Once Jeffrey made up his mind, it was clear that no one could shake his *resolve* to attend the concert. _____

    _____

10. After arriving late on her first day, Michelle knew she was *fortunate* to be given another opportunity to prove herself at the job. _____

    _____

Restatement Context Clues

Restatement context clues help define an unknown word by restating the meaning with different words. You might think of restatement context clues as synonyms. Though it is not always the case, the word used to restate the meaning is often a synonym. Read the sentence that follows for an illustration of restatement context clues. The unknown word is *stupendous*.

> Running a marathon is an incredible feat for the average person, so for the double amputee, it was even more of a *stupendous* accomplishment.

Now that you've read the sentence, see if you can identify the restatement context clue.

If you chose "incredible," then you are correct. *Stupendous* means incredible.

As you begin to use this strategy, keep in mind that restatement context clues, like definition context clues, are sometimes set off by punctuation. However, because this is not always the case, be on the lookout for restatements in the form of synonyms and explanatory word groups. Practice identifying restatement context clues in the following exercise.

Read each of the following sentences. First, identify the restatement context clues for the *italicized* word. Next, restate the meaning of the italicized word on the line that follows the sentence(s).

Exercise 3.6

Try not to look up any words in the dictionary; instead, rely only on the clues offered in the sentence(s).

1. Jose couldn't believe the main office was so *hectic*. He'd never experienced such an active and lively atmosphere. _____

    _____

2. The police officer asked the neighbor three times if the music had *abated*, and three times the neighbor confirmed that the music had not stopped—it actually became louder, he said. _____

    _____

3. There are many regulations against the distribution and selling of gasoline; for example, it is *prohibited* to transport gasoline in unauthorized containers. _____

    _____

4. Most general practice doctors do well in diagnosing familiar ailments like the common cold, but they are less *competent* in diagnosing lesser-known diseases. _____

    _____

5. Teenagers are generally very eager to *obtain* their driver's license, but once they get it, life turns out to be much the same as before. _____

    _____

6. Even though Sarah and David argue about nearly everything, they will never admit that they are *incompatible*. _____

    _____

7. If you were a real *denizen* of Key West and not a tourist, you would know that the people who actually live here don't care to have plastic pink flamingos on their lawns these days. _____

    _____

8. Much to the dismay of the victim's family, the federal judge *upheld* the lower court's ruling, thus indicating his full support of the state's right to dismiss the charges. _____

    _____

9. There are few things I *abhor* more than being lied to; in fact, my friends would rather hurt my feelings than risk making me angry with them for telling a little white lie. _____

    _____

10. In today's technologically savvy world, teens have many ways to *correspond* with their friends—I mean, who has the time to write an e-mail or make a phone call, they ask. _____

    _____

USING WORD PARTS

Using **word parts** to help you understand the meaning of an unknown word is another great strategy. This strategy is a bit like learning addition and subtraction: once you know the addition and subtraction basics, you can build on them to understand a number of more complex mathematical operations. Likewise, once you know key roots, prefixes, and suffixes, you can break words into less complex parts and also use word parts to create more complex words.

Here's a quick example. Consider the prefix *re-*, which means again or back. Now look at these words:

- Reuse
- Remake
- Rethink
- Retake
- Redo

Since you now know that *re-* means again or back, you have the tools to understand any one of these words.

- Reuse means to use again
- Remake means to make again
- Rethink means to think again
- Retake means to take back
- Redo means to do again

Let's look more closely at word parts. There are three word parts that we will examine, and they fit together rather neatly. A **prefix** attaches to the front of a word or root word and alters the meaning. A **suffix** attaches to the end of a word or root word and also changes the meaning of a word. A **root** is a part of a word and contains the core meaning. Prefixes and suffixes do not stand alone; they are always meant to be combined with a word to create a new word. Roots also do not stand alone.

Here's an illustration of how these word parts fit together.

PREFIX + WORD ROOT + SUFFIX = NEW WORD

Word parts can be an effective strategy for expanding your vocabulary. And memorizing some of the more common word parts will go a long way in increasing your ability to recognize and understand new vocabulary. The lists that follow will offer you a place to begin with roots, prefixes, and suffixes. All of these word parts come from either Latin or Greek.

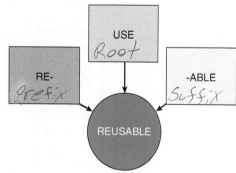

FIGURE 3.1

Table 3.1 Roots

Root	Meaning	Example Words
-anthrop-	human	misanthrope, philanthropy, anthropomorphic
-cept-	to take	accept, receptive, reception
-chron-	time	anachronism, chronic, chronicle, synchronize, chronometer
-cis-, -cid-	to cut, to kill	incisor, scissor, homicide, suicide
-dem-	people	democracy, demography, demagogue, endemic, pandemic
-dict-	to say	contradict, dictate, diction, edict, predict
-duc-	to lead, bring, take	deduce, produce, reduce
-fac-, -fici-, -fec-	to make, to do	facile, fiction, factory, fact
-gress-	to walk	digress, progress, transgress
-ject-	to throw	eject, inject, interject, project, reject, subject
-lat-	to carry	lateral, bilateral, latent
-leg-	law	legal, legislate, legislature, legitimize
-log-, -logo-	word	catalog, prologue, epilogue
-mit-, -mis-	to send, to do	transmit, mission, omission
-morph-	form	amorphous, metamorphic, morphology
-nav-, -naut-	to sail, boat	navigate, naval, nautical
-path-	feeling, suffering	empathy, sympathy, apathy, apathetic, psychopathic
-ped-, -pod-	foot	pedal, pedestrian, podiatrist
-pedo-, -ped-	child, children	pediatrician, pedagogue
-pel-	to drive	compel, dispel, impel, repel
-pend-	to hang	append, depend, impend, pendant, pendulum
-philo-, -phil-	having a strong affinity or love for	philanthropy, philharmonic, philosophy
-port-	to carry	comport, deport, export, import, report, support
-pos-	to put	compose, depose, oppose

Root	Meaning	Example Words
-press-	press	express, depress, impress, suppress
-rupt-	break	disrupt, interrupt, erupt
-scrib-, -script-	to write	describe, description, prescribe, prescription, subscribe, subscription, transcribe, transcription
-ten-, -tend-, -tain-	hold	tenable, maintain, contain, contend, pretend
-tract-	to pull, drag, draw	attract, contract, detract, extract, protract, retract, traction
-vert-	to turn	convert, divert, invert, revert
-vis-, -vid-	to see	vision, vista, visit, video

Table 3.2 Prefixes

Prefix	Meaning	Example Words
a-, an-	without	achromatic, amoral, atypical, asymptomatic
ad-	to, toward	admit, adjust, adhere
anti-, ant-	opposite; opposing	anticrime, antipollution, antacid
aud-, audi-, aur-	to hear	audience, auditory, audible, auditorium, audiovisual, audition, auricular
auto-	self, same	autobiography, automatic, autopilot
bio-, bi-	life, living organism	biology, biography, biophysics, biotechnology, biopsy
co-	together	coauthor, coeditor, copilot
con-, com-	with	complete, compel, conscious, condense, confess, confirm
de-	away, off; generally indicates reversal or removal in English	deactivate, defrost, decompress, detract
di-	two, across	direct, dissect, divert
dis-	not, apart	disbelief, discomfort, discredit, disrepair, disrespect
ex-, e-	out of, from	except, eject, external
geo-	Earth; geography	geography, geophysics, geopolitics

Prefix	Meaning	Example Words
hetero-	other	heterogeneous, heterosexual, heterodox
homo-	same	homonym, homosexual, homogenized, homophone
hyper-	excessive, excessively	hyperactive, hypercritical, hypersensitive
in-, im-	into, not	inject, impose, impossible, impolite
inter-	between, among	international, interfaith, intertwine, interject
micro-	small	microcosm, microeconomics, microscope
mono-	one, single, alone	monochrome, monosyllable, monoxide
multi-	many	multiple, multiply, multitask
neo-	new, recent	neonatal, neophyte, neoconservatism, neofascism
non-	not	nonessential, nonmetallic, nonresident, nonviolence, nonskid, nonstop
ob-	to, toward	obstacle, obvious, object
pan-	all	panorama, panchromatic, pandemic, pantheism
post-	after	postdate, postwar, postnasal, postnatal
pre-	before	preconceive, preexist, premeditate, predispose, prepossess, prepay
pro-	near, support, forward	proceed, promote, prolife
re-	again; back, backward	rearrange, rebuild, recall, remake, rerun, rewrite
sub-	under	submarine, subsoil, subway, subhuman, substandard
thermo-, therm-	heat	thermal, thermometer, thermostat
trans-	across, beyond, through	transatlantic, transpolar

Table 3.3 Suffixes

Suffix	Meaning	Example Words
-able, -ible	forms adjectives and means "capable or worthy of"	likable, flexible
-al	relating to (adj.)	polar, solar, aural
-ary, -ory	connected to, place	stationary, oratory, laboratory
-ation	forms nouns from verbs	creation, civilization, automation, speculation, information
-duct	carry, lead	conduct, deduct
-fy, -ify	forms verbs and means "to make or cause to become"	purify, beautify, multiply, humidify
-gram	something written or drawn, a record	cardiogram, telegram
-graph	something written or drawn; an instrument for writing, drawing, or recording	monograph, phonograph, seismograph
-ia, -y	condition (noun)	nostalgia, mania, anarchy, democracy
-ism	forms nouns and means "the act, state, or theory of"	criticism, optimism, capitalism
-ist	forms agent nouns (one who does or one who prefers)	conformist, copyist, cyclist, classist, sexist
-ive	relating to (adj.)	reactive, active, protective
-ize	forms verbs from nouns and adjectives	jeopardize, legalize, modernize, emphasize, hospitalize, computerize
-logue	speech, discourse; to speak	monologue, dialogue, travelogue
-logy	study of, science of	phraseology, biology, dermatology
-ly	makes an adverb	sleepily, tenderly, friendly, angrily
-ment	forms nouns from verbs	entertainment, amazement, statement, banishment
-meter, -metry	measuring device; measure	spectrometer, geometry, kilometer, parameter, perimeter

Suffix	Meaning	Example Words
-oid	forms adjectives and nouns and means "like, resembling," or "shape"	humanoid, spheroid, trapezoid
-ous	full of, characteristic of	ambiguous, delicious
-phile	one that loves or has a strong affinity for; loving	audiophile, Francophile
-phobe, -phobia	one that fears a specified thing; an intense fear of a specified thing	homophobe, homopho-bia, xenophobe, xenophobia
-phone	sound; device that receives or emits sound; speaker of a language	homophone, geophone, telephone, Francophone
-tion, -ion, -sion	condition (noun)	action, motion, decision
-ty, -ity	forms nouns from adjectives	subtlety, certainty, cruelty, frailty, loyalty, royalty; eccentricity, electricity, peculiarity, similarity, technicality

While the preceding list is not exhaustive, it includes many of the more common roots, prefixes, and suffixes. Let's take a look at two examples of how words can be deciphered by using word parts.

	prefix	root word	suffix	
reusable	re	use	able	= able to be used again
Definition	*again*	*put into action*	*capable of*	

	prefix	root word	suffix	
nonviolent	non	violent		= not using physical force
Definition	*not*	*using physical force*		

As you can see, breaking the words into their parts simplifies words that may have once appeared complex. While it may take some practice breaking down words as done in the charts above, it becomes easier once you memorize common word parts.

Exercise 3.7   **Use the roots, prefixes, and suffixes in the provided tables to aid you in deciphering the words in the exercise that follow. Determine the meaning of each of the words by analyzing its word parts.**

Fill in the chart just as demonstrated in the preceding examples. Remember that not all word parts are used for each word. Also, be creative in your interpretation of the word's meaning once you have the definition of the word parts.

	prefix	root word	suffix	
1. intercept				
Definition				

	prefix	root word	suffix	
2. transform				
Definition				

	prefix	root word	suffix	
3. digress				
Definition				

	prefix	root word	suffix	
4. monologue				
Definition				

	prefix	root word	suffix	
5. banishment				
Definition				

	prefix	root word	suffix	
6. indispensable				
Definition				

	prefix	root word	suffix	
7. retain				
Definition				

	prefix	root word	suffix	
8. postwar				
Definition				

	prefix	root word	suffix	
9. compel				
Definition				

	prefix	root word	suffix	
10. deduct				
Definition				

USING DICTIONARY DEFINITIONS

Looking for a word in the dictionary may have been the first strategy you ever learned to understand unfamiliar words. This strategy is still very helpful in many cases, so don't think that your oldest strategy is no longer useful. Instead of disregarding the old strategy, let's look at ways of enhancing it with other strategies to aid you in selecting the most appropriate dictionary definition.

Parts of Speech

The **part of speech** of a word indicates how the word should be used in a sentence. When you look up a word in the dictionary, immediately following the pronunciation key is the part of speech. Keep in mind, however, that some words may be used as different parts of speech, depending on the context. Table 3.4 highlights the ten parts of speech, how they are commonly abbreviated in a dictionary, their usage, and an example.

Table 3.4

Part of Speech	Abbreviation	USAGE	EXAMPLE
verb	v.	action or state	think, buy, have
transitive verb	v.t.	expresses an action and a direct object receives the action	take (my car), want (a soda), paint (the room)
intransitive verb	v.i.	expresses an action but is not followed by a direct object	arrive, die, sneeze
noun	n.	person or thing	car, dog, house
adjective	adj.	describes a noun	hot, small
adverb	adv.	describes a verb, adverb, or adjective	slowly, quickly
pronoun	pron.	replaces a noun	she, he, you
preposition	prep.	links a noun to another word	to, on, over
interjection	interj.	short exclamation	Oh! Ha! Well!
conjunction	conj.	joins sentences, clauses, or words	and, but, so

Now, to fully grasp this strategy, let's examine the dictionary entry of an actual word. Here's how the entry for the word *impart* looks in a dictionary:

im·part (im-pärt´) *v.t.* **1**, make known; tell. **2**, give; bestow; share. —**im˝par·ta´tion**, *n.*

As you can see, *impart* is a transitive verb. Transitive means that it generally has a direct object. Direct objects receive the action of a verb. For example, you might *impart* wisdom. The part of speech, a transitive verb, tells you how to use *impart* in any given sentence.

Multiple Definitions

If you refer to the entry for the word *impart* once again, you will notice that there are two options for the definition. Which one do you use? Well, like everything else in this chapter, it depends on the context. Let's look at an example.

> My first college roommate was a senior, and she was able to *impart* to me all the tips and secrets she'd learned during her time at the college.

For this particular sentence, which definition of *impart* is most appropriate? If you said definition 2, or "give," then you are correct. To check your work, insert the definition into the sentence and see if it makes sense.

> My first college roommate was a senior, and she was able to *give* to me all the tips and secrets she'd learned during her time at the college.

As you can see, this does make sense.

Let's practice this strategy with another word. Here is a dictionary snapshot.

pi´ous (pī əs) *adj.* **1,** godly; devout. **2,** pretending piety. —**pi´ous·ness**, *n.*

> When I went there, she was a *pious*, warm, and tender-hearted woman. (Douglass)

Now that you've read the sentence, use the dictionary snapshot to select the appropriate definition for the word *pious*. If you selected the first definition, "godly; devout," then you are correct. But let's insert the definition into the sentence just to be sure it makes sense.

> When I went there, she was a *devout*, warm, and tender-hearted woman.

Once again, the definition we selected is a good fit. With practice, locating the appropriate definition can be relatively simple if you consider the context in which the word is used.

Practice locating the appropriate dictionary definition in the following exercise. All of the words used in this exercise come from the reading selection "Learning to Read and Write" by Frederick Douglass. The full reading is included at the end of this chapter in Strategies in Action.

Exercise 3.8   Read each of the following sentences. First, use the snapshots of dictionary definitions to verify the part of speech of the *italicized* word. Next, select the definition that best fits the context of the sentence in which the word is used. Write that definition on the line that follows the sentence.

---

apt *adj.* **1,** suited to its purpose. **2,** quick in learning. **3,** having a tendency; inclined. —**apt´ness,** *n*

brute (broot) *n.* **1,** a beast. **2,** a savage, cruel person. —*adj.* like a beast; not sensitive or reasoning.

chat´tel (chat´əl) *n.* a movable piece of personal property. 🗗 *cattle*

com·pli´ant (kəm-plī-ənt) *adj.* complying; yielding to the wishes of others. —**com·pli´ance,** *n.*

de·nun˝c·i·a´tion (dj-nun˝sė-ā´shən) *n.* act or result of denouncing. —**de·nun´ciate,** *v.t.*—**de·nun´ci·a·to·ry** (-ətôr-ė), *adj.*

dis˝po·si´tion (dis˝pə-zish´ən) *n.* **1,** an arrangement of parts. **2,** definite settlement; ultimate destination. **3,** innate temper; natural tendency of the mind.

e·man´ci·pate˝ (i-man´si-pāt˝) *v.t.* set free from a restraint; liberate. —**eman˝ci·pa´tion,** *n.* —**eman´ci·pa˝tor,** *n.*

pre´cept (prē´sept) *n.* a rule for moral conduct; maxim. —**pre·cep´tor,** *n.*

strat´a·gem (strat´ə-jəm) *n.* a means of deception; a trick.

> **stratagem, strategy**
> Although these two words are often used as synonyms, they have distinct meanings. A *stratagem* is a trick intended to deceive, whereas *strategy* is the science of tactical planning. Both words derive from Greek *stratēgós,* general of an army.

te´di·ous (tē´dė-əs) *adj.* long, slow, and tiresome. —**te´di·ous·ness,** *n.*

1. She was an *apt* woman; and a little experience soon demonstrated, to her satisfaction, that education and slavery were incompatible with each other. _____

_____

2. Under its influence, the tender heart became stone, and the lamblike *disposition* gave way to one of tiger-like fierceness. _____

_____

_____

3. She now commenced to practice her husband's *precepts.* _____

_____

_____

4. It was at least necessary for her to have some training in the exercise of irresponsible power, to make her equal to the task of treating me as though I were a *brute.* _____

_____

5. My mistress, who had kindly commenced to instruct me, had, in *compliance* with the advice and direction of her husband, not only ceased to instruct, but had set her face against my being instructed by any one else.

_____

_____

6. In accomplishing this, I was compelled to resort to various *stratagems.* _____

_____

_____

7. In entering upon the duties of a slaveholder, she did not seem to perceive that I sustained to her the relation of a mere *chattel*, and that for her to treat me as a human being was not only wrong, but dangerously so. _____

_____

8. The slave was made to say some very smart as well as impressive things in reply to his master—things which had the desired though unexpected

effect; for the conversation resulted in the voluntary *emancipation* of the slave on the part of the master. _____

_____

9. What I got from Sheridan was a bold *denunciation* of slavery, and a powerful vindication of human rights. _____

_____

10. Thus, after a long, *tedious* effort for years, I finally succeeded in learning how to write. _____

_____

Vocabulary Strategies Review
Combined Practice 1

Read the following excerpt (the full short story is in Chapter 2), and use the vocabulary strategies from this chapter to define the selected words.

The Story of an Hour (excerpt)

By Kate Chopin

_____

She was young, with a fair, calm face, whose lines bespoke **repression** and even a certain strength. But now there was a dull stare in her eyes, whose gaze was fixed away off yonder on one of those patches of blue sky. It was not a glance of reflection, but rather indicated a suspension of intelligent thought.

There was something coming to her and she was waiting for it, fearfully. What was it? She did not know; it was too subtle and elusive to name. But she felt it, creeping out of the sky, reaching toward her through the sounds, the scents, the color that filled the air.

Now her bosom rose and fell tumultuously. She was beginning to recognize this thing that was approaching to possess her, and she was **striving** to beat it back with her will—as powerless as her two white slender hands would have been.

When she abandoned herself a little whispered word escaped her slightly parted lips. She said it over and over under her breath:

"free, free, free!" The **vacant** stare and the look of terror that had followed it went from her eyes. They stayed **keen** and bright. Her pulses beat fast, and the **coursing** blood warmed and relaxed every inch of her body.

She did not stop to ask if it were or were not a monstrous joy that held her. A clear and exalted **perception enabled** her to dismiss the suggestion as trivial.

She knew that she would weep again when she saw the kind, tender hands folded in death; the face that had never looked save with love upon her, fixed and gray and dead. But she saw beyond that bitter moment a long **procession** of years to come that would belong to her absolutely. And she opened and spread her arms out to them in welcome.

There would be no one to live for during those coming years; she would live for herself. There would be no powerful will bending hers in that blind **persistence** with which men and women believe they have a right to **impose** a private will upon a fellow-creature. A kind intention or a cruel intention made the act seem no less a crime as she looked upon it in that brief moment of **illumination**.

And yet she had loved him—sometimes. Often she had not. What did it matter! What could love, the unsolved mystery, count for in the face of this possession of self-assertion which she suddenly recognized as the strongest **impulse** of her being!

Word	Definition	Strategy Used
example	*illustration*	*general sense context clue*
1. repression		
2. striving		
3. vacant		
4. keen		
5. coursing		
6. perception		
7. enabled		
8. procession		
9. persistence		
10. impose		
11. illumination		
12. impulse		

Read the following excerpt (the full article is in Chapter 2), and use the vocabulary strategies from this chapter to define the selected words.

Building Safe Schools for Girls in War Zones (excerpt)

by Anna Mulrine

Hard climb. There were times when Mortenson, an **avid** mountain climber who worked in hospital emergency rooms to fund his passion, wasn't sure he would be able to start a school in the small Pakistani village where he found himself exhausted and lost after a failed attempt to **ascend** the **notorious** K2 Himalayan **summit.** But he was determined to return the generosity the villagers had shown him. "I kind of had to give up everything, and sell all my possessions, until things started to change around," he says. After hearing of his efforts, American schoolchildren stepped in. Their 62,400 donated pennies helped to build his first school. The villages are supplied with masons, carpenters, and teacher training. Villages must provide free labor, wood, and land.

He now visits about 200 schools a year throughout the United States, from kindergartens to the Air Force Academy, to speak about his efforts to educate **impoverished** children. Pennies for Peace will be in some 20,000 schools next year, giving rise to what Mortenson hopes will become a new generation of leaders in the United States who will take up the cause of global education. "Women who have an education are not likely to **condone** their son getting into violence," he says. "I've seen that very **vividly.**"

In Afghanistan in 2000, there were 800,000 children in school, nearly all boys. Today, there are 8.4 million children in school, including 2.5 million girls. "That's the greatest increase in school enrollment of any country in modern history, but very few people in America seem to be aware of it." Mortenson hopes to **remedy** that through his work in the years to come.

Word	Definition	Strategy Used
example	*illustration*	*general sense context clue*
1. avid		
2. ascend		

Word	Definition	Strategy Used
3. notorious		
4. summit		
5. impoverished		
6. condone		
7. vividly		
8. remedy		

KEY TERM REVIEW

These key terms will be defined by example. Add your own examples when none are provided.

Context Clues—select a sentence from the chapter to serve as an example of the different types of context clues.

- **Example context clues**

- _____
  _____

- **Contrast context clues**

- _____
  _____

- **Definition context clues**

- _____
  _____

- **General sense context clues**

- _____
  _____

- **Restatement context clues**

- _____
  _____

Word Parts—an example of how the word part is used is provided. Define the words using the provided word parts.

- **Root**—pandemic = pan - dem - ic

- **Prefix**—confirm = con - firm

- **Suffix**—amazement = amaze - ment

Dictionary Definitions—an example of the part of speech is provided.

- **Parts of speech**
  - noun—stadium, car, person
  - verb—run, grab, sleep, love
    - transitive—to set (down), to take (the job)
    - intransitive—gamble, talk
  - pronoun—he, she, they
  - adjective—fancy, delightful
  - adverb—awkwardly, quickly
  - preposition—to, on, below
  - conjunction—and, but, for
  - interjection—Oh! Ha! Eh!

STRATEGIES IN ACTION

Nearly two hundred years ago, a young man named Frederick was introduced to the written word. Read the following selection from *Narrative of the Life of Frederick Douglass, an American Slave* and see how he taught himself to decipher the marks and scratches we understand to be the written word.

As you read Douglass's story, you may feel an odd sense of déjà vu. There's a good reason for that: some of the vocabulary words used in the previous exercises, especially Exercise 3.8, were drawn from "Learning to Read and Write." So, as you read, check your earlier work if you encounter an unknown word; chances are that you've already defined it.

Learning to Read and Write

By Frederick Douglass

Frederick Douglass (1818–1895) was born into slavery in Tuckahoe, Maryland. He met his mother only a few times in his youth because she'd been sent to work on a distant plantation soon after his birth. As a young slave, Douglass was spared some of the physical cruelties of slavery, but he did suffer the mental anguish the system imposed, such as not knowing his mother, having his birth date withheld from him, and seeing and hearing the horrible beatings other slaves endured. Despite the challenges of his situation, Douglass lived to be a free man. He became a world-renowned speaker against slavery, an American statesman, and an author of three books. This selection is from his first autobiography, published in 1845, Narrative of the Life of Frederick Douglass, an American Slave. *The selection takes place in Baltimore at a home to which Douglass had been sent when he was about seven years old to care for the couple's young son.*

Based on the author's bio and the title, what do you think this reading will be about?

I lived in Master Hugh's family about seven years. During this time, I succeeded in learning to read and write. In accomplishing this, I was compelled to resort to various stratagems. I had no regular teacher. My mistress, who had kindly commenced to instruct me, had, in compliance with the advice and direction of her husband, not only ceased to instruct, but had set her face against my being instructed by any one else. It is due, however, to my mistress to say of her, that she did not adopt this course of treatment immediately. She at first lacked the depravity indispensable to shutting me up in mental darkness. It was at least necessary for her to have some training in the exercise of irresponsible power, to make her equal to the task of treating me as though I were a brute.

My mistress was, as I have said, a kind and tenderhearted woman; and in the simplicity of her soul she commenced, when I first went to live with her, to treat me as she supposed one human being ought to treat another. In entering upon the duties of a slaveholder, she did not seem to perceive that I sustained to her the relation of a mere chattel, and that for her to treat me as a human being was not only wrong, but dangerously so. Slavery proved as injurious to her as it did to me. When I went there, she was a pious, warm, and tender-hearted woman. There was no sorrow or suffering for which she had not a tear. She had bread for the hungry, clothes for the naked, and comfort for every mourner that came within her reach. Slavery soon proved its ability to divest her of these heavenly qualities. Under its influence, the tender heart became stone, and the lamblike disposition gave way to one of tiger-like fierceness. The first step in her downward course was in her ceasing to instruct me. She now commenced to practice her husband's precepts. She finally became even more violent in her opposition than her husband himself. She was not satisfied with simply doing as well as he had commanded; she seemed anxious to do better. Nothing seemed to make her more angry than to see me with a newspaper. She seemed to think that here lay the danger. I have had her rush at me with a face made all up of fury, and snatch from me a newspaper, in a manner that fully revealed her apprehension. She was an apt woman; and a little experience soon demonstrated, to her satisfaction, that education and slavery were incompatible with each other.

From this time I was most narrowly watched. If I was in a separate room any considerable length of time, I was sure to be suspected of having a book, and was at once called to give an account of myself. All this, however, was too late. The first step had been taken. Mistress, in teaching me the alphabet, had given me the *inch,* and no precaution could prevent me from taking the *ell.*

The plan which I adopted, and the one by which I was most successful, was that of making friends of all the little white boys whom I met in the street. As many of these as I could, I converted into teachers. With their kindly aid, obtained at different times and in different places, I finally succeeded in learning to read. When I was sent of errands, I always took my book with me, and by going one part of my errand quickly, I found time to get a lesson before my return. I used also to carry bread with me, enough of which was always in the house, and to which I was always welcome; for I was much better off in this regard than many of the poor white children in our neighborhood. This bread I used to bestow upon the hungry little urchins, who, in return, would give me that more valuable bread of knowledge. I am strongly tempted to give the names of two or three of those little boys, as a testimonial of the gratitude and affection I bear them; but prudence forbids;—not that it would injure me, but it might embarrass them; for it is almost an unpardonable offence to teach slaves to read in this Christian country. It is enough to say of the dear little fellows, that they lived on Philpot Street, very near Durgin and Bailey's ship-yard. I used to talk this matter of slavery over with them. I would sometimes say to them, I wished I could be as free as they would be when they got to be men. "You will be free as soon as you are twenty-one, *but I am a slave for life!* Have not I as good a right to be free as you have?" These words used to trouble them; they would express for me the liveliest sympathy, and console me with the hope that something would occur by which I might be free.

I was now about twelve years old, and the thought of being *a slave for life* began to bear heavily upon my heart. Just about this time, I got hold of a book entitled "The Columbian Orator." Every opportunity I got, I used to read this book. Among much of other interesting matter, I found in it a dialogue between a master and his slave. The slave was represented as having run away from his master three times. The dialogue represented the conversation which took place between them, when the slave was retaken the third time. In this dialogue, the whole argument in behalf of slavery was brought forward by the master, all of which was disposed of by the slave. The slave was made to say some very smart as well as impressive things in reply to his master—things which had the desired though unexpected effect; for the conversation resulted in the voluntary emancipation of the slave on the part of the master.

In the same book, I met with one of Sheridan's mighty speeches on and in behalf of Catholic emancipation. These were choice documents to me. I read them over and over again with una-bated interest. They gave tongue to interesting thoughts of my own soul, which had frequently flashed through my mind, and died away for want of utterance. The moral which I gained from the dialogue was the power of truth over the conscience of even a slaveholder. What I got from Sheridan was a bold denunciation of slavery, and a powerful vindication of human rights. The reading of these docu-ments enabled me to utter my thoughts, and to meet the arguments brought forward to sustain slavery; but while they relieved me of one difficulty, they brought on another even more painful than the one of which I was relieved. The more I read, the more I was led to abhor and detest my enslavers. I could regard them in no other light than a band of successful robbers, who had left their homes, and gone to Africa, and stolen us from our homes, and in a strange land reduced us to slavery. I loathed them as being the meanest as well as the most wicked of men.

As I read and contemplated the subject, behold! that very discon-tentment which Master Hugh had predicted would follow my learning to read had already come, to torment and sting my soul to unutterable anguish. As I writhed under it, I would at times feel that learning to read had been a curse rather than a blessing. It had given me a view of my wretched condition, without the remedy. It opened my eyes to the horrible pit, but to no ladder upon which to get out. In moments of agony, I envied my fellow-slaves for their stupidity. I have often wished myself a beast. I preferred the condition of the meanest reptile to my own. Any thing, no matter what, to get rid of thinking! It was this everlasting thinking of my condition that tormented me. There was no getting rid of it. It was pressed upon me by every object within sight or hearing, animate or inanimate. The silver trump of freedom had roused my soul to eternal wakefulness. Freedom now appeared, to disappear no more forever. It was heard in every sound, and seen in every thing. It was ever present to torment me with a sense of my wretched condition. I saw nothing without seeing it, I heard nothing without hearing it, and felt nothing without feeling it. It looked from every star, it smiled in every calm, breathed in every wind, and moved in every storm.

I often found myself regretting my own existence, and wishing myself dead; and but for the hope of being free, I have no doubt but that I should have killed myself, or done something for which I should have been killed. While in this state of mind, I was eager to hear any one speak of slavery. I was a ready listener. Every little while, I could hear something about the abolitionists. It was some time before I found what the word meant. It was always used in such connections as to make it an interesting word to me. If a slave ran away and succeeded in getting clear, or if a slave killed his master, set fire to a barn, or did any thing very wrong in the mind of a slaveholder, it was spoken of as the fruit of *abolition*. Hearing the word in this connection very often, I set about learning what it meant. The dictionary afforded me little or no help. I found it was "the act of abolishing;" but then I did not know what was to be abolished. Here I was perplexed. I did not dare to ask any one about its meaning, for I was satisfied that it was something they wanted me to know very little about. After a patient waiting, I got one of our city papers, containing an account of the number of petitions from the north, praying for the abolition of slavery in the District of Columbia, and of the slave trade between the States. From this time I understood the words *abolition* and *abolitionist,* and always drew near when that word was spoken, expecting to hear something of importance to myself and fellow-slaves. The light broke in upon me by degrees.

I went one day down on the wharf of Mr. Waters; and seeing two Irishmen unloading a scow of stone, I went, unasked, and helped them. When we had finished, one of them came to me and asked me if I were a slave. I told him I was. He asked, "Are ye a slave for life?" I told him that I was. The good Irishman seemed to be deeply affected by the statement. He said to the other that it was a pity so fine a little fellow as myself should be a slave for life. He said it was a shame to hold me. They both advised me to run away to the north; that I should find friends there, and that I should be free. I pretended not to be interested in what they said, and treated them as if I did not understand them; for I feared they might be treacherous. White men have been known to encourage slaves to escape, and then, to get the reward, catch them and return them to their masters. I was afraid that these seemingly good men might use me so; but I nevertheless remembered their advice, and from that time I resolved to run away. I looked forward to a time at which it would be safe for me to escape. I was too young to think of doing so immediately; besides, I wished to learn how to write, as I might have occasion to write my own pass. I consoled myself with the hope that I should one day find a good chance. Meanwhile, I would learn to write.

The idea as to how I might learn to write was suggested to me by being in Durgin and Bailey's ship-yard, and frequently seeing the ship carpenters, after hewing, and getting a piece of timber ready for use, write on the timber the name of that part of the ship for which it was intended. When a piece of timber was intended for the larboard side, it would be marked thus—"L." When a piece was for the starboard side, it would be marked thus—"S." A piece for the larboard side forward, would be marked thus—"L. F." When a piece was for starboard side forward, it would be marked thus—"S. F." For larboard aft, it would be marked thus—"L. A." For starboard aft, it would be marked thus—"S. A." I soon learned the names of these letters, and for what they were intended when placed upon a piece of timber in the ship-yard. I immediately commenced copying them, and in a short time was able to make the four letters named. After that, when I met with any boy who I knew could write, I would tell him I could write as well as he. The next word would be, "I don't believe you. Let me see you try it." I would then make the letters which I had been so fortunate as to learn, and ask him to beat that. In this way I got a good many lessons in writing, which it is quite possible I should never have gotten in any other way. During this time, my copy-book was the board fence, brick wall, and pavement; my pen and ink was a lump of chalk. With these, I learned mainly how to write. I then commenced and continued copying the Italics in Webster's Spelling Book, until I could make them all without looking on the book. By this time, my little Master Thomas had gone to school, and learned how to write, and had written over a number of copy-books. These had been brought home, and shown to some of our near neighbors, and then laid aside. My mistress used to go to class meeting at the Wilk Street meetinghouse every Monday afternoon, and leave me to take care of the house. When left thus, I used to spend the time in writing in the spaces left in Master Thomas's copy-book, copying what he had written. I continued to do this until I could write a hand very similar to that of Master Thomas. Thus, after a long, tedious effort for years, I finally succeeded in learning how to write.

***

Understanding Context

1. What particular circumstances did Douglass need to confront as he sought to learn to read and write?

2. Was Douglass externally or internally motivated? Explain your response.

3. Did the reading material Douglass encountered affect his understanding of the world? Explain your response.

Vocabulary in Context

As indicated previously, many of the challenging words appearing in "Learning to Read and Write" were discussed in the exercises given previously in this chapter. Still, there may have been a few words that gave you pause. What were they? List at least five words that were unfamiliar to you in this selection, and also write their definitions. Use context clues or one of the other vocabulary strategies to define these words.

1. _____

2. _____

3. _____

4. _____

5. _____

Checking In

1. What is the most surprising information you discovered about Frederick Douglass? Why was it surprising?

2. Do you think there are any connections between Frederick Douglass's and Sherman Alexie's experiences? (Sherman Alexie's essay is in Chapter 1.)

Getting the Point

1. ____ What did Douglass's mistress do when he first began living with her?
   a) She told him the rules of slavery.
   b) She began teaching him.
   c) She showed him how to cook for the family.
   d) She treated him as a brute.

2. ____ Why did Douglass's mistress change her treatment of Douglass?
   a) Her husband told her to.
   b) Douglass wasn't grateful enough.
   c) The reason is not given.
   d) The mistress began reading a book on slavery.

3. ____ What was Douglass's plan to learn to read?
   a) He didn't have a plan to learn to read.
   b) He convinced his master's young son to teach him how to read.
   c) He befriended the poor white boys in his neighborhood for lessons.
   d) He would sneak to the library and read books when he had time.

4. ____ How did Douglass feel after learning to read and discovering certain facts about slavery?
   a) He felt that education was the best way to be happy.
   b) He felt depressed and trapped by his situation as a slave.
   c) He felt grateful that he had a mistress and master who were kind.
   d) He felt no differently than he had before learning to read.

5. ____ How was Douglass's plan to learn to write similar to his earlier method of learning to read?
   a) Both plans depended on the boys in his neighborhood for lessons.
   b) Both plans required him to go to the library when he could.
   c) Both plans were conducted at the shipyards where he worked.
   d) Both plans relied on his mistress teaching him what she knew.

6. ____ What do Douglass's efforts to learn to read and write reveal about him?
   a) He was an ungrateful person for tricking his mistress.
   b) He was fortunate to have a kind mistress.
   c) He was a lucky person.
   d) He was a very determined person.

STRATEGIES IN ACTION

The Ways We Lie

by Stephanie Ericsson

Stephanie Ericsson (1953–) began her writing career in television. She has worked for an award-winning screenwriter and worked as a screenwriter for the popular sitcom Mork & Mindy *(starring Robin Williams). In 1988, she wrote* Companion Through the Darkness *from the journals she kept after her husband's sudden death, and it became an instant classic on grief from the moment it was published in 1993. Her work includes "The Ways We Lie" and* ShameFaced. *She is also the editor of two books by Stephen Zuckerman:* New Clichés for the 21st Century *and* Doc, What's Up?

Review the words in Vocabulary in Context which follow this reading. Mark or highlight those words as you read.

The bank called today, and I told them my deposit was in the mail, even though I hadn't written a check yet. It'd been a rough day. The baby I'm pregnant with decided to do aerobics on my lungs for two hours, our three-year-old daughter painted the living-room couch with lipstick, the IRS put me on hold for an hour, and I was late to a business meeting because I was tired. [1]

I told my client that traffic had been bad. When my partner came home, his haggard face told me his day hadn't gone any better than mine, so when he asked, "How was your day?" I said, "Oh, fine," knowing that one more straw might break his back. A friend called and wanted to take me to lunch. I said I was busy. Four lies in the course of a day, none of which I felt the least bit guilty about. [2]

We lie. We all do. We exaggerate, we minimize, we avoid confrontation, we spare people's feelings, we conveniently forget, we keep secrets, we justify lying to the big-guy institutions. Like most people, I indulge in small falsehoods and still think of myself as an honest person. Sure I lie, but it doesn't hurt anything. Or does it? [3]

I once tried going a whole week without telling a lie, and it was paralyzing. I discovered that telling the truth all the time is nearly impossible. It means living with some serious consequences: The bank charges me $60 in overdraft fees, my partner keels over when I tell him about my travails, my client fires me for telling her I didn't feel like being on time, and my friend takes it personally when I say I'm not hungry. There must be some merit to lying. [4]

But if I justify lying, what makes me any different from slick politicians or the corporate robbers who raided the S&L industry? Saying it's okay to lie one way and not another is hedging. I cannot seem to escape the voice deep inside me that tells me: When someone lies, someone loses. What far-reaching consequences will I, or others, pay as a result of my lie? Will someone's trust be destroyed? Will someone else pay my penance because I ducked out? We must consider the meaning of our actions. Deception, lies, capital crimes, and misdemeanors all carry meanings. *Webster's* definition of *lie* is specific:

1. a false statement or action especially made with the intent to deceive;
2. anything that gives or is meant to give a false impression.

A definition like this implies that there are many, many ways to tell a lie. Here are just a few. [5]

The White Lie

The white lie assumes that the truth will cause more damage than a simple, harmless untruth. Telling a friend he looks great when he looks like hell can be based on a decision that the friend needs a compliment more than a frank opinion. But, in effect, it is the liar deciding what is best for the lied to. Ultimately, it is a vote of no confidence. It is an act of subtle arrogance for anyone to decide what is best for someone else. [6]

Yet not all circumstances are quite so cut-and-dried. Take, for instance, the sergeant in Vietnam who knew one of his men was killed in action but listed him as missing so that the man's family would receive indefinite compensation instead of the lump-sum pittance the military gives widows and children. His intent was honorable. Yet for twenty years this family kept their hopes alive, unable to move on to a new life. [7]

> *A man who won't lie to a woman has very little consideration for her feelings.*
> —*Bergen Evans*

Facades

Et tu, Brute?
—Caesar

We all put up facades to one degree or another. When I put on a suit to go to see a client, I feel as though I am putting on another face, obeying the expectation that serious businesspeople wear suits rather than sweatpants. But I'm a writer. Normally, I get up, get the kid off to school, and sit at my computer in my pajamas until four in the afternoon. When I answer the phone, the caller thinks I'm wearing a suit (though the UPS man knows better). [8]

But facades can be destructive because they are used to seduce others into an illusion. For instance, I recently realized that a former friend was a liar. He presented himself with all the right looks and the right words and offered lots of new consciousness theories, fabulous books to read, and fascinating insights. Then I did some business with him, and the time came for him to pay me. He turned out to be all talk and no walk. I heard a plethora of reasonable excuses, including in-depth descriptions of the big break around the corner. In six months of work, I saw less than a hundred bucks. When I confronted him, he raised both eyebrows and tried to convince me that I'd heard him wrong, that he'd made no commitment to me. A simple investigation into his past revealed a crowded graveyard of disenchanted former friends. [9]

Ignoring the Plain Facts

*Well, you must
understand that
Father Porter is only
human.*
*—A Massachusetts
priest*

In the '60s, the Catholic Church in Massachusetts began hearing complaints that Father James Porter was sexually molesting children. Rather than relieving him of his duties, the ecclesiastical authorities simply moved him from one parish to another between 1960 and 1967, actually providing him with a fresh supply of unsuspecting families and innocent children to abuse. After treatment in 1967 for pedophilia, he went back to work, this time in Minnesota. The new diocese was aware of Father Porter's obsession with children, but they needed priests and recklessly believed treatment had cured him. More children were abused until he was relieved of his duties a year later. By his own admission, Porter may have abused as many as a hundred children. [10]

Ignoring the facts may not in and of itself be a form of lying, but consider the context of this situation. If a lie is a false action done with the intent to deceive, then the Catholic Church's conscious covering for Porter created irreparable consequences. The church became a co-perpetrator with Porter. [11]

Deflecting

I've discovered that I can keep anyone from seeing the true me by being selectively blatant. I set a precedent of being up-front about intimate issues, but I never bring up the things I truly want to hide; I just let people assume I'm revealing everything. It's an effective way of hiding. [12]

Any good liar knows that the way to perpetuate an untruth is to deflect attention from it. When Clarence Thomas exploded with accusations that the Senate hearings were a "high-tech lynching," he simply switched the focus from a highly charged subject to a radioactive subject. Rather than defending himself, he took the offensive and accused the country of racism. It was a brilliant maneuver. Racism is now politically incorrect in official circles—unlike sexual harassment, which still rewards those who can get away with it. [13]

Some of the most skilled deflectors are passive-aggressive people who, when accused of inappropriate behavior, refuse to respond to the accusations. This you-don't-exist stance infuriates the accuser, who, understandably, screams something obscene out of frustration. The trap is sprung and the act of deflection successful, because now the passive-aggressive person can indignantly say, "Who can talk to someone as unreasonable as you?" The real issue is forgotten and the sins of the original victim become the focus. Feeling guilty of name-calling, the victim is fully tamed and crawls into a hole, ashamed. I have watched this fighting technique work thousands of times in disputes between men and women, and what I've learned is that the real culprit is not necessarily the one who swears the loudest. [14]

Omission

Omission involves telling most of the truth minus one or two key facts whose absence changes the story completely. You break a pair of glasses that are guaranteed under normal use and get a new pair, without mentioning that the first pair broke during a rowdy game of basketball. Who hasn't tried something like that? But what about omission of information that could make a difference in how a person lives his or her life? [15]

For instance, one day I found out that rabbinical legends tell of another woman in the Garden of Eden before Eve. I was stunned. The omission of the Sumerian goddess Lilith from Genesis—as well as her demonization by ancient misogynists as an embodiment of female evil—felt like spiritual robbery. I felt like I'd just found out my mother was really my stepmother. To take seriously the tradition that Adam was created out of the same mud as his equal counterpart, Lilith, redefines all of Judeo-Christian history. [16]

> *When you have no basis for an argument, abuse the plaintiff.*
> —Cicero

> *The cruelest lies are often told in silence.*
> —R.L. Stevenson

Some renegade Catholic feminists introduced me to a view of Lilith that had been suppressed during the many centuries when this strong goddess was seen only as a spirit of evil. Lilith was a proud goddess who defied Adam's need to control her, attempted negotiations, and when this failed, said adios and left the Garden of Eden. [17]

This omission of Lilith from the Bible was a patriarchal strategy to keep women weak. Omitting the strong-woman archetype of Lilith from Western religions and starting the story with Eve the Rib has helped keep Christian and Jewish women believing they were the lesser sex for thousands of years. [18]

Stereotypes and Clichés

Stereotype and cliché serve a purpose as a form of shorthand. Our need for vast amounts of information in nanoseconds has made the stereotype vital to modern communication. Unfortunately, it often shuts down original thinking, giving those hungry for the truth a candy bar of misinformation instead of a balanced meal. The stereotype explains a situation with just enough truth to seem unquestionable.[19]

All the "isms"—racism, sexism, ageism, et al.—are founded on and fueled by the stereotype and the cliché, which are lies of exaggeration, omission, and ignorance. They are always dangerous. They take a single tree and make it a landscape. They destroy curiosity. They close minds and separate people. The single mother on welfare is assumed to be cheating. Any black male could tell you how much of his identity is obliterated daily by stereotypes. Fat people, ugly people, beautiful people, old people, large-breasted women, short men, the mentally ill, and the homeless all could tell you how much more they are like us than we want to think. I once admitted to a group of people that I had a mouth like a truck driver. Much to my surprise, a man stood up and said, "I'm a truck driver, and I never cuss." Needless to say, I was humbled. [20]

Groupthink

Irving Janis, in Victims of Group Think, defines this sort of lie as a psychological phenomenon within decision-making groups in which loyalty to the group has become more important than any other value, with the result that dissent and the appraisal of alternatives are suppressed. If you've ever worked on a committee or in a corporation, you've encountered groupthink. It requires a combination of other forms of lying—ignoring facts, selective memory, omission, and denial, to name a few. [21]

Where opinion does not exist, the status quo becomes stereotyped and all originality is discouraged.
—Bertrand Russell

Who is more foolish, the child afraid of the dark, or the man afraid of the light?
—Maurice Freehill

The textbook example of groupthink came on December 7, 1941. From as early as the fall of 1941, the warnings came in, one after another, that Japan was preparing for a massive military operation. The navy command in Hawaii assumed Pearl Harbor was invulnerable—the Japanese weren't stupid enough to attack the United States' most important base. On the other hand, racist stereotypes said the Japanese weren't smart enough to invent a torpedo effective in less than 60 feet of water (the fleet was docked in 30 feet); after all, US technology hadn't been able to do it. [22]

On Friday, December 5, normal weekend leave was granted to all the commanders at Pearl Harbor, even though the Japanese consulate in Hawaii was busy burning papers. Within the tight, good-ole-boy cohesiveness of the US command in Hawaii, the myth of invulnerability stayed well entrenched. No one in the group considered the alternatives. The rest is history. [23]

Out-and-Out Lies

Of all the ways to lie, I like this one the best, probably because I get tired of trying to figure out the real meanings behind things. At least I can trust the bald-faced lie. I once asked my five-year-old nephew, "Who broke the fence?" (I had seen him do it.) He answered, "The murderers." Who could argue? [24]

At least when this sort of lie is told it can be easily confronted. As the person who is lied to, I know where I stand. The bald-faced lie doesn't toy with my perceptions—it argues with them. It doesn't try to refashion reality, it tries to refute it. Read my lips.... No sleight of hand. No guessing. If this were the only form of lying, there would be no such things as floating anxiety or the adult-children-of-alcoholics movement. [25]

> *The only form of lying that is beyond reproach is lying for its own sake.*
> —Oscar Wilde

Dismissal

Dismissal is perhaps the slipperiest of all lies. Dismissing feelings, perceptions, or even the raw facts of a situation ranks as a kind of lie that can do as much damage to a person as any other kind of lie. [26]

The roots of many mental disorders can be traced back to the dismissal of reality. Imagine that a person is told from the time she is a tot that her perceptions are inaccurate. "Mommy, I'm scared." "No you're not, darling." "I don't like that man next door, he makes me feel icky." "Johnny, that's a terrible thing to say, of course you like him. You go over there right now and be nice to him." [27]

> *Pay no attention to that man behind the curtain! I am the Great Oz!*
> —The Wizard of Oz

I've often mused over the idea that madness is actually a sane reaction to an insane world. Psychologist R. D. Laing supports this hypothesis in Sanity, Madness and the Family, an account of his investigation into the families of schizophrenics. The common thread that ran through all of the families he studied was a deliberate, staunch dismissal of the patient's perceptions from a very early age. Each of the patients started out with an accurate grasp of reality, which, through meticulous and methodical dismissal, was demolished until the only reality the patient could trust was catatonia. [28]

Dismissal runs the gamut. Mild dismissal can be quite handy for forgiving the foibles of others in our day-to-day lives. Toddlers who have just learned to manipulate their parents' attention sometimes are dismissed out of necessity. Absolute attention from the parents would require so much energy that no one would get to eat dinner. But we must be careful and attentive about how far we take our "necessary" dismissals. Dismissal is a dangerous tool, because it's nothing less than a lie. [29]

Delusion

I could write the book on this one. Delusion, a cousin of dismissal, is the tendency to see excuses as facts. It's a powerful lying tool because it filters out information that contradicts what we want to believe. Alcoholics who believe that the problems in their lives are legitimate reasons for drinking rather than results of the drinking offer the classic example of deluded thinking. Delusion uses the mind's ability to see things in myriad ways to support what it wants to be the truth. [30]

But delusion is also a survival mechanism we all use. If we were to fully contemplate the consequences of our stockpiles of nuclear weapons or global warming, we could hardly function on a day-to-day level. We don't want to incorporate that much reality into our lives because to do so would be paralyzing. [31]

Delusion acts as an adhesive to keep the status quo intact. It shamelessly employs dismissal, omission, and amnesia, among other sorts of lies. Its most cunning defense is that it cannot see itself. [32]

These are only a few of the ways we lie. Or are lied to. As I said earlier, it's not easy to entirely eliminate lies from our lives. No matter how pious we may try to be, we will still embellish, hedge, and omit to lubricate the daily machinery of living. But there is a world of difference between telling functional lies and living a lie. Martin Buber once said, "The lie is the spirit committing treason against itself." Our acceptance of lies becomes a cultural cancer that eventually shrouds and reorders reality until moral garbage becomes as invisible to us as water is to a fish. [33]

How much do we tolerate before we become sick and tired of being sick and tired? When will we stand up and declare our right to trust? When do we stop accepting that the real truth is in the fine print? Whose lips do we read this year when we vote for president? When will we stop being so reticent about making judgments? When do we stop turning over our personal power and responsibility to liars? [34]

Maybe if I don't tell the bank the check's in the mail I'll be less tolerant of the lies told me every day. A country song I once heard said it all for me: "You've got to stand for something or you'll fall for anything." [35]

The liar's punishment [...] is that he cannot believe anyone else.
—*George Bernard Shaw*

***

Vocabulary in Context

Locate the following words (the paragraph location is provided) within the essay by Stephanie Ericsson. Using strategies covered in this chapter, define the word. Then, identify the strategy that you used to define the word.

Word in Context	Definition	Strategy Used
plethora, par. 9	*assortment*	*general sense context clue*
haggard, par. 2		
indulge, par. 3		
travails, par. 4		
frank, par. 6		
pittance, par. 7		
facades, par. 9		
irreparable, par. 11		
blatant, par. 12		
perpetuate, par. 13		
deflect, par. 13		
demonization, par. 16		
misinformation, par. 19		
mused, par. 28		
foibles, par. 29		
reticent, par. 34		

Checking In

1. Before you began reading this essay, what was your opinion of "white lies" and other lies that seem to be a necessity of social life? Did your view change after reading Ericsson's essay?

2. Of the types of lies Ericsson discusses, which one have you used most often? Keep in mind, as Ericsson said, that we all lie in some way.

Getting the Point

3. After listing and describing all of the various ways that people lie to each other, Ericsson brings it all together to make a point. What is that point?

Delving Deeper

4. Review the quotations that open each of Ericsson's sections. Select two of the quotations, and explain how each relates to the type of lie being discussed in that section.

Technology Tip

After reading the essay "The Ways We Lie," go to a news site on the Internet to locate an article in which someone reportedly lied about something. Briefly describe the situation you discovered and explain how the lie illustrates one of the ways of lying discussed in the essay.

 For support in meeting this chapter's objectives, go to MyReadingLab and select **Vocabulary**

4 Comprehension Strategies: Main Ideas

Learning Objectives

In this chapter you will:

- Identify the topic of paragraphs and longer selections.
- Use identifying questions to find stated main ideas.
- Use identifying questions to compose implied main ideas.
- Identify the central point of longer selections.

All truths are easy to understand once they are discovered; the point is to discover them.

—Galileo Galilei

GETTING THE POINT

Imagine this: you have been talking to your friend Stephanie, and she's describing her visit to the dentist. She tells you how she sat for a few minutes in the waiting room, how she chatted with the dental assistant after being taken to the examination room, how her dentist is so nice, and a whole bunch of other details about her visit. At first you listen intently, waiting for the punch line, the surprise—something! Finally, as she's telling you what the dentist talked about while he filled her cavity, you blurt out, "Come on, Steph! What are you getting at? What's the point?"

Does your outburst make you a bad friend? Does it mean you're not a good listener? More likely, it means neither of those things. Rather, it highlights something we all desire and need in our communication—namely, that it has a point. Maybe you are doing your friend Stephanie a favor by letting her know that she's wandering around in a story rather than getting to the actual point she wants to make.

As the scenario with Stephanie and her dental visit illustrates, listeners and readers tend to lose interest in a story that does not have a point. The very essence of communication is to convey an idea to another person. If there is no idea, there is no need for communication. Necessarily, then, as readers and listeners, we seek out the point in every communication, whether it's made by a friend on the telephone, hinted at in a magazine you scan while standing in line at the grocery store, or discussed in the textbook you have for your psychology class. There is always a point, and we, as readers, need to be able to find it.

Understanding the point is a major stage in developing reading effectiveness. Once you have identified the major point of someone's communication, you are free to notice other things about it, such as whether or not you agree and whether it is interesting or not. For now, we will focus on this first stage: getting the point. This chapter will offer you the strategies you need to master this stage of the reading process.

Here's what will be covered in Chapter 4:

Identifying a Topic
- General versus specific

Identifying a Main Idea
- Stated main ideas
- Implied main ideas
- Central points

Identifying Topics and Main Ideas in Context

Identifying a Topic

A **topic** is the subject of a reading selection, whether it is a paragraph, a book, a newspaper article, or a research paper. The topic is what the author is talking about. The topic is general in nature and could be developed in several ways, depending on the author's purpose. Initially, however, you as the reader simply need to grasp the big picture: what is the author talking about? It is helpful to keep in mind that a topic is only a word or phrase; it is not a complete idea.

As just mentioned, one characteristic of topics is that they are general. To illustrate this idea of general versus specific, consider Practice 1.

Practice 1

First identify, in a word or two, what each of the following lists describes. Write each description in the spaces provided. Next, select any word from List A and compare it to the word you wrote on the line. Which is more specific?

List A describes _dog breeds_

Beagle

Pit bull

Boxer

Poodle

Bulldog

Golden retriever

Yorkshire terrier

Doberman pincher

Labrador retriever

German shepherd

List B describes _animals_

Hamsters

Cats

Horses

Elephants

Seals

Pigs

Bears

Cows

Birds

Wolves

If you described List A as "dogs" or "dog breeds," then any one of the breeds in the list will be more specific than your description. This is because the description you wrote is essentially the topic—and a topic is general. If you do the same thing with List B, your description will be more general than any of the words in List B. For example, if you described List B as "animals," that description is more general than, for example, the entry "Cows."

You have just identified the difference between general and specific in relation to topics. Any selection's topic will be general, and the remainder of the selection will expand on the topic in some specific way.

Distinguishing between general and specific ideas is the first step in identifying the topic. The next step is to ask, "What is the author talking about?" This question, and an awareness of the level of specificity of ideas, will lead you to the topic of a selection.

Let's look at a reading and put these strategies in action. This selection is from a textbook on developing arguments. Read the paragraph and identify the topic.

Practice 2

Paragraph A

Take another moment to consider words that come to mind when you think of dialogue: discussion, listening, interaction, and understanding. By definition, a dialogue includes more than one voice, and those voices are responsive to each other. When we have a dialogue with someone, we don't simply present our own views. We may disagree, but we take turns so that no one voice monopolizes the conversation. The object of a dialogue is not to win or lose; the object is to communicate our ideas and to listen to what the other person has to say in response.

Who or what is the author talking about in this paragraph?

dialogue

Strategy Tip

If an idea is repeated often, that idea is likely the topic of the selection.

If you answered "dialogue," then you are correct. Not only is it the topic of the paragraph, it is the idea that is mentioned most often: four times. Sometimes the number of times the author mentions an idea can suggest to you what the topic is. That is true in this case.

Identifying a Main Idea

Now that we've discussed how to identify topics, let's discuss how to identify main ideas. The **main idea** is the point the author wishes to communicate about the topic. As mentioned in the opening of this chapter, every communication has a point. The **point** is what you are meant to understand or know after the communication is made. Often the main idea is stated directly, but you will find that is not always the case.

A useful strategy to employ when trying to identify a main idea is to ask questions. Let's call the two questions the **Identifying Questions** (see Figure 4.1). You've already used the question that leads you to the topic: **Who or what is the author talking about?** The next question to ask is, **"What point is the author making about the topic?"** Combining your two answers to the Identifying Questions will allow you to compose the main idea. If the main idea is stated, you then look for this idea as expressed in the reading. While your phrasing of the main idea may differ from the wording of the author, the general sense of both main ideas should be the same.

To illustrate, reread Paragraph A and ask the Identifying Questions. We've already answered the first question, so now you answer the second.

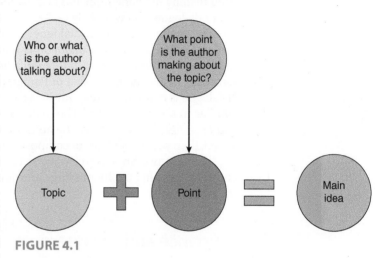

FIGURE 4.1

Paragraph A

Take another moment to consider words that come to mind when you think of <u>dialogue</u>: discussion, listening, interaction, and understanding. By definition, a <u>dialogue</u> includes more than one voice, and those voices are responsive to each other. When we have a <u>dialogue</u> with someone, we don't simply present our own views. We may disagree, but we take turns so that no one voice monopolizes the conversation. The object of a <u>dialogue</u> is not to win or lose; the object is to communicate our ideas and to listen to what the other person has to say in response.

Notice that "dialogue" is mentioned four times.

1. What is the author talking about in this paragraph? _____

2. What point is the author making about the topic? _____

_____

After reading the paragraph and looking for the point the author is making about dialogue, you will likely realize that the author is defining dialogue. So, what is the definition of dialogue? According to the author, in the last sentence: "The object of a dialogue is not to win or lose; *the object is to communicate our ideas and to listen to what the other person has to say in response.*" Thus, the main idea of Paragraph A is a definition of dialogue: "Dialogue is communicating our ideas and listening to what another person has to say in response." The main idea is stated in this paragraph, so you need only identify where the author has said it. If the main idea is not stated, then you would have to compose the main idea in your own words.

The next two brief exercises will offer you an opportunity to become comfortable using the Identifying Questions to find the topic and identify the main idea.

Exercise 4.1

Finance and the Internet

by Jean Folkerts, Stephen Lacy, and Ann Larabee

from the textbook *The Media in Your Life*

M ore Internet users now trust computer systems to handle their financial transactions. In December 2006, 35 percent of bills were paid online, up from 25 percent the year before. Consumers also use the Internet to make deposits, check their credit histories, submit their tax forms, and play the stock market. Some large banks, such as ING Direct, have only an online presence and no brick and mortar sites. The rise of online banking and other financial activities is having an effect on labor, since fewer employees are needed to handle routine transactions. However, knowledgeable employees are still in demand for customer service. The shift in investment strategies to online trading may also have global impacts. *The New York Times* columnist Thomas Friedman has argued that online trading allows individuals to participate in the global economy as never before, and that, taken collectively, the "electronic herd" can have a powerful effect on global markets.

1. Who or what are the authors talking about? _____

_____

2. What point are the authors making about the topic? _____

    _____

    _____

3. Which statement from the selection best expresses the main idea as
    you've identified it? _____

    _____

Superman and Me (excerpt)

By Sherman Alexie

Sherman J. Alexie, Jr. (1966–) is a Spokane/Coeur d'Alene Indian. He grew
up on the Spokane Indian Reservation in Wellpinit, Washington, about 50
miles northwest of Spokane, Washington. Approximately 1,100 Spokane
Tribal members live there.

My father, who is one of the few Indians who went to Catholic
school on purpose, was an avid reader of westerns, spy thrillers,
murder mysteries, gangster epics, basketball player biographies
and anything else he could find. He bought his books by the pound at
Dutch's Pawn Shop, Goodwill, Salvation Army and Value Village. When
he had extra money, he bought new novels at supermarkets, convenience
stores and hospital gift shops. Our house was filled with books. They were
stacked in crazy piles in the bathroom, bedrooms and living room. In a fit
of unemployment-inspired creative energy, my father built a set of bookshelves and soon filled them with a random assortment of books about
the Kennedy assassination, Watergate, the Vietnam War and the entire
23-book series of the Apache westerns. My father loved books, and since I
loved my father with an aching devotion, I decided to love books as well.

1. Who or what is the author talking about? *Alexie is*
    referring to his father.

2. What point is the author making about the topic? _____

    _____

3. Which statement from the selection best expresses the main idea as
    you've identified it? _____

    _____

Implied Main Ideas

In both fiction and nonfiction, it is very common to find that the main idea of a work is unstated. These types of main ideas are called **implied main ideas.** To **imply** is to suggest or hint; authors imply main ideas by offering examples, ideas, and details that suggest the point they wish to communicate. The reader must actively connect the stated information to compose an accurate implied main idea. Sometimes, combining a few sentences from the reading will create the implied main idea. As well, adding a word or two to a stated sentence is sometimes enough to compose the implied main idea. Keep in mind that since both of these strategies require you to compose the main idea, the main idea is still categorized as unstated or implied—even if part of it is stated.

Regardless of whether the main idea is completely unstated or partially stated, you'll want to employ the Identifying Questions to determine the topic and the point before composing your implied main idea. Be sure that the Identifying Questions have led you to the appropriate conclusion, since there will be no explicit statement from the author to reassure you. Later, in Chapter 5, we will discuss supporting details and how they can be used to identify the implied main idea. In the meantime, use active reading strategies and the Identifying Questions to recognize and compose implied main ideas.

> **Collaboration Opportunity**
>
> Discuss this fable with other students to get help in composing the main idea.

Exercise 4.3

To practice composing implied main ideas, read the following selection and answer the questions that follow.

The Lion and the Boar

Translated by George Flyer Townsend

This brief tale is from Aesop's Fables, a collection of stories that has been gathered from around the world and passed on from generation to generation. A fable is a tale that often features animals speaking and acting as humans would. The fables are meant to comment upon our universal human condition.

On a summer day, when the great heat induced a general thirst, a Lion and a Boar came at the same moment to a small well to drink. They fiercely disputed which of them should drink first, and were soon engaged in the agonies of a mortal combat. On their stopping on a sudden to take a breath for the fiercer renewal of the strife, they saw Vultures waiting in the distance to feast on the one which should fall first. They at once made up their quarrel, saying, "It is better for us to make friends, than to become the food of Crows or Vultures."

1. Who or what is the author talking about? _____

    _____

2. What point is the author making about the topic? _____

    _____

    _____

3. Write the main idea as you've identified it through the Identifying
    Questions. _____

    _____

As you may have noticed, identifying a main idea is a little trickier when it is implied and when the subject is fictional, as in this fable. Still, consider the descriptive note provided before the fable, which gives you some hint as to how you should understand the story. The note indicates that the tale is somehow representative of human values. The title too offers you a clue; it tells you who or what the author is talking about. Of course, the lion and the boar are representative of people, but ask yourself, what type of people? In this fable, people who want the same limited resource—water from a small well. The lion and the boar begin fighting for the water, but soon they see vultures circling in anticipation. What does this suggest to the two fighters? Use your answer to this question to state the main idea of this fable.

What follows are two short passages for which you can practice identifying and composing *implied* main ideas.

Exercise 4.4

Plant Success in Ecosystems

By Edward Bergman and William Renwick

from the textbook *Geography: People, Places and Environment*

The success of one species over another is the result of competition. In the case of plants, this competition is for light, water, nutrients, and space. Although plants require all these factors to grow, in any ecosystem one factor usually is restricted, which forces competition and adaptation. For example, in an arid environment, plants compete for scant water but do not need to compete for the abundant sunlight. In a humid environment, water is abundant, but plants must compete for sunlight. An area with adequate water and light may have poor soils, so plants must compete for nutrients. Through evolution, the plants that have adapted their life forms, physiological characteristics, and reproductive mechanisms that allow them to succeed in particular environments have survived. The plants that compete best in an environment dominate the ground cover there.

1. In what type of class might you read this selection? _____

_____

2. Use context clues to define the following words from the selection.

arid: _____

dominate: _____

3. Who or what are the authors talking about? _____

4. What point are the authors making about the topic? _____

_____

_____

5. Use your responses to the Identifying Questions to compose the implied main idea of this paragraph. _____

_____

Exercise 4.5

The Lark and the Farmer

Translated by George Flyer Townsend

This brief tale is from Aesop's Fables, a collection of stories that has been gathered from around the world and passed on from generation to generation. A fable is a tale that often features animals speaking and acting as humans would. The fables are meant to comment upon our universal human condition.

A Lark had made her nest in the early spring on the young green wheat. The brood had almost grown to their proper strength, and attained the use of their wings and the full plumage of their feathers, when the owner of the field, overlooking his crop, now quite ripe, said "The time is come when I must send to all my neighbors to help me with my harvest." One of the young Larks heard his speech, and related it to his mother, inquiring of her to what place they should move for safety. "There is no occasion to move yet, my son," she replied; "the man who only sends to his friends to help him with his harvest is not really in earnest."

The owner of the field again came a few days later, and saw the wheat shedding the grain from excess of ripeness, and said, "I will come myself tomorrow with my laborers, and with as many reapers as I can hire, and will get in the harvest." The Lark on hearing these words said to her brood, "it is time now to be off, my little ones, for the man is in earnest this time; he no longer trusts to his friends, but will reap the field himself."

1. Why does the young lark think his family must move? _____

    _____

    _____

2. What does the mother lark mean when she says, "The man who only sends to his friends to help him with his harvest is not really in earnest"? _____

    _____

    _____

3. Use context clues to define the following words from the selection.

    brood: _____

    plumage: _____

    earnest: _____

4. Who or what is this fable about? (*Hint:* Who are the main characters?) _____

    _____

    _____

5. What point does the farmer's situation illustrate? _____

    _____

    _____

6. Use your responses to the Identifying Questions to compose the implied main idea of this fable. _____

    _____

    _____

Identifying Central Points

The terms *main idea* and *implied main idea* are widely accepted to refer to the author's key point or overall idea. However, there is another commonly used term: the *central point*. The most important distinction between a central point and a main idea is the breadth of their coverage. Essentially, a main idea is the key point of a paragraph. In multi-paragraph readings there are often many main ideas—in a sense, nearly every paragraph has a main idea. To make a clear distinction between the main idea of a single paragraph and the overall main idea of an entire reading, the term **central point** is used. Thus, a central point often refers to the overall point or key idea of a longer text. You might discuss, for example, the central point of a single essay, an article, or even a collection of essays written by the same author. To avoid misunderstanding, read instructions carefully to determine whether you need to identify the main idea of a paragraph or the overall main idea (central point) of an entire selection. In most readings, you will need to understand and identify both the main ideas of paragraphs and the central point of the overall work.

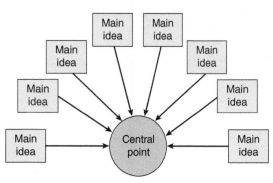

FIGURE 4.2

Identifying Topics and Main Ideas in Context

Thus far we have been discussing finding a topic and a main idea as if a reading selection floats alone in a world all its own. In actuality this is rarely the case. You will encounter a wealth of information before you even get to the material you are meant to read. Consider, for instance, that a *section* of a textbook is in a *chapter* of the textbook, which itself is a *book* that you purchased for your *history* class. All of those pieces fit together to create a context for reading. So, there is much more contextual information surrounding a section, a chapter, and a textbook than just the reading material itself.

As discussed in Chapter 1, the context sets the stage for what is to follow. A student rarely approaches a reading task in an academic setting that doesn't have a specific context. When you add to context the pre-reading strategies that you will employ before you read, you give yourself even more information. If, for example, you ask the right questions during the pre-reading stage, you will likely already know the topic of the reading material before you begin to read it. This means you need only identify the point the author is making about that topic before you locate or compose the main idea.

Identifying topics and main ideas and composing implied main ideas will become easier with practice and a set of strategies to guide you as you read. Keep in mind, too, that while we are discussing the reading process in stages, in reality the process becomes fluid, like one sweeping movement—like riding a bike.

So, as you position yourself on this bike and get ready to pedal your way through the exercises that follow, use all the contextual clues provided to you, as well as the strategies highlighted in this chapter, to identify and compose main ideas.

Read these four passages and complete the questions following them. The questions for these reading selections will call upon all of the strategies you have learned in Chapter 4.

Exercise 4.6

Ethnobotany

by Paul G. Hewitt, Suzanne Lyons, John Suchocki, and Jennifer Yeh

from the textbook *Conceptual Integrated Science*

Human societies use plants in many different ways—for food, medicine, shelter, clothing, tools, ceremonial functions,—and other purposes. Ethnobotany is the study of how people use plants, and ethnobotanists generally conduct their work by interviewing local peoples and studying their traditions and habits. Paleoethnobotanists focus on plant use in prehistoric times by examining seeds, pollen, wood, and other plant remains found at archaeological sites.

Although ethnobotanists are interested in all types of plant use, the study of medicinal plants, with its potential for social and economic benefit, has always been of particular interest. In fact, ethnobotanical investigations have led to the development of numerous important medicines. Quinine, the first antimalarial drug, comes from the bark of cinchona trees, long used in native Peruvian medicine to treat fever, digestive ailments, and malaria. Aspirin originally came from willow bark, which has been used for thousands of years to relieve pain. More recently, Madagascar periwinkle, a plant used by several native peoples for diabetes and other conditions, provided two new cancer drugs.

Scientists pursuing drug development have traditionally relied on the knowledge of local healers in their search for promising plants. However, the development of modern drugs from medicinal plant compounds leads to a difficult ethical issue. What are the rights of indigenous peoples, and how can these be protected? Critics are quick to point to the fact that cancer drugs developed from Madagascar periwinkle produced over a billion dollars in profit for the pharmaceutical giant Eli Lilly, but nothing for traditional societies in Madagascar. Some drug developers now attempt to ensure that local peoples also benefit. For example, when the AIDS Research Alliance found an anti-HIV compound in a Samoan medicinal tree, the group made direct contributions to the village where the tree was known and also promised 20 percent of the profits from drugs that are eventually developed. Unfortunately, because of the ongoing loss of native cultures and the extinction of plant species through deforestation and habitat destruction, it is all too likely that many medically useful species will never be known.

Questions for Exercise 4.6: "Ethnobotany"

1. What is ethnobotany? _____

_____

2. How do ethnobotanists conduct their work? _____

_____

_____

3. What is the main idea of paragraph 2? _____

_____

4. What is the main idea of paragraph 3? _____

_____

_____

5. ____ Which of the following statements best expresses the central point of this passage?
   a) Ethnobotanists' study of and search for medicinal plants has social and economic benefits, but it also presents ethical issues when foreign interests profit from resources and information taken from native populations.
   b) Ethnobotany is the study of how people use plants, and ethnobotanists generally conduct their work by interviewing local peoples and studying their traditions and habits.
   c) Scientists pursuing drug development have traditionally relied on the knowledge of local healers in their search for promising plants.

d) Although ethnobotanists are interested in all types of plant use, the study of medicinal plants, with its potential for social and economic benefit, has always been of particular interest.

Exercise 4.7

The Placebo Effect

by Paul G. Hewitt, Suzanne Lyons, John Suchocki, and Jennifer Yeh

from the textbook *Conceptual Integrated Science*

A patient with knee pain goes in for surgery. He receives anesthesia, and cuts are made around his knee where the surgical instruments will be inserted. Afterwards, the surgery appears to be successful—both pain and swelling are greatly diminished. What's unusual about this story? Nothing, except that the operation was a sham. Cuts were made around the patient's knee, but nothing happened after that. Why does the patient feel so much better? Because of a phenomenon known as the placebo effect.*

Placebo is Latin for "I shall please." It refers to the once regular practice in which doctors prescribed sugar pills to patients whom they otherwise couldn't help. Although this is now considered unethical, it doesn't change the fact that sugar pills did often help. The placebo effect is defined as the improvement patients experience when they are given a treatment with no relevance to their medical problem.

Placebos appear to work for a wide variety of conditions and are usually far better than no treatment at all. In a study of patients with Parkinson's disease, for example, a placebo worked just as well as medication in inducing the release of dopamine by the brain. Placebos have also been found to work as well as modern antidepressants in the treatment of depression. The placebo effect is certainly real, though placebos work better for some maladies than others. Placebos appear

---

*Patients enrolled in these types of clinical studies—which are usually designed to examine the effectiveness of a surgery, drug, or other treatments—are aware that they are participating in a clinical study and that they might be assigned to a "sham" treatment group. If the surgery or other treatment performs no better than the placebo (as occurred in this case), the conclusion is that the treatment is not effective. Testing treatments against placebos is important precisely because the placebo effect can be very powerful. Of course, if there is already a proven treatment for a particular condition, new treatments can be tested against the established one.

to be particularly effective for conditions related to the nervous system, including pain, depression, anxiety, headaches, fatigue, and gastrointestinal symptoms. For most of these conditions, placebos have about 30–50 percent effectiveness—nearly as good as "real" treatments in some cases. Placebos are also believed to account for the "success" of certain alternative remedies with no medical basis.

The placebo effect is one of the oddest phenomena in medicine. What causes it? This question has not been fully answered and is the object of continued study. However, several possible mechanisms have been suggested. One idea is that the placebo effect operates through the release of endorphins. Release of the body's natural opiates would explain why placebos are so good at treating pain. Further evidence comes from the fact that placebos become much less effective as painkillers when patients are given a drug that blocks the opiate receptors. However, because the placebo effect works for many symptoms other than pain, this can't be the whole story. Another idea is that receiving a placebo reduces stress, allowing the immune system to function more effectively. Numerous studies have shown that stress reduces the immune system's capabilities—consequently, stress relief would be expected to improve its function. Still, there must be more to it than this because the placebo effect is very specific—it doesn't help with all your ailments, only the one you think you're being treated for. There is no getting around the fact that a person's expectations somehow lie at the crux of the placebo effect. Some scientists have argued that the placebo effect is a conditioned reflex. The patient has, through numerous experiences with doctors, pills, injections, and so on, been conditioned to expect a positive effect after medical treatment. And somehow, the nervous system has become wired to comply.

Interestingly, studies have also demonstrated a "nocebo effect," sometimes called the placebo effect's "evil twin." Expectations of negative effects are realized too. For example, people on placebos often develop negative "side effects" from their treatments. Side effects of real medications may sometimes be caused by the nocebo effect as well. For example, studies have repeatedly shown that patients who were warned of specific side effects tend to experience them much more often than patients who weren't warned. The nocebo effect can be even more serious. One study showed that women who believed they were vulnerable to heart disease were four times as likely to die of it as women who didn't believe they were vulnerable, but had similar risk factors. The nocebo effect may also account for the effectiveness of voodoo death curses. Never underestimate the power of the mind.

Questions for Exercise 4.7: "The Placebo Effect"

1. ____ In what type of course might you read this selection?
   a) a history course
   b) a science course
   c) a chemistry course
   d) a computer course

2. ____ What is a pre-reading question you can ask to help your understanding of this article?
   a) Who wrote this article?
   b) When was this article written?
   c) What is a placebo?
   d) What was wrong with the patient?

3. What is the definition of "sham" as it is used in paragraph 1? _____

   _____

4. What is the placebo effect? _____

   _____

5. What is the stated main idea of paragraph 3? _____

   _____

   _____

6. What is the definition of "maladies" as it is used in paragraph 3? _____

   _____

   _____

7. ____ What is the implied main idea of paragraph 4?
   a) Placebos have also been found to work as well as modern antidepressants in the treatment of depression.
   b) The placebo effect is one of the oddest phenomena in medicine.
   c) Another idea is that receiving a placebo reduces stress, allowing the immune system to function more effectively.
   d) The placebo effect is not fully understood, although many possible explanations have emerged from continued study.

8. What is the nocebo effect? _____

   _____

   _____

9. Explain how the nocebo effect might contribute to the effects of a "voodoo death curse" as suggested in this selection. _____

_____

_____

_____

10. What is the implied central point of this selection? _____

_____

_____

Exercise 4.8

Prejudice and Discrimination

By James M. Henslin

from the textbook *Sociology, A Down to Earth Approach*

Prejudice and discrimination are common throughout the world. In Mexico, Mexicans of Hispanic descent discriminate against Mexicans of Native American descent; in Israel, Ashkenazi Jews, primarily of European descent, discriminate against Sephardi Jews from the Muslim world. In some places, the elderly discriminate against the young; in others, the young discriminate against the elderly. And all around the world, men discriminate against women.

Discrimination is an *action*—unfair treatment directed against someone. Discrimination can be based on many characteristics: age, sex, height, weight, skin color, clothing, speech, income, education, marital status, sexual orientation, disease, disability, religion, and politics. When the basis of discrimination is someone's perception of race, it is known as **racism.** Discrimination is often the result of an *attitude* called **prejudice**— a prejudging of some sort, usually in a negative way. There is also *positive prejudice*, which exaggerates the virtues of a group, as when people think that some group (usually their own) is more capable than others. Most prejudice, however, is negative and involves prejudging a group as inferior.

As with our other attitudes, we are not born with prejudice. Rather, we learn prejudice from the people around us. In a fascinating study, sociologist Kathleen Blee (2005) interviewed women who were members of the KKK and Aryan Nations. Her first finding is of the "ho hum" variety: Most women were recruited by someone who already belonged to the group. Blee's second finding, however, holds a surprise: Some women learned to be racists *after* they joined the group. They were attracted to the group not because it matched their racist beliefs but because someone they liked belonged to it. Blee found that their racism was not the *cause* of their joining but, rather, the *result* of their membership.

It is amazing how much prejudice people can learn. In a classic article, psychologist Eugene Hartley (1946) asked people how they felt about several racial and ethnic groups. Besides Negroes, Jews, and so on, he included the Wallonians, Pireneans, and Danireans—names he had made up. Most people who expressed dislike for Jews and Negroes also expressed dislike for these three fictitious groups.

Hartley's study shows that prejudice does not depend on negative experiences with others. It also reveals that people who are prejudiced against one racial or ethnic group also tend to be prejudiced against other groups. People can be, and are, prejudiced against people they have never met—and even against groups that do not exist!

Questions for Exercise 4.8: "Prejudice and Discrimination"

1. What does the first paragraph communicate about prejudice and discrimination? _____

_____

_____

2. According to this selection, how is prejudice different than discrimination?

_____

_____

_____

3. _____ If a manager of a clothing store refuses to hire women who reveal that they have young children, this is
   a) his right as a manager.
   b) a type of prejudice.
   c) an act of discrimination.
   d) an example of racism.

4. What point is the author making in paragraph 3? _____

_____

_____

5. What does "fictitious" mean as it is used in paragraph 4? _____

_____

_____

6. ____ Which statement best expresses the implied main idea of paragraphs 4 and 5?

   a) It is amazing how much prejudice a person can learn.

   b) Hartley's study shows that people who are prejudiced toward one group are likely to be prejudiced toward other groups, whether or not they have had negative experiences with those groups.

   c) Hartley's study shows that prejudice does not depend on negative experiences with others.

   d) Most people who expressed dislike for Jews and Negros also expressed dislike for these three fictitious groups.

7. What is the implied central point of this selection? _____

   _____

   _____

Exercise 4.9

Feelers

by John Gould

_____

"An entomologist, did you say?" says Harlan, incredulous. He's been here at the Bougainvillea Resort and Spa about an hour and already something wild is happening to him. "From the Greek *entomon*, insect? From the neuter of *entomos*, cut up, from *temnein*, to cut?"

"Um, I guess so," says the woman standing next to him—head cocked, arms akimbo—before the rack of brochures. "Bugs."

"Because you see I'm an etymologist," says Harlan. "Entomologist, etymologist, don't you think that's kind of uncanny?"

"Etymologist?" says the woman. "Like, words?"

"Right," says Harlan. "From the Greek *etymon*, from *etymos*, true, and of course *logion*, diminutive of *logos*"—no way to stop himself when he's wound this tight—"a saying, especially a saying of Christ's. Can I buy you a drink?"

"Sure," says the woman. "My name's Miriam."

"Harlan," says Harlan.

They place their orders—gin and tonic for Harlan, virgin Caesar for Miriam ("Hal" from Harlan)—and wander out onto a little patio overlooking one of the pools. It's dusk, but birds still—mockingbirds, presumably, as promised by the resort's literature. Poring over the pamphlet at home a few weeks ago, Harlan strove to imagine the mockingbird's evening cry. He failed. Failure comes easily to Harlan. Most recently he failed at marriage. This trip, an impulsive purchase which will max out all three of his credit cards, was inspired by the arrival of his divorce papers.

Harlan and Miriam take seats at a lime table by a potted palm with a view of the setting sun—a hot-pink smear over the tennis courts—cross their legs and start chatting. During their conversation they discover all sorts of things about one another. They discover that they're both from Toronto, that they've both just arrived at the Bougainvillea Resort and Spa, that they were both on the same flight, Harlan in seat 7E (seven, coincidentally, being the most blessed of all numbers according to the faith of her fathers, to say nothing of her mothers), Miriam in seat 34D (Harlan's eyebrows going up here—the figure's just about right, judging by the trippy distortion of the stripes on her blouse). They discover that Harlan had the chicken, Miriam the pasta. They discover that neither of them ever goes on a vacation like this, or has a spouse, or a child.

Inevitably, though, the things they discover about one another are way outnumbered by the things they don't discover about one another. For example, Miriam doesn't discover that as a boy Harlan indulged in a dark practice for which he later coined the term *ento-mosadism*—yanking not the limbs but the antennae, the fine feelers, from various creepy-crawlies. Nor does she discover that Harlan is here recovering from his botched marriage, a knowledge which, a couple of months down the road, will fill her with remorse. Harlan, for his part, doesn't discover that as a girl Miriam consistently mis-heard the Torah passage, "I will make him an help meet for him" (God taking pity on his lonesome man of clay), as "I will make him an elk meat form." Worse, perhaps, he doesn't discover that Miriam is here recovering (still) from the loss of her child, a baby girl known as Toots who died at the age of three hours, before she could get herself a proper name—all of this nine years ago now, when Miriam was twenty-five years old. A couple of months down the road this knowledge will inspire in him a sense of awe for the human heart—Miriam's, for example, and his own—the depth to which it can be damaged, the weird miracle of its healing.

For the next ten days, though, the two will flourish in a state of blissful ignorance of these and umpteen other details. They'll come to adore one another's little quirks, the affected way Harlan has of twirl-ing his walking stick—a brass-and-mahogany heirloom from somebody else's family he scooped at a swap meet years ago, and has never since gone without—or the way Miriam bares her teeth like a baboon on the cusp of each orgasm.

"Love," Harlan will sigh, "from the Old English *lufu*, akin to the Latin *lubere*, to please."

A couple of months from now, when Miriam dumps Harlan, she'll do it with a gift, a plastic terrarium which will appear, at first, to be bereft of life. Taped to the glass will be this note:

> *Harlan, my dear, this is a carausius morosus, a "walking stick"—thought you'd enjoy the wordplay. I've named her Toots, after the little girl I lost many years ago. I'm sorry I could never bring myself to tell you. She likes brambles, please, fresh every day. She'll have babies, even though she has no mate. Do you know the word parthenogenesis? Of course you do. I'm afraid that pill I popped every morning wasn't THE pill, as I let you assume, it was just something for my allergies. Again, I'm sorry. I wanted your height, and your intellect—a flair for the humanities to balance out my science. And anyway I liked you, I really did. I swear to God I won't come after you for child support. Please just forgive me, if you can, and then forget us. Love, Babs*

Eventually Harlan will spot her, a greenish bug about the length of his pinky, a stick with six stick-legs and two antennae. "Hello, Toots," he'll say. "Parthenogenesis," he'll say, "from the Greek *parthenos*, virgin, and Latin *genesis*. Virgin birth, baby." Harlan will wonder whether he's ever had anything irreplaceable, whether he's lost it. Brambles? he'll wonder. Where the hell am I going to find brambles in this town?

Questions for Exercise 4.9: "Feelers"

1. Reread the opening of this story. What do the context clues suggest an "entomologist" is? What about an "etymologist"? _____

    _____

    _____

    _____

2. The author writes that Harlan and Miriam "discover all sorts of things about one another." What does that statement, and the details that follow, imply about what is happening between Harlan and Miriam? _____

    _____

    _____

    _____

3. ____ The reader learns about Miriam's lost child, Toots. What does this information suggest about Miriam?
   a) She was once married.
   b) She is a good person.
   c) She has had sadness in her life.
   d) She doesn't want to have more children.

4. Reread the note Miriam leaves for Harlan. What major fact does she reveal to Harlan in that good-bye note? _____

   _____

   _____

5. What does "botched" mean as it is used in paragraph 10: "Harlan is here recovering from his *botched* marriage"? _____

   _____

   _____

6. ____ Which of these statements expresses one of the central messages in this short story?
   a) Inevitably, though, the things they discover about one another are way outnumbered by the things they don't discover about one another.
   b) Harlan will wonder whether he's ever had anything irreplaceable, whether he's lost it.
   c) They discover that neither of them ever goes on a vacation like this, or has a spouse, or a child.
   d) This knowledge will inspire in him a sense of awe for the human heart—Miriam's, for example, and his own—the depth to which it can be damaged, the weird miracle of its healing.

KEY TERM REVIEW

Using the chapter as your reference, create your own definitions of the following key terms.

1. Topic
2. Main idea
3. Identifying Questions
4. Imply
5. Implied main idea
6. Central point

Other Noteworthy Ideas: Write down anything else from this chapter you'd like to quickly reference.

CHAPTER 4: STRATEGY QUIZ

Books and Social Change
by Jean Folkerts, Stephen Lacy, and Ann Larabee

from the textbook *The Media in Your Life*

The first mass-market bestseller in the United States was Harriet Beecher Stowe's *Uncle Tom's Cabin*, published in 1852. Written for a popular audience, the novel was a powerful indictment of slavery that energized the abolition movement. Like many nineteenth-century novels, *Uncle Tom's Cabin* began in **serialized** form, appearing in the *National Era,* an abolitionist weekly. Stage plays and minstrel shows based on the story immediately began to appear and became popular entertainment. After publication in book form, the novel sold 20,000 copies within 3 weeks, and 300,000 within the first year. Stowe earned more than any other American or European author had on a single book. *Uncle Tom's Cabin* had its critics, who accused Stowe of exaggerating and writing with an overly emotional, sentimental woman's hand. In the South, the book was received with denial and anger. Students at the University of Virginia publicly burned it, and peddlers were sometimes driven from Southern towns where they attempted to distribute it. Despite more recent criticisms of the book's racial stereotyping, *Uncle Tom's Cabin* has remained a classic because of its enormous popular influence on a vital national issue.

The expansion of the book publishing industry provided opportunities for other writers dedicated to freedom and social justice for African Americans. Slave narratives—first-hand accounts of life under the slave system—were published and widely circulated by abolitionists. Some of these books and pamphlets reached sales of tens of thousands of copies and influenced works like *Uncle Tom's Cabin*. One of the most famous was the *Narrative of the life of Frederick Douglass,* written by an escaped slave who became the country's most influential African-American voice, speaking for the Union cause and advising President Lincoln. After the Civil War, Douglass remained a tireless advocate of social justice, speaking and writing on black voting rights, urban development, economic opportunity, and women's rights. He reached his audience through his autobiographies, newspaper articles, and lectures, eventually taking his message abroad. Other former slaves continued to publish accounts of their experience, providing an important witness to history, ensuring that the nation would never forget the evils of slavery.

Paperbacks and Popular Culture

The development of the paperback book industry signaled to society that books were no longer for elites only and that the middle and lower classes would read popular fiction. For many years, books had belonged to the elites, and access to "refined" and "socially respectable" forms of reading reinforced elite values. The development of inexpensive paperbacks created the perception of pandering to popular taste and appealing to those who could be entertained by formulaic fiction. Accessibility to reading material helped to expand the middle class, but it also challenged elite social control. The result was a *democratization of knowledge,* or expansion of information to a wide group of individuals.

Economic and political conditions fueled the development of paperbacks. First distributed before the Civil War, paperbacks benefited from the less expensive printing technology associated with newspapers and from a lack of government regulation. Because the U.S. government refused to recognize foreign copyrights, books from other countries could be cheaply reproduced as paperbacks.

Further, newspapers printed cheap editions of French and English novels that masqueraded as newspapers so they could be distributed by newsboys and sold in the mail using inexpensive newspaper rates. Later in the nineteenth century, publishers printed books that resembled pamphlets and tried to distribute them as magazines. The practice ended in 1901 when the postmaster general declared that book publishers could not use second-class mailing rates under any conditions. Publishers took their case to court but ultimately lost. By 1914, *book distribution* finally gained a favorable mailing status. The move laid the groundwork for the development of book clubs in the 1920s, which promoted popular consumption of best-sellers as well as histories and biographies. Publishers sold hardback books through the clubs, successfully competing with the paperback industry.

Popular Paperback Formats

The growth of the paperback industry stirred the debate over *quality versus quantity,* and in 1884 *Publishers Weekly* reported, "In the rage for cheapness, we have sacrificed everything for slop, and a dainty bit of bookmaking is like a jewel in the swine's snout."

During the Civil War, publishers encouraged inexpensive, relatively short fiction that became known as the **dime novel;** it was a form well suited to popular taste. Soldiers in the field wanted to fill their time, and reading provided portable entertainment. Between 1860 and 1861 alone The Beadle Brothers sold four million copies of formulaic pocket-size novels written with specific plots focusing on romance and violence similar to the plots of television entertainment or the romance novels of today.

Paperback stories reflected men and women in factories and fictionalized situations they might encounter in that new world of work. The stories were produced through what writers often called the **fiction factory,** in which publishers dictated the story lines, characters, plots, and sometimes specific scenes. The stories were aimed at the working class: mechanics, farmers, traveling salesmen, shop and factory workers, secretaries, and domestic servants. The story lines included traditional, heroic war and frontier stories, as well as tales of outlaws, detectives, male factory operatives, and young women who worked in the mills. Religious themes declined, but the virtue of women remained a hot topic. "Fiction that heroized women outside the domestic sphere," writes literary scholar Christine Bold, "offered working-class women some kind of accommodation and justification, some means of negotiating the transition from private to public."

Questions for "Books and Social Change"

1. _____ To find the topic of this passage, which of these questions should you ask?
   a) Who is Harriet Beecher Stowe?
   b) Who are the writers or authors of this passage?
   c) Who or what is the passage about?
   d) What is the point the authors are making in this passage?

2. _____ What is the topic of this entire passage?
   a) Harriet Beecher Stowe
   b) people and paperbacks
   c) books and social change
   d) popular culture and slavery

3. _____ What is the topic of paragraph 2?
   a) Frederick Douglass
   b) the expansion of book publishing
   c) Uncle Tom's Cabin
   d) writers of slave narratives

4. _____ According to the passage, who were the main readers of books *before* paperback books?
   a) schoolchildren
   b) society's elites
   c) educated Southerners
   d) businessmen

5. ____ What is the "democratization of knowledge"?
   a) economic and political conditions that fuel development
   b) the expansion of information to a wide group of individuals
   c) the development of the paperback book industry
   d) accessibility of reading materials to women

6. ____ Which of the following statements best explains what this quotation means: "In the rage for cheapness, we have sacrificed everything for slop, and a dainty bit of bookmaking is like a jewel in the swine's snout"?
   a) People are enraged that books are being made to look cheap.
   b) Publishers are sacrificing quality in order to produce cheaper books.
   c) People like to buy cheap pork products rather than books.
   d) Cheaper books have allowed people to spend more money on jewels.

7. ____ What is the stated main idea of the last paragraph of this selection?
   a) Paperback stories reflected men and women in factories and fictional-ized situations they might encounter in that new world of work.
   b) Fiction factories produced many novels during this time.
   c) The story lines included traditional, heroic war and frontier stories, as well as tales of outlaws, detectives, male factory operatives, and young women who worked in the mills.
   d) Religious themes declined, but the virtue of women remained a hot topic.

8. ____ What is a "dime novel"?
   a) a novel that isn't worth a dime
   b) a form well suited to popular taste
   c) war stories that soldiers like to read
   d) inexpensive, relatively short fiction

9. ____ Which of the following could serve as an appropriate title for this selection?
   a) Dime Novels in the United States
   b) Publishing a Best Seller
   c) How Books Changed Society
   d) Book Publishing and Women

10. ____ Which of these statements best expresses the implied central point of this passage?
   a) The expansion of the book publishing industry provided opportunities for other writers dedicated to freedom and social justice for African Americans.
   b) Books have played a significant role in shaping and reflecting major social and cultural changes in American society.
   c) Accessibility to reading material helped to expand the middle class, but it also challenged elite social control.
   d) Paperback stories reflected men and women in factories and fictional-ized situations they might encounter in that new world of work.

STRATEGIES IN ACTION

What I've Learned from Men

by Barbara Ehrenreich

Barbara Ehrenreich (1941–) is a social critic and essayist. Her book Nickel and Dimed *(2002) was a national best seller in the United States. She is a prolific journalist who peppers her writing with a sardonic sense of humor. Ehrenreich attended Reed College and later obtained a PhD in biology from the Rockefeller University in New York City. She eventually decided not to become a research scientist, however. Instead, she became involved in politics as an activist for social change. From 1991 to 1997, she was a regular columnist for* Time. *Currently, Ehrenreich is regular columnist with* The Progressive. *Ehrenreich has also written for the New York Times, Mother Jones, The Atlantic Monthly, Ms., New Republic, Z Magazine, In These Times, Salon.com, and other publications. The essay "What I've Learned from Men" was originally published in* Ms. *magazine in 1985. Here, Ehrenreich discusses what she feels women would do well to learn from men.*

> Barbara Ehrenreich is well-known for her sharp humor. Look for examples of this humor as you read this essay.

---

1   For many years I believed that women had only one thing to learn from men: how to get the attention of a waiter by some means short of kicking over the table and shrieking. Never in my life have I gotten the attention of a waiter, unless it was an off-duty waiter whose car I'd accidentally scraped in a parking lot somewhere. Men, however, can summon a maitre d' just by thinking the word "coffee," and this is a power women would be well advised to study. What else would we possibly want to learn from them? How to interrupt someone in mid-sentence as if you were performing an act of conversational euthanasia? How to drop a pair of socks three feet from an open hamper and keep right on walking? How to make those weird guttural gargling sounds in the bathroom?

2   But now, at mid-life, I am willing to admit that there are some real and useful things to learn from men. Not from all men—in fact, we may have the most to learn from some of the men we like the least.

This realization does not mean that my feminist principles have gone soft with age: what I think women could learn from men is how to get tough. After more than a decade of consciousness-raising, assertiveness training, and hand-to-hand combat in the battle of the sexes, we're still too ladylike. Let me try that again—we're just too damn ladylike.

3   Here is an example from my own experience, a story that I blush to recount. A few years ago, at an international conference held in an exotic and luxurious setting, a prestigious professor invited me to his room for what he said would be an intellectual discussion on matters of theoretical importance. So far, so good. I showed up promptly. But only minutes into the conversation—held in all-too-adjacent chairs—it emerged that he was interested in something more substantial than a meeting of minds. I was disgusted, but not enough to overcome 30-odd years of programming in ladylikeness. Every time his comments took a lecherous turn, I chattered distractingly; every time his hand found its way to my knee, I returned it as if it were something he had misplaced. This went on for an unconscionable period (as much as 20 minutes); then there was a minor scuffle, a dash for the door, and I was out—with nothing violated but my self-esteem. I, a full-grown feminist, conversant with such matters as rape crisis counseling and sexual harassment at the workplace, had behaved like a ninny—or, as I now understand it, like a lady.

4   The essence of ladylikeness is a persistent servility masked as "niceness." For example, we (women) tend to assume that it is our responsibility to keep everything "nice" even when the person we are with is rude, aggressive, or emotionally AWOL. (In the above example, I was so busy taking responsibility for preserving the veneer of "niceness" that I almost forgot to take responsibility for myself.) In conversations with men, we do almost all the work: sociologists have observed that in male-female social interactions it's the woman who throws out leading questions and verbal encouragements ("So how did you feel about that?" and so on) while the man, typically, says "Hmmmm." Wherever we go, we're perpetually smiling—the on-cue smile, like the now outmoded curtsy, being one of our culture's little rituals of submission. We're trained to feel embarrassed if we're praised, but if we see a criticism coming at us from miles down the road, we rush to acknowledge it. And when we're feeling aggressive or angry or resentful, we just tighten up our smiles or turn them into rueful little moues. In short, we spend a great deal of time acting like wimps.

5   For contrast, think of the macho stars we love to watch. Think, for example, of Mel Gibson facing down punk marauders in "The Road Warrior" ... John Travolta swaggering his way through the early

scenes of "Saturday Night Fever" … or Marlon Brando shrugging off the local law in "The Wild One." Would they simper their way through tight spots? Chatter aimlessly to keep the conversation going? Get all clutched up whenever they think they might—just might—have hurt someone's feelings? No, of course not, and therein, I think, lies their fascination for us.

6   The attraction of the "tough guy" is that he has—or at least seems to have—what most of us lack, and that is an aura of power and control. In an article, feminist psychiatrist Jean Baker Miller writes that "a Woman's using self-determined power for herself is equivalent to selfishness [and] destructiveness"—an equation that makes us want to avoid even the appearance of power. Miller cites cases of women who get depressed just when they're on the verge of success—and of women who do succeed and then bury their achievement in self-deprecation. As an example, she describes one company's periodic meetings to recognize outstanding salespeople: when a woman is asked to say a few words about her achievement, she tends to say something like, "Well, I really don't know how it happened. I guess I was just lucky this time." In contrast, the men will cheerfully own up to the hard work, intelligence, and so on, to which they owe their success. By putting herself down, a woman avoids feeling brazenly powerful and potentially "selfish"; she also does the traditional lady's work of trying to make everyone else feel better ("She's not really so smart, after all, just lucky").

7   So we might as well get a little tougher. And a good place to start is by cutting back on the small acts of deference that we've been programmed to perform since girlhood. Like unnecessary smiling. For many women—waitresses, flight attendants, receptionists—smiling is an occupational requirement, but there's no reason for anyone to go around grinning when she's not being paid for it. I'd suggest that we save our off-duty smiles for when we truly feel like sharing them, and if you're not sure what to do with your face in the meantime, study Clint Eastwood's expressions—both of them.

8   Along the same lines, I think women should stop taking responsibility for every human interaction we engage in. In a social encounter with a woman, the average man can go 25 minutes saying nothing more than "You don't say?" "Izzat so?" and, of course, "Hmmmm." Why should we do all the work? By taking so much responsibility for making conversations go well, we act as if we had much more at stake in the encounter than the other party—and that gives him (or her) the power advantage. Every now and then, we deserve to get more out of a conversation than we put into it: I'd suggest not offering information you'd rather not share ("I'm really terrified that my sales plan won't

work") and not, out of sheer politeness, soliciting information you don't really want ("Wherever did you get that lovely tie?"). There will be pauses, but they don't have to be awkward for you.

9   It is true that some, perhaps most, men will interpret any decrease in female deference as a deliberate act of hostility. Omit the free smiles and perky conversation-boosters and someone is bound to ask, "Well, what's come over you today?" For most of us, the first impulse is to stare at our feet and make vague references to a terminally ill aunt in Atlanta, but we should have as much right to be taciturn as the average (male) taxi driver. If you're taking a vacation from smiles and small talk and some fellow is moved to inquire about what's "bothering" you, just stare back levelly and say, the international debt crisis, the arms race, or the death of God.

10   There are all kinds of ways to toughen up—and potentially move up—at work, and I leave the details to the purveyors of assertiveness training. But Jean Baker Miller's study underscores a fundamental principle that anyone can master on her own. We can stop acting less capable than we actually are. For example, in the matter of taking credit when credit is due, there's a key difference between saying "I was just lucky" and saying "I had a plan and it worked." If you take the credit you deserve, you're letting people know that you were confident you'd succeed all along, and that you fully intend to do so again.

11   Finally, we may be able to learn something from men about what to do with anger. As a general rule, women get irritated: men get mad. We make tight little smiles of ladylike exasperation; they pound on desks and roar. I wouldn't recommend emulating the full basso profundo male tantrum, but women do need ways of expressing justified anger clearly, colorfully, and, when necessary, crudely. If you're not just irritated, but pissed off, it might help to say so.

12   I, for example, have rerun the scene with the prestigious professor many times in my mind. And in my mind, I play it like Bogart. I start by moving my chair over to where I can look the professor full in the face. I let him do the chattering, and when it becomes evident that he has nothing serious to say, I lean back and cross my arms, just to let him know that he's wasting my time. I do not smile, neither do I nod encouragement. Nor, of course, do I respond to his blandishments with apologetic shrugs and blushes. Then, at the first flicker of lechery, I stand up and announce coolly, "All right, I've had enough of this crap." Then I walk out—slowly, deliberately, confidently. Just like a man.

13   Or—now that I think of it—just like a woman.

***

Vocabulary in Context

Use the vocabulary strategies covered in Chapter 3 to identify a *synonym* (word with the same meaning) for the words that follow. Use the vocabulary strategies as much as possible before you refer to a dictionary.

1. A few years ago, at an international conference held in an exotic and luxurious setting, a *prestigious* professor invited me to his room for what he said would be an intellectual discussion on matters of theoretical importance. (par. 3)

   _____

2. But only minutes into the conversation—held in all-too-*adjacent* chairs—it emerged that he was interested in something more substantial than a meeting of minds. (par. 3)

   _____

3. Every time his comments took a *lecherous* turn, I chattered distractingly; every time his hand found its way to my knee, I returned it as if it were something he had misplaced. (par. 3)

   _____

4. This went on for an *unconscionable* period (as much as 20 minutes); then there was a minor scuffle, a dash for the door, and I was out—with nothing violated but my self-esteem. (par. 3)

   _____

5. The essence of ladylikeness is a persistent *servility* masked as "niceness." (par. 4)

   _____

6. Wherever we go, we're perpetually smiling—the on-cue smile, like the now outmoded *curtsy*, being one of our culture's little rituals of submission. (par. 4)

   _____

7. And when we're feeling aggressive or angry or resentful, we just tighten up our smiles or turn them into *rueful* little moues. (par. 4)

   _____

8. And when we're feeling aggressive or angry or resentful, we just tighten up our smiles or turn them into rueful little *moues*. (par. 4)

   _____

9. Miller cites cases of women who get depressed just when they're on the verge of success—and of women who do succeed and then bury their achievement in *self-deprecation*. (par. 6)

   _____

10. And a good place to start is by cutting back on the small acts of *deference* that we've been programmed to perform since girlhood. (par. 7)

_____

11. For most of us, the first impulse is to stare at our feet and make vague references to a terminally ill aunt in Atlanta, but we should have as much right to be *taciturn* as the average (male) taxi driver. (par. 9)

_____

12. There are all kinds of ways to toughen up—and potentially move up—at work, and I leave the details to the *purveyors* of assertiveness training. (par. 10)

_____

13. I wouldn't recommend *emulating* the full basso profundo male tantrum, but women do need ways of expressing justified anger clearly, colorfully, and, when necessary, crudely. (par. 11)

_____

14. I wouldn't recommend emulating the full *basso profundo* male tantrum, but women do need ways of expressing justified anger clearly, colorfully, and, when necessary, crudely. (par. 11)

_____

15. Nor, of course, do I respond to his *blandishments* with apologetic shrugs and blushes. (par. 12)

_____

Vocabulary Crossword

Using the vocabulary from the exercises in this chapter and "What I've Learned from Men," complete the crossword puzzle. Note that not all of the words in the list will be used.

prestigious	unconscionable	rueful	deference	emulate
adjacent	servility	moue	taciturn	basso profundo
arid	dominate	brood	plumage	earnest
lecherous	curtsy	self-deprecation	purveyor	blandishment

CROSSWORD CLUES (DEFINITIONS)

ACROSS	DOWN
1. dry	2. family of young birds
3. submissiveness	4. regretful
6. control	5. flattering speech
7. imitate	8. bow made by women by bending the knee
9. feathers	10. little grimace
11. lewd	13. provider, seller
12. respect	14. silent
15. esteemed	

Checking In

1. Reread the first paragraph. What is Ehrenreich's attitude toward men? What details support your response?

2. What did you expect from this essay after you read its title? Were you surprised by anything Ehrenreich says? Explain your thoughts.

Getting the Point

3. Why does Ehrenreich include her experience with the "professor" (par. 3)?

4. Why does Ehrenreich think women act so "nice"? Refer to specific details in the essay to support your response.

5. What is Ehrenreich's central point?

Delving Deeper

6. Ehrenreich describes actors who have played tough guys in movies. What tough guy from a movie would you use as an example? Describe why you think this actor/character is a "tough guy."

7. Have you ever witnessed a woman being "nice" when she should have been "tough"? Describe what you noticed and how you felt about the situation at the time.

Writing Connection

What have you learned from the opposite sex? Describe at least two qualities or characteristics. Explain how you've seen the opposite sex display those qualities or characteristics as well as how you have adopted those mannerisms for yourself.

STRATEGIES IN ACTION

The Men We Carry in Our Minds

by Scott Russell Sanders

Scott Russell Sanders (1945–) was born in Memphis, Tennessee, and grew up in a poor rural family. A scholarship student, he graduated first in his class from Brown University. Now a professor of English at Indiana University, he has written science fiction, folk tales, children's stories, essays, and novels. Among his many books are Stone Country *(1985), about Indiana's limestone region; the novel* The Invisible Company; *and the essay collection* The Force of Spirit *(2000). "The Men We Carry in Our Minds" appeared in his 1987 collection* The Paradise of Bombs. *Sanders writes here of his childhood growing up amid poor working-class families.*

Have you ever been surprised by how others see the world differently than you do? Consider that idea as you read this essay.

1   The first men, besides my father, I remember seeing were black convicts and white guards, in the cottonfield across the road from our farm on the outskirts of Memphis. I must have been three or four. The prisoners wore dingy gray-and-black zebra suits, heavy as canvas, sodden with sweat. Hatless, stooped, they chopped weeds in the fierce heat, row after row, breathing the acrid dust of boll-weevil poison. The overseers wore dazzling white shirts and broad shadowy hats. The oiled barrels of their shotguns flashed in the sunlight. Their faces in memory are utterly blank. Of course those men, white and black, have become for me an emblem of racial hatred. But they have also come to stand for the twin poles of my early vision of manhood—the brute toiling animal and the boss.

2   When I was a boy, the men I knew labored with their bodies. They were marginal farmers, just scraping by, or welders, steel workers, carpenters; they swept floors, dug ditches, mined coal, or drove trucks, their forearms ropy with muscle; they trained horses, stoked furnaces, built tires, stood on assembly lines wrestling parts onto cars and refrigerators. They got up before light, worked all day long whatever the weather, and when they came home at night they looked as though somebody had been whipping them. In the evenings and on weekends they worked on their own places, tilling gardens that were lumpy with clay, fixing broken-down cars, hammering on houses that were always too drafty, too leaky, too small.

3   The bodies of the men I knew were twisted and maimed in ways visible and invisible. The nails of their hands were black and split, the hands tattooed with scars. Some had lost fingers. Heavy lifting had given many of them finicky backs and guts weak from hernias. Racing against conveyor belts had given them ulcers. Their ankles and knees ached from years of standing on concrete. Anyone who had worked for long around machines was hard of hearing. They squinted, and the skin of their faces was creased like the leather of old work gloves. There were times, studying them, when I dreaded growing up. Most of them coughed, from dust or cigarettes, and most of them drank cheap wine or whiskey, so their eyes looked bloodshot and bruised. The fathers of my friends always seemed older than the mothers. Men wore out sooner. Only women lived into old age.

4   As a boy I also knew another sort of men, who did not sweat and break down like mules. They were soldiers, and so far as I could tell they scarcely worked at all. During my early school years we lived on a military base, an arsenal in Ohio, and every day I saw GIs in the guard-shacks, on the stoops of barracks, at the wheels of olive drab Chevrolets. The chief fact of their lives was boredom. Long after I left the Arsenal I came to recognize the sour smell the soldiers gave off as that of souls in limbo. They were all waiting—for wars, for transfers, for leaves, for promotions, for the end of their hitch—like so many braves waiting for the hunt to begin. Unlike the warriors of older tribes, however, they would have no say about when the battle would start or how it would be waged. Their waiting was broken only when they practiced for war. They fired guns at targets, drove tanks across the churned-up fields of the military reservation, set off bombs in the wrecks of old fighter planes. I knew this was all play. But I also felt certain that when the hour for killing arrived, they would kill. When the real shooting started, many of them would die. This was what soldiers were for; just as a hammer was for driving nails.

5   Warriors and toilers: those seemed, in my boyhood vision, to be the chief destinies for men. They weren't the only destinies, as I learned from having a few male teachers, from reading books, and from watching television. But the men on television—the politicians, the astronauts, the generals, the savvy lawyers, the philosophical doctors, the bosses who gave orders to both soldiers and laborers—seemed as remote and unreal to me as the figures in tapestries. I could no more imagine growing up to become one of these cool, potent creatures than I could imagine becoming a prince.

6   A nearer and more hopeful example was that of my father, who had escaped from a red-dirt farm to a tire factory, and from the assembly line to the front office. Eventually he dressed in a white shirt and tie. He carried himself as if he had been born to work with his mind. But his body, remembering the earlier years of slogging work, began to give out on him in his fifties, and it quit on him entirely before he turned sixty-five. Even such a partial escape from man's fate as he had accomplished did not seem possible for most of the boys I knew. They joined the Army, stood in line for jobs in the smoky plants, helped build highways. They were bound to work as their fathers had worked, killing themselves or preparing to kill others.

7   A scholarship enabled me not only to attend college, a rare enough feat in my circle, but even to study in a university meant for the children of the rich. Here I met for the first time young men who had assumed from birth that they would lead lives of comfort and power.

And for the first time I met women who told me that men were guilty of having kept all the joys and privileges of the earth for themselves. I was baffled. What privileges? What joys? I thought about the maimed, dismal lives of most of the men back home. What had they stolen from their wives and daughters? The right to go five days a week, twelve months a year, for thirty or forty years to a steel mill or a coal mine? The right to drop bombs and die in war? The right to feel every leak in the roof, every gap in the fence, every cough in the engine, as a wound they must mend? The right to feel, when the layoff comes or the plant shuts down, not only afraid but ashamed?

8   I was slow to understand the deep grievances of women. This was because, as a boy, I had envied them. Before college, the only people I had ever known who were interested in art or music or literature, the only ones who read books, the only ones who ever seemed to enjoy a sense of ease and grace were the mothers and daughters. Like the men-folk, they fretted about money, they scrimped and made-do. But, when the pay stopped coming in, they were not the ones who had failed. Nor did they have to go to war, and that seemed to me a blessed fact. By comparison with the narrow, ironclad days of fathers, there was an ex-pansiveness, I thought, in the days of mothers. They went to see neigh-bors, to shop in town, to run errands at school, at the library, at church. No doubt, had I looked harder at their lives, I would have envied them less. It was not my fate to become a woman, so it was easier for me to see the graces. Few of them held jobs outside the home, and those who did filled thankless roles as clerks and waitresses. I didn't see, then, what a prison a house could be, since houses seemed to me brighter, handsomer places than any factory. I didn't realize—because such things were never spoken of—how often women suffered from men's bullying. I did learn about the wretchedness of abandoned wives, single mothers, widows; but I also learned about the wretchedness of lone men. Even then I could see how exhausting it was for a mother to cater all day to the needs of young children. But if I had been asked, as a boy, to choose between tending a baby and tending a machine, I think I would have chosen the baby. (Having now tended both, I know I would choose the baby.)

9   So I was baffled when the women at college accused me and my sex of having cornered the world's pleasures. I think something like my bafflement has been felt by other boys (and by girls as well) who grew up in dirtpoor farm country, in mining country, in black ghet-tos, in Hispanic barrios, in the shadows of factories, in Third World nations—any place where the fate of men is as grim and bleak as the fate of women. Toilers and warriors. I realize now how ancient these identities are, how deep the tug they exert on men, the undertow of a

thousand generations. The miseries I saw, as a boy, in the lives of nearly all men I continue to see in the lives of many—the body-breaking toil, the tedium, the call to be tough, the humiliating powerlessness, the battle for a living and for territory.

10 When the women I met at college thought about the joys and privileges of men, they did not carry in their minds the sort of men I had known in my childhood. They thought of their fathers, who were bankers, physicians, architects, stockbrokers, the big wheels of the big cities. These fathers rode the train to work or drove cars that cost more than any of my childhood houses. They were attended from morning to night by female helpers, wives and nurses and secretaries. They were never laid off, never short of cash at month's end, never lined up for welfare. These fathers made decisions that mattered. They ran the world.

11 The daughters of such men wanted to share in this power, this glory. So did I. They yearned for a say over their future, for jobs worthy of their abilities, for the right to live at peace, unmolested, whole. Yes, I thought, yes yes. The difference between me and these daughters was that they saw me, because of my sex, as destined from birth to become like their fathers, and therefore as an enemy to their desires. But I knew better. I wasn't an enemy, in fact or in feeling. I was an ally. If I had known, then, how to tell them so, would they have believed me? Would they now?

***

Vocabulary in Context

Use the vocabulary strategies covered in Chapter 3 to *define* these words from the essay. The paragraph in which the word is used is given in parentheses. Use the vocabulary strategies as much as possible before you refer to a dictionary.

Once you feel confident about your definition, use the words below to complete the sentences that follow.

emblem (par. 1)
maimed (par. 3)
tapestries (par. 5)
slogging (par. 6)
baffled (par. 7)
grievances (par. 8)
fretted (par. 8)
expansiveness (par. 8)
wretchedness (par. 8)
tedium (par. 9)

1. It is hard to believe that the man who had been the star quarterback of the football team has fallen into a state of such poverty and _____.

2. Denise reached across the table for Mike's hand, her eyes filling with tears, and Mike knew she was completely _____ as to why he wanted to end the relationship.

3. Lena had three little dogs, and she _____ over all three as if they were infants.

4. Yesterday I received an official-looking email—it had my bank's _____ and colors—asking me to log into my account to verify recent transactions.

5. The defense lawyer shook his head as he took his seat; there was no doubt that the officer's testimony had seriously _____ his client's chances of being found innocent.

6. To relieve the _____ and earn a few extra dollars, Mr. Burns's character suggests—what else?—robbing a bank. (Glenn Ruffenach, "The Oscar for Best Retiree Goes to…")

7. A typical winter morning in Michigan is bound to find school-age children _____ to school with sleepy faces and overstuffed book bags.

8. Police officers are asking Idaho lawmakers to make their home phone numbers and addresses private, saying it's too easy for people with _____ to harass officers at home. (Associated Press)

9. Above them the walls are covered in beads, near musical instruments like an Iraqi *oud*—similar to a lute—paintings, knives and _____. (Sarah Maslin Nir, "Their Corner of the World")

10. Florida's coral reefs are considered a unique natural heritage area in the United States for their proximity to the coast and their _____, running from north of Miami in the Atlantic Ocean to the Gulf of Mexico. (Agence France-Presse)

Checking In

1. The title of this essay is "The Men We Carry in Our Minds." What do you think this title means? What does it mean to you? _____.

2. In your pre-reading of this essay, what stood out most about the author, Scott R. Sanders? Did you read anything about Sanders that influenced how you understood his essay? Explain your response. _____.

Getting the Point

3. Based on the men Sanders saw as a young boy, describe his primary image of manhood. Sanders's image developed as he grew up.

4. Describe the images of women that Sanders saw when he was a child.

5. Why did Sanders find the women and men he met at college surprising and puzzling?

6. What point do you think Sanders wants to reveal in this essay?

Writing Connection

Whether you are male or female, do you think that the men you saw while growing up influenced who you believed you could be as an adult? In responding to this question, be sure to describe these men and how they did or did not influence you in some way.

For support in meeting this chapter's objectives, go to MyReadingLab and select **Main Idea**

5 Comprehension Strategies: Supporting Details

Learning Objectives

In this chapter you will:

- Understand the role of supporting details.
- Distinguish between major and minor details.
- Identify supporting details in narrative and expository writing.
- Use supporting details to find main ideas.

Reading is to the mind what exercise is to the body.
—Joseph Addison

SUPPORTING DETAILS

A Doppler radar, like the one pictured on the previous page, is used to create images of precipitation and storms. In fact, Doppler radars provide many of the weather-related images you see on the nightly news. The radar is actually housed within the large sphere that sits atop the steel frame. Without the steel frame, the radar wouldn't have the correct vantage point to do its job. Interesting, perhaps, but how does all this relate to the reading process in general and to supporting details in particular?

Chapter 4 focused on the main idea and how to identify it. The main idea is like the Doppler radar enclosed within the big white sphere. Like the radar, the main idea provides a view of all that surrounds it. But notice again the frame holding up the radar. This frame, or scaffolding, has only one purpose: to support the Doppler radar. In this same way, as you will see, supporting details have one primary goal: to support the main idea. So, while supporting details may not have a starring role in a selection, they do serve a vital function. Try to keep the image of the massive, white sphere with a crisscross of steel beams supporting it in mind as you think about the key role that supporting details play in a reading selection.

Here's what you can expect in Chapter 5:

Understanding Supporting Details
- Major details
- Minor details

Identifying Supporting Details in Narrative Writing

Identifying Supporting Details in Expository Writing

Using Supporting Details to Find Main Ideas

UNDERSTANDING SUPPORTING DETAILS

Supporting details are ideas that support, develop, and expand the main idea. Examples, facts, statistics, reasons, and definitions are all supporting details. These supporting details are often called major details and minor details. **Major details** are those details that directly support and expand the main idea. **Minor details** support major details by adding interest and specificity to an idea. Minor details answer the questions who, what, where, when, why, and how. In this way, minor details expand on major details. Keep in mind, however, that while minor details add substance to a reading, they are not essential to understanding the main idea.

Visualizing the role of supporting details may be helpful in understanding how they relate to the main idea, so think of the relationship between a main idea, major details, and minor details as a four-legged table. The

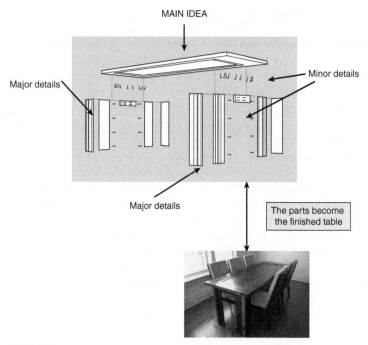

FIGURE 5.1

tabletop is the main idea, the four legs are the major details, and the nails, screws, and joints that hold the legs to the tabletop are the minor details. And even though each piece of the table is distinct, each piece relies on the others to complete the project—the table. A reading selection, no matter how long, generally works the same way. Figure 5.1 illustrates how a table is constructed and how the parts interact, just as a main idea, major details, and minor details interact.

The table analogy is a great way to visualize the relationship between supporting details and the main idea because supporting details hold up the main idea.

IDENTIFYING SUPPORTING DETAILS IN NARRATIVES

In fiction and narrative nonfiction, such as, respectively, a short story and a personal essay, a major detail may be a dialogue between two characters that shows a growing love between them. Or a major detail could be two detectives' discussion of a key suspect. It could even be a description of a house. The key to identifying major details in narratives is to consider how they relate to the big picture, or the major focus of the story. When you read a scene, a dialogue, or a description, you must consider how it is related to the focus of the narrative (the focus is likely to be the main idea, but more on that soon). To see how this works, read this passage from a novel:

> I had to go down to my aunt's house to get my car then *I drove back up the quarter to Miss Emma's.* Usually she was waiting for me, but not today. *I sat out there in the car a good five minutes, but no Miss Emma.* I didn't want to blow the horn; I thought that might show impatience and disrespect. But still no Miss Emma. The door was shut and the only thing to give the place any sign of life was a trickle of white smoke rising occasionally out of the chimney. *After sitting out there another couple of minutes*, I put the patience and respect aside. I pressed the horn hard and long enough for everybody in the quarter to hear it. (Ernest J. Gaines)

What do you think is the primary focus in this selection? Taken as a whole, the focus seems to be that the narrator is waiting to pick up Miss Emma. Re-read the selection and identify the details that suggest the narrator is waiting. Those details have been italicized for you. These are the major details in this selection. This example demonstrates how major details support the main idea, the major focus, in a narrative. These major details describe what the narrator is doing—waiting. Most of the remaining details in the selection give further explanation of the waiting: how long and how impatiently. These are the minor details; while they add interest and distinction to the scene, it is most important that the reader understand that the narrator is waiting for Miss Emma. That is what the major details show the reader.

IDENTIFYING SUPPORTING DETAILS IN EXPOSITORY WRITING

In expository nonfiction, those ideas, reasons, examples, and descriptions that directly support the main idea are the major details. What these major details are depends on the type of expository material. In a textbook, major details could be the scenarios or cases the author offers to illustrate a definition. In a newspaper article, the facts of a situation may be the major details, with the more specific information being the minor details. Keep in mind that minor details are the same in any type of reading: they are generally very specific pieces of information that come after major details. Minor details do not directly support the main idea; instead, they help paint the picture or add weight to the major details, which do directly support the main idea. Here is a brief selection from an article on homeless college students. Read the selection and look for the supporting details. Then, distinguish between the major and the minor details.

Asad Dahir has also spent time on the streets.[1] "I've been homeless more than one time and in more than one country," Dahir wrote on his scholarship application.[2] Originally from Somalia, he and his family fled their homeland due to civil war and ended up in a refugee camp in neighboring Kenya.[3] After more than a year in the camp, he and his thirteen-year-old brother were resettled, first in Atlanta and later in Ohio.[4] There, high housing costs once again rendered the pair homeless.[5] (Eleanor J. Bader, "Homeless on Campus")

In this passage the main idea is Dahir's homelessness. This is stated in the first sentence of the paragraph. The second sentence is a major detail. It tells the reader directly that Dahir has been homeless—more than once and in more than one country. The third, fourth, and fifth sentences are minor details that expand on the specific occasions and locations of Dahir's homelessness. This paragraph illustrates a common example of how the main idea and supporting details are used in expository writing.

Overall, identifying supporting details in narrative and expository material is more alike than it is different. However, it is helpful to see how the details are presented in each type of reading material.

To see how supporting details appear in action, read the following selection. In the questions that follow this selection, some of the information has been identified for you. Use the provided information to identify the minor supporting details.

Practice 1

Shooting an Elephant (excerpt)

By George Orwell

This excerpt is taken from an essay written in 1936 about an incident that occurred in Burma, now called Myanmar. At the time of the events in this essay, the British held power in many parts of Asia, including Burma and India. The writer was a British officer stationed in a small town.

In Moulmein, in lower Burma, I was hated by large numbers of people—the only time in my life that I have been important enough for this to happen to me. I was sub-divisional police officer of the town, and in an aimless, petty kind of way anti-European feeling was very bitter. No one had the guts to raise a riot, but if a European woman went through the bazaars alone somebody would probably spit betel juice over her dress. As a police officer I was an obvious target and was baited whenever it seemed safe to do so. When a nimble Burman tripped me up on the football field and the referee (another Burman) looked the other way, the crowd yelled with hideous laughter. This happened more than once. In the end the sneering yellow faces of young men that met me everywhere, the insults hooted after me when I was at a safe distance, got badly on my nerves. The young Buddhist priests were the worst of all. There were several thousands of them in the town and none of them seemed to have anything to do except stand on street corners and jeer at Europeans.

1. Who or what is the author talking about? _____

2. What point is the author making about the topic? _____

3. Is the main idea ⦿ stated or ☐ implied? If stated, identify the main idea in the selection. _____

4. Provided here is a major detail. Locate a minor detail that supports this major detail.

   Major Detail: I was sub-divisional police officer of the town, and … anti-European feeling was very bitter. _____

   Minor Detail: _____

   _____

5. Provided here is a major detail. Locate a minor detail that supports this major detail.

   Major Detail: As a police officer I was an obvious target and was baited whenever it seemed safe to do so. _____

   Minor Detail: _____

   _____

In this exercise, you may have found that having the main idea and major details identified made it easier to locate the minor details. The major details identified here further establish the situation that the young police officer faced in town. The minor details, remember, are meant to support the major details. For the major detail identified in question 4, the minor detail is: "No one had the guts to raise a riot, but if a European woman went through the bazaars alone somebody would probably spit betel juice over her dress." This expands on the idea that anti-British sentiment was present and affected anyone British. In question 5, there are a number of

> ### Strategy Tip
>
> Supporting details always lead the way to the main idea. If they do not, you may need to refocus your attention to find the appropriate main idea.

minor details that support that major detail. You might have identified the incident when the police officer was tripped or the insults he heard constantly. This selection demonstrates how minor details add specificity to major details. As well, you may have noticed that the major details are necessary for understanding, while the minor details are supplementary.

USING SUPPORTING DETAILS TO FIND MAIN IDEAS

Supporting details really do give legs to a main idea; without supporting details there is no real sense of where the author is going. In fact, supporting details do such a great job of communicating the essence of a main idea that many authors leave the main idea out. Instead, they choose supporting details that will **imply** (suggest) the main idea.

This leads us to another strategy: using supporting details to identify the main idea. Whether or not the main idea is stated, the major details will be supporting it. So, if you have identified a statement as a main idea, but you can't find any support for that idea, then you might have made a mistake. On the flipside, if you have identified a main idea and all the support lines up beneath it (like the legs of a table), then you are probably right on target.

The following passage from the textbook *Sociology, A Down to Earth Approach* by James M. Henslin makes a point that is unstated. Read the passage and compose an implied main idea for the passage. Pay particular attention to the underlined ideas.

> Sociologist Randall Collins (1979) observed that <u>industrialized nations have become *credential societies*</u>. By this he means that <u>employers use diplomas and degrees as *sorting devices* to determine who is eligible for a job</u>. Because employers don't know potential workers, <u>they depend on school to weed out the incapable</u>. For example, when you graduate from college, <u>potential employers will presume that you are a responsible person</u>—that you have shown up for numerous classes, have turned in scores of assignments, and have demonstrated basic writing and thinking skills. They will then graft their particular job skills onto this <u>foundation, which has been certified by your college</u>.

Implied Main Idea: _____

_____

_____

A main idea for the provided passage could be something like this: "Today's employers depend on degrees and diplomas to certify knowledge and character." Generally, the supporting details are pointing to the idea that diplomas and degrees certify that a person has attained something of value, some training that will make him or her a good employee.

While many reading materials will be more complicated and lengthier than the exercise you just completed, the principle is the same: use the supporting details to see which way the wind is blowing. Once you do that, you will be able to identify the main idea, whether it's stated or implied. This is true in both fiction and nonfiction, academic and nonacademic texts.

Here are three more brief readings in which you can practice identifying main ideas and supporting details. Read the selections and answer the questions for each.

> **Identifying & Composing Main Ideas**
> Use Context
> Use Active Reading Strategies
> Use Identifying Questions
> Use Supporting Details

EXPOSITORY   Exercise 5.1

The Internet Economy

by Larry Long and Nancy Long

adapted from the textbook *Computers: Information Technology in Perspective*

The World Wide Web and Internet browsers catapulted the Internet into every phase of our information society. The result is that the money flow associated with the Internet industry is growing more than 10 times as fast as the general U.S. economy. The Internet industry is defined by those companies that are wholly online or have a significant presence online in conjunction with traditional bricks-and-mortar companies.

The Internet economy is now larger than the airline industry and is approaching the size of the publishing industry. Over a million new jobs in the U.S. alone can be linked directly to Internet businesses. Tens of thousands of companies are writing job descriptions for the first time for Internet-related jobs. Fortune 500-size companies can have 30 or more job descriptions for Internet-related jobs.

To see the relationships between the topic, main idea, and supporting details, complete this outline for the passage "The Internet Economy."

What is the topic of this passage? _____

_____

I. Compose the implied main idea. _____

_____

_____

_____

1. Major Detail: _____

_____

_____

2. Major Detail: _____

_____

_____

_____

3. Major Detail: _____

_____

_____

    a) Minor Detail: _____

    _____

    _____

    b) Minor Detail: _____

    _____

    _____

NARRATIVE

Two Ways of Seeing a River (excerpt)

by Mark Twain

from *Life on the Mississippi*
This passage describes a transformation that occurred for the author after he became the captain of a steamboat that sailed upon the Mississippi River.

Now when I had mastered the language of this water and had come to know every trifling feature that bordered the great river as familiarly as I knew the letters of the alphabet, I had made a valuable acquisition. But I had lost something, too. I had lost something which could never be restored to me while I lived. All the grace, the beauty, the poetry, had gone out of the majestic river!

I still kept in mind a certain wonderful sunset which I witnessed when steam boating was new to me. A broad expanse of the river was turned to blood; in the middle distance the red hue brightened into gold, through which a solitary log came floating, black and conspicuous; in one place a long, slanting mark lay sparkling upon the water; in another the surface was broken by boiling, tumbling rings, that were as many-tinted as an opal; where the ruddy flush was faintest, was a smooth spot that was covered with graceful circles and radiating lines, ever so delicately traced; the shore on our left was densely wooded and the somber shadow that fell from this forest was broken in one place by a long, ruffled trail that shone like silver; and high above the forest wall a clean-stemmed dead tree waved a single leafy bough that glowed like a flame in the unobstructed splendor that was flowing from the sun. There were graceful curves, reflected images, woody heights, soft distances, and over the whole scene, far and near, the dissolving lights drifted steadily, enriching it every passing moment with new marvels of coloring.

While this passage is very descriptive, there is still a topic, a main idea, and supporting details. Read carefully to distinguish the main idea from the major and minor details.

1. What is the topic of this passage? _____

_____

2. What point is the author making about the topic? _____

_____

3. Compose the implied main idea of this passage. (*Hint:* The main idea is suggested in a few sentences.) _____

_____

_____

_____

4. Locate and write here a major detail from this selection. _____

_____

_____

_____

5. Locate and write here two minor details from this selection. _____

_____

_____

_____

Exercise 5.3 NARRATIVE

A Mere Prophecy (excerpt)

by Stephen Crane

from *The Red Badge of Courage*
This is an excerpt from the novel *The Red Badge of Courage* and is set in the American Civil War. In the novel, a young soldier struggles with his fear.

When the youth awoke it seemed to him that he had been asleep for a thousand years, and he felt sure that he had opened his eyes upon an unexpected world. Gray mists were slowly shifting before the first efforts of the sun rays. An impending splendor could be seen in the eastern sky. An icy dew had chilled his face, and immediately upon arousing he curled farther down into his blanket. He stared for a while at the leaves overhead, moving in a heraldic wind of the day.

The distance was splintering and blaring with the noise of fighting. There was in the sound an expression of a deadly persistency, as if it had not begun and was not to cease.

About him were the rows and groups of men that he had dimly seen the previous night. They were getting a last draught of sleep before the awakening. The gaunt, careworn features and dusty figures were made plain by this quaint light at the dawning, but it dressed the skin of the men in corpselike hues and made the tangled limbs appear pulseless and dead.

The youth started up with a little cry when his eyes first swept over this motionless mass of men, thick-spread upon the ground, pallid, and in strange postures. His disordered mind interpreted the hall of the forest as a charnel place. He believed for an instant that he was in the house of the dead, and he did not dare to move lest these corpses start up, squalling and squawking.

In a second, however, he achieved his proper mind. He swore a complicated oath at himself. He saw that this somber picture was not a fact of the present, but a mere prophecy.

1. ____ What is happening in the first paragraph of the passage?

   a) The youth is dreaming.   c) The rain has just stopped.

   b) The youth is getting dressed.   d) The youth is waking up.

2. ____ Which of the following choices describes these two sentences from the first paragraph? "Gray mists were slowly shifting before the first efforts of the sun rays. An impending splendor could be seen in the eastern sky." These two sentences are

   a) part of the main idea.   c) minor details.

   b) major details.   d) not important.

3. ____ What does the second paragraph tell the reader?

   a) that the youth is very afraid

   b) that a battle is occurring nearby

   c) that death is persistently on the youth's mind

   d) that the battle is almost over

4. ____ Which word best describes the way the sleeping soldiers are portrayed in paragraph 3?

   a) deathly   c) fresh

   b) tired   d) drowsy

5. ____ Which of these sentences from paragraph 4 is a major detail?

   a) The youth started up with a little cry when his eyes first swept over this motionless mass of men, thick-spread upon the ground, pallid, and in strange postures.

   b) His disordered mind interpreted the hall of the forest as a charnel place.

   c) He believed for an instant that he was in the house of the dead, and he did not dare to move lest these corpses start up, squalling and squawking

   d) All of the sentences are major details.

6. ____ Which word or phrase gives the best context clue for the word "charnel" as used in paragraph 4?

   a) corpses   c) house of the dead

   b) forest   d) somber picture

7. ____ Which statement best captures the meaning of the last line of the passage?

   a) The youth realizes that not all the soldiers are dead.

   b) The youth believes that at some point, all the soldiers will die in battle.

   c) The youth is hoping that they will all make it home safely.

   d) The youth is mad at himself for having imagined such a horrible thing.

8. Compose the implied main idea of this passage. _____

   _____

   _____

CHAPTER 5 STRATEGY QUIZ

This short story by Yann Martel requires the reader to fill in a few missing ideas. However, with close attention to the many details that are given, a very odd and disturbing story emerges.

We Ate the Children Last

by Yann Martel

I   The first human trial was on Patient D, a fifty-six-year-old male, single and childless, who was suffering from colon cancer. He was a skeletal man with white, bloodless skin who could no longer ingest even clear fluids. He was aware that his case was terminal and he waived all rights to legal redress should the procedure go wrong. His recovery was astounding. Two days after the operation, he ate six lunch meals in one sitting. He gained twenty-four kilos in two weeks. Clearly, his liver, pancreas, and gallbladder, the source of greatest worry, had adapted to the transplant. The only side effect noted at the time concerned his diet. Patient D rapidly came to dislike sweet dishes, then spicy ones, then cooked food altogether. He began to eat bananas and oranges without peeling them. A nurse reported that one morning she found him eating the flowers in his room.

2   The French medical team felt vindicated. Until then, the success rate of full-organ xenografts was zero; all transplants of animal organs to humans—the hearts, livers, and bone marrow of baboons, the kidneys of chimpanzees—had failed. The only real achievement in the field was the grafting of pigs' heart valves to repair human hearts, and, to a lesser extent, of pigs' skin onto burn victims. The team decided to examine the species more closely. But the process of rendering pigs' organs immunologically inert proved difficult, and few organs were compatible. The potential of the pig's digestive system, despite its biological flexibility, stirred little interest in the scientific community, especially among the Americans; it was assumed that the porcine organ would be too voluminous and that its high caloric output would induce obesity in a human. The French were certain that their simple solution to the double problem—using the digestive system of a smaller, pot-bellied species of pig—would become the stuff of scientific legend, like Newton's apple. "We have put into this man a source of energy both compact and powerful—a Ferrari engine!" boasted the leader of the medical team.

3   Patient D was monitored closely. When asked about what he ate, he was evasive. A visit to his apartment three months after the operation revealed that his kitchen was barren; he had sold everything in it, including fridge and stove, and his cupboards were empty. He finally confessed that he went out at night and picked at garbage. Nothing pleased him more, he said, than to gorge himself on putrid sausages, rotten fruit, moldy brie, baguettes gone green, skins and carcasses, and other soured leftovers and kitchen waste. He spent a good part of the night doing this, he admitted, since he no longer felt the need for much sleep and was embarrassed about his diet. The medical team would have been concerned except that his hemoglobin count was excellent, his blood pressure was ideal, and further tests revealed what was plain to the eye: the man was bursting with good health. He was stronger and fitter than he had been in all his life.

4   Regulatory approval came swiftly. The procedure replaced chemotherapy as the standard treatment for all cancers of the digestive tract that did not respond to radiotherapy.

5   *Les Bons Samaritains*, a lobby group for the poor, thought to apply this wondrous medical solution to a social problem. They suggested that the operation be made available to those receiving social assistance. The poor often had unwholesome diets, at a cost both to their health and to the state, which had to spend so much on medical care. What better, more visionary remedy than a procedure that in reducing food budgets to nothing created paragons of fitness? A cleverly orchestrated campaign of petitions and protests—"*Malnutrition: zero! Deficit: zero!*" read the banners—easily overcame the hesitations of the government.

6   The procedure caught on among the young and the bohemian, the chic and the radical, among all those who wanted a change in their lives. The opprobrium attached to eating garbage vanished completely. In short order, the restaurant became a retrograde institution, and the eating of prepared food a sign of attachment to deplorable worldly values. A revolution of the gut was sweeping through society. "*Liberte! Liberte!*" was the cry of the operated. The meaning of wealth was changing. It was all so heady. The telltale mark of the procedure was a scar at the base of the throat; it was a badge we wore with honor.

7   Little was made at the time of a report by the *Societe protectrice des animaux* on the surprising drop in the numbers of stray cats and dogs. Garbage became a sought-after commodity. Unscrupulous racketeers began selling it. Dumps became dangerous places. Garbage collectors were assaulted. The less fortunate resorted to eating grass.

8   Then old people began vanishing without a trace. Mothers who had turned away momentarily were finding their baby carriages empty. The government reacted swiftly. In a matter of three days, the army descended upon every one of the operated, without discrimination between the law-abiding and the criminal. The newspaper *Le Cochon Libre* tried to put out a protest, but the police raided their offices and only a handful of copies escaped destruction. There were terrible scenes during the roundup: neighbors denouncing neighbors, children being separated from their families, men, women and children being stripped in public to look for telling scars, summary executions of people who tried to escape. Internment camps were set up, nearly always in small, remote towns: Les Milles, Gurs, Le Vernet d'Ariege, Beaune-la-Rolande, Pithiviers, Recebedou.

9   No provisions were made for food in any of the camps. The story was the same in all of them: first the detainees ate their clothes and went naked. Then the weaker men and women disappeared. Then the rest of the women. Then more of the men. Then we ate those we loved most.

The last known prisoner was an exceptional brute by the name of Jean Proti. After forty-one days without a morsel of food except his own toes and ears, and after thirty hours of incessant screaming, he died.

10 I escaped. I still have a good appetite, but there is a moral rot in this country that even I can't digest. Everyone knew what happened, and how and where. To this day everyone knows. But no one talks about it and no one is guilty. I must live with that.

Questions for "We Ate the Children Last"

1. ____ According to paragraph 1, what was done to Patient D?
    a) He was told he had colon cancer.
    b) He was deprived of all cooked food.
    c) He was given a trial operation for his colon cancer.
    d) He was subjected to skin grafting for skin cancer.

2. ____ What is the topic of this short story?
    a) an experimental surgery using a pig's digestive system
    b) Patient D's recovery from colon cancer.
    c) the moral rot at the center of this society
    d) the French medical team's experiments with pigs

3. ____ According to paragraph 3, why were the scientists and doctors unconcerned that Patient D was eating garbage?
    a) People can eat whatever they want.
    b) Patient D was eating garbage only from healthy restaurants.
    c) They did not want to ruin their scientific breakthrough.
    d) Patient D was in terrific health despite eating garbage.

4. ____ Based on the details provided in this story, where does the main action take place?
    a) New York   c) South Africa
    b) Russia   d) France

5. ____ What is the implied main idea of paragraph 5?
    a) A lobby group for the poor decided to apply this solution to a social problem, and they used petitions and protests to convince the government to allow the surgery for the poor.
    b) The poor did not eat well, so they were chosen to have this operation.
    c) The government allowed the new surgery to be used on people receiving social assistance because the surgery would save money and increase the poor's overall health.
    d) *Les Bons Samaritains* convinced poor people that they would feel better and spend less money on food if they had this new surgery.

6. _____ What does "opprobrium" mean as used in paragraph 6?
   a) danger   c) disapproval
   b) disease   d) disobedience

7. _____ In paragraph 7, the narrator says, "Dumps became dangerous places. Garbage collectors were assaulted." Which of the following statements best explains what the two sentences imply?
   a) Many people did not like eating garbage.
   b) The people eating garbage could become violent.
   c) People were not willing to pay for their food.
   d) If people were not fed properly, they would hunt for food.

8. _____ According to the details in paragraph 8, why did the army get involved and round up the garbage eaters?
   a) The army got involved because old people began vanishing without a trace.
   b) The army got involved because garbage eaters were stealing too much garbage.
   c) The army got involved because neighbors were no longer being kind to one another.
   d) The army got involved because the garbage eaters were starting to eat other people.

9. _____ Which of the following details does *not* suggest the terrible truth about the diet of the garbage eaters?
   a) Cats and dogs began disappearing.
   b) Patient D was in good health.
   c) Patient D ate "skins and carcasses."
   d) Old people began to disappear.

10. _____ What do the details in the last paragraph of this story suggest about the narrator?
    a) He is someone who had the operation.
    b) He tried to warn people about the dangers of the operation.
    c) He is Jean Proti, the last survivor of the camps.
    d) He is Patient D.

KEY TERM REVIEW

Using the chapter as your reference, create your own definitions of the following key terms.

1. Supporting details
2. Major details
3. Minor details
4. Imply

STRATEGIES IN ACTION

The Tell-Tale Heart

by Edgar Allan Poe

Edgar Allan Poe (1800–1849) was a fiction writer, editor, critic, and poet. His personal life was constantly tinged with sorrow and loss, beginning with the death of his parents when he was only ten years old. From an early age, Poe had a strong interest in poetry and continued to write in verse throughout his life. His most famous poem, The Raven, is still read widely today. Poe is also known for his contributions to suspenseful fiction and detective stories. Poe has been described as a melancholy and other-worldly man who was deeply interested in the shadows cast by life. Many of his tales focus upon the horrors that emerge from those shadows. "The Tell-Tale Heart" was published in 1843 and is one of Edgar Allan Poe's more widely known short stories.

Consider the title of this short story. As you read, try to determine whose heart it is that tells a tale.

1   TRUE!—nervous—very, very dreadfully nervous I had been and am; but why will you say that I am mad? The disease had sharpened my senses—not destroyed—not dulled them. Above all was the sense of hearing acute. I heard all things in the heaven and in the earth. I heard many things in hell. How, then, am I mad? Hearken! and observe how healthily—how calmly I can tell you the whole story.

2   It is impossible to say how first the idea entered my brain; but once conceived, it haunted me day and night. Object there was none. Passion there was none. I loved the old man. He had never wronged me. He had never given me insult. For his gold I had no desire. I think it was his eye! yes, it was this! He had the eye of a vulture—a pale blue eye, with a film over it. Whenever it fell upon me, my blood ran cold; and so by degrees—very gradually—I made up my mind to take the life of the old man, and thus rid myself of the eye forever.

3   Now this is the point. You fancy me mad. Madmen know nothing. But you should have seen me. You should have seen how wisely I proceeded—with what caution—with what foresight—with what dissimulation I went to work! I was never kinder to the old man than

during the whole week before I killed him. And every night, about midnight, I turned the latch of his door and opened it—oh so gently! And then, when I had made an opening sufficient for my head, I put in a dark lantern, all closed, closed, that no light shone out, and then I thrust in my head. Oh, you would have laughed to see how cunningly I thrust it in! I moved it slowly—very, very slowly, so that I might not disturb the old man's sleep. It took me an hour to place my whole head within the opening so far that I could see him as he lay upon his bed. Ha! would a madman have been so wise as this, And then, when my head was well in the room, I undid the lantern cautiously—oh, so cautiously—cautiously (for the hinges creaked)—I undid it just so much that a single thin ray fell upon the vulture eye. And this I did for seven long nights—every night just at midnight—but I found the eye always closed; and so it was impossible to do the work; for it was not the old man who vexed me, but his Evil Eye. And every morning, when the day broke, I went boldly into the chamber, and spoke courageously to him, calling him by name in a hearty tone, and inquiring how he has passed the night. So you see he would have been a very profound old man, indeed, to suspect that every night, just at twelve, I looked in upon him while he slept.

4   Upon the eighth night I was more than usually cautious in opening the door. A watch's minute hand moves more quickly than did mine. Never before that night had I felt the extent of my own powers—of my sagacity. I could scarcely contain my feelings of triumph. To think that there I was, opening the door, little by little, and he not even to dream of my secret deeds or thoughts. I fairly chuckled at the idea; and perhaps he heard me; for he moved on the bed suddenly, as if startled. Now you may think that I drew back—but no. His room was as black as pitch with the thick darkness, (for the shutters were close fastened, through fear of robbers,) and so I knew that he could not see the opening of the door, and I kept pushing it on steadily, steadily.

5   I had my head in, and was about to open the lantern, when my thumb slipped upon the tin fastening, and the old man sprang up in bed, crying out—"Who's there?"

6   I kept quite still and said nothing. For a whole hour I did not move a muscle, and in the meantime I did not hear him lie down. He was still sitting up in the bed listening;—just as I have done, night after night, hearkening to the death watches in the wall.

7   Presently I heard a slight groan, and I knew it was the groan of mortal terror. It was not a groan of pain or of grief—oh, no!—it was the low stifled sound that arises from the bottom of the soul when overcharged with awe. I knew the sound well. Many a night, just at

midnight, when all the world slept, it has welled up from my own bosom, deepening, with its dreadful echo, the terrors that distracted me. I say I knew it well. I knew what the old man felt, and pitied him, although I chuckled at heart. I knew that he had been lying awake ever since the first slight noise, when he had turned in the bed. His fears had been ever since growing upon him. He had been trying to fancy them causeless, but could not. He had been saying to himself—"It is nothing but the wind in the chimney—it is only a mouse crossing the floor," or "It is merely a cricket which has made a single chirp." Yes, he had been trying to comfort himself with these suppositions: but he had found all in vain. All in vain; because Death, in approaching him had stalked with his black shadow before him, and enveloped the victim. And it was the mournful influence of the unperceived shadow that caused him to feel—although he neither saw nor heard—to feel the presence of my head within the room.

8   When I had waited a long time, very patiently, without hearing him lie down, I resolved to open a little—a very, very little crevice in the lantern. So I opened it—you cannot imagine how stealthily, stealthily—until, at length a simple dim ray, like the thread of the spider, shot from out the crevice and fell full upon the vulture eye.

9   It was open—wide, wide open—and I grew furious as I gazed upon it. I saw it with perfect distinctness—all a dull blue, with a hideous veil over it that chilled the very marrow in my bones; but I could see nothing else of the old man's face or person: for I had directed the ray as if by instinct, precisely upon the damned spot.

10   And have I not told you that what you mistake for madness is but over-acuteness of the sense?—now, I say, there came to my ears a low, dull, quick sound, such as a watch makes when enveloped in cotton. I knew that sound well, too. It was the beating of the old man's heart. It increased my fury, as the beating of a drum stimulates the soldier into courage.

11   But even yet I refrained and kept still. I scarcely breathed. I held the lantern motionless. I tried how steadily I could maintain the ray upon the eve. Meantime the hellish tattoo of the heart increased. It grew quicker and quicker, and louder and louder every instant. The old man's terror must have been extreme! It grew louder, I say, louder every moment!—do you mark me well I have told you that I am nervous: so I am. And now at the dead hour of the night, amid the dreadful silence of that old house, so strange a noise as this excited me to uncontrollable terror. Yet, for some minutes longer I refrained and stood still. But the beating grew louder, louder! I thought the heart must burst. And now a

new anxiety seized me—the sound would be heard by a neighbor! The old man's hour had come! With a loud yell, I threw open the lantern and leaped into the room. He shrieked once—once only. In an instant I dragged him to the floor, and pulled the heavy bed over him. I then smiled gaily, to find the deed so far done. But, for many minutes, the heart beat on with a muffled sound. This, however, did not vex me; it would not be heard through the wall. At length it ceased. The old man was dead. I removed the bed and examined the corpse. Yes, he was stone, stone dead. I placed my hand upon the heart and held it there many minutes. There was no pulsation. He was stone dead. His eye would trouble me no more.

12   If still you think me mad, you will think so no longer when I describe the wise precautions I took for the concealment of the body. The night waned, and I worked hastily, but in silence. First of all I dismembered the corpse. I cut off the head and the arms and the legs.

13   I then took up three planks from the flooring of the chamber, and deposited all between the scantlings. I then replaced the boards so cleverly, so cunningly, that no human eye—not even his—could have detected any thing wrong. There was nothing to wash out—no stain of any kind—no blood-spot whatever. I had been too wary for that. A tub had caught all—ha! ha!

14   When I had made an end of these labors, it was four o'clock— still dark as midnight. As the bell sounded the hour, there came a knocking at the street door. I went down to open it with a light heart,—for what had I now to fear? There entered three men, who introduced themselves, with perfect suavity, as officers of the police. A shriek had been heard by a neighbor during the night; suspicion of foul play had been aroused; information had been lodged at the police office, and they (the officers) had been deputed to search the premises.

15   I smiled,—for what had I to fear? I bade the gentlemen welcome. The shriek, I said, was my own in a dream. The old man, I mentioned, was absent in the country. I took my visitors all over the house. I bade them search—search well. I led them, at length, to his chamber. I showed them his treasures, secure, undisturbed. In the enthusiasm of my confidence, I brought chairs into the room, and desired them here to rest from their fatigues, while I myself, in the wild audacity of my perfect triumph, placed my own seat upon the very spot beneath which reposed the corpse of the victim.

16   The officers were satisfied. My manner had convinced them. I was singularly at ease. They sat, and while I answered cheerily, they chatted of familiar things. But, ere long, I felt myself getting pale and wished

them gone. My head ached, and I fancied a ringing in my ears: but still they sat and still chatted. The ringing became more distinct:—It continued and became more distinct: I talked more freely to get rid of the feeling: but it continued and gained definiteness—until, at length, I found that the noise was not within my ears.

17   No doubt I now grew very pale;—but I talked more fluently, and with a heightened voice. Yet the sound increased—and what could I do? It was a low, dull, quick sound—much such a sound as a watch makes when enveloped in cotton. I gasped for breath—and yet the officers heard it not. I talked more quickly—more vehemently; but the noise steadily increased. I arose and argued about trifles, in a high key and with violent gesticulations; but the noise steadily increased. Why would they not be gone? I paced the floor to and fro with heavy strides, as if excited to fury by the observations of the men—but the noise steadily increased. Oh God! what could I do? I foamed—I raved—I swore! I swung the chair upon which I had been sitting, and grated it upon the boards, but the noise arose over all and continually increased. It grew louder—louder—louder! And still the men chatted pleasantly, and smiled. Was it possible they heard not? Almighty God!—no, no! They heard!—they suspected!—they knew!—they were making a mockery of my horror!—this I thought, and this I think. But anything was better than this agony! Anything was more tolerable than this derision! I could bear those hypocritical smiles no longer! I felt that I must scream or die! and now—again!—hark! louder! louder! louder! louder!

18   "Villains!" I shrieked, "dissemble no more! I admit the deed!—tear up the planks! here, here!—It is the beating of his hideous heart!"

***

Vocabulary in Context

Use the vocabulary strategies covered in Chapter 3 to identify a *synonym* (word with the same meaning) of the words that follow.

____ 1. Above all was the sense of hearing *acute.* I heard all things in the heaven and in the earth. (par. 1)

     a) keen   b) painful

____ 2. *Hearken!* and observe how healthily—how calmly I can tell you the whole story. (par. 1)

     a) pay attention   b) come quickly

_____ 3. It is impossible to say how first the idea entered my brain; but once *conceived*, it haunted me day and night. (par. 2)

   a) to become pregnant   b) formed in the mind

_____ 4. Now this is the point. You *fancy* me mad. Madmen know nothing. (par. 3)

   a) make   b) assume

_____ 5. You should have seen how wisely I proceeded—with what caution— with what foresight—with what *dissimulation* I went to work! (par. 3)

   a) disinterest   b) concealment

_____ 6. Oh, you would have laughed to see how *cunningly* I thrust it in! I moved it slowly—very, very slowly, so that I might not disturb the old man's sleep. (par. 3)

   a) swiftly   b) deceitfully

_____ 7. And this I did for seven long nights—every night just at midnight— but I found the eye always closed; and so it was impossible to do the work; for it was not the old man who *vexed* me, but his Evil Eye. (par. 3)

   a) annoyed   b) challenged

_____ 8. And every morning, when the day broke, I went boldly into the cham- ber, and spoke courageously to him, calling him by name in a *hearty* tone, and inquiring how he has passed the night. (par. 3)

   a) cheerful   b) frightful

_____ 9. Never before that night had I felt the extent of my own powers—of my *sagacity*. (par. 4)

   a) intelligence   b) strength

_____ 10. I could *scarcely* contain my feelings of triumph. (par. 4)

   a) quietly   b) barely

_____ 11. Presently I heard a slight groan, and I knew it was the groan of mortal terror. It was not a groan of pain or of grief—oh, no!—it was the low stifled sound that arises from the bottom of the soul when overcharged with *awe*. (par. 7)

   a) fear and wonder   b) anger and disgust

_____ 12. Many a night, just at midnight, when all the world slept, it has *welled* up from my own bosom, deepening, with its dreadful echo, the ter- rors that distracted me. (par. 7)

   a) risen   b) deflate

_____ 13. He had been saying to himself—"It is nothing but the wind in the chimney—it is only a mouse crossing the floor," or "It is merely a cricket which has made a single chirp." Yes, he had been trying to comfort himself with these *suppositions*: but he had found all in vain. (par. 7)

   a) guesses   b) fears

_____14. And it was the mournful influence of the *unperceived* shadow that caused him to feel—although he neither saw nor heard—to feel the presence of my head within the room. (par. 7)

a) not received   b) unobserved

_____15. When I had waited a long time, very patiently, without hearing him lie down, I resolved to open a little—a very, very little *crevice* in the lantern. (par. 8)

a) small flame   b) slight space

_____16. I saw it with perfect *distinctness*—all a dull blue, with a hideous veil over it that chilled the very marrow in my bones; but I could see nothing else of the old man's face or person: for I had directed the ray as if by instinct, precisely upon the damned spot. (par. 9)

a) clarity   b) distance

_____17. I then smiled *gaily*, to find the deed so far done. (par. 11)

a) cheerfully   b) viciously

_____18. There entered three men, who introduced themselves, with perfect *suavity*, as officers of the police. (par. 14)

a) suspicion   b) confidence

_____19. I took my visitors all over the house. I *bade* them search—search well. (par. 15)

a) dared   b) invited

_____20. In the enthusiasm of my confidence, I brought chairs into the room, and desired them here to rest from their fatigues, while I myself, in the wild *audacity* of my perfect triumph, placed my own seat upon the very spot beneath which reposed the corpse of the victim. (par. 15)

a) boldness   b) ignorance

_____21. In the enthusiasm of my confidence, I brought chairs into the room, and desired them here to rest from their fatigues, while I myself, in the wild audacity of my perfect triumph, placed my own seat upon the very spot beneath which *reposed* the corpse of the victim. (par. 15)

a) rested   b) hid

_____22. No doubt I now grew very pale;—but I talked more *fluently*, and with a heightened voice. (par. 17)

a) spoken easily   b) spoken carefully

_____23. I gasped for breath—and yet the officers heard it not. I talked more quickly—more *vehemently*; but the noise steadily increased. (par. 17)

a) crazily   b) forcefully

_____ 24. I arose and argued about trifles, in a high key and with violent _gesticulations_; but the noise steadily increased. (par. 17)

    a) curses   b) motions

_____ 25. "Villains!" I shrieked, "_dissemble_ no more! I admit the deed!—tear up the planks! here, here!—It is the beating of his hideous heart!" (par. 18)

    a) take apart patiently   b) conceal true feelings

Checking In

1. According to the narrator (the person telling the story), what does he _not_ want the reader to think? Why?

2. Why does the narrator wish to kill the old man?

Getting the Point

3. Reread paragraph 3. What do you think the main idea of that paragraph is? What supporting details suggest that main idea? Be specific and refer to the story.

4. Why didn't the narrator kill the old man sooner? What was stopping him?

5. What are the two factors that push the narrator to finally commit the horrible crime?

6. How would you describe the narrator's attitude when the police officers initially arrived and he began to show them around the house?

Delving Deeper

7. In paragraph 7, the reader sees the narrator reacting to the old man's fear. What does the narrator's reaction reveal about him?

8. Refer to the title of this short story once again. How do you think the title connects to the events that occur in paragraphs 16–17? Refer specifically to the story to explain your point.

9. What do you think is the overall message of this story? Consider your responses to all the previous questions as you develop your answer.

STRATEGIES IN ACTION

The *CSI* Effect
by Kit R. Roane

Kit R. Roane is a journalist, screenwriter, and photographer who has written on various subjects, including politics, international affairs, and crime. He has been a senior writer for U.S. News & World Report, *a staff writer for the* New York Times, *and a contributor to the* Chicago Tribune, *among other periodicals and newspapers. This article was first published in* U.S. News & World Report *in April 2005 and is currently part of a criminal justice anthology,* Critical Issues in Criminal Justice. *Roane's article discusses the effects television crime dramas have had upon the criminal justice system.*

> Do you know what *CSI* refers to? If you do not, be sure to use your Internet saavy to find out.

1   On TV, it's all slam-dunk evidence and quick convictions. Now juries expect the same thing and that's a big problem.

2   Picture this: A middle-aged woman from out of town digs into a bowl of chili at a fast-food restaurant in California. Each bite is more delicious than the last. She chews. She savors. Then something goes terribly wrong. She spits. She screams. She vomits. All eyes focus on the table, where a well-manicured fingertip peeks out from a mound of masticated chili. Lights and sirens. Forensic experts troll for evidence. Pimple-faced fry cooks are lined up. Fingers are pointed, and fingers are counted. The nub is popped into an evidence bag to make the forensic rounds. A fingerprint is taken to run through a national database. DNA tests are done. Detectives search for clues.

3   If this were an episode of *CSI: Crime Scene Investigation*—and it might well become one—the well-coiffed technicians who star in the show would solve the mystery lickety-split. Fingerprints or DNA evidence would identify the victim, a leggy blond, within 45 minutes. Then, in a twist, a smudge of blood still under the nail would lead to her killer, a jealous fashion photographer, unwilling to let go of his star.

4   But this is real life. Anna Ayala reported her disturbing find at a Wendy's restaurant late last month. And as of last week, investigators were still stumped. Ayala hasn't confessed to any fraud. The fry cooks all had their fingers. The print wasn't a match. And the DNA test still hadn't come back from the lab. On CBS's *CSI*, the forensic science is sexy, fast, and remarkably certain, a combination that has propelled the three-show franchise to top ratings, attracting nearly 60 million viewers a week. The whole investigation genre is hot, from NBC's *Law & Order* series on down to the documentary-like re-creations of A&E's *Forensic Files*. America is in love with forensics, from the blood spatter and bone fragments of TV's fictional crime scenes to the latest thrust and parry at the Michael Jackson trial.

5   That's good, right? Jurors are smarter, and understaffed government crime labs are using the trend to seek more funding. But not so fast. Stoked by the technical wizardry they see on the tube, many Americans find themselves disappointed when they encounter the real world of law and order. Jurors increasingly expect forensic evidence in every case, and they expect it to be conclusive.

"Your *CSI* Moment"

6   Real life and real death are never as clean as *CSI*'s lead investigator, Gil Grissom, would have us believe. And real forensics is seldom as fast, or as certain, as TV tells us. Too often, authorities say, the science is unproven, the analyses unsound, and the experts unreliable. At a time when the public is demanding *CSI*-style investigations of even common crimes, many of the nation's crime labs—underfunded, undercertified, and under attack—simply can't produce. When a case comes to court, "jurors expect it to be a lot more interesting and a lot more dynamic," says Barbara LaWall, the county prosecutor in Tucson, Arizona. "It puzzles the heck out of them when it's not."

7   A disappointed jury can be a dangerous thing. Just ask Jodi Hoos. Prosecuting a gang member in Peoria, Illinois, for raping a teenager in a local park last year, Hoos told the jury, "You've all seen *CSI*. Well, this is your *CSI* moment. We have DNA." Specifically, investigators had matched saliva on the victim's breast to the defendant, who had denied touching her. The jury also had gripping testimony from the victim, an emergency-room nurse, and the responding officers. When the jury came back, however, the verdict was not guilty. Why? Unmoved by the DNA evidence, jurors felt police should have tested "debris" found in the victim to see if it matched soil from the park. "They said they knew from *CSI* that police could test for that sort of thing," Hoos said. "We had his DNA. We had his denial. It's ridiculous."

8   Television's diet of forensic fantasy "projects the image that all cases are solvable by highly technical science, and if you offer less than that, it is viewed as reasonable doubt" says Hoos's boss, Peoria State's Attorney Kevin Lyons. "The burden it places on us is overwhelming." Prosecutors have a name for the phenomenon: "the *CSI* effect."

9   Some of the "evidence" the *CSI* shows tout—using a wound to make a mold of a knife, or predicting time of death by looking at the rate at which a piece of metal might rust—is blatant hokum, experts say. But more and more, police and prosecutors are waking up to the need to cater to a jury's heightened expectations. That means more visual cues, with PowerPoint and video presentations, and a new emphasis during testimony on why certain types of evidence haven't been presented. If there are no fingerprints in evidence, more prosecutors are asking investigators to explain why, lest jurors take their absence as cause for doubt.

10   The same goes for DNA or gunshot residue. Joseph Peterson, acting director of the Department of Criminal Justice at the University of Illinois-Chicago, says DNA is rarely culled from crime scenes and analyzed. Crime scenes today are much like they were in the 1970s, Peterson says, when his studies found that fingerprints and tool marks were the most common types of evidence left at crime scenes. Blood was found only 5 percent of the time, usually at murder scenes.

11   Like crime scenes, many crime labs also haven't changed that much—at least in one respect. Many are still understaffed, and they often don't receive all of the relevant physical evidence from the crime scene, either because police investigators don't know what they're looking for or because they figure—possibly wrongly—that the case is strong enough without it. A crime lab's bread and butter is testing drugs found at crime scenes, doing toxicology screens, and comparing fingerprints. DNA matches are way down the list, mainly because they're time consuming and expensive. How much time? A Cape Cod trash hauler gave police a DNA sample in March 2004. The lab was backlogged. Last week, after it was finally analyzed, he was arrested for the 2002 murder of fashion writer Crista Worthington.

12   Defense attorneys, predictably, are capitalizing on the popularity of shows like *CSI,* seizing on an absence of forensic evidence, even in cases where there's no apparent reason for its use. In another Peoria case, jurors acquitted a man accused of stabbing his estranged girlfriend because police didn't test her bloody bedsheets for DNA. The man went back to prison on a parole violation and stabbed his ex again when he got out—this time fatally.

13   The *CSI* effect was raised in the acquittal last month of actor Robert Blake in the murder of his wife. The L.A. district attorney called the jurors "incredibly stupid," but jurors noted that the former Baretta

star was accused of shooting his wife with an old Nazi-era pistol that spewed gunshot residue. Blake's skin and clothes, a juror told *U.S. News*, had "not one particle."

"On Thin Ice"

14 Still, forensic evidence and expert testimony can add a lot of weight. Confronted with a possible fingerprint or DNA match, many defendants will plead guilty instead of risking a trial and the possibility of a heavier penalty.

15 At trial, many juries tend to believe forensic experts and the evidence they provide—even when they shouldn't. Sandra Anderson and her specially trained forensic dog, Eagle, are a case in point. Dubbed a canine Sherlock Holmes, Eagle and his trainer were the darlings of prosecutors and police across the country. They appeared on TV's *Unsolved Mysteries* and headlined forensic science seminars. The dog seemed to have a bionic nose, finding hidden traces of blood evidence, which Anderson duly corroborated in court. In one case, Eagle's million-dollar nose gave police enough for a search warrant after he found damning evidence in the house of a biochemist suspected of murdering his wife. Plymouth, Mich., Police Lt. Wayne Carroll declared at the time: "Before we brought that dog down there, we were on thin ice." Anderson and Eagle, however, were frauds. After she admitted planting blood on a hacksaw blade during the investigation of the suspect, Azizul Islam, he was granted a new trial last year. It was one of several cases in which Anderson faked evidence. She is now serving a 21-month prison term after pleading guilty to obstruction of justice and making false statements. Lawyers and forensic experts say Anderson is just one of the more bizarre cases of forensic specialists lying under oath, misreading test results, or overstating evidence.

16 In recent years, the integrity of crime labs across the country, including the vaunted FBI crime lab, have come under attack for lax standards and generating bogus evidence. One problem is that crime labs don't have to be accredited. All DNA labs seeking federal funding will have to be accredited by next year, but roughly 30 percent of the publicly funded crime labs operating in the United States today have no certification, a recent Justice Department study found. The FBI's lab gained accreditation in 1998, after it was embarrassed by a series of foul-ups. A Houston lab sought accreditation this year, following a scandal that has so far resulted in the release of two men from prison and cast doubt on the lab's other work.

17 Dozens of coroners, crime lab technicians, police chemists, forensic anthropologists, crime reconstruction experts, and other forensic specialists, meanwhile, have been fined, fired, or prosecuted for lying

under oath, forging credentials, or fabricating evidence. It's hard to find anyone in law enforcement who can't recite a story of quackery on the stand or in the lab. Forensic practitioners say the popularity of the field may make things even worse, noting that new forensics-degree programs are cropping up all over the place, some turning out questionable candidates. "For some reason, the forensic sciences have always had their fair share of charlatans," says Max Houck, director of the Forensic Science Initiative at West Virginia University. "Because of the weight the analysis is now given, professional ethics and certification of labs has never been more important."

"Dead-Bang Evidence"

18   One of the most infamous charlatans worked his magic just down the road from Houck at the West Virginia State Police lab. Fred Zain, who died in 2002, was a forensics star, a lab chemist who testified for prosecutors in hundreds of cases in West Virginia and Texas, sending some men to death row. No one ever bothered to look at his credentials—including the fact that he had failed organic chemistry—or review his test results. When two lab workers complained that they had seen Zain record results from a blank test plate, they were ignored. Zain was undone when DNA test results performed on Glen Woodall—serving a prison term of 203 to 335 years—proved that he could not have committed two sexual assaults for which he'd been convicted. Zain had told the jury that the assailant's blood types "were identical to Mr. Woodall's." After Woodall's conviction was overturned, in 1992, the West Virginia Supreme Court of Appeals ordered a full review of Zain's work. Its conclusion? The convictions of more than 100 people were in doubt because of Zain's "long history of falsifying evidence in criminal prosecutions." Nine more men have since had their convictions overturned.

19   Forensic science experts say the solution is to tighten standards for experts and increase funding for crime labs. A consortium of forensic organizations is lobbying Congress now to do both. "In many places, crime labs are the bastard stepchildren of public safety," says Barry Fisher, a member of the Forensic Science Consortium and director of the L.A. County Sheriff's Department crime lab. Asked about the importance of mandatory certification, he adds: "I don't know if I would go to a hospital that wasn't accredited. The same goes with labs."

20   Some forensic experts, however, question the value of certification. Psychologist Steve Eichel, a longtime critic of what he calls "checkbook credentials," secured credentials for his cat—"Dr. Zoe D. Katze"—from

four major hypnotherapy and psychotherapy associations. Critics have questioned the rigor of the American College of Forensic Examiners International, the largest forensic certifier in the country. Its founder, Robert O'Block, who was charged with plagiarism and fired from the criminal justice department at Appalachian State University shortly before starting the organization, strongly denies assertions that he runs a certification mill, blaming those accusations on disgruntled competitors; the Appalachian incident, he says, was retaliation for reporting improper academic practices.

21   Even accredited crime labs, however, can make mistakes. Most publicly accredited labs gauge their proficiency through declarative tests, where lab workers know they're being tested. Although most labs do well on such tests, some experts question their ability to judge labs' day-to-day performance. And even in declarative tests, deficiencies can be glaring. According to 2004 proficiency results from one private testing service reviewed by *U.S. News*, a few labs failed to properly match samples on simple DNA tests, mysteriously came to the right result after making the wrong interpretation of the data, or accidentally transposed the information from one sample onto another. In a ballistics test, one lab matched a slug with the wrong test gun.

22   Such errors can have real-world consequences in court. In 1999, a Philadelphia crime lab accidentally switched the reference samples of a rape suspect and the alleged victim, then issued a report pointing to the defendant's guilt. Last year, a false fingerprint match led the FBI to wrongfully accuse an Oregon lawyer—and converted Muslim—of complicity in the al Qaeda-linked Madrid train bombings. The FBI later blamed the foul-up on the poor quality of the fingerprint image. "There are a number of cases that deal with what on the surface ought to be dead-bang evidence," says Fisher. "But it turns out it was the wrong result. Improper testing or improper interpretation of data left the innocent convicted."

23   For all the setbacks and scandals, science has made considerable progress in the courts since the advent of forensic investigation. In the 1600s, the evidence against two London "witches" accused of causing children to vomit bent pins and a twopenny nail was ... a bunch of bent pins and a twopenny nail. So it must have seemed fairly revolutionary in the 1800s when a Brussels chemist named Jean Servais Stas devised a way to separate a vegetable poison from the stomach of a countess's brother to prove how he had been killed. Or when an English investigator around the same time solved the case of a murdered maid by matching a corduroy patch left in the mud at the crime scene to the pants of a laborer working some nearby fields.

"Obvious" Problems

24   That doesn't mean forensics can always be believed, however, even when the data are accurate. As Sherlock Holmes said, "There is nothing more deceptive than an obvious fact." DNA is a case in point. While DNA testing is the most accurate of the forensic sciences, experts can make vastly different interpretations of the same DNA sample. Criminal justice experts say most lawyers and judges don't know enough about any of the forensic sciences to make an honest judgment of the veracity of what they are told. Prosecutor Mike Parrish in Tarrant County, Texas, decided to get a second opinion on his DNA evidence in a capital murder case three years ago after the local police lab amended its result to more strongly link his suspect to the crime. Suspicious, Parrish had the sample reanalyzed by the county medical examiner, whose results were much less definitive. In the end, Parrish said, because of the conflicting DNA reports, he chose not to seek the death penalty.

25   Other forensic tests are even more open to interpretation. Everything from fingerprint identification to fiber analysis is now coming under fire. And rightly so. The science is inexact, the experts are of no uniform opinion, and defense lawyers are increasingly skeptical. Fingerprint examiners, for instance, still peer through magnifying glasses to read faint ridges.

26   Many of these techniques and theories have never been empirically tested to ensure they are valid. During much of the past decade, coroners have certified the deaths of children who might have fallen down steps or been accidentally dropped as "shaken baby" homicides because of the presence of retinal hemorrhages—blood spots—in their eyes. Juries bought it. Noting that new research casts grave doubt on the theory, Joseph Davis, the retired director of Florida's Miami-Dade County Medical Examiner's Office and one of the nation's leading forensics experts, compares proponents of shaken-baby syndrome to "flat Earthers" and says its use as a prosecution tool conjures up "shades of Salem witchcraft" trials.

27   The list goes on. Ear prints, left behind when a suspect presses his ear to a window, have been allowed as evidence in court, despite the fact that there have been no studies to verify that all ears are different or to certify the way ear prints are taken. The fingerprint match, once considered unimpeachable evidence, is only now being closely scrutinized. The National Institute of Justice offered grants to kick-start the process this year. Other "experts" have pushed lip-print analysis, bite-mark analysis, and handwriting analysis with degrees of certainty that just don't exist, critics say.

28   Microscopic hair analysis was a staple of prosecutions until just a few years ago and was accorded an unhealthy degree of certitude. "Hair comparisons have been discredited almost uniformly in court," says Peterson

of the University of Illinois-Chicago. "There are many instances where science has not come up to the legal needs," adds James Starrs, professor of forensic sciences and law at George Washington University. Everyone, including the jury, wants certainty. But it seldom exists in forensics. So the expert, says Starrs, "always needs to leave the possibility of error."

***

Vocabulary in Context

Using the vocabulary from "The CSI Effect," complete the crossword puzzle.

masticate (2)	phenomenon (8)	corroborate (16)	veracity (24)
troll (2)	hokum (9)	lax (16)	grave (26)
parry (4)	culled (10)	charlatans (17)	conjure (26)
conclusive (5)	spew (13)	advent (23)	

CROSSWORD CLUES (DEFINITIONS)

ACROSS	DOWN
1. a fraud	2. the arrival or beginning of
3. accuracy	4. to call to mind
5. collected	8. serious
6. chew	9. an unexplained happening
7. decisive	
11. to confirm	10. careless
15. to answer evasively	12. to expel
	13. nonsense
	14. to search for

Checking In

1. Based on the title of this article, what ideas did you already have about the subject?

2. What was your reaction to the opening story in paragraphs 2–3? Why do you think the author chose to begin the article this way? Explain your response.

Getting the Point

3. What is the main point of paragraphs 6–8? What supporting details back up your response?

4. Discuss two major problems that have arisen due to the increased focus on forensic evidence.

5. Why are examples like that of Fred Zain such a concern to law enforcement and prosecutors? Explain your response.

Delving Deeper

6. Within the article, the author twice refers to the accusations made against women believed to be witches. He makes the first reference in paragraph 23 and the second in paragraph 26. What is the intended effect the author hopes to achieve by using these references?

7. Considering all the various points made in this article, do you think the author advocates forensic evidence or policies guiding forensic evidence being used differently? Refer to specific details that support your response.

Writing Connection

The author of "The CSI Effect" discusses how police investigations and criminal prosecutions have been affected by the CSI effect. Do you think reality dramas on television, such as *The Real Housewives* ... or *The Bachelor*, have affected expectations in other areas of "real" life? Give examples to support your view.

For support in meeting this chapter's objectives, go to MyReadingLab and select **Supporting Details**

6 Writing About Reading

Learning Objectives

In this chapter you will:

- Demonstrate the ability to summarize concisely and accurately.
- Understand the types of questions used to develop comprehension, analysis, and application abilities.
- Understand how making connections among reading selections supports comprehension.

I write entirely to find out what I'm thinking, what I'm looking at, what I see and what it means.

—*Joan Didion*

Reading and writing are opposite sides of the same coin. Truly, it is hard to discuss one without the other. Writing about what you have read will feature heavily in your academic career; it is one of the primary methods of evaluation in some courses. Furthermore, writing about what you have read fosters thinking about what you have read. And there is nothing more likely to improve your comprehension than thoughtfully considering the material. This chapter, thus, is devoted to four methods of writing about reading. You will practice each of the methods with the readings in this textbook. In fact, writing is so important that many of the exercises in this textbook require you to write responses rather than to select options from a multiple-choice list.

Here's what will be covered in Chapter 6:

Writing about Reading

- Summaries
- Questions
- Writing connections
- Thematic links

Summaries

If this chapter were a website, the summary would be the most frequently visited page. It hardly matters who you are and what you need to accomplish; creating a summary seems to play a part in any activity. From impromptu movie recaps to closing summations in a courtroom, the summary is the true indication of whether or not "you get it." While it seems that informal and formal summaries can be found everywhere, learning how to write a summary is not so easily found. Writing a summary is not especially complicated, but there are some guidelines to consider. And like most things, it becomes easier with time and practice. The general principles for writing a summary are the same for any type of reading material, but there are distinctions to be made among the summaries of expository nonfiction, fiction, and narrative nonfiction.

Let's consider writing a summary for expository nonfiction material first. To illustrate this discussion, please refer to the Chapter 8 article "Student Abuse of Prescription Drugs on Rise." The first thing to do is set the context by stating the who, what, and where of the selection to be summarized. This can be done simply: "Allison Loudermilk's article on college students and prescription drugs in

General Summary Writing Principles

- Do state the basics: who, what, and where.
- Do include the main idea and any themes.
- Do include major details.
- Do state the author's implied ideas.
- Do include concluding thoughts and suggestions.
- Do use your own words.
- Do keep it focused and concise.
- Do **not** express your opinions or reactions.
- Do **not** include minor details.

The Red and Black...." Opening with the basic facts of the text keeps you focused on your goal, and doing so leads you right to the next item to include—the main idea. After the main idea, include the supporting details and any relevant implied ideas. Keep in mind that while you are relating the author's ideas, you are *using your own words.* This is not, however, the time for your opinions about and reactions to the author's ideas. Keep the summary objective. After you have included the supporting details, close the summary with any final insights, recommendations, or suggestions the author made. Let's give it a try with the article by Allison Loudermilk (go to page 252 for the article). After you've read the article, use the general principles to write a summary in the space provided. You can use the opening line provided previously to get started.

Allison Loudermilk's article on college students and prescription drugs in
The Red and Black

Practice 1

_____

_____

_____

_____

_____

_____

_____

How did you fare? Compare your summary with the one given here. Remember, as you write more summaries, you will become more adept at it. And if you are already doing well, then you will only get better.

Summary: "Student Abuse of Prescription Drugs on Rise"

Allison Loudermilk's article on college students and prescription drugs in *The Red and Black* reported the increased abuse of prescription drugs like Adderall, Vicodin, and Xanax on the college campus. While the problem is growing, health officials, on and off campus, are still struggling to address the issue. A major hindrance in the fight against this trend is the relative availability of prescription drugs from friends, family, and online pharmacies. The culture of drugs that is present on college campuses also makes it unlikely that addictions will be self-reported, although evaluation and counseling are available to students who request it.

Writing a summary for fiction and narrative nonfiction is only slightly different from writing a summary for expository writing. For a narrative text like a novel, short story, or memoir, the best summary maintains a sense of the narrative flow that is present in the material. This does not mean you have to write as if you were the author; rather, you preserve the storytelling aspect as you relate the main idea and major details. Another difference between narrative summaries and expository summaries is what you include. In narrative summaries you do need to mention pivotal moments or scenes, but only the most important ones. You also should indicate how the story is resolved or how it ends. The resolution is the equivalent of the concluding remarks in an expository summary.

Let's practice writing a narrative summary. Refer to Chapter 7 and the myth of "Pygmalion and Galatea." To demonstrate narrative flow and how to set context, the first few lines are completed for you. Complete the remainder of summary. Be sure to include the most important actions or events in the story.

Practice 2

Summary: "Pygmalion and Galatea"

In the ancient myth of Pygmalion and Galatea, the reader first meets the young sculptor Pygmalion when he is at the height of his art and his disdain for women. For unknown reasons, Pygmalion decides to create a statue whose beauty would be unrivaled in art or life. In his artistic devotion to this masterpiece, the artist is absolute. In fact, he falls hopelessly in love with his own lifeless creation.

_____

_____

_____

_____

_____

_____

_____

_____

_____

_____

Questions

Summary may be the most common type of writing about reading, but it is not the only type. As you may have already noticed, answering questions is another way of responding to reading. In particular, comprehension and analysis questions are used to focus the reader's attention on key ideas. If you did not use active reading and comprehension strategies while you were reading, you will certainly need them to respond thoughtfully to comprehension and analysis questions. In general, comprehension questions seek to assess how well you understood the ideas expressed by the author; comprehension questions basically evaluate whether or not you got the point. Analysis questions require you to delve deeper into the implied meaning of the text, to draw conclusions and make predictions, to make connections among the ideas in the text, and to analyze the techniques the author used to convey ideas. You've already had practice answering comprehension questions for the readings in the previous chapters. The next two chapters will provide you with additional strategies to answer a variety of analysis questions.

Writing Connections

Writing connections is a way for you to relate to a reading and to explore your own experiences. These types of questions will allow you to understand central points and themes more intimately and with more insight.

Reader's Response Journals are another way to write about what you've read. Journals are often written for the instructor in a course and can focus on personal reactions to and reflections about the text or evaluations and creative interpretations of the text. A journal may include one focus or many. One of the primary aims of journals is to generate thinking about the text. The readings in the following chapters and in Part 2 will offer opportunities for you to write Reader's Response Journal entries.

Thematic Links

A benefit and pleasure inherent in reading literature is the richness of the material. In literature you will find the breadth of the human experience explored. This exploration will unearth a wealth of themes to discuss and investigate further. Consequently, another type of writing used in this textbook is centered on thematic links. Based on the ideas that are generated from the readings in Parts 2 and 3 of this text, you will have the opportunity to make broader

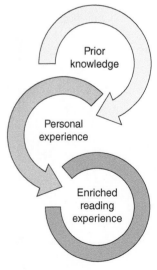

FIGURE 6.1

connections to the themes you explore. In fact, the readings in Part 2 were chosen, in part, for their thematic links to the books and novels discussed in Part 3.

STRATEGIES IN ACTION

Student Obesity Linked to Proximity to Fast-food Outlets

by Jerry Hirsch

Jerry Hirsch is a business writer for the Los Angeles Times. *This article was published on March 23, 2009.*

> What do you already know about fast food and obesity?

1 Barely 300 feet separate Fullerton Union High School from a McDonald's restaurant on Chapman Avenue. Researchers say that's boosting the odds that its students will be super-sized.

2 Teens who attend classes within one-tenth of a mile of a fast-food outlet are more likely to be obese than peers whose campuses are located farther from the lure of quarter-pound burgers, fries and shakes.

3 Those are the findings of a recent study by researchers from UC Berkeley and Columbia University seeking a link between obesity and the easy availability of fast food. The academics studied body-fat data from more than 1 million California ninth-graders over an eight-year period, focusing on the proximity of the school to well-known chains including McDonald's, Burger King, KFC, Taco Bell and Pizza Hut.

4 Their conclusion: Fast food and young waistlines make lousy neighbors.

5 The presence of an outlet within easy walking distance of a high school—about 530 feet or less—resulted in a 5.2% increase in the incidence of student obesity compared with the average for California youths, a correlation deemed "sizable" according to the findings.

6 The link vanished when these fast-food joints were located farther from campus, presumably because students couldn't easily reach them.

Nor was it present in schools located near full-service eateries, whose prices and service times don't typically match student budgets, tastes or schedules.

7   "Fast food offers the most calories per price compared to other restaurants, and that's combined with a high temptation factor for students," said Stefano DellaVigna, a UC Berkeley economist and one of the paper's authors.

8   The researchers said cities concerned about battling teen obesity should consider banning fast-food restaurants near schools.

9   At Fullerton Union, one-third of the ninth-graders examined over the eight-year study period were obese. That compares with a 27% rate at La Habra High School over the same period. Located just six miles from Fullerton Union, La Habra High has similar demographics, but its neighboring fast-food eateries are situated farther from the entrance to its campus.

10   Fullerton Union ninth-grader Anyea Wilson said she's consumed more McDonald's fare than ever before since starting at the school last year.

11   "I get ice cream, French fries, double cheeseburgers, all that stuff," the student said. "I know it's not very good for you, but I eat it because that is the closest place to school."

12   Sophomore Daniel Bannes is partial to cheeseburgers, fries and what he and his friends call the Hulk, a large drink containing a sugary mix of orange Hi-C and blue Powerade.

13   Daniel said he had stopped ordering Big Macs because he was worried about the calories; a single sandwich packs 540 of them. Still, he likes having McDonald's so close.

14   "We all hang there after school and kick it," Daniel said.

15   The findings are likely to fuel the debate over what's driving America's obesity epidemic.

16   Concerned about growing rates of diabetes and heart disease—particularly among young people—state and local governments nationwide are taking aim at fatty, high-calorie foods.

17   California has been one of the most aggressive. Students can no longer purchase soda or junk food in Golden State schools. Some districts won't allow bake sales. California has banned artery-clogging trans fats, and Los Angeles has a one-year moratorium on new fast-food outlets in a 32-square-mile area of South L.A.

18   More than a dozen states and numerous cities are pondering legislation patterned after a new California law forcing chain restaurants to list calorie counts on their menus.

19   But blaming restaurants for the nation's weight problem strikes many as misguided. Obesity can be a product of a variety of factors, experts say, including genetics, lack of exercise and household nutrition. Courts have struck down patrons' attempts to sue restaurant chains for making them fat.

20 Not every group living or working in areas where fast food is plentiful experiences a higher incidence of obesity. The report's authors studied weight data for pregnant women, another group for which statistics are easily available. They found a much smaller correlation between the expectant mothers' weight gain and their proximity to the same type of burger, chicken and pizza restaurants.

21 The high schoolers studied appeared more susceptible to the temptations of fast food.

22 "School kids are a captive audience. They can't go very far from school during lunch, but adults can get in their car and have more choices," said Janet Currie of Columbia University, a co-author.

23 Researchers examined body-fat data taken from the mandatory fitness tests administered to all ninth-graders enrolled in California's public schools. Schools use a variety of methods, including skin-fold calipers. Using that device, a measure of more than 32% body fat for ninth-grade girls and more than 25% for boys is considered obese. The average is 25% for girls and 15% for boys, according to state guidelines.

24 The tests take place in the spring, giving the students about 30 weeks of exposure to the fast-food restaurants near their campuses before body-fat measures are recorded. The study looked at data from more than 1,000 public high schools. About 80 of them had a fast-food establishment within a tenth of a mile of their campuses, a large enough sample to make the findings valid, DellaVigna said.

25 Latino and female students were the most susceptible to weight gain, according to the study.

26 At Fullerton Union, students learn about nutrition in health classes, and the school tries to serve healthful fare, said Principal Catherine Gach. But the school has little control over what happens outside its gates.

27 Gach said freshmen aren't supposed to leave campus at lunch, but she admitted that some sneak out from time to time. Others stop by McDonald's before or after school.

28 The Oak Brook, Ill.-based fast-food giant declined to discuss the issues raised by the study, such as store location and teen obesity, saying only that it offers a variety of food choices.

29 Taco Bell, another chain mentioned in the study, said that its core market is males 18 to 34 and that it doesn't specifically target kids. The Irvine-based chain provides customers with nutritional information and a variety of low-fat offerings, said Rob Poetsch, a Taco Bell spokesman. It's also adding calorie information to its menu boards.

30 The finding that students who are constantly exposed to fast food are more likely to be fat "should not be a surprise," said Brenda Roche, a registered dietitian at UC Cooperative Extension in Los Angeles County.

31   "If you put a McDonald's in front of a school, kids will eat there," she said. "Obesity is as much a factor of environment as it is a matter of choice."

32   But there's hope for high school students hooked on burgers and fries, said Robert Hemedes, a partially reformed fast-food junkie. "Now that I am older and I saw how it can impact the waistline, I no longer order the larger sizes and I make sure to exercise," said Hemedes, a human resources worker in Los Angeles. Last week he ate at McDonald's but limited his order to a regular hamburger and small fries. The $2.07 bill fit his budget, he said, "saving me money so I can go out with my foodie friends to a better restaurant on the weekend."

***

Vocabulary in Context

Use the vocabulary strategies covered in Chapter 3 to identify a *synonym* (word with the same meaning) for the words that follow. For each word, you will be given a choice of possible synonyms; select the one that best fits the context of the sentence.

_____ 1. Teens who attend classes within one-tenth of a mile of a fast-food outlet are more likely to be obese than peers whose campuses are located farther from the *lure* of quarter-pound burgers, fries and shakes. (par. 2)

   a) enticement   b) trickery

_____ 2. The presence of an outlet within easy walking distance of a high school—about 530 feet or less—resulted in a 5.2% increase in the incidence of student obesity compared with the average for California youths, a *correlation* deemed "sizable" according to the findings. (par. 5)

   a) connection   b) number

_____ 3. The link vanished when these fast-food joints were located farther from campus, *presumably* because students couldn't easily reach them. (par. 6)

   a) most naturally   b) most likely

_____ 4. California has banned artery-clogging trans fats, and Los Angeles has a one-year *moratorium* on new fast-food outlets in a 32-square-mile area of South L.A. (par. 17)

   a) freeze   b) monitor

_____ 5. More than a dozen states and numerous cities are *pondering* legislation patterned after a new California law forcing chain restaurants to list calorie counts on their menus. (par. 18)

   a) considering   b) policing

____ 6. Courts have struck down *patrons'* attempts to sue restaurant chains for making them fat. (par. 19)

a) pretenders   b) customers

____ 7. They found a much smaller correlation between the expectant mothers' weight gain and their *proximity* to the same type of burger, chicken and pizza restaurants. (par. 20)

a) nearness   b) potential

____ 8. The high schoolers studied appeared more *susceptible* to the temptations of fast food. (par. 21)

a) suitable   b) vulnerable

Checking In

1. How did your pre-existing ideas about fast food and obesity affect your understanding of this selection?

2. Would this selection be considered narrative nonfiction or expository nonfiction? How do you know?

Getting the Point

3. What is the central point of this selection? What main ideas develop that central point?

4. Write a summary of this article.

5. How is the information in paragraph 6 related to the information in paragraph 5?

6. How is the information in paragraph 9 related to the central point?

Delving Deeper

7. In paragraph 31, Brenda Roche said, "If you put a McDonald's in front of a school, kids will eat there" and added, "Obesity is as much a factor of environment as it is a matter of choice." Is she supporting the study's findings or contradicting them?

8. According to the article, why are teenagers more likely to be affected by the nearness of fast food?

The Writing Connection

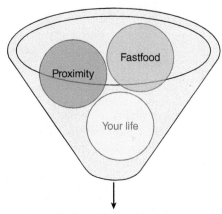

Reader's Response Journal

Based on your own experience, discuss whether or not the proximity of fast food influences your eating habits. Talk specifically about incidents or examples from your life.

STRATEGIES IN ACTION

Perspectives on Corporate Social Responsibility

by Courtland L. Bovee, John V. Thill, and Michael H. Mescon

from *Excellence in Business*

"Perspectives on Corporate Social Responsibility" is from the textbook Excellence in Business. This textbook is designed for students who will be future professionals and consumers. No matter where students go to work after graduation, they'll be competing against the best business talent the world has to offer. The good news is that they already know more about business than they might think. The secret is to help them re-imagine their experiences as consumers and employees from the perspective of entrepreneurs or business executives. Excellence in Business is designed to do just that—in fact, no other textbook helps students make the leap from consumer to professional in so many creative ways. This selection from Excellence in Business focuses on the changing view of the corporation's social responsibility to the public it serves.

> What do you expect from the business in your community? What is their responsibility to you?

1   Conflicts over ethics and social responsibility are often fueled by differing perspectives on the issues at hand. People with equally good intentions can arrive at different conclusions based on different assumptions about business's role in society. These perspectives can be grouped into three general categories: (1) the only responsibility of business is to make money, (2) business has a larger responsibility to society—and ethical behavior leads to financial success, and (3) businesses must balance social responsibility and financial objectives.

The Traditional Perspective: The Business of Business Is Making Money

2   The classic perspective on this issue states that the sole responsibility of business is to make money for the investors who put their money at risk to fund companies. This stance seems blunt, but it can be more subtle than you might think at first glance. In the 19th and early 20th centuries, the prevailing view among U.S. industrialists was that business had only one responsibility: to make a profit. "The public be damned," said railroad tycoon William Vanderbilt, "I'm working for the shareholders." *Caveat emptor*—"Let the buyer beware"—was the rule of the day. If you bought a product, you paid the price and took the consequences.

3   In 1970, influential economist Milton Friedman updated this view by saying "There is only one social responsibility of business: to use its resources and engage in activities designed to increase its profits so long as it stays within the rules of the game, which is to say, engages in open and free competition without deception or fraud." Friedman argued that only real people, not corporations, could have responsibilities and that dividends and profit maximization would allow the shareholders to contribute to the charities and causes of their choice. As he saw it, the only social responsibility of business was to provide jobs and pay taxes.

4   The subtlety that is sometimes overlooked by critics of business is that companies cannot fund the many good things businesses today are expected to provide—decent wages, health care, child care, community assistance, philanthropy, and so on—if they don't make enough money

to do so. The benefits of a healthy economy are numerous, from lower crime rates to better education, but socially healthy economies cannot exist without financially healthy companies because business is the primary generator of wealth in the economy.

The Contemporary Perspective: Ethics Pays

5   Most people in the United States, as much as 95 percent of the population according to one survey, now reject the notion that a corporation's only role is to make money. In the last couple of decades, a new view of corporate social responsibility has replaced the classic view in the minds of many people both inside and outside business. This perspective states that not only do businesses have a broader responsibility to society, doing good for society helps companies do well for themselves. In other words, ethics pays.

6   Many investors and managers now support a broader view of social responsibility. They argue that a company has an obligation to society beyond the pursuit of profits and that becoming more socially responsible can actually improve a company's profits. This line of thinking is best captured by a *New York Times* headline: "Do Good? Do Business? No, Do Both!" "You can't put one in front of the other. You can't be successful if you can't do both," says Seth Goldman, co-founder of Honest Tea, a company that manufactures barely sweetened ice tea and totally biodegradable tea bags. In other words, companies must be profitable businesses to advance their social mission, and their socially responsible activities should enhance the business.

7   Companies that support this line of thinking link the pursuit of socially responsible goals with their overall strategic planning. Such socially responsible companies are just as dedicated to building a viable, profitable business as they are to hewing to a mission—and they think strategically to make both happy. Increasingly, companies and employees are caring about their community and want to be a part of the greater cause. They want to be good corporate citizens and satisfy shareholders' needs for a return on their investment. Still finding the right balance can be challenging.

8   Exactly how much can businesses contribute to social concerns? This is a difficult decision for most companies because they have limited resources. They must allocate their resources to a number of goals, such as upgrading facilities and equipment, developing new products, marketing existing products, and rewarding employee efforts, in addition to contributing to social causes. This juggling act is a challenge that every business faces. For example, if a company consistently ignores its

stakeholders, its business will suffer and eventually fold. If the company disregards society's needs (such as environmental concerns), voters will clamor for laws to limit the offensive business activities, consumers who feel their needs and values are being ignored will spend their money on a competitor's products, investors who are unhappy with the company's performance will invest elsewhere, and employees whose needs are not met will become unproductive or will quit and find other jobs. Stakeholders' needs sometimes conflict. In such cases, which stakeholders should be served first—society, consumers, investors, or employees?

An Emerging Perspective: Dynamically Balancing Ethics and Profits

9   Some business theorists now promote a third view, that ethics needs to be one of the cornerstones of business but that in the real world, profits and ethics are often at odds. Managers need to evaluate every situation within the context of the organization's "moral personality." In some cases, the ethical approach will pay off financially as well, but in others it won't. The decision by 3M to discontinue Scotchgard Fabric Protector is a noteworthy example of this perspective. The government did not order 3M to stop manufacturing products (such as Scotchgard) containing perfluorooctane sulfonate (PFOs), and there was no evidence as yet that PFOs harmed humans. But when traces of the chemical showed up in humans, 3M decided to pull the plug on the product and not wait until scientific evidence might someday link PFOs to a disease. This decision cost 3M $500 million in annual sales because the company did not have a substitute product to fill Scotchgard's void. Even though the decision had painful financial implications, it fit the moral personality that 3M's leaders want to maintain for the organization.

***

Vocabulary in Context

Use the vocabulary strategies covered in Chapter 3 to decipher the meaning of the following words. Use the vocabulary strategies as much as possible before you refer to a dictionary.

1. Conflicts over ethics and social responsibility are often fueled by differing *perspectives* on the issues at hand. (par. 1) _____

_____

2. This *stance* seems blunt, but it can be more subtle than you might think at first glance. (par. 2) _____

_____

3. The subtlety that is sometimes overlooked by critics of business is that companies cannot fund the many good things businesses today are expected to provide—decent wages, health care, child care, community assistance, *philanthropy*, and so on—if they don't make enough money to do so. (par. 4) _____

_____

4. Most people in the United States, as much as 95 percent of the population according to one survey, now reject the *notion* that a corporation's only role is to make money. (par. 5) _____

_____

5. Such socially responsible companies are just as dedicated to building a *viable*, profitable business as they are to hewing to a mission—and they think strategically to make both happy. (par. 7)

practical, _____

_____

6. They must *allocate* their resources to a number of goals, such as upgrading facilities and equipment, developing new products, marketing existing products, and rewarding employee efforts, in addition to contributing to social causes. (par. 8) _____

_____

7. If the company disregards society's needs (such as environmental concerns), voters will *clamor* for laws to limit the offensive business activities.... (par. 8) _____

_____

Checking In

1. Did you adjust your strategies when you realized this was a textbook selection? If so, how did you adjust? If not, why not?

2. Is the publishing information that precedes the selection necessary to understand the key ideas of this selection?

3. Did you feel that you had a prior knowledge advantage or disadvantage regarding this topic? Explain your response.

Getting the Point

4. How is the idea of "social responsibility" defined in this selection? You may refer to the reading, but use your own words as much as possible.

5. What are the perspectives on social responsibility that are discussed in this selection?

6. If you were a business owner and you felt that your primary responsibility to the community was to run a profitable business, with which perspective would you most likely agree?

7. What role does the company 3M play in the discussion of ideas presented in this selection? In other words, why are the actions of that company discussed?

8. What is the central point of this selection? What main ideas back up your response? Be specific.

Delving Deeper

9. Consider the various perspectives presented in this reading. Which perspective do the authors appear to favor? Explain your reasoning by referring to the selection.

For support in meeting this chapter's objectives, go to MyReadingLab and select **Outlining and Summarizing**

7 Critical Reading Strategies

Learning Objectives

In this chapter you will:

- Identify patterns of development and relationships among ideas.
- Use transitional words to identify patterns and relationships in reading selections.
- Identify and analyze the narrative conventions used in reading selections.
- Draw appropriate inferences and conclusions and make predictions based on provided information.

Reading without reflecting is like eating without digesting.

—Edmund Burke

C ritical reading strategies are necessary in your development as an accomplished reader. Critical reading requires you to think as you read, to reflect when you finish, and to review with insight. In short, critical reading demands that you read with a magnifying glass—you must become a detective on an elite squad that scours the scene for evidence of a point, an elusive point.

As a newly appointed word detective, having an awareness of the common conventions of writing and having a creative mind will be key to your success. The strategies discussed in this chapter may be the most challenging to master; many readers struggle with the more nuanced elements of reading because so much happens between the lines. However, as an adult making your way through the world, you have, undoubtedly, begun to realize that so much of what you experience leads you to the hidden rules and unstated requirements that you must, nonetheless, understand before you achieve success. Consider, for example, when you first realized that successful relationships require you to be a mind reader. You may not have known that mind reading was even possible, but now you know that it is not only possible, but expected! As you'll see while working through the material in this chapter, reading the *word* with all its hidden meanings will require some of the same strategies that you've developed to read the *world* with all its hidden meanings. But luckily, the strategies offered here are more easily developed than mind reading is.

Here's what will be covered in Chapter 7:

Making Connections

- Identifying patterns of development
- Identifying relationships
- Transitional phrases and signal words
- Identifying narrative conventions
- Connecting ideas

Making Inferences

- Making inferences
- Drawing conclusions
- Making predictions

MAKING CONNECTIONS

The human mind is constructed to look for patterns. We like to know what to expect, and patterns help us figure out how new information or ideas relate to what we already know. Wanting to know what's in store does not end when we begin to read. The idea is to become more aware of this need and to bring it to the forefront of our minds. In Chapters 4 and 5, we focused on identifying key elements of a text such as the main idea and supporting details. This chapter will build on that work; now we will begin to examine the way an author has shaped the main idea and supporting details and the overall effect that these ideas have on us. To do this, we will make connections among the ideas; some connections will be clearly evident and others will be implied.

Identifying Patterns of Development

One way to begin understanding how a text is constructed is to note how the author has organized the ideas. Writers rely on common conventions to get their points across, and some of the most common conventions are patterns of development. A **pattern of development** is a systematic way of developing ideas to make a point. Table 7.1 provides an overview of the most common patterns of development, a brief definition of each pattern, and an example of a main idea using the given pattern.

Identifying Relationships

Even with a dominant pattern of development, writers must still ensure that readers understand how one idea is related to another. This is the **relationship** between sentences or ideas and how one idea connects to another idea. A relationship can be expressed in a number of ways, and relationships between sentences or ideas help authors communicate clear points. Relationships are often identified by the same features and signal words that identify patterns of development. Here is an instance of two sentences that express a relationship:

> Most animals are uniquely adapted to their environment. The polar bear, for example, has white fur so that it blends into a snowy landscape.

How is the second sentence related to the first? It provides an example of how one animal, the polar bear, is uniquely adapted to its environment. So the sentences show a relationship of generalization and example or, simply put, a pattern of illustration.

Transitional Phrases and Signal Words

To assist readers in identifying patterns and relationships, writers use transitions to signal and make clear the connections among the ideas, or sentences, in a text. **Transitional phrases and signal words** move the reader from one idea to the next and identify the relationship of one idea to another. Very often, transitional phrases and signal words indicate the

Table 7.1

Pattern	Definition	Example
Cause and Effect	Builds a point with a focus on causes and/or effects.	The primary causes of global warming are...
Comparison and Contrast	Builds a point by discussing similarities and/or differences.	There are many differences between capitalist and socialist economies.
Listing	Builds a point by listing ideas in no particular order.	Women have achieved social advancement in times of great change. During the Civil War, the industrial revolution, and World War I, women began working...
Time Order and Process	Both of these build a point with a focus on time and sequence.	Before you can become a surgeon, you must first...
Narration	Builds a point through storytelling.	I never understood the importance of honesty until...
Generalization and Example (Illustration)	Builds a point by making a general statement that is followed by specific examples.	Most animals are uniquely adapted to their environment. The polar bear, for example, is...
Definition and Example (Illustration)	Builds a point by providing a definition that is followed by examples of that definition.	A wind instrument is a musical instrument that produces sound when air is blown against a sharp edge or through a reed. A flute is a type of wind instrument.
Description	Builds a point through description with references to the senses (touch, sight, smell, etc.).	Amidst the stark beauty of the towering snow banks and sparkling ice floes, Leonard began to see...

relationship of supporting details to the main idea. Without transitions, writing may be jumpy, disjointed, and hard to follow.

Table 7.2 identifies some commonly used transitional phrases and signal words. The transitions are grouped by the patterns and relationships they often signify. Keep in mind that some transitional words can be used to show multiple patterns and relationships, so understanding the general meaning of a sentence is necessary to know the intended pattern or relationship.

Table 7.2

Pattern/Relationship	Transitional Phrases and Signal Words
Cause	■ In the event that, as / so long as, for the purpose of, with this intention, in order to, in view of, If... then, unless, when, whenever, since, while, because of, as, since, while, lest, in case, provided that
Effect	■ Accordingly, as a result, consequently, for this reason, for this purpose, hence, otherwise, so then, subsequently, therefore, thus, thereupon, wherefore.
Comparison	■ Also, while, in the same way, like, as, similarly, likewise, in like fashion, in like manner, analogous to.
Contrast	■ On the contrary, contrarily, notwithstanding, but, however, nevertheless, in spite of, in contrast, yet, on one hand, on the other hand, rather, or, nor, conversely, at the same time, while this may be true.
Listing & Illustration	■ And, in addition to, furthermore, moreover, besides, than, too, also, another, equally important, again, further, last, finally.
	■ As well as, next, likewise, similarly, in fact, consequently, in the same way, for example, for instance, thus, therefore, otherwise.
Time Order & Process	■ After, afterward, before, then, once, next, last first, second, at first, formerly, rarely, usually, finally, soon, meanwhile, at the same time
	■ During, most important, later, ordinarily, afterwards, generally, in order to, subsequently, previously, immediately, eventually, concurrently, simultaneously.
Narration	■ At the present time, from time to time, at the same time, to begin with, until now, as soon as, in the meantime, in a moment, without delay, in the first place, all of a sudden, immediately.
Description	■ Words that describe the senses: to see, hear, smell, feel & taste.
	■ Quickly, finally, after, later, until, since, then, before, when, once, about, next, now, suddenly, during, instantly, ordinarily, typically, usually.

Practice 1

Using Table 7.2 as a guide, look over the following four excerpts to see how transitional phrases and signal words are used to indicate a pattern or relationship between ideas. First identify the transitional phrase or signal word. Then state the pattern or relationship present in the excerpt.

1. Most animals are uniquely adapted to their environment. The polar bear, **for example,** has white fur so that it blends into a snowy landscape.

   Illustration.

2. Women have achieved social advancement in times of great change. **For instance,** during the Civil War, the industrial revolution, and World War I, women joined the workforce in numbers previously unseen.

Illustration

3. In the beginning, communication was linked to transportation because information could travel only as fast as a horse and rider. Eventually, the link between communication and transportation was broken in 1844 when Samuel Morse opened the nation's first telegraph line.

4. She could see in the open square before her house the tops of trees that were all aquiver with the new spring life. The delicious breath of rain was in the air. In the street below a peddler was crying his wares. The notes of a distant song which some one was singing reached her faintly, and countless sparrows were twittering in the eaves.

Exercise 7.1   The following selection from a history book provides an opportunity for you to practice the critical reading strategies covered thus far.

Higher Education and the Professions

by S. J. Kleinberg

from _Women in the United States 1830–1945_

Women of all races had to fight hard for access to advanced education. In 1858 the Michigan Board of Regents refused a woman's application, claiming it needed more time to consider the issue. The University of Iowa admitted women in that year, while Wisconsin took female students on its normal school course in 1863. The University of Michigan finally accepted women in 1870 when only two-fifths of the 582 colleges and universities in the United

States admitted women. By 1890, the number of institutions of higher education had doubled and over three-fifths accepted female applicants. At the beginning of the twentieth century almost all publicly funded institutions of higher education took women, albeit many demanded higher entry qualifications from them to keep their numbers down, a practice that continued well past the middle of the twentieth century.

Numerous state universities diverted women to teacher training or home economics and worried that too many women students would undermine an institution's appeal to men. Military academies and institutions modeled upon them, such as Texas A & M and the Citadel, barred women until 1960s equal opportunities legislation prised their doors open. Some southern states maintained women's colleges, and a number of private colleges, including Harvard, Tufts, and Columbia, opened "sister" institutions which accommodated women's demands for education in separate and unequal facilities.

Opponents of women's higher education used biological and sociological arguments. The author of *Sex in Education* (1873) believed study diverted blood from the reproductive organs and nervous system and would undermine women's health and ability to reproduce. The first generations of college-educated women formed strong female friendships, had lower marriage rates, and fewer children than their contemporaries. Women's colleges founded in the 1870s and 1880s perceived their mission as educating women without undermining their health, childbearing proclivities, or femininity, introducing rigorous intellectual programs but also acting *in loco parentis* and regulating their students' social behavior.

Many women attended normal schools or colleges in order to become teachers, and their dominance in the teaching profession increased in the late nineteenth and early twentieth centuries. In 1870, women comprised 61 percent of all teachers, rising steadily to 86 percent by 1920. Women's place in the classroom seemed assured since school boards felt they could pay them meager wages, yet advancement in colleges and universities came more slowly, especially at the higher degree and faculty level. In this same 50-year span, the proportion of undergraduate degrees awarded to women doubled, from 15 to 31 percent; their proportion of masters' or second professional degrees rose from 19 percent (in 1900) to 30 percent in 1920, and female doctorates increased from 6 to 15 percent.

[1]Many higher educational institutions discriminated against female faculty on the basis of their looks or marital status, and married women were routinely refused appointment or promotion. [2]One of the first female graduates from Howard University, Lucy Ella Moten, was appointed to head the Miner Normal School in 1883 over the trustees' objection that she was too pretty to be authoritative. [3]Even some women's colleges refused to hire women who had married, assuming that they

would place their "self-elected home duties" before their academic work. [4]Nevertheless, the proportion of female academics rose in these years, although it stayed significantly below that of teachers. [5]In 1870, about 12 percent of university teachers were women, rising to 26 percent by 1920.

Answer the following questions based on the reading "Higher Education and the Professions."

1. What is the central point of this selection?

    Women wanting access to education.

2. Identify two of the main ideas that support the central point of this selection.

    _____

3. In paragraph 3, which pattern of development is primarily used?

    _____

4. In paragraph 4, which pattern of development is primarily used?

    _____

5. In paragraph 5, what is the relationship of sentences 2 and 3 to sentence 1?

    _____

6. In paragraph 5, what is the relationship of sentence 4 to sentence 1?

    _____

    _____

    _____

7. In paragraph 5, what is the signal word used in sentence 4?

    Exception

8. In paragraph 5, what is the relationship of sentence 5 to sentence 4?

*A result of how female aca-
demic rose over the years.*

IDENTIFYING NARRATIVE CONVENTIONS

In fiction and narrative nonfiction (memoirs, for example), the dominant pattern of development is narration. However, as with any other type of writing, authors of fiction and narratives willfully move among the patterns, depending on what needs to be communicated. Nonetheless, in fiction and narrative nonfiction, there are some particular conventions that you will find helpful to know. **Narrative conventions** refer to techniques used by writers to communicate ideas. While the terms used to identify these conventions may be new to you, the concept is not. Many of the conventions are present in the movies and television shows that you watch regularly.

The four conventions to be examined are:

- Conflict
- Point of view
- Setting
- Scenes

Conflict.   Let's begin with conflict. The core action of any story is the engagement of conflicts. A **conflict** is a tension that exists between a character and some other force. This force could be another character, an emotion, an external circumstance, or a personal flaw. Conflict can be further broken down into external conflicts and internal conflicts. An external conflict is something that confronts a character—like an angry boss, a rival, or a burglar. It could also be a circumstance such as losing one job and needing to find another or a desire to save a rainforest from being destroyed. On the other hand, an internal conflict occurs within the person; in a sense, the person is fighting with himself or herself. This type of conflict may show up as a personal flaw or personality weakness. A character could be a coward in the face of danger or too shy to ask the woman he loves for a date. Internal conflicts can be just as hard to overcome as external conflicts. The boiled-down description of conflict is that the character wants something but cannot obtain it. This creates tension, interest, and drive in a narrative. The **plot,** the series of events that make up the story, will complicate and add to the conflicts, and when all the conflicts have been resolved, the narrative ends. The **resolution** of a conflict simply means that the conflict is no longer affecting the characters. Note that resolution does not indicate success or failure, just completion. Some common conflicts are man versus self, woman versus society, man versus nature, woman versus time, and man versus beast.

Point of View. This convention is generally easy to identify. The **point of view** is the vantage point from which the story is told. There are two aspects of point of view. One involves language and perspective—whether the story is told from the first-person, the second-person, or the third-person point of view. First-person narratives use "I." Second-person narratives use "you." And third-person narratives use "he" or "she." The second aspect of point of view is which character is telling the story. This aspect can be tricky to determine when the author switches the point of view among different characters. Depending on how many clues are given prior to the switch in point of view, it may confuse readers when a new perspective emerges. Overall, as a reader of narratives, you must be aware of the point of view the writer is employing, and you must also note any changes that occur. A shift in point of view is usually made to deepen the story in some way.

> **Point of View**
>
> First Person—I am waiting.
> Second Person—You are waiting.
> Third Person—She is waiting.

Setting. The **setting** of a narrative is the place where and the time when the action occurs. Some narratives have a static setting—one place, one span of time. Other narratives move from place to place and shift among time periods. As well, you will find some settings, while static, unfamiliar because they are foreign to you in location and/or time. Frederick Douglass's autobiography, part of which you read in Chapter 3, was set in the early 1800s. That's a time unfamiliar to most people. Sometimes the setting is so distinctive that, like a character, it takes on an existence all its own. In all cases, setting is a critical aspect of storytelling and should be examined, especially when the setting is unfamiliar to you.

Scenes. The units of action and reaction that occur within a narrative are called **scenes.** A scene is composed of an action, something that happens, and a reaction to what happened. Consider this: a man walks into a bar and punches another man. The man who was punched recovers from the hit and then *reacts* to the attack (the action). That, in essence, is the composition of a scene and the central movement of a narrative: a story progresses through a series of scenes that build to a **climax** (a high point) and resolution (a settling of conflicts). Because scenes, as well as settings, are integral to movies and television shows, you are already familiar with the concept of them. When reading critically, however, it is important to notice the progression of scenes and how they affect the plot. If you think of the plot as a brick wall, then scenes are the individual bricks in that brick wall. But if you are

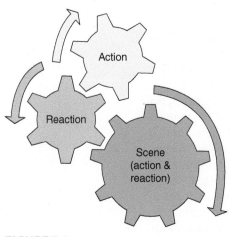

FIGURE 7.1

mainly aware of the huge wall, you may not realize that it is composed of brick after brick after brick. The same is true of scenes. It may be easier in a movie to note the progression of action and reaction in scenes because there are clear visual clues to mark transitions as the plot progresses. In a written narrative, however, the clues are there but are often more subtle. For this reason, it is necessary to look more closely for scenes that are pivotal or turning points. **Pivotal scenes** are those scenes that change the course of events significantly; they may have a considerable emotional impact on the character(s), or they may occasion a major change in events. Whichever is the case, pivotal scenes are the hinges upon which a story swings. Training your mind to locate and take note of these scenes is an important step in increasing your reading effectiveness.

> **Pivotal Scenes**
>
> A pivotal scene is a turning point in a narrative. Often they signal the beginning or ending of a conflict.

Finally, there is one particular type of scene that, when used effectively, is a powerful authorial tool: the **flashback.** The flashback is a scene that returns to an previous time and reveals events and motivations that are relevant to the present circumstances of the character(s). Necessarily then, it is crucial to take note of flashback scenes.

Being aware of these four conventions of the narrative— conflict, point of view, setting, and scenes—will positively impact your ability to read and understand the ideas an author is communicating. Similar to patterns of development, these conventions of storytelling give a particular shape to the point the author wants to make; understanding these conventions also gives you the resources to decipher that message.

Connecting Ideas

Writers not only have patterns and conventions to support the ideas they want to communicate to readers; they also have language itself as a major tool. Now, it may seem obvious that writers use language; however, I have a wholly different meaning in mind. In using language, writers *select* language, *craft* language, and *play with* language. They do this to sharpen and heighten the outcome of the effect that their words, collectively, create. As a reader, if you begin to notice the ways that a writer is hinting and suggesting ideas through certain linguistic choices, then you have another strategy to utilize to make connections. As stated previous, you as a reader are like a detective on a case. You must look under every bed and examine every

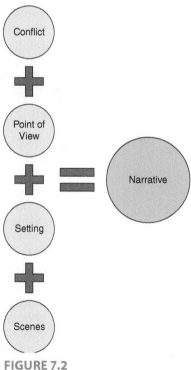

FIGURE 7.2

object for clues, for patterns, for connections. The clues that are given in language often show up as recurring ideas. To delve deeper into your reading experience, you'll need to read with an awareness of these recurring ideas.

Recurring ideas are those images, feelings, and events/actions that continually surface, sometimes subtly, in a text. For example, any one of the movies made about the superhero Superman touches on the idea of sacrifice: the sacrifices he makes for others and the sacrifice his parents made in sending him to our world alone. This is a recurring idea, and this type of recurring idea is called a theme. A **theme** is a concern that the story deals with in many ways and is often bigger in scope than the main idea. A single paragraph or a single scene may have a main idea to communicate, but the sum of all the paragraphs and scenes will contribute to the theme. Identifying a theme requires you to keep in mind preceding ideas and connect them to a current point. In other words, you must make connections between what you are reading in the moment and what you read moments before.

Themes are often a universal principle or ideal. A few examples of themes are "love conquers all," "friendship is forever," "blood is thicker than water," and "treat others as you wish to be treated." Themes can also be actions that turn into broader ideas like "betrayal," "loyalty," "sacrifice," and "survival." Even if you do not identify a theme, you are still likely to understand a reading; however, your reading experience and understanding will be deepened if you do identify the theme. In some cases, the ability to read at the level that allows you to identify a theme may be the minimum requirement for successful completion of an academic course.

Other types of recurring ideas show up as images, feelings, and events or actions. **Recurring images** are often descriptions and phrases that the author repeats throughout the work to highlight visual clues. In the movie *Titanic*, the diamond worn by the young woman is a recurring image of enduring beauty and love. In both fiction and nonfiction, images are used to convey powerful emotions, and repetition of an image can reinforce a theme.

Feelings or emotions can also be used to create an atmosphere or aura in a text. In a textbook on sociology, for example, the author may consistently refer to the negative and positive impacts that social pressure exerts on the emotional state of individuals. The author may do this to impress upon readers the significant role that society plays in our development as individuals. Recurring feelings or emotions can also be heightened to the level of a theme.

Finally, authors may highlight **recurring actions/events** to reveal themes. Actions or events are not simply recycled; rather, the author writes these actions/events in such a manner that they mirror each other in discreet ways that an alert reader can detect. The effects of this are a sense of continuity and an expanded engagement with the text. Depending on the importance of the recurring actions or events, they can be heightened to the level of a theme themselves.

All of these recurring ideas operate on the level of language: the author's language choices. It is thus the reader's job to make the connections and see the broader implications of the recurring ideas and themes.

Using the key terms and strategies covered in this section about narrative conventions, read the myth of Pygmalion and answer the questions that follow.

Exercise 7.2

Pygmalion and Galatea

by Edith Hamilton

from *Mythology: Timeless Tales of Gods and Heroes*

A gifted young sculptor of Cyprus, named Pygmalion, was a woman-hater. *Detesting the faults beyond measure which nature has given to women,* he resolved never to marry. His art, he told himself, was enough for him. Nevertheless, the statue he made and devoted all his genius to was that of a woman. Either he could not dismiss what he so disapproved of from his mind as easily as from his life, or else he was bent on forming a perfect woman and showing men the deficiencies of the kind they had to put up with.

However that was, he labored long and devotedly on the statue and produced a most exquisite work of art. But lovely as it was he could not rest content. He kept on working at it and daily under his skillful fingers it grew more beautiful. No woman ever born, no statue ever made, could approach it. When nothing could be added to its perfections, a strange fate had befallen its creator: he had fallen in love, deeply, passionately in love, with the thing he had made. It must be said in explanation that the statue did not look like a statue; no one would have thought it was ivory or stone, but warm human flesh, motionless for a moment only. Such was the wondrous power of this disdainful young man. The supreme achievement of art was his, the art of concealing art.

But from that time on, the sex he scorned had their revenge. No hopeless lover of a living maiden was ever so desperately unhappy as Pygmalion. He kissed those enticing lips—they could not kiss him back; he caressed her hands, her face—they were unresponsive; he took her in his arms—she remained a cold and passive form. For a time he tried to pretend, as children do with their toys. He would dress her in rich robes, trying the effect of one delicate or glowing color after another, and imagine she was pleased. He would bring her the gifts real maidens love, little birds and gay flowers and the shining tears of amber Phaethon's sisters weep, and then dream that she thanked him with eager affection. He put her to bed at night, and tucked her in all soft and warm, as little girls do their dolls. But he was not a child; he could not keep on pretending. In the end he gave up. He loved a lifeless thing and he was utterly and hopelessly wretched.

This singular passion did not long remain concealed from the Goddess of Passionate Love. Venus was interested in something that seldom came her way, a new kind of lover, and she determined to help a young man who could be enamored and yet original.

The feast day of Venus was, of course, especially honored in Cyprus, the island which first received the goddess after she rose from the foam. Snow-white heifers whose horns had been gilded were offered in numbers to her; the heavenly odor of incense was spread through the island from her many altars; crowds thronged her temples; not an unhappy lover but was there with his gift, praying that his love might turn kind. There too, of course, was Pygmalion. He dared to ask the goddess only that he might find a maiden like his statue, but Venus knew what he really wanted and as a sign that she favored his prayer the flame on the altar he stood before leaped up three times, blazing into the air.

Very thoughtful at this good omen Pygmalion sought his house and his love, the thing he had created and given his heart to. There she stood on her Pedestal, entrancingly beautiful. He caressed her and then he started back. Was it self-deception or did she really feel warm to his touch? He kissed her lips, a long lingering kiss, and felt them grow soft beneath his. He touched her arms, her shoulders; their hardness vanished. It was like watching wax soften in the sun. He clasped her wrist; blood was pulsing there. Venus, he thought. This is the goddess's doing. And with unutterable gratitude and joy he put his arms around his love and saw her smile into his eyes and blush.

Venus herself graced their marriage with her presence, but what happened after that we do not know, except that Pygmalion named the maiden Galatea, and that their son, Paphos, gave his name to Venus' favorite city.

Answer the following questions based on the reading "Pygmalion and Galatea."

1. What is the central point of this selection?

   _____

2. What are the main ideas that support the central point in this selection?

   _____

3. Is this story told in the first-, second-, or third-person point of view? From which character's perspective is the story primarily told?

   _____

4. Is there a shift in the point of view? If so, to whom does it shift?

   _____

5. What is the major conflict of this story? How do you know?

   _____

6. What is the setting of the story? Is the setting important to the events of the story?

   _____

7. Describe a pivotal scene in the story, and explain why it is pivotal.

   _____

8. Describe an image that recurs in this story.

   _____

9. What is an idea that recurs in this story?

   _____

10. Suggest a possible theme and explain what details support that theme.

_____

MAKING INFERENCES

Making inferences is necessary to reading critically. An **inference** involves stating the unknown based on known information. An inference is an informed guess: you have some information, but not enough to be certain of your conclusion. To continue with the detective analogy, just imagine how much a detective infers in order to solve a case. As the detective is gathering evidence for the case, he has gaps in his knowledge that can be bridged only with creative thinking and by making connections among the evidence he does have. Likewise, readers must use what they know to figure out what they don't know.

We have already begun to explore making inferences. In Chapter 4, you worked with implied main ideas. An author implies meaning; a reader infers meaning. The relationship between implying and inferring is similar to the relationship between giving and taking. A writer implies or gives hints and suggestions, and a reader infers or takes the hints or suggestions and makes meaning from them. So in Chapter 5, when you used supporting details to figure out implied main ideas, you were, in fact, inferring the main idea. When a main idea is unstated, you need to verify your inferences by looking as closely as possible at the details you have.

When reading literature, both nonfiction and fiction, making inferences is part of the task of reading well. We have discussed narrative conventions and practiced identifying them. As you will see, these conventions are related to the work of making inferences.

Drawing Conclusions

When you are reading, ideas begin to accumulate in ways that suggest a point. The suggestion of an idea or point can be enhanced by the author's use of a pattern such as cause and effect or comparison and contrast. When the author employs a pattern, you can often connect the dots and make a conclusion about an implied point. A **conclusion** is a type of inference that is made after an identifiable set of clues is presented that make a point seem likely. Review this brief selection to see this idea in action.

Sex, Lies and Conversation (excerpt)

by Deborah Tannen

I was addressing a small gathering in a suburban Virginia living room—a women's group that had invited men to join them. Throughout the evening, one man had been particularly talkative, frequently offering ideas and anecdotes, while his wife sat silently beside him on the couch. Toward the end of the evening, I commented that women frequently complain that their husbands don't talk to them. This man quickly concurred. He gestured toward his wife and said, "She's the talker in our family." The room burst into laughter; the man looked puzzled and hurt. "It's true," he explained. "When I come home from work I have nothing to say. If she didn't keep the conversation going, we'd spend the whole evening in silence."

In this selection, the room "burst into laughter" after the man said his wife is talkative. Why? According to the details given, the man had been talking all evening while his wife sat silently. Thus, we can infer that the group couldn't believe that the wife was "the talker" in their family, and so the group laughed when the husband said she was. This is drawing a conclusion. While it may sound tricky when it is defined, in actuality, it is something that occurs naturally when you read critically.

Making inferences and drawing conclusions in nonfiction (like the Tannen selection) and fiction is one thing. What about making inferences in a textbook reading? While more straightforward in their intentions (to instruct and inform), textbook authors have adopted many characteristics of general-interest reading material. For example, textbooks often have sidebars that feature short articles or essays that are more relatable or personal than the broader academic discussion. Besides this, textbooks have become more narrative and conversational as they strive to keep the interest of readers who are also consumers. For these reasons, applying some of the same strategies used to understand and analyze literature is helpful with textbooks as well.

The following selection from a criminal justice textbook offers you an opportunity to practice your newly minted critical reading techniques. This selection is typical of the kind of article that is included in a textbook. Read the selection and answer the questions that follow.

Exercise 7.3

Inmates Go to Court for the Right to Use Internet

by Kevin Johnson

in the textbook *Criminal Justice Today* by Frank Schmalleger

When a friend sent Georgia inmate Danny Williams some legal research that had been downloaded from the Internet...state prison guards confiscated the package.

Prison officials said the material was prohibited under a 5-year-old regulation that, according to state Department of Corrections Commissioner James Donald, bars inmates from receiving any printed material downloaded from the Internet. The policy is designed to prevent inmates from gaining access to material on the Internet that could compromise security—bombmaking instructions, for example.

Now, Williams is challenging the policy in federal court, the latest in a series of cases in which inmates are seeking changes in prison regulations or state law to try to use the Internet to do research or communicate with the outside world.

State and federal inmates do not have direct access to computers. However, some have used written correspondence with friends or family members to set up and maintain websites and e-mail accounts to air grievances, solicit legal assistance and express political views. Legal challenges such as Williams'—along with recent reports that several death-row inmates in Texas have posted personal profiles on the social networking site MySpace.com—have ignited a national debate over speech rights and how much contact prisoners should be allowed with the public in the Internet age.

John Boston, a prisoners' rights advocate in New York, says inmates' use of the Internet—albeit indirectly—represents a matter of simple free speech that should be protected.

However, Andy Kahan, director of Houston's crime victims office, says some of that speech, potentially viewable around the world, could reinjure victims.

"It's like getting (harmed) all over again," Kahan says.

In some states, crime victims and prison officials have launched legal and informal campaigns to block all access to the Internet by inmates. Those strategies, however, have been largely unsuccessful:

— In a case similar to Williams' challenge in Georgia, a federal appeals court in California two years ago sided with an inmate who was barred under state prison regulations from receiving printed copies of Internet-generated documents through regular mail. Prison authorities feared that the materials could contain coded messages.

— In Arizona, prisoners' rights groups successfully challenged a state law that once banned inmates from exchanging written mail with Internet service providers or establishing profiles on websites through outside contacts.

The Arizona law, overturned in 2003, called for additional disciplinary sanctions against inmates if they were found to have corresponded with Internet providers or requested that "any person access a provider's website."

The Arizona Department of Corrections, according to court documents, had imposed sanctions against at least five inmates "because their names appeared on Internet websites."

A similar issue surfaced this month in Texas, when Kahan discovered that 30 death-row inmates had profiles on MySpace.com.

"Is it (MySpace's) policy to give killers a platform for all the world to see?" Kahan says. "I'm asking MySpace to take a stand. Do they want convicted killers to infiltrate a system geared to young people?"

Among the most notorious inmates featured on the site is Randy Halprin, 29. He was a member of the "Texas 7," a group of inmates who escaped from the state prison system in 2000 and went on a murderous rampage.

The group was involved in the fatal shooting of a police officer during a botched robbery near Dallas. Halprin was sentenced to death for his role in the slaying.

On MySpace, Halprin established a profile, which included a gallery of photographs chronicling his life from childhood to a current photo of a smiling Halprin on death row. The page is no longer accessible to the public.

Texas Department of Criminal Justice spokeswoman Michelle Lyons says that for years, death row inmates have been using relatives and others to post information on their behalves. "We cannot police the Internet for what outsiders are posting," she says.

MySpace spokesman Jeff Berman says the site is reviewing profiles posted on behalf of inmates and says it will "remove any that violate our terms of service, such as hate speech, advocating violence and threatening conduct.

"Unless you violate the terms of service or break the law, we don't step in the middle of free expression," Berman says. "There's a lot on our site we don't approve of in terms of taste or ideas, but it's not our role to be censors."

Jayne Hawkins says she believes MySpace should do more to discourage inmate profiles. Her son, Aubrey Hawkins, was the police officer killed in the robbery that involved Halprin.

"Websites that allow criminals are helping them turn into romantic figures; that is so detrimental to our children," Hawkins says.

"This kind of thing dishonors Aubrey. What should happen on death row is that these people should sit behind a locked door, and we should be allowed to forget about them."

Answer the following questions based on the reading "Inmates Go to Court for the Right to Use Internet."

1. What is the central point of this selection?

   _____

2. What are two ways that inmates are gaining access to the Internet, according to this article?

   _____

3. Why do some people support an inmate's use of the Internet?

   _____

____ 4. Based on the provided information, what can you conclude about John Boston's beliefs?

   a) He feels most inmates are actually not guilty.

   b) He believes inmates should have freedom of speech.

    c) He supports only those inmates who have a chance of parole.

    d) He believes inmates should not have their mail restricted or searched.

_____ **5.** What can be inferred about Andy Kahan's beliefs regarding inmates?

    a) He believes inmates' rights should not hurt or negatively impact crime victims.

    b) He doesn't think inmates deserve to be given any rights.

    c) He believes that inmates who committed violent crimes should be on death row.

    d) He believes inmates should be isolated and kept behind locked doors.

_____ **6.** What position is MySpace taking in this debate about inmates' right to Internet access?

    a) MySpace seems to support the inmates' right to the Internet.

    b) MySpace wants to block inmates from posting or using the site.

    c) MySpace suggested the inmates use Facebook instead of their site.

    d) MySpace has not taken a stand on the issue.

Making Predictions

The final frontier of this chapter is the realm of predictions. **Predictions** are also a type of inference: predictions seek to anticipate what will happen. We spoke of predicting in Chapter 2 as a way of preparing yourself for the reading experience. At that time, it was mentioned that we would return to the discussion of prediction in a later chapter; well, this is that chapter. Predictions, like conclusions, allow your mind to race ahead of the text and pave the way for events and ideas that are likely to follow. The key word is "likely." As anyone who has ever visited a fortune-teller knows, just because Madame Lalafalo predicted you would win the lottery, that doesn't mean you will definitely do so. With that fact notwithstanding, prediction is still a helpful strategy for readers. Predicting encourages you to bring various ideas and details together and try to make sense of them. Even if your prediction turns out not to be true, predicting still motivated you to focus on the particulars and read carefully. In the event that your prediction is accurate, well, you will feel like an especially skillful reader.

To expand on the idea of prediction, consider the myth of Midas. You may be familiar with the story of Midas from one of the many variations that have been told over the years. If you are not familiar with Midas, this exercise will allow you to become familiar.

Midas

by Edith Hamilton

from *Mythology: Timeless Tales of Gods and Heroes*

Midas, whose name has become a synonym for a rich man, had very little profit from his riches. The experience of possessing them lasted for less than a day and it threatened him with speedy death. He was an example of folly being as fatal as sin, for he meant no harm; he merely did not use any intelligence. His story suggests that he had none to use.

He was King of Phrygia, the land of roses, and he had great rose gardens near his palace. Into them once strayed old Silenus who intoxicated as always, had wandered off from Bacchus' train where he belonged and lost his way. The fat drunkard was found asleep in a bower of roses by some of the servants of the palace. They bound him with rosy garlands, set a flowering wreath on his head, woke him up, and bore him in this ridiculous guise to Midas as a great joke. Midas welcomed him and entertained him for ten days. Then he led him to Bacchus, who, delighted to get him back, told Midas whatever wish he made would come true. Without giving a thought to the inevitable result Midas wished that whatever he touched would turn into gold. Of course Bacchus in granting the favor foresaw what would happen....

The tale of Midas continues, but what do you predict the god Bacchus saw in Midas's future? What do you think will happen once Midas is given his wish? Write your predictions on the lines that follow.

_____

_____

_____

Now, let's see what actually happens to Midas.

Midas

by Edith Hamilton

from *Mythology: Timeless Tales of Gods and Heroes*

... Of course Bacchus in granting the favor foresaw what would happen at the next meal, but Midas saw nothing until the food he lifted to his lips became a lump of metal. Dismayed and very hungry and thirsty, he was forced to hurry off to the god and implore him to take his favor back. Bacchus told him to go wash in the source of the river Pactolus and he would lose the fatal gift. He did so, and that was said to be the reason why gold was found in the sands of the river.

How did your predictions match up with the actual events of the myth? If you have read or been told this story before, you may have drawn from your prior knowledge to make your predictions. But even if you had never heard of the Midas myth before this reading, a few speculations about where such a golden touch would lead are not hard to imagine. It is worth noting that this version of the Midas myth is the classic rendering. Other versions may be more similar to the predictions you made. For example, many retellings of this myth have Midas touching various objects as he rejoices in his newfound ability. Once he tries to eat his food, he becomes worried. But his worry quickly turns to horror when his dear daughter approaches him and he turns her to gold, too.

Predicting, drawing conclusions, and making general inferences are important aspects of critical reading. The most effective way to become skilled in the use of these strategies is to practice them. In fact, practice is the most effective way to become skilled in any of the strategies discussed in this chapter and the other chapters. After the review of key terms on the pages that follow, you will find additional readings with which to get started on your mastery of the critical reading strategies covered in this chapter. These readings will require you to put all your strategies to work. But first, take the Strategy Quiz.

CHAPTER 7 STRATEGY QUIZ

This short story by Andrew Lam showcases, in a creative way, the art of prediction. Read the story carefully, annotating as you read. Then use the critical reading strategies discussed in this chapter to answer the questions that follow the reading.

The Palmist

by Andrew Lam

The palmist closed up early because of the pains. He felt as if he was being roasted, slowly, from the inside out. By noon he could no longer focus on his customers' palms, their life and love lines having all failed to point to any significant future, merging instead with the rivers and streams of his memories.

Outside, the weather had turned. Dark clouds hung low, and the wind was heavy with moisture. He reached the bus stop's tiny shelter when it began to pour. He didn't have to wait long, however. The good old 38 Geary pulled up in a few minutes, and he felt mildly consoled, though sharp pains flared and blossomed from deep inside his bowels like tiny geysers and made each of his three steps up the bus laborious.

It was warm and humid on the crowded bus, and a fine mist covered all windows. The palmist sat on the front bench facing the aisle, the one reserved for the handicapped and the elderly. A fat woman who had rosy cheeks and who did not take the seat gave him a dirty look. It was true: his hair was still mostly black, and he appeared to be a few years short of senior citizenship. The palmist pretended not to notice her. Contemptuously, he leaned back against the worn and cracked vinyl and smiled to himself. He closed his eyes. A faint odor of turned earth reached his nostrils. He inhaled deeply and saw again a golden rice field, a beatific smile, a face long gone: his first kiss.

The rain pounded the roof as the bus rumbled toward the sea.

At the next stop, a teenager got on. Caught in the downpour without an umbrella, he was soaking wet, and his extra-large T-shirt, which said play hard…. stay hard, clung to him. It occurred to the palmist that this was the face of someone who hadn't yet learned to be fearful of the weather. The teenager stood, towering above the palmist and blocking him from seeing the woman, who, from time to time, continued to glance disapprovingly at him.

So young, the palmist thought: the age of my youngest son, maybe, had he lived. The palmist tried to conjure up his son's face, but could not. It had been some years since the little boy drowned in the South China Sea, along with his two older sisters and their mother. The palmist had escaped on a different boat, a smaller one that had left a day after his family's boat, and, as a result, reached America alone.

Alone, thought the palmist and sighed. Alone.

It was then that his gaze fell upon the teenager's hand and he saw something. He leaned forward and did what he had never done before on the 38 Geary. He spoke up loudly, excitedly.

"You," he said in his heavy accent. "I see wonderful life!"

The teenager looked down at the old man and arched his eyebrows.

"I'm a palmist. Maybe you give me your hand?" the palmist said.

The teenager did nothing. No one had ever asked to see his hand on the bus. The fat woman snickered. Oh, she'd seen it all on the 38 Geary. She wasn't surprised. "This my last reading: no money, free, gift for you," the palmist pressed on. "Give me your hand."

"You know," the teenager said, scratching his chin. He was nervous. "I don't know." He felt as if he'd been caught inside a moving greenhouse and that, with the passengers looking on, he had somehow turned into one of its most conspicuous plants.

"What—what you don't know?" asked the palmist. "Maybe I know. Maybe I answer."

"Dude," the teenager said, "I don't know if I believe in all that hocus-pocus stuff." And, though he didn't say it, he didn't know whether he wanted to be touched by the old man with wrinkled, bony hands and nauseating tobacco breath. To stall, the teenager said, "I have a question, though. Can you read your own future? Can you, like, tell when you're gonna die and stuff?" Then he thought about it and said, "Nah, forget it. Sorry, that was stupid."

The bus driver braked abruptly at the next stop, and all the people standing struggled to stay on their feet. But those near the front of the bus were also struggling to listen to the conversation. "No, no, not stupid," said the palmist. "Good question. Long ago, I asked same thing, you know. I read same story in many hands of my people: story that said something bad will happen. Disaster. But in my hand here, I read only good thing. This line here, see, say I have happy family, happy future. No problem. So I think: me, my family, no problem. Now I know better: all hands affect each other, all lines run into each other, tell a big story. When the war ended in my country, you know, it was so bad for everybody. And my family? Gone, gone under the sea. You know, reading palm not like reading map." He touched his chest. "You feel and see here in heart also, in guts here also, not just here in your head. It is—how d'you say— atuition?"

"Intuition," the teenager corrected him, stifling a giggle.

"Yes," nodded the palmist. "Intuition."

The teenager liked the sound of the old man's voice. Its timbre reminded him of the voice of his long-dead grandfather, who also came from another country, one whose name had changed several times as a result of wars.

"My stop not far away now," the palmist continued. "This your last chance. Free. No charge."

"Go on, kiddo," the fat woman said, nudging the boy with her elbow and smiling. She wanted to hear his future. "I've been listening. It's all right. He's for real, I can tell now."

That was what the boy needed. "OK," he said, then opened his right fist like a flower and presented it to the palmist. The old man's face burned with seriousness as he leaned down and traced the various lines and contours and fleshy knolls on the teenager's palm. He bent the boy's wrist this way and that, kneaded and poked the fingers and knuckles as if to measure the strength of his resolve. In his own language, he made mysterious calculations and mumbled a few singsong words to himself.

Finally, the palmist looked up and, in a solemn voice, spoke. "You will become artist. When twenty-five, twenty-six, you're going to change very much. If you don't choose right, oh, so many regrets. But don't be afraid. Never be afraid. Move forward. Always. You have help. These squares here, right here, see, they're spirits and mentors, they come protect, guide you. When you reach mountain-top, people everywhere will hear you, know you, see you. Your art, what you see, others will see. Oh, so much love. You number one someday."

Inspired, the palmist went on like this for some time. Despite his pains, which flared up intermittently, the old man went on to speak of the ordinary palms and sad faces he had read, the misfortunes he had seen coming and the wondrous opportunities squandered as a result of fear and distrust. Divorces, marriages, and deaths in families—of these, he had read too many. Broken vows, betrayals, and adulteries—too pedestrian to remember. Twice, however, he held hands that committed unspeakable evil, and each time, he was sick for a week. And once, he held the hand of a reincarnated saint. How many palms had he read since his arrival in America?

"Oh, so many," he said, laughing, "too many. Thousands. Who care now? Not me."

When the palmist finished talking, the teenager retrieved his hand and looked at it. It seemed heavy and foreign. Most of what the palmist had said made no sense to him. Sure he loved reading a good book now and then—reading was like being inside a cartoon—but he loved cartoons even more. And even if he got good grades, he hated his stupid English classes, though it's true that he did write poetry—but only for himself. He also played the piano. A singer? Maybe a computer graphic artist? Maybe a movie star? He didn't know. Everything was still possible. Besides, turning twenty-five was so far away—almost a decade.

Before she got off the bus, the fat lady touched the teenager lightly on the shoulder. "Lots of luck, kiddo," she said and smiled a sad, wistful smile.

Nearing his stop, the palmist struggled to get up, wincing as he did. The teenager helped him and wanted to say some thing, but he did not. When the bus stopped, he flashed a smile instead and waved to the palmist, who, in turn, gave him a look that he would later interpret as that of impossible longing. Later he would also perceive the palmist as the first of many true seers in his life and realize that, in the cosmic sense of things, their encounter was inevitable. At that moment, however, all he saw was a small and sad-looking old man whose eyes seemed on the verge of tears as he quietly nodded before stepping off the bus and into the downpour.

The teenager lived near the end of the line, past the park. As usual, the bus was nearly empty on this stretch, and he moved to the bench the palmist had occupied. He could still feel the warmth of the vinyl and felt insulated by it somehow.

With nearly everyone gone, he grew bored. He turned to the befogged window behind him and drew a sailor standing on a sloop and holding a bottle. The ocean was full of dangerous waves. The boat, it seemed, was headed toward a girl who had large round breasts and danced in a hula skirt on a distant shore. He drew a few tall mountains and swaying palm trees behind her. He hesitated before mischievously giving her two, three more heads and eight or nine more arms than she needed to entice the drunken sailor to her island. And then he pulled back to look at what he had done: the scene made him chuckle to himself.

Through his drawing, the teenager saw a rushing world of men, women, and children under black, green, red, blue, polka-dotted umbrellas and plastic ponchos. He watched until the people and storefront windows streaked into green: pine trees, fern groves, placid lakes, and well-tended grass meadows. The park ... beyond which was the sea.

The rain tapered off, and a few columns of sunlight pierced the gray clouds, setting the road aglow like a golden river. The boy couldn't wait to get off the bus and run or do something—soar above the clouds if he could. In the sky, jumbo jets and satellites gleamed. People were talking across borders, time zones, oceans, continents. People were flying to marvelous countries, to mysterious destinies.

With repeated circular movements of his hand, he wiped away sailor, boat, waves, and girl. Where the palmist's thumbnail had dug into the middle of his palm and made a crescent moon, he could still feel a tingling sensation. "A poet... not!" he said to himself and giggled. Then he shook his head and looked at his cool, wet palm before wiping it clean on his faded Levi's.

Questions for "The Palmist"

1. What is another name for a "palmist"? _____

_____

2. What can you infer about the palmist's original country? _____

_____

3. What is it that seems to especially draw the palmist to the teenager? ____

_____

_____

4. ____ The palmist tells the teenager, "I read same story in many hands of my people: story that said something bad will happen. Disaster. But in my hand here, I read only good thing." The palmist says more about this. How does his response answer the teenager's question about the palmist reading his own future?

   a) It does not answer the question because the palmist is rambling.

   b) The palmist means that you have to read palms in the context of other people and your intuition to understand even your own future.

    c) The palmist means that you cannot read your own future, even with intuition, since he read his own future so badly.

    d) The response does not really answer the question because the palmist speaks in riddles.

5. What encourages the teenager to let the palmist read his palm? _____

_____

_____

6. What does the palmist see in the teenager's future? _____

_____

_____

7. ____ Which of the following statements is a detail that implies how intensely the palmist connects to people when he reads their palms?

    a) Finally, the palmist looked up and, in a solemn voice, spoke.

    b) It was then that his gaze fell upon the teenager's hand and he saw something.

    c) Twice, however, he held hands that committed unspeakable evil, and each time, he was sick for a week.

    d) Inspired, the palmist went on like this for some time.

8. ____ The teenager affects both the palmist and the fat lady. Which of these emotions is *not* implied by their reactions to the teenager?

    a) jealousy

    b) hope

    c) longing

    d) wistfulness

9. Identify and discuss something that the teenager does, sees, or says that suggests his potential as an artist. _____

_____

_____

_____

10. ____ Which of the following can you conclude about the teenager based on the information provided in the story?

    a) He thinks the palmist is a foolish old man.

    b) He doesn't believe anything the palmist says since he doesn't understand it.

    c) He believes what the palmist says but is too afraid of the future to say so.

    d) He believes what the palmist says but cannot yet imagine it happening.

KEY TERM REVIEW

Using the chapter as your reference, match the key term with its definition.

Key Term	Definition
1. Pattern of development ____	**a)** the place where and time when a story's action occurs
2. Relationships ____	**b)** a concern that a story deals with in many ways and is often bigger in scope than the main idea
3. Transitional phrases and signal words ____	**c)** a scene that returns to an previous time and reveals events and motivations that are relevant to the present circumstances of the character(s)
4. Narrative conventions ____	**d)** an idea that continually surfaces, sometimes subtly, in a text
5. Conflict ____	**e)** a type of inference that seeks to anticipate what will happen in the future
6. Resolution ____	**f)** an idea developed by stating the unknown based on information that is known
7. Plot ____	**g)** word(s) that move(s) the reader from one idea to the next and signal the relationship of one idea to another
8. Point of view ____	**h)** a type of inference that is made after an identifiable set of clues is presented that make a point seem likely
9. Setting ____	**i)** when a conflict is no longer at play, or it has been dealt with by the character(s)
10. Scenes ____	**j)** descriptions and phrases that the author repeats over time to highlight visual clues about a theme or point
11. Pivotal scene ____	**k)** a series of scenes that build to a high point
12. Flashback ____	**l)** techniques used by writers to communicate ideas in fiction and nonfiction
13. Theme ____	**m)** an action or event which mirrors or repeats a previous action or event
14. Recurring idea ____	**n)** the scene that changes the course of events significantly
15. Recurring image ____	**o)** a tension that exists between a character and some other force
16. Inference ____	**p)** the units of action and reaction that occur within a narrative
17. Conclusion ____	**q)** a systematic way of developing ideas to make a point
18. Prediction ____	**r)** the series of events that make up a story
19. Climax ____	**s)** the vantage point from which a story is told
20. Recurring action/event ____	**t)** how one idea connects to another

STRATEGIES IN ACTION

Seeing the World Whole

by Natasha Singh

Natasha Singh (1973–) was born in Jasper, Alberta, Canada. She received her MFA from Sarah Lawrence College and has since taught creative writing at Rutgers University and the Collegiate School. She currently teaches South Asian literature and creative writing at the Branson School in Ross, California.

Singh has received several writing grants including the Canada Council Grant for fiction. Recent essays and/or excerpts of her work have appeared in ThreePenny Review, Crab Orchard Review, Glimmer Train, South Asian Review, *and the* New York Times. *She is currently completing a memoir.*

In "Seeing the World Whole," Singh examines how a father and daughter see each other as fragments. Blindness, she suggests, can happen to any of us.

> Based on the author's bio and the title, what do you think this reading will be about?

---

1   Before my father lost his eye, he saw the world whole. His dreams lived along the lines of railway tracks; they were dressed in silver and traversed the arched back of Rajasthan to Tamil Nadu. Before my father lost his eye, he dreamed of being a train conductor, and then he glanced upward and his dreams became silver birds that flew up and disappeared through clouds, leaving gaping holes like open mouths in the sky. "Or a pilot," he once confided in me. "I wanted to see the world." But his world, then, was a perfect circle comprised of left and right. If he glanced straight ahead, I bet he saw both his shoulders—the open windows on either side. But after he lost his eye, my father had to turn around to see openings, to find doors. He had to shift himself, his face, the tilt of his head to see the whole. If the world was a movie that you and I can see, my father only saw half of it.

2   His other eye was made of glass. It was a smooth colored marble that I saw him take out from time to time. The first time he did this, I must have been about six. While at a stop sign, he turned his head and

cupped his palm over his eye; and then I saw a glimpse of it—a flash of white and brown—as he rolled it around in his handkerchief. When a car behind him honked, he jumped, and for a brief second I saw a bright pink pocket where his eye should have been. An empty hole. I don't remember asking him about what I'd seen; I only remember his eyelashes sticking to his glass eyeball like skinny black bars—his drooping eyelid that reminded me of a camel's eye.

3   In my little girl world, my father never slept. When he asked me to tell him stories, I would perch on the edge of his bed and narrate worlds comprised of roaming elk, bear, and elephants—a mishmash of animals plucked from Jasper and India. I threw in Gods and Goddesses and made them dance for him. I spun worlds made from silver thread and gold needles. I talked and talked and never stopped, thinking that he was listening. His snores never clued me in. When I grew tired of telling, I would look at him in exasperation, only to see his eye staring back at me. That searchlight which never turned off.

4   My father sees the world in parts. He sees himself as half a man. He has lived, he says, half a life. After he lost his eye, he returned to boarding school where boys filled his water glass with urine—where he was tripped, pushed, and locked inside closets—where having one eye was the same as having one leg, one arm. No mouth. Then he will purse his lips and say, "I do not want to talk of these things anymore. I do not want to remember." So, I pick up the pieces and construct the jigsaw puzzle that is his life. I know that he ran away from boarding school, ran miles, and never returned. I know that he refused to marry lest he contaminate a woman's life. But when he was forty, my grandmother forced him. Had she not, perhaps my father would still be living in a large empty home in India. And I, of course, would never have been born. I don't know much else: I know little of my father's life as a boy. I know little of his time as a young man. The only story he repeats for me time and time again is the story of how he lost his eye.

5   Every time my father tells me, he weeps as if it is the first telling. When he finishes, he always cautions me, "Never tell your sister or brother," but I half suspect that he tells them the same thing. He says he fell asleep one afternoon beneath a neem tree, and when he awoke he looked upward. A sliver of sky fell into his eye. Baffled, he rubbed, but he couldn't get the clouds out. He was chloroformed and operated on, and as he recovered, numerous fingers poked and prodded around his eye, which then became infected. He tells me that the poking and prodding was what did it, for not too soon after, he felt his eyeball slide down the inside of his face. I do not know whether that is even possible, but he remembers it that way. When he first told me this, I imagined

a giant tear making its way down behind the skin—the face—so that only my father could feel it, know its vanishing. He screamed, and when they tried to put it back in, he fought against being chloroformed again. His legs and arms shot out of their own accord, and that's when his eye fell out. He saw it, he tells me. He saw it roll down his chest and away from him, across the floor. And dragging behind it, I imagine, he saw the other half of his life.

6   Whenever I see my father, I want to uncover the world he must have seen for himself as a young boy. Not the immediate world of his village made of narrow paths of cobblestone and dust; not the world of rickshaw drivers, chai wallahs, samosa wallahs—all the wallahs selling their wares—but the world he imagined he would live into some day. A future where he saw his face as beautiful, majestic, and whole. A world where he married young, where women flocked to him like he was a Bollywood film hero, where his family treated him as the eldest son and not the cripple. It was a world where dreams were not dreams but actual windows you could climb through. Where barriers were made of glass and not skinny black bars.

7   My father is eighty-two now, and, still, he rarely leaves the house. He has always sought refuge away from people; his solace has lain in newspapers, magazines, and the blue hypnotic eye of the television screen. From a stationary position, safe inside his home, behind closed doors and closed windows, he has read intensely of other worlds. He has watched dynamic lives unfold in Hindi serials. He has looked around at his wife and children and reduced us to half when, really, we were always whole. His hair is shockingly white, and if we walk down the street hand in hand, people turn to stare. He is really that frail, that beautiful. Once, when I held his head between my palms, I thought it was as light as eggshells. He is kinder now, gentler. Old age has removed rough edges and softened places once hard as stone. He cries more often; in fact, he cries frequently. My father makes up for lost time by weeping into his hands and into my ears.

8   In my family, we do not speak of his eye. My mother has always told us not to. It is only recently that I asked to see it. My father and I were sitting on the sofa in the living room. The sun was coming in, and it was just the two of us. He had finished telling me the story of his eye again, and I pointed in its direction. "May I?" And my father, as if he'd been waiting to be asked this question his whole life, nodded, and with a familiar and ancient gesture, he cupped his palm over his eye and removed that marble. Without a word, he handed it to me and I held it in my palm. It was warm and wet, and I longed to trace that empty place in my father's face. I longed to bury my heart there or plant a kiss

in that sea of baby pink. Instead, I cradled that glass marble and closed my eyes. It was his other half I was holding there: the father I had never met, the man he never became, the boy who'd stayed in school. The human being who'd never hid. It was a long time before either of us spoke. And finally he said it: small words. Quiet words. And maybe, just maybe, I am making them up because I want to believe them. "You can see me now, beti," he said. "You can see." And for that second that stretched into forever, I really believed I could.

***

Vocabulary in Context

Use the vocabulary strategies covered in Chapter 3 to decipher the meaning of the following words. Use the vocabulary strategies as much as possible before you refer to a dictionary.

1. His dreams lived along the lines of railway tracks; they were dressed in silver and *traversed* the arched back of Rajasthan to Tamil Nadu. (par. 1)

   _____

2. But his world, then, was a perfect circle *comprised* of left and right. (par. 1)

   _____

3. When he asked me to tell him stories, I would perch on the edge of his bed and narrate worlds comprised of roaming elk, bear, and elephants—a *mishmash* of animals plucked from Jasper and India. (par. 3)

   _____

4. I know that he refused to marry lest he *contaminate* a woman's life. (par. 4)

   _____

5. His legs and arms shot out of their own *accord*, and that's when his eye fell out. (par. 5)

   _____

6. Not the immediate world of his village made of narrow paths of cobblestone and dust; not the world of rickshaw drivers, chai wallahs, samosa wallahs—all the *wallahs* selling their wares—but the world he imagined he would live into some day. (par. 6)

   _____

7. A world where he married young, where women *flocked* to him like he was a Bollywood film hero, where his family treated him as the eldest son and not the cripple. (par. 6)

   _____

8. He has always sought *refuge* away from people; his solace has lain in news-papers, magazines, and the blue hypnotic eye of the television screen. (par. 7)

   _____

9. From a *stationary* position, safe inside his home, behind closed doors and closed windows, he has read intensely of other worlds. (par. 7)

   _____

10. And maybe, just maybe, I am making them up because I want to believe them. "You can see me now, *beti*," he said. "You can see." (par. 8)

    _____

Checking In

1. How accurate was your pre-reading prediction of the focus of this selection?
2. Would this selection be considered fiction or nonfiction? How do you know?

Getting the Point

3. What do you think the author wants the reader to understand after reading this selection? What details support that idea?

4. What is the setting of this selection? Does it change during the story?

5. From whose point of view is the story told? Does the point of view shift?

6. Identify two pivotal scenes and explain their importance to the story.

7. What do you think a major conflict in this story is? How is it resolved?

Delving Deeper

8. How would you describe the author's relationship with her father? Does it change during the course of the essay? Explain your response.

9. How did others' treatment affect the father in his young life? Use details from the selection to support your response.

10. Identify a recurring image in this selection.

11. Identify a recurring feeling or emotion in this selection.

12. Consider the main idea and the recurring images and emotions you've written about. Based on these elements, what theme do you feel is present? Explain how you see this theme in the selection.

The Writing Connection

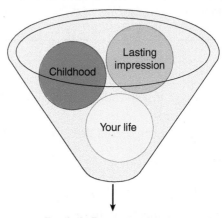

Reader's Response Journal

Based on your own experience, write about some event or person from your childhood that had a lasting impact on how you think of yourself. Talk specifically about how the incident or person affected your life.

STRATEGIES IN ACTION

Edison and the Electric Industry

by Gary Cross and Rick Szostak

from *Technology and American Society: A History*

Technology and American Society *offers a global perspective on the development of American technology. This textbook is structured around a historical narrative detailing major technological transformations over the last three centuries. With coverage devoted to both dramatic breakthroughs and incremental innovations,* Technology and American Society *analyzes the cause-and-effect relationship of change and its role in the constant drive toward improvement and modernization. This selection about Thomas Edison is from the chapter on the second industrial revolution, which began in the mid-1800s.*

What do you already know about Thomas Edison? Jot down your ideas and read on to see if those ideas are accurate.

1   Thomas Alva Edison (1847–1931) was a legend in his own time, for he epitomized the characteristics that nineteenth-century Americans admired about themselves. Despite his lack of formal education or family wealth, his pluck and luck brought him fame and fortune. He was admired as a traditional individualist, whose hard work and practicality produced striking success. He lacked a systematic background in science, and was incapable of adjusting personally to the corporate hierarchy. But Edison was also modern, in tune with the most advanced technology of his time, skilled in addressing the demands of the market, and able to organize a team of specialists to help him innovate. Edison helped fund the journal *Science* in its early days, and sought (often in vain) the respect of scientists, but he emphasized that he cared about whether things worked, not why. In these ways, Edison could be called a transitional figure, with one foot in the era of the prescientific "tinkerer" and another in the age of the corporate inventor.

2   Edison was close to the cutting edge of technology in his time. In his late teens he began working as an itinerant telegraph operator and, like others, he devoted much thought to improving the telegraph. Edison reached maturity just as electricity was on the threshold of revolutionizing the way power was generated and utilized. His first patent, in 1868 (when he was twenty-one), was for a system to electronically tabulate votes in the legislature. When members of Congress proved uninterested, he vowed never again to waste his time on a technical development without first ascertaining that there was a market for it. The following year he moved to New York, perhaps with the expectation that he would best be able to find both financial backing and potential markets there. His first profitable innovation was an improved stock ticker, for which he received the then-astonishing sum of $40,000. He was amazed at this offer, and became even more committed to a career as an inventor. These funds provided the basis for his inventing enterprise.

3   Edison quickly recognized that modern inventing required the skills of specialists. Among those on his staff who originally were hired to produce stock tickers were at least three who would achieve fame in their own right: John Kreusi, who would work with Edison at Menlo Park, and later be chief engineer at General Electric; Sigmund

Bergmann, who would establish a large electrical manufacturing concern in Germany; and Johann Schukert, who founded another German manufacturing firm that became Siemens-Schukert.

4   Edison was not well-fitted to the corporate hierarchy himself, and was uncomfortable in the day-to-day business of managing a modern organization. Instead he devoted himself to a series of research labs, which he called invention factories, to develop a wide range of marketable products. After a couple of years of operating a small laboratory in Newark, New Jersey, Edison established the much larger Menlo Park laboratory in 1876. Still, his staff never numbered many more than fifty. Edison always referred to these people as "friends and coworkers." He drove them hard (or, as one worker described it, made the work so interesting they chose to work long hours), but also sang songs and smoked cigars with them during late-evening breaks. In so doing, he showed that innovation could be managed—his lab was not the first in the United States, but was for many decades the largest and most successful.

5   In the early 1870s, Edison patented a number of improvements to the telegraph that allowed two messages to be sent in each of two directions over the same wire at the same time, rather than only one in one direction as previously. After quadrupling the productivity of telegraph cables, Edison, at the suggestion of Western Union—which provided much financing of Edison's research—turned his attention to the telephone, and developed a much more sensitive carbon-based transmitter and receiver (initially in an attempt to get around the Bell patent). He developed the first phonograph in 1877. Edison had had earlier thoughts about the telephone, but had doubted its commercial value; likewise, Bell had conceived of the phonograph, but doubted that there was a market for it.

6   Rather than developing the phonograph's market potential, Edison shifted immediately to inventing electric lighting. This project illustrates Edison's talent as an organizer. Although he often spoke critically of pure scientists, he soon added a chemist and physicist to the staff, along with an array of machinists and various specialists in electricity and metals. At Menlo Park, precise measuring devices were mounted on vibrationless tables anchored to the earth. Edison was justifiably proud of the $40,000 worth of equipment in his lab, as well as his vast library of scientific and technical material. He noted that his researchers were guided by scientific insights such as Ohm's Law and Joule's Law. Still, he was much less open to the pursuit of basic scientific research than would be the case in later industrial research labs.

7   Edison and his laboratory staff began to focus their energy on the problem of electric lighting in 1878, despite the fact that Edison had little experience with either lighting or electric power generation. The

popularity of urban gas lighting (both indoor and outdoor) convinced him of the commercial potential. Arc lamps, in which a bright light was created by electric current bridging a gap between pieces of charcoal, were employed for external lighting in some cities, but they were inappropriate for the home market. Edison studied the potential market for lighting lower Manhattan, and estimated the price at which this could be profitable. This was a truly modern approach to invention, for Edison was concerned not merely with producing a practical electric illumination, but he also recognized that he had to develop a method of low-cost electricity generation and transmission.

8   The first trick was, naturally, the light itself. Early in the century, it had been shown that various materials gave off light—became incandescent—when an electric current was passed through them. Most, however, quickly burned up. Edison experimented with a number of filament materials, including platinum. We do not know exactly how the process of choosing materials for experiment was guided. Chemistry doubtless played some role, even though Edison captured the public imagination with stories that he tested thousands of types of vegetation. In the end, carbon (which was used in other Edison creations, such as the telephone transmitter) proved to have the resistance necessary for a commercially feasible electric lamp. It would not only last many hours but would require little electric current. Edison was only successful, though, by creating a better vacuum within the lightbulb, so that the carbon did not oxidize.

9   The filament in turn determined the nature of other components of the system. The generator, in particular, had to be capable of producing a small current of high voltage. Edison recognized that generators designed for arc lights were inappropriate to his purpose. His team soon produced a generator that more than doubled the output of its predecessors. Between the generator and the light, Edison's lab had to develop new junction boxes, switches, and especially meters. Fuses were invented to prevent overload and reduce the risk of fire (which naturally made potential consumers of this new product anxious). In those days before plastic, insulating miles of wiring also presented difficulties; cardboard was used before low-cost natural rubber became available.

10   Menlo Park was shut down after five years and hundreds of patents. In 1881, Edison shifted his efforts to the operation of his electric lighting system in New York. In 1886, Edison returned to his first love and opened the even larger West Orange Laboratory. He foresaw its main goal as the development of new electric apparatuses for both home and workplace, and wanted to be able to combine innovation and manufacturing on the same site.

11 Because the new venture was much larger than the one in Menlo Park, Edison found himself increasingly playing the role of manager and businessman. He could no longer play an active, guiding role in the many research projects his lab undertook. He struggled with the question of how much freedom to give his staff. At one time, more than seventy different research projects were underway. This was likely too many. West Orange was still responsible for numerous improvements to electrical systems, the creation of a mass-market phonograph, the storage battery, and the movie camera. These innovations kept Edison in the public eye through World War I.

12 Still, none of Edison's later inventions had the success of his earlier triumphs. In part this was because Edison did not recognize the potential market for the phonograph and movie camera, as he had the lightbulb. Whereas the lightbulb replaced gas lighting, the phonograph and movie camera were novelties. Edison geared the phonograph toward a business market for dictation, and thought that people would want to watch movies individually rather than on a large screen. He remained a folk hero until his death in 1931, and was a close friend of such modem industrialists as Henry Ford and Harvey Firestone. Ironically, the large integrated corporations that these men represented had ushered in a new era of industrial research with little place for a facility such as Edison's.

13 Edison General Electric and Thomas Houston merged to form General Electric in 1892. The new GE company would take a very different approach to research than did Edison. Its research lab, set up in 1901, was much more focused than was Edison's, concentrating on developing and protecting its strong position in the lightbulb market. GE developed an improved carbon filament in 1905. Filaments based on the newly isolated tungsten further doubled energy efficiency in 1912; and when in 1913 GE wound tungsten filaments into tight coils and filled the bulbs with argon and nitrogen, efficiency improved another 50 percent. These improvements (along with cheaper electricity) reduced the cost of lighting by three-quarters between 1910–1930, and lightbulb use multiplied sixteen times.

14 General Electric's lab did slowly branch out from research focused on the lightbulb. It was responsible for major advances in AC electricity transmission. It developed X rays. It produced . . . many of the components essential to radio. Success with X rays and radio encouraged an even broader approach to research after World War I. This was accomplished, however, in a quite different environment from Edison's labs. Research was pursued in line with the productive capabilities of the firm. Goals were quite clearly set from above. Edison's hostility to basic scientific research was replaced by a willingness to embrace such basic research, if it would aid the commercial activities of the firm in the long run. Laboratory reports,

which Edison had shunned, were expected. Although Edison had paved the way for the modern industrial research lab, it would take a form that he would scarcely recognize. It did, though, continue Edison's practice of bringing together researchers with differing areas of expertise.

***

Vocabulary in Context

Use the vocabulary strategies covered in Chapter 3 to decipher the meaning of the following words. Use the vocabulary strategies as much as possible before you refer to a dictionary.

1. Thomas Alva Edison (1847–1931) was a legend in his own time, for he *epitomized* the characteristics that nineteenth-century Americans admired about themselves. (par. 1)

2. Despite his lack of formal education or family wealth, his *pluck* and luck brought him fame and fortune. (par. 1)

3. He lacked a systematic background in science, and was incapable of adjusting personally to the corporate *hierarchy*. (par. 1)

4. In these ways, Edison could be called a *transitional* figure, with one foot in the era of the prescientific "tinkerer" and another in the age of the corporate inventor. (par. 1)

5. In his late teens he began working as an *itinerant* telegraph operator and, like others, he devoted much thought to improving the telegraph. (par. 2)

6. Edison reached maturity just as electricity was on the *threshold* of revolutionizing the way power was generated and utilized. (par. 2)

7. His first patent, in 1868 (when he was twenty-one), was for a system to electronically *tabulate* votes in the legislature. (par. 2)

8. When members of Congress proved uninterested, he vowed never again to waste his time on a technical development without first *ascertaining* that there was a market for it. (par. 2)

9. After *quadrupling* the productivity of telegraph cables, Edison, at the suggestion of Western Union—which provided much financing of Edison's research—turned his attention to the telephone....(par. 5)

_____

10. Early in the century, it had been shown that various materials gave off light—became *incandescent*—when an electric current was passed through them. (par. 8)

_____

11. In the end, carbon (which was used in other Edison creations, such as the telephone transmitter) proved to have the resistance necessary for a commercially *feasible* electric lamp. (par. 8)

_____

12. His team soon produced a generator that more than doubled the output of its *predecessors.* (par. 9)

_____

13. He foresaw its main goal as the development of new electric *apparatuses* for both home and workplace, and wanted to be able to combine innovation and manufacturing on the same site. (par. 10)

_____

14. Whereas the lightbulb replaced gas lighting, the phonograph and movie camera were *novelties.* (par. 12)

_____

15. Edison's hostility to basic scientific research was replaced by a willingness to embrace such basic research, if it would aid the commercial activities of the firm in the long run. Laboratory reports, which Edison had *shunned,* were expected. (par. 14)

_____

Checking In

1. Knowing that this selection is from a textbook, did you prepare to read it differently than how you would prepare to read fiction or nonfiction? Explain your reasoning.

2. Consider the textbook from which this reading about Edison was selected. What did you expect the focus of this reading to be, given that context?

Getting the Point

3. According to this selection, what was a major motivation for Edison as an inventor? Be specific and refer to the reading.

4. Why did Edison feel separate from the scientific community? Be specific and refer to the reading.

5. What is the primary pattern of development in this reading? What supporting details back up your response?

6. What is the central point of this selection?

Delving Deeper

7. According to this selection, Edison invented two products whose potential he underestimated. What were the two products, and how did he underestimate their potential?

For support in meeting this chapter's objectives, go to MyReadingLab and select **Critical Thinking**

8 Critical Thinking Strategies

Learning Objectives

In this chapter you will:

- Identify an author's purpose.
- Determine an author's tone.
- Identify the audience of a text.
- Evaluate texts for elements of reliability.
- Evaluate texts for elements of point of view.

Though this be madness, yet there is method in't.

—William Shakespeare

The layers of meaning that seem to continually spring forth from a writer's pen have occasionally evoked despair and fatigue in the struggling reader. Yet, as an observer of sorrowful Prince Hamlet once noted, "There is method in't." The aim of this textbook is to assist you in recognizing the method behind the written word. This chapter will continue in that charge by going even more deeply into the "madness" of the author's world and revealing his/her strategies. To begin this process, you will need to utilize not only critical reading strategies, but critical thinking strategies as well. These critical thinking strategies are advanced techniques that will help you dig into a text and reap all that the author has planted.

Here's what will be covered in Chapter 8:

The Author's Strategies

- Identifying purpose
  - Pattern of development
  - Publishing medium
  - Writing style and focus
- Identifying audience
- Identifying tone
  - Denotation
  - Connotation

Evaluating Arguments

- Reliability
  - Author's credibility
  - Balance of facts and opinions
  - Timeliness of information
- Point of View
  - Objectivity–subjectivity range
    - Bias
  - Language choices
  - Assumptions

THE AUTHOR'S STRATEGIES

When you receive an assignment or a project from your professor and begin to work on it, the first thing you probably do is strategize. You consider what is expected of you, what you want to accomplish (maybe what grade you want), and how you will accomplish it. Authors do the same thing. And like you, after strategizing about a task or assignment, they use the methods that will best accomplish the overall goal. While you may not have given names to what you focus on when you figure out how to complete an assignment, there are terms for this focusing when an author strategizes. Generally, an author considers purpose, audience, and tone when he/she is developing a writing project. Necessarily, then, it is the job of a critical reader and thinker to consider those elements when reading an author's work.

Identifying Purpose

An author's **purpose** in writing is his/her reason for communicating and what he/she hopes to accomplish with that communication. To find an author's purpose, consider these elements:

- Pattern of development
- Publishing medium
- Writing style and focus

If you have been practicing critical reading strategies, you will likely have already gathered important clues about the author's purpose. Do you remember the patterns of development discussed in Chapter 7? Those same patterns will indicate the author's purpose. Consider, for example, an author who experienced a harrowing escape from kidnappers when she was thirteen and has now written a memoir about that episode in her life. Why do you think she wrote the memoir? A few likely guesses are: to share her experience, to warn others, or to entertain readers with the adventurousness of her story. Without further information, we can't say for sure, but we do know that she is *narrating* her story, and that offers the first clue into her purpose. Often narrative nonfiction, like a memoir, sheds light on a unique experience—or, in other words, informs readers.

Considering the pattern of development that is primarily used in a text will put you one step ahead, but it will not take you all the way. For one thing, there may be more than one pattern used in a text—whether the text is a paragraph, a chapter, an entire book, or a work of any other length. This leads to the next indicator: the medium of the reading material. You'll want to note the **publishing medium** (the type of publication through which the author has shared or published his/her work). Is it in a newspaper, a newsmagazine, a collection of essays, a textbook, or a posting on a personal blog? The publishing medium will offer more information about the author's purpose, as certain mediums have a purpose that is implicit, or already present. Take, for instance, a piece in your local newspaper: you know it is meant to inform the reader. Table 8.1 duplicates the table from Chapter 1 that describes certain types of reading material and their common purposes. In Chapter 1 this table was presented as a way to help you understand the context of the reading material; it is still being used for context, but now we are focusing on the publishing medium especially.

If we go back to the memoir about the young girl who escaped kidnappers and consider her purpose again, we can see that this table indicates that memoirs are often written to share information or to entertain.

Table 8.1

Reading Material	Writing Style	Purpose
textbook	academic	instruction
short story	literary	entertainment
newspaper	expository	information
novel	literary	entertainment
scholarly journal	academic/scholarly	information/instruction
magazine	expository	entertainment/information
memoir	expository/literary	information/entertainment
blog	expository/personal	information/entertainment
online news report	expository	information
personal web page	expository/personal	entertainment/information

This supports the purpose we'd suggested earlier after determining that the memoir was a narrative.

The writing style and focus of a text are also primary indicators of purpose. The writing style of a text may be shaped by the publishing medium. If you refer to Table 8.1 again, you will see that the writing style is given for various types of reading material you might encounter. Additionally, what the author chooses to focus upon in a text is also indicative of purpose. Using the memoir of the botched kidnapping again, if the author focuses on the ways in which school officials did not protect her, then you might infer that she is exposing the weaknesses of a system that is supposed to keep kids safe. Table 8.2 identifies the five primary purposes for writing and the focus each one generally maintains.

Table 8.2   Writing to …

Persuade/Convince	Advocates the author's position or ideas Attempts to alter or influence the reader's view or course of action Evaluates or judges
Describe	Describes using the five senses Uses metaphors, similes, analogies, and other figurative language Paints a verbal picture
Inform/Expose	Explains and discusses ideas Presents information objectively Gives examples Gives definitions or characteristics Analyzes or questions ideas
Narrate	Tells a story Uses chronological order Details the basic facts of an incident or event
Entertain	Uses humor Amuses Covers light or noncontroversial subjects

Identifying Audience

Now that you've gathered information to determine the author's purpose, there's another question to ask: who is the intended audience? The intended **audience** is the group of people who will most likely be interested in and read the material. Your responsibility is to identify who that audience is. To do this, you will need to keep in mind all the elements that you noted when you determined the purpose. Then you will take it one step further and consider who would be a likely audience given all those elements. Here are a few examples of the types of audiences a writer may gear his/her writing toward:

- a general audience (a nationwide newspaper or magazine);
- a specific individual (a letter to a newspaper editor);
- a specific audience (from a particular historical era or cultural background);
- a sympathetic audience (a group the author identifies with);
- a skeptical or unsupportive audience (a group the author wants to persuade);
- a targeted audience (an advertisement during prime-time television).

Sometimes identifying the audience can be quite easy. For example, if you pick up a magazine with images of teen idols on the cover, you can assume the articles will be geared toward teens.

Determining the intended audience is often done in conjunction with determining the author's purpose.

Identifying Tone

The final element of an author's strategies that we will focus on is **tone.** The tone can be defined as the author's attitude and mood toward the subject, and the stance taken toward the audience. One way to consider tone is to think of the emotional quality of a speaker's words and voice. So much is conveyed by a person's voice—a shout versus a whisper, a snicker versus a chuckle—and in the selection of one word over another. Consequently, both elements, the spoken words and the way the words are spoken, impact the ultimate meaning you hear. In the same way, authors use the written word, and the attitude or mood implicit in those words, to express tone to readers. A writer's tone may fall anywhere in the range of human emotions. For example, the tone of a reading can be vindictive, cautious, carefree, resigned, straightforward, furious, excited, or admiring.

To determine the author's tone, examine the author's purpose, audience, and language. When examining the author's language, pay particular attention to words' denotations and connotations. The **denotation** is the literal, dictionary definition of a word. The **connotation** includes the denotation and adds the emotional weight of a word. Consider, for example, this statement: Laura has a *large* wardrobe. As a reader, you understand that Laura has a lot of clothes. Now think about this sentence: Laura has a *ridiculous* wardrobe. In this second description of Laura's wardrobe, there is a sense of disapproval or disdain conveyed by the word *ridiculous*. That is the power of word choice and the emotional weight that connotation carries. Thus, when identifying tone, observe both what the author says and how the author says it.

The following two selections will offer you an opportunity to practice identifying an author's strategies. Read each selection and answer the questions that follow.

Exercise 8.1

Lethal Dose: Agents Poison Wildlife on Public Lands

from *Nature's Voice "for NRDC's 1.3 Million Members and Online Activists"*
Natural Resources Defense Council: The Earth's Best Defense

It can take minutes or even hours, but no matter how quickly it comes, the death is never painless. The body is seized with violent convulsions; the eyes roll back in the head. And amid all the thrashing, there's the constant, desperate gasping for breath. This is death by the lethal toxin Compound 1080—one of two poisons that kill some 13,000 animals every year on our public lands, including ecologically important predators like coyotes, wolves, bears, bobcats and foxes. And believe it or not, American taxpayers are footing a big part of the bill.

Wildlife Services, a division of the Department of Agriculture, spends $100 million annually to kill millions of wild animals. As part of that program, toxic poisons are strewn across public wild lands by government agents. They deploy two of the world's most lethal toxins, Compound 1080 and sodium cyanide, intending to kill would-be predators that might threaten livestock. NRDC is fighting to put an end to this deadly misuse of our tax dollars.

"The government shouldn't be doing the dirty work of agri-business, especially on our own public lands," said Louisa Willcox, NRDC senior wildlife advocate. "These poisons are indiscriminate. They'll kill any animal that comes in contact with them." That includes hundreds of non-target animals, as well as people's pets. In Oregon, Amanda Wood Kingsley was exposed to sodium cyanide after her dog Ruby stumbled upon a government-set trap. It took a full 15 minutes for Ruby to die as Amanda desperately tried to save her life. Ruby had tripped an M-44, a spring-loaded device that shoots a pellet of sodium cyanide directly into the animal's mouth. The EPA has rated both sodium cyanide and Compound 1080 in Toxicity Category I, the highest degree of acute toxicity. Compound 1080 is so lethal that a single teaspoonful can kill 100 people. Many other countries have banned its use.

"We're paying to poison our own public lands, even though there are effective alternatives for controlling predators that are far less harmful," said Willcox. "Our public forests and lands exist for our enjoyment and the preservation of nature. They should be safe places for wildlife, our pets and our families." Tens of thousands of NRDC (Natural Resource Defense Council) Members and online activists have taken action and petitioned Secretary of Agriculture Tom Vilsack to stop this needless killing.

Answer the following questions using the strategies to identify purpose, audience, and tone.

1. What do you think is the purpose of this article? Discuss the elements of the article that influence your response. _____

   _____

   _____

2. Who is the intended audience? How do you know? _____

   _____

   _____

3. Describe the author's tone. Indicate which words or phrases help reveal the tone. _____

   _____

   _____

Exercise 8.2

Reading Textbooks: Textbooks Are Not Meatloaf

by Saundra K. Ciccarelli and J. Noland White

from *Psychology: An Exploration*

There are two common mistakes that people make in regard to reading a textbook. The first mistake is simple: Many people don't bother to read the textbook before going to the lecture that will cover that material. Trying to get anything out of a lecture without reading the material first is like trying to find a new, unfamiliar place without using a map or any kind of directions. It's easy to get lost. This is especially true because of the assumption that most instructors make when planning their lectures: They assume that the students have already read the assignment. The instructors then use the lecture to go into detail on the information the students supposedly got from the reading. If the students haven't done the reading, the instructor's lecture isn't going to make a whole lot of sense.

The second mistake that most people make when reading textbook material is to try to read it the same way they would read a novel: They start at the first page and read continuously. With a novel it's easy to do this because the plot is usually interesting and people want to know what happens next, so they keep reading. It isn't necessary to remember every little detail—all they need to remember are the main plot points. One could say that a novel is like meatloaf—some meaty parts with lots of filler. Meatloaf can be eaten quickly, without even chewing for very long.

With a textbook, the material may be interesting but not in the same way that a novel is interesting. A textbook is a big, thick steak—all meat, no filler. Just as a steak has to be chewed to be enjoyed and to be useful to the body, textbook material has to be "chewed" with the mind. You have to read slowly, paying attention to every morsel of meaning.

Answer the following questions using the strategies to identify purpose, audience, and tone.

1. What do you think is the purpose of this article? Discuss the elements of the article that influence your response. _____

_____

_____

2. Who is the intended audience? How do you know? _____

_____

_____

3. Describe the author's tone. Indicate which words or phrases help reveal the tone. _____

_____

_____

EVALUATING ARGUMENTS

Reading critically and thinking critically require a lot of a student. They are not passive activities; focused engagement with the text is absolutely necessary. Similar to the judges on televised competitions like *American Idol*, critical readers and thinkers must evaluate what is before them and decide whether or not it is worthy of serious consideration. In the course of your college career and beyond, information of all sorts will come before you. Consequently, you must develop ways to separate the good from the bad, the relevant from the irrelevant, the useful from the not useful. In addition to the author's strategies about which you just learned, looking at the reliability and objectivity of a text will take you quite far in determining what information to remember and what information to forget. While you will certainly evaluate fiction for particular elements, the primary focus of the discussion that follows is nonfiction, with an emphasis on persuasive and argumentative writing.

Reliability

The **reliability** of a text is determined by three factors:

- author's credibility;
- balance of facts and opinions;
- timeliness of information.

First, let's consider the author's **credibility.** The word "credibility" is derived from the Latin word *credere*, to believe. Credibility is, thus, believability. When you examine what an author has written, you want to evaluate his/her credibility. For example, what gives this author the authority to talk about this particular topic? What experience or education stands behind the author? What research has informed the author's thinking? These are questions that evaluate an author's credibility.

Consider, for example, how you determine from whom you will accept or seek advice. If you are buying a new car, do you ask your friend Eddie, who plays the guitar and cares only about music, or do you ask your uncle, who rebuilds classic cars as his hobby? Who would you consider the more credible advisor? In this case, it would be your uncle since he knows so much about cars. In the same way that you evaluate the source of personal advice, evaluate the information provided to you by authors. Not everyone is an expert in, or even knowledgeable about, the topics he/she chooses to write about. It is your responsibility to search for the most credible authors.

> **Determining Author Credibility**
> ■ What gives the author the authority to talk about this topic?
> ■ What experience or education stands behind the author?
> ■ What research has informed the author's thinking?

Another aspect of reliability depends upon the balance of facts and opinions in a text. A **fact** is something that can be proven or disproven. Facts are objective. Most measurements are factual; you can measure the distance from New York to Michigan. **Opinions** are ideas based on a person's preferences, beliefs, or evaluations; opinions are subjective. A person may believe that New York is a better state than Michigan without ever considering why New York is better. Without supporting reasons that are factual, the person's view that New York is a better state is an opinion. Everyone has opinions, but they are not always reliable or suitable for someone else to believe or depend upon. Facts are needed for reliability.

A reliable text has a balance of facts and opinions. There is no magic number or percentage regarding the correct balance; basically, what's correct depends on the subject matter and the purpose for which you are reading. However, even though there is no magic number, a correct balance can still be determined. Imagine that you are researching global warming for an ecology course and you locate two articles. In the first article, the author argues that global warming is a serious threat to humankind. He discusses the many ways that humans depend on the environment. He offers all these ideas based on his own experience as an individual who also relies on the environment. The second article also discusses the risk that global warming poses to humankind. But this author focuses on the threat of rising sea levels as glaciers in the North and South Poles continue to melt. She includes statistics and data from researchers who have studied the melting glaciers. This author indicates that based on the threat of rising sea levels alone, global warming is something to take seriously. Considering these brief summaries of the two articles, which appears to have a better balance of facts

and opinions? In this case, the second article seems to be more balanced and, thus, more reliable as a source of information.

So far you have explored evaluating a text's reliability by examining the author's credibility and weighing the balance of fact and opinion. The third element in determining the reliability of a text is the timeliness of the information. **Timeliness** is how up-to-date and accurate factual information is. Some topics do not change significantly no matter how much time passes, and some topics change every day. Most topics, of course, are somewhere in between. In any case, an active reader must consider the timeliness of the material.

To illustrate this idea, imagine that you are researching the cell phone usage of teens in high school. Would you rely on statistics you gathered from a book printed in 1978? Hopefully, you would not. Those statistics would be irrelevant to your needs because cell phones were not widely used in 1978. (The first person to make a phone call using a cellular phone was Martin Cooper, when he tested his cellular phone prototype in 1973.) Consequently, the timeliness of any information you obtained from sources that are not relatively current—within a one- or two-year range—would not suit the needs of your research. This is where timeliness comes into play. Like facts and opinions and an author's credibility, there is no fixed marker for timeliness; however, depending on the needs of the reader, a suitable balance for each of these three reliability factors can be determined.

Point of View

Point of view is the vantage point from which a story is told or the angle from which an author approaches a topic. The author's point of view impacts the text in a number of ways. In fiction and narrative nonfiction, the character telling the story generally is a sign of the point of view. The point of view may shift to another character at times, but readers are generally aware of the perspective from which they are being told the story. In nonfiction, some readers assume that the author's point of view, or perspective, is neutral and objective. This is not always the case; in argumentative writing, for example, the author doesn't intend to have a point of view that is neutral. Thus, considering aspects of the author's point of view is crucial when evaluating a text, especially an argumentative or persuasive text. One should consider the:

- objectivity–subjectivity range;
- language choices;
- assumptions.

Objectivity and subjectivity are the most critical aspects of point of view to consider. **Objectivity** is defined as a state of being based on facts and observable factors, free from personal thoughts and emotions. As Joe

Friday, from the 1950s detective show *Dragnet*, would advise, "All we want are the facts, ma'am." Objective writing is mainly lacking the personal prejudices and biases that individuals naturally bring to an issue. **Subjectivity** is defined as being rooted or grounded in the individual's experiences, perceptions, and, often, prejudices and biases, too. As thinking individuals, everyone brings a certain amount of subjectivity to an issue; however, the goal in some writing, especially journalistic and scientific writing, is to be as objective as possible when handling a topic. This allows readers to determine for themselves what to think about the information presented.

Given that you are likely to come across writing from a variety of sources, it is helpful for you to be able to read a text and evaluate how objective or subjective it is. To do this, you might consider the publishing medium (Was the text published in a national newsmagazine like *Newsweek*? Did a community-based advocacy group publish the text?) and examine the point of view of that medium. Another way to evaluate the level of objectivity/subjectivity is to consider the proportion of factual information to opinions. You will find that the balance of facts and opinions contributes to the level of objectivity or subjectivity present in a text. An author's presenting only opinions may indicate that there are no facts that support his/her point of view. Or, at the other extreme, there may be too many facts that oppose the author's point of view. An author who seeks to be objective has no problem presenting both sides of an issue. So, if an author's point of view leans too far in either direction—slanted in favor of a topic or issue or slanted against a topic or issue—he/she is showing **bias.** Keep in mind that depending on your purpose for reading, you may find some subjectivity acceptable, and even preferable in some instances. Bias is not necessarily negative; it is, however, something that critical readers should be aware of.

The author's **language choices** also influence the point of view. Such choices are not random. When you select one word over another, you consider the likely effect of your language choice. Think about what goes through your mind when a dear friend asks you to evaluate her new pair of jeans. "How do I look?" your friend asks. Do you blurt out the first thing that enters your mind, or do you consider the most appropriate way to describe what you see? How you respond to questions like this may explain whether your friends find you kind and thoughtful or blunt and insensitive. In the same way, a writer considers the impact of the language he/she uses.

Many words carry two meanings: the denotation and connotation. You read about this previously in the chapter in the discussion of tone. The denotation is the literal, dictionary definition of a word. A word's connotation includes the denotation and adds the emotional weight of a word.

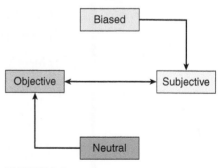

FIGURE 8.1

Being described as *charming* is one thing; being described as *slick* is another. Charming sounds pleasant and engaging and has a positive emotional value. Slick sounds sneaky and snake-like and has a negative emotional value. Yet, both words denote someone who is persuasive. This illustration is meant to remind you of the way language can shape emotion and meaning for the reader. Thus, as a critical thinker and reader, you must consider the language choices of an author. Some questions you might ask as you note the author's language choices:

- Does the author consistently use language that excites the emotions?
- Does the author use overly positive or negative language?
- Does the author make comparisons or references to ideas or things that have strong emotional connections? (For example, comparing person X to a famous person known for drug abuse might cause a reader to have a slightly negative view of person X.)

The final aspect to consider with point of view is the issue of assumptions. **Assumptions** are ideas that one assumes to be true or takes for granted. If you assume that all people who dress a certain way will act a certain way, then you will behave in accordance with your assumption. In the same way, authors may assume that readers believe certain things, have experienced certain things, or are afraid of certain things. This allows authors to call upon the subjectivity of readers—all the thoughts, emotions, prejudices, and biases everyone has—without appearing to be subjective themselves. However, critical readers and thinkers do not allow such manipulations to go unnoticed. Looking for these embedded or hidden assumptions can uncover important information necessary to understand an author's point of view.

Since new ideas need reinforcement to take root, the following reading is provided to offer you just the sort of reinforcement that developing critical thinkers need. Read the selection and answer the questions that follow.

Exercise 8.3

The Trouble with Troubled Teen Programs

by Maia Szalavitz

from *Reason* (excerpt)

Maia Szalavitz is a journalist who covers health, science, and public policy. She is winner of the 2005 Edward M. Brecher Award for Achievement and coauthor of Recovery Options: The Complete Guide. *She has written for the* New York Times, *the* Washington Post, Newsday, New York Magazine, New Scientist, Newsweek,

Elle, Salon, Redbook, and other major publications. She has also worked in television for ABC and PBS, among other stations. Her books include Help at Any Cost: How the Troubled Teen Industry Cons Parents and Hurts Kids *(2006) and* Born for Love: Why Empathy Is Essential—and Endangered *(2010), which she coauthored.*

---

1   The state of Florida tortured 14-year-old Martin Lee Anderson to death for trespassing. The teen had been sentenced to probation in 2005 for taking a joy ride in a Jeep Cherokee that his cousins stole from his grandmother. Later that year, he crossed the grounds of a school on his way to visit a friend, a violation of his probation. His parents were given a choice between sending him to boot camp and sending him to juvenile detention. They chose boot camp, believing, as many Americans do, that "tough love" was more likely to rehabilitate him than prison.

2   Less than three hours after his admission to Florida's Bay County Sheriff's Boot Camp on January 5, 2006, Anderson was no longer breathing. He was taken to a hospital, where he was declared dead early the next morning.

3   A video recorded by the camp shows up to 10 of the sheriff's "drill instructors" punching, kicking, slamming to the ground, and dragging the limp body of the unresisting adolescent. Anderson had reported difficulty breathing while running the last of 16 required laps on a track, a complaint that was interpreted as defiance. When he stopped breathing entirely, this too was seen as a ruse.

4   Ammonia was shoved in the boy's face; this tactic apparently had been used previously to shock other boys perceived as resistant into returning to exercises. The guards also applied what they called "pressure points" to Anderson's head with their hands, one of many "pain compliance" methods they had been instructed to impose on children who didn't immediately do as they were told.

5   All the while, a nurse in a white uniform stood by, looking bored. At one point she examined the boy with a stethoscope, then allowed the beating to continue until he was unconscious. An autopsy report issued in May—after an initial, disputed report erroneously attributed Anderson's death to a blood disorder—concluded that he had died of suffocation, due to the combined effects of ammonia and the guards' covering his mouth and nose.

6   Every time a child dies in a tough love program, politicians say—as Florida Gov. Jeb Bush initially did on hearing of Anderson's death—that it is "one tragic incident" that should not be used to justify

shutting such programs down. But there have now been nearly three dozen such deaths and thousands of reports of severe abuse in programs that use corporal punishment, brutal emotional attacks, isolation, and physical restraint in an attempt to reform troubled teenagers.

7   Tough love has become a billion-dollar industry. Several hundred programs, both public and private, use the approach. Somewhere between 10,000 and 100,000 teenagers are currently held in treatment programs based on the belief that adolescents must be broken (mentally, and often physically as well) before they can be fixed. Exact numbers are impossible to determine, because no one keeps track of the kids in these programs, most of which are privately run. The typical way to end up in a government-run program, such as the camp where Martin Lee Anderson was killed, is for a court to give you the option of going there instead of prison. The typical way to end up in a private program is to be sent there by your parents, though judges and public schools have been known to send kids to private boot camps as well. Since they offer "treatment" some of the private centers are covered by health insurance.

8   In the nearly five decades since the first tough love residential treatment community, Synanon, introduced the idea of attack therapy as a cure for drug abuse, hundreds of thousands of young people have undergone such "therapy." These programs have both driven and been driven by the war on drugs. Synanon, for example, was aimed at fighting heroin addiction, its draconian methods justified by appeals to parents' fears that drugs could do far worse things to their children than a little rough treatment could. The idea was that only a painful experience of "hitting bottom" could end an attachment to the pleasures of drugs.

9   But like the drug war itself, tough love programs are ineffective, based on pseudoscience, and rooted in a brutal ideology that produces more harm than most of the problems they are supposedly aimed at addressing. The history of tough love shows how fear consistently trumps data, selling parents and politicians on a product that hurts kids.

Answer the following questions using critical reading strategies to determine reliability and point of view.

1. Based on the information you have about the author of this selection, do you think she is a credible writer for this topic? Explain your reasoning.

   _____

   _____

   _____

2. Review the first five paragraphs of this selection. In your assessment, does the author employ facts or opinions to convey what happened to

Martin Lee Anderson? Point to particular statements of either facts or opinions to support your response. _____

_____

_____

3. Review the author's language choices. Point to three places where she uses a word that carries strong connotations, and discuss the effect of the word choice. _____

_____

_____

4. Would you consider this selection to be objective or subjective? Why?

_____

_____

_____

5. Examine the way the author develops her points and how she presents information to the reader. Can you determine any assumptions the author makes concerning what readers may already believe or feel about tough love boot camps? _____

_____

_____

CHAPTER 8 STRATEGY QUIZ

Read the article and answer the questions that follow. Use all of the critical thinking strategies discussed in this chapter.

Inventive Ways to Land a Cool Job

by Pol T. Keeley

Pol T. Keeley was born in Dublin, Ireland. He has worked as a recruitment consultant as well as working within the education and ESL industry as a marketing representative, trainer, and writer. He also writes for a number of lifestyle magazines and publications. His recent work includes writing travel and music scripts for the MTV HD Uncompressed travel and lifestyles show. Keeley is a former professional racing cyclist and is still very active on two wheels. He divides his time between New York City and Kent, England.

Like most things in life, when it comes to getting your foot in the career door, securing your grip on the recruitment ladder, and smooching ahead in advertising, it doesn't harm your chances to be proactive as soon as you can get your skates on. If you're fresh out of college or grad school, or just looking to boost your job status, an original approach—if and when appropriate—will go a long way in getting you noticed.

The Basics

Ask any reputable recruitment consultant, proven business leader, or seasoned business professional worth their salt what it takes to get the career ball rolling and they will all tell you fairly similar things. You've got to be able to build, establish, and maintain a network, all of which can be potential job sources or leads when making the right connections. Have faith in the "word of mouth" channels as convenient and multitasking options—let those who like you say all kinds of glowing things about your strengths and promise to people in higher or attractive places. Just remember to have done something good beforehand that is at the very least worthy of mention! Most employers would naturally rather save themselves the time and hassle of adverting for positions if they can learn about your good self through a mutual friend who holds you in high regards or admires what you stand for.

Once you have made connections, showcase the usual pillars or stalwarts in your character (think of them as the usual suspects in the career dating game as you flirt with one potential employer to the next) to aid your resume and cover letter tactics. These namely include being proactive and in touch with what's going on in the job market, building bridges between your previous experience and what you can offer the company you wish to dazzle, and thoroughly researching your hunting ground without resorting to plain stalking (imagine the interviewer's reaction as he's adamant he saw you the week before lurking in the company parking lot, and then delivering the Friday afternoon office pizzas).

One thing to also bear in mind when job hunting is that you will have to use common sense when paying attention to the fine art of being bold while at the same time not being underhanded, menacing, or teetering on coming across as downright stubborn. If they politely show you the door after your well-intended game plan, be sure to do your homework to see if there is indeed another window of opportunity through which you can come back in.

Location, Location, Location

Working in a restaurant or food eatery frequented by the kinds of people of a particular industry you aspire to is one of the handy ways of meeting people who may be able to provide you with a useful lead or stepping stone. Keep your eyes and ears open to find out about possible openings and what's generally moving and shaking in the sector. Be careful not to ask for a job there and then, but do show boldness—or some sassiness dressed as a professional clout—in adequate doses to express your interest and show you know what's going on. Such tactics can be very rewarding, especially as networking exercises.

If you've read any guide on how to influence people and make a lasting impression, extending your comfort zone to strike up some good old-fashioned conversation can provide worthwhile experiences. Meeting people on trains and planes, in train stations and airports, or any kind of potential meeting place is basically an invitation to strike up a bit of friendly and sincere dialogue—the emphasis being on engaging in meaningful dialogue and listening rather than monologue accounts of your career stats—that can pay dividends later on. Seizing the initiative, and subsequent moment, to get talking to a senior business person or director may just be the networking jewel that could lead to further correspondence and even an interview later on. Everyone knows that people love to talk, but knowing when and how to act is key. Networking can take place anywhere, whether at a relevant industry seminar or function, online (especially if the social networking channels you use demonstrate adequate business flair), or in transport meeting areas. Moreover, if it's financially viable to get in your car—or on a plane—to meet prospective employers and people in the industry circles you aspire to be a part of, this again could prove to be a tasty networking trip. One example shows how a UK banker who wanted to get into the film finance industry showed his initiative by flying to California for a series of meetings he'd organized beforehand. Three of the meetings turned into opportunities and he accepted a job ten days later.

Bold Moves

Like job hunters, most employers read the job sections of the trade press and online job portals. One example of an enterprising candidate who wanted to demonstrate a competitive advantage tells of how he placed an ad in the jobs section, listing his strengths in a particular way—bold but on point. This advertisement jumped out at prospective employers who remarked on his initiative and creative approach. Another example highlights an attention-grabbing public gesture. A Polish computer programmer looking for work in Warsaw managed to get his name and basic strengths on a few massive billboards (picture, if

you can, a giant, glorified business card that looked great) around the city center, both in Polish and English. He was then interviewed on a local radio station to discuss why and how he had chosen this tactic. He simply replied that he hadn't seen anyone else try that when looking for a job. In a way, this demonstrated a kind of dual-format public relations exercise as well as a flair for advertising that simply got people looking and talking.

Other inventive ways to land a dream job could be in the writing of a business plan or business proposal to prospective employers. This definitely shows a bold character, but done properly can be pulled off with a great deal of panache. One such story is told by Colin Barrow (via MSN website), visiting fellow at the Cranfield School of Management. An MBA student decided to write a sincere and well-thought-out business plan for an independent airline. The premise for this came from the student's love of piloting in general, as well as some industrious background research in the airline's history and what was going on in the industry at the time. The independent airline venture capital company graciously acknowledged the business plan and politely "filed" it away. Lucky they did, as a year later something cropped up that led them to call the student with an offer for him to run a feeder airline being operated by Caledonian Airlines.

Most of us know that at some point we may have to be willing to work for nothing and go beyond the call of duty in order to get ahead. Another useful exercise in writing skills is to write to a prospective employer and ask (convince, persuade) them or charm them into allowing you to work with them for a brief yet dynamic period of time. Once accepted (who doesn't love freebies—employers are no different!), again use that as a networking opportunity to get to know the kinds of people you aspire to be yourself, demonstrating a professionally sincere yet human account of yourself. If they don't hire you or offer you something else, they may know someone else who would. Another creative example is how Sarah Williams won a television quiz show in the UK called Jet Set, which gave her a taste for a different job and life. Asked how it all came to fruition and blossomed thereafter, Sarah replied, "I kept in touch with the presenter and eventually got some work experience with the production company, 12 Yard. I spent two weeks organizing contestants and hospitality." That willingness to work selflessly paid off and Sarah is now a personal assistant and administrator for the production company.

As they say, every little bit helps, and a touch of flair and honest initiative can go a long way in securing a great new job. At the very least, it can put you in the right direction and keep those networking skills polished and ready for the arrival of that golden opportunity.

Questions for "Inventive Ways to Land a Cool Job"

1. ____ . Which of the following sentences best states the main idea of the second paragraph?

   a) You've got to be able to build, establish, and maintain a network, all of which can be potential job sources or leads when making the right connections.

   b) Have faith in the "word of mouth" channels as convenient and multitasking options—let those who like you say all kinds of glowing things about your strengths and promise to people in higher or attractive places.

   c) Ask any reputable recruitment consultant, proven business leader, or seasoned business professional worth their salt what it takes to get the career ball rolling and they will all tell you fairly similar things.

   d) Most employers would naturally rather save themselves the time and hassle of adverting for positions if they can learn about your good self through a mutual friend who holds you in high regards or admires what you stand for.

2. ____ What is the purpose of this article?

   a) to convince

   b) to inform

   c) to entertain

   d) to expose

3. ____ Who is the intended audience?

   a) retirees

   b) first-year college students

    c) textbook readers

    d) job seekers

4. ____ Which of the following choices best describes the author's tone?

    a) argumentative

    b) informative and friendly

    c) serious

    d) concerned and cautious

5. ____ Based on the information you have about the author of this article, do you think he is a credible writer on this topic?

    a) Yes, he writes very well.

    b) No, it is clear that he has no experience.

    c) Yes, his bio shows that he would be considered an expert in this field.

    d) No, getting a job is different for each person.

6. ____ What is one of the ways that the author establishes a balance of facts and opinions?

    a) He does not establish a balance.

    b) He uses examples of real job seekers.

    c) He suggests asking a recruitment consultant or business leader for advice.

    d) He says that working in a restaurant is a good way to network.

7. ____ Which of the following words carries negative connotations?

    a) researching

    b) flair

    c) stalking

    d) adamant

8. ____ Would you consider this article to be objective or subjective?

    a) completely objective

    b) completely subjective

    c) mostly objective

    d) mostly subjective

9. ____ How does the picture of the job seeker's billboard support, if it does, the author's point?

    a) It doesn't help; there was no reason to include it.

    b) It gives an example of a bad idea.

    c) It provides visual proof of the author's point.

    d) It gives the author credibility as a photographer.

10. ____ Which of the following sentences best expresses the central point of this article?

   a) Everyone knows that people love to talk, but knowing when and how to act is key.

   b) If you're fresh out of college or grad school, or just looking to boost your job status, an original approach—if and when appropriate—will go a long way in getting you noticed.

   c) Like job hunters, most employers read the job sections of the trade press and online job portals.

   d) Most employers would naturally rather save themselves the time and hassle of adverting for positions if they can learn about your good self through a mutual friend.

KEY TERM REVIEW

Using the chapter as your reference, match the key terms with the definitions in the opposite column.

Key Term	Definition
1. Purpose ____	a) to tell a story
2. Publishing medium ____	b) the author's believability
3. Persuade/convince ____	c) an author's reason for communicating and what the author hopes to accomplish with the communication
4. Describe ____	d) based on credibility, balance of facts and opinions, and timeliness
5. Inform/expose ____	e) the author's attitude and mood toward the subject, and the stance taken toward the audience
6. Narrate ____	f) to advocate the author's position or ideas; to evaluate or judge
7. Entertain ____	g) slanted in favor of a topic or issue or slanted against a topic or issue
8. Audience ____	h) the literal, dictionary definition of a word
9. Tone ____	i) to cover light or noncontroversial subjects; to amuse
10. Denotation ____	j) the group of people who will most likely be interested in and read the material
11. Connotation ____	k) how up-to-date and accurate factual information is
12. Reliability ____	l) a state of being rooted or grounded in the individual's experiences, perceptions, prejudices, and biases

(continued)

Key Term	Definition
13. Credibility ____	**m)** an idea that can be proven or disproven
14. Fact ____	**n)** the vantage point from which a story is told or the angle from which an author approaches a topic
15. Opinion ____	**o)** the type of publication in which a work is distributed
16. Timeliness ____	**p)** to use the five senses and figurative language to paint a verbal picture
17. Point of view ____	**q)** an idea that one assumes to be the truth or takes for granted
18. Objectivity ____	**r)** an idea based on a person's preferences, personal beliefs, or evaluations or on an individual's perception
19. Subjectivity ____	**s)** a state of being based on facts and observable factors, free from personal thoughts and emotions
20. Bias ____	**t)** the dictionary meaning and the emotional weight of a word
21. Assumption ____	**u)** to explain and discuss ideas

STRATEGIES IN ACTION

Student Abuse of Prescription Drugs on Rise

by Allison Loudermilk

Allison Loudermilk was a student at the University of Georgia at Athens when she published this article in 2006. The Red and Black newspaper is an independently published, student-run enterprise. The Red and Black's mission is to provide a professional and valuable journalistic experience for students on staff, and an objective and reputable source of news for the university community.

What do you think this reading will be about?

1   College students are turning to a new type of drug to get high. Although alcohol and marijuana remain the substances most likely to be misused by college students at 87 and 49 percent respectively, prescription medications are close behind at 31 percent.

2   The annual *Monitoring the Future* study, regarded as the gold standard for tracking drug trends among American students, reports 14.4 percent of college students misused Vicodin or some other prescription narcotic at least once in 2005, up from 13.8 percent in 2004. Misuse of tranquilizers or downers, such as Xanax, jumped to 11.9 percent, up from 10.6 percent in 2004. Use of the stimulant Ritalin dropped, from 4.7 percent in 2004 to 4.2 percent in the past year.

3   Doctors often prescribe Vicodin, a narcotic similar to Percocet and OxyContin, to patients with severe pain. Xanax, a central nervous system depressant, is often used to treat anxiety or panic attacks. Ritalin and Adderall are commonly prescribed for attention deficit hyperactivity disorder or ADHD. All possess the potential for abuse.

4   "This is a rising epidemic," said Dr. John Knight, founder of the Center for Adolescent Substance Abuse Research at Children's Hospital Boston. "Everyone is a little unclear on how to deal with this," Knight said in Atlanta on Oct. 8 during a speech to the American Academy of Pediatrics.

5   Although University health officials don't have concrete numbers on increases on campus, they believe the pattern holds true in Athens. The University Health Center counsels students who abuse prescription medications. These students tend to have problems with alcohol or illicit drugs as well, said Erin English, the center's alcohol, tobacco and other drugs health educator. English didn't have data on drug abuse at the University but said students have told staff that prescription stimulants and narcotics are becoming bigger on campus.

6   Signs of misuse include upping dosage, injecting or snorting meds or asking for early refills, said Dr. Sharon Levy, Knight's colleague and co-presenter at the pediatrics conference. A student prescribed Ritalin for ADHD may take extra pills so he can pull an all-nighter before an exam, said Levy, a pediatrician and instructor at the Harvard Medical School researching adolescent substance abuse.

7   Occasional misuse can lead to more serious drug abuse, such as grinding up Ritalin and snorting it. When abuse escalates to this level, young people may go missing from school, home or work, endanger their health or get into legal trouble, Levy said.

8   Because prescription medications are easy to get online or through parents and friends, their potential for abuse increases, said Levy.

9   And some students mistakenly assume these drugs are safe because doctors prescribe them, according to a study published in April in *The New England Journal of Medicine*. Health experts said students who abuse these drugs can be hard to spot.

10   "You can't tell by looking at someone whether they're using or abusing. You have really functional drug abusers and addicts out there," English said.

11   [1]Some students said they weren't surprised that prescription medications are making the rounds on campus. [2]Jo Lee, a senior from Thomasville, said Adderall, Paxil and Prozac are prescription drugs students abuse. [3]Lee said people sometimes take prescription medications before they go out and mix them with drinks, while others pop Adderall to study. [4]"I would say Adderall would be the biggest," she said. [5]And it's not hard to get. [6]Students with prescriptions will sell pills for $5 or $10 each to earn extra cash, Lee said.

12   Jeremy Vig, a senior from Lawrenceville, said he has noticed students misusing prescription medications such as Adderall, speed-type drugs and pain pills. "I'm sure everyone knows finals week is the big week that people are looking for that kind of stuff," Vig said.

13   English said students concerned about their drug use should get a professional, confidential evaluation available through the counseling and psychiatric services at the University Health Center.

14   "It's very easy for people with abuse or addiction problems to rationalize their problem, which makes it hard for them to see that there is a problem."

***

Vocabulary in Context

Use the vocabulary strategies covered in Chapter 3 to decipher the meaning of the following words. Use the vocabulary strategies as much as possible before you refer to a dictionary.

1. The annual *Monitoring the Future* study, regarded as the *gold standard* for tracking drug trends among American students, reports 14.4 percent of college students misused Vicodin or some other prescription narcotic at least once in 2005, up from 13.8 percent in 2004. (par. 2)

_____

2. Use of the *stimulant* Ritalin dropped, from 4.7 percent in 2004 to 4.2 percent in the past year. (par. 2)

_____

3. Xanax, a central nervous system depressant, is often used to treat *anxiety* or panic attacks. (par. 3)

_____

4. Although University health officials don't have *concrete* numbers on increases on campus, they believe the pattern holds true in Athens. (par. 5)

_____

5. Some students said they weren't surprised that prescription medications are *making the rounds* on campus. (par. 10)

_____
_____

Checking In

1. How accurate was your pre-reading prediction of the focus of this selection?

2. Would this selection be considered fiction or nonfiction? How do you know?

3. What was the publishing medium of this selection, and when was it published?

4. Is the publishing information relevant to understanding the key ideas of this selection?

Getting the Point

5. What is the central point of this selection?

6. In paragraph 3, what point is the author making? Which pattern of development is used to make that point?

7. In paragraph 6, what point is the author making? Which pattern of development is used to make that point?

8. In paragraph 10, what is the relationship of sentence 6 to sentence 1?

Delving Deeper

9. In paragraph 6, Dr. Levy said, "When abuse escalates to this level, young people may go missing from school, home or work, endanger their health or get into legal trouble." What conclusion can you draw from this statement?

10. Based on the students' responses in paragraphs 10–11, what can you infer about students' attitudes toward prescription drugs?

Evaluating the Author's Strategies

11. What effect do you think the author sought in publishing this article? Discuss the details that contribute to your response.

12. Who was the intended audience for this article? How do you know?

13. What is the author's tone? Provide examples of words that support your answer.

14. Are there sufficient facts presented in this article? Does the author present an objective or a subjective viewpoint?

Technology Tip

Select a web page of your choice. Evaluate the web page using the strategies for evaluating an argument as discussed in this chapter. Be sure to:

- Provide a link to the website or web page.
- Address the author's strategies.
- Address reliability and point of view.

STRATEGIES IN ACTION

On the Threshold
by Mike Rose

from *Why School? Reclaiming Education for All of Us*

Mike Rose (1944–) is the son of Italian immigrants. He was born in Altoona, Pennsylvania, and raised in Los Angeles, California. While his early academic career was challenging, Rose went on to earn his bachelor's degree, two master's degrees, and a doctorate degree. In his forty years as an educator, he has taught in a range of educational settings, from kindergarten to job training and adult literacy programs. He is currently on the faculty of the UCLA Graduate School of Education and Information Studies.

Rose has written a number of books and articles on language, literacy, and cognition and has received a Guggenheim Fellowship and numerous other awards and honors. He is the author of ten books, including Lives on the Boundary: The Struggles *and* Achievements of America's Underprepared *and* Why School? Reclaiming Education for All of Us.

In describing his reasons for writing Why School?, *from which this selection comes, Rose says the book "comes from a professional lifetime in classrooms, creating and running educational programs, teaching and researching, writing and thinking about education and human development. It offers a series of appeals for big-hearted social policy and an embrace of the ideals of democratic education—from the way we define and structure opportunity to the way we respond to a child adding a column of numbers. Collectively, the chapters provide a bountiful vision of human potential, illustrated through the schoolhouse, the work place, and the community."*

> Considering the biographical information on Mike Rose, how do you think he feels about education?

1   Food wrappers and sheets of newspaper were blowing in the wet wind across the empty campus. It was late in the day, getting dark fast, and every once in a while I'd look outside the library—which was pretty empty too—and imagine the drizzly walk to the car, parked far away.

2   Anthony was sitting by me, and I was helping him read a flyer on the dangers of cocaine. He wanted to give it to his daughter. Anthony was enrolled in a basic skills program, one of several special programs at this urban community college. Anthony was in his late-thirties, had some degree of brain damage from a childhood injury, worked custodial jobs most of his life. He could barely read or write, but was an informed, articulate guy, listening to FM radio current affairs shows while he worked, watching public television at home. He had educated himself through the sources available to him, compensating for the damage done.

3   The librarian was about to go off shift, so we gathered up our things—Anthony carried a big backpack—and headed past her desk to the exit. The wind pushed back on the door as I pushed forward, and I remember thinking how dreary the place was, dark and cold. At that moment I wanted so much to be home.

4   Just then a man in a coat and tie came up quickly behind us. "Hey man," he said to Anthony, "you look good. You lose some weight?" Anthony beamed, said that he had dropped a few pounds and that things were going o.k. The guy gave Anthony a cupping slap on the shoulder, then pulled his coat up and walked head down across the campus.

5   "Who was that?" I asked, ducking with Anthony back inside the entryway to the library. He was one of the deans, Anthony said, but, well, he was once his parole officer, too. He's seen Anthony come a long way. Anthony pulled on the straps of his backpack, settling the weight more evenly across his shoulders. "I like being here," he said in his soft, clear voice. "I know it can't happen by osmosis. But this is where it's at."

6   I've thought about this moment off and on for twenty years. I couldn't wait to get home, and Anthony was right at home. Fresh from reading something for his daughter, feeling the clasp on his shoulder of both his past and his future, for Anthony a new life was emerging on the threshold of a chilly night on a deserted campus.

7   These few minutes remind me of how humbling work with human beings can be. How we'll always miss things. How easily we get distracted—my own memories of cold urban landscapes overwhelmed the moment.

8   But I also hold onto this experience with Anthony for it contains so many lessons about development, about resilience and learning, about the power of hope and a second chance. It reminds us too of the importance of staying close to the ground, of finding out what people are thinking, of trying our best—flawed though it will be—to understand the world as they see it ... and to be ready to revise our understanding. This often means taking another line of sight on what seems familiar, seeing things in a new light.

9   And if we linger with Anthony a while longer, either in the doorway or back inside at a library table, we might get the chance to reflect on the basic question of what school is for, the purpose of education. What brought Anthony back to the classroom after all those years? To help his economic prospects, certainly. Anthony wanted to trade in his mop and pail for decent pay and a few benefits. But we also get a glimpse as to why else he's here. To be able to better guide his daughter. To be more proficient in reading about the events swirling around him—to add reading along with radio and television to his means of examining the world. To create a new life for himself, nurture this emerging sense of who he can become.

***

Vocabulary in Context

Use the vocabulary strategies covered in Chapter 3 to decipher the meaning of the following words. Use the vocabulary strategies as much as possible before you refer to a dictionary.

1. He had educated himself through the sources available to him, *compensating* for the damage done. (par. 2) _____

_____

2. "I know it can't happen by *osmosis*. But this is where it's at." (par. 5) _____

   _____

   _____

3. But I also hold onto this experience with Anthony for it contains so many lessons about development, about *resilience* and learning, about the power of hope and a second chance. (par. 8) _____

   _____

4. It reminds us too of the importance of staying close to the ground, of finding out what people are thinking, of trying our best—*flawed* though it will be—to understand the world as they see it … and to be ready to revise our understanding. (par. 8) _____

   _____

5. To be more *proficient* in reading about the events swirling around him—to add reading along with radio and television to his means of examining the world. (par. 9) _____

   _____

6. To create a new life for himself, *nurture* this emerging sense of who he can become. (par. 9) _____

   _____

Checking In

1. Consider the title of this essay. What does it mean to be "on the threshold"?

2. Would this selection be considered narrative or expository nonfiction? How do you know?

Getting the Point

3. What actions occur in this essay? Are those actions the focus of the essay? Explain your response.

4. The author does not state in this essay what his connection or relationship is to Anthony. Based on the supporting details, what do you think the relationship between Anthony and the author is?

5. What is the central point of this selection? What supporting details develop that idea?

6. Write a summary of this essay.

Delving Deeper

7. The last sentence of paragraph 8 states, "This often means taking another line of sight on what seems familiar, seeing things in a new light." What do you think this means?

Evaluating the Author's Strategies

8. Consider the information given about the author and his statement regarding the book *Why School?* Based on those considerations, who is the audience for this essay? What could be the author's purpose in sharing this story? Use the supporting details from the essay to back up your conclusion.

9. Does Mike Rose present an objective or a subjective point of view? How do you know?

The Writing Connection

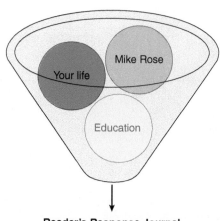

Reader's Response Journal

Mike Rose says that this experience with Anthony has stayed in his mind for many years. Reflect on the experiences you have had in your educational career. Write about an interaction or experience that you had with someone—a teacher, a professor, a counselor, or an administrator—who made an unexpected, lasting impression on you.

   For support in meeting this chapter's objectives, go to MyReadingLab and select **Purpose and Tone**

PART 2 Short Readings

Graywolf: A Romance

by Annie Seikonia

About the Author

Annie Seikonia (1961–) lives on the coast of Maine. She is a writer, artist, and poet who has a degree in English literature from the University of Southern Maine. She has written articles for the *Casco Bay Weekly* and the *Maine Times.* Her poetry has been published in *Café Review* and *Janus Head,* and one of her flash fiction pieces was selected as an Editor's Pick by the online journal *flashquake.*

An avid reader, Seikonia likes to incorporate elements of the supernatural and magical into her fiction. In *Graywolf: A Romance,* the idea of having an ideal friend takes on an unexpected twist.

Before You Read

Does the picture of Graywolf remind you of anything that you've read about or seen before?

Thematic Links

- Friendship
- Relationships

Part 3 Book Link

- *The Kite Runner*

Graywolf: A Romance

By Annie Seikonia

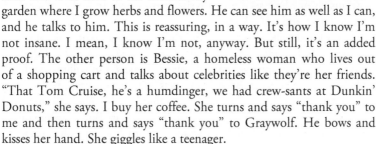

1   Graywolf and I walk around the cove, along the boulevard. It is brisk and windy and he has his woolen hood up. Not that anyone can see him anyway, except me. Lots of children have invisible friends. Then they grow up. I guess I didn't. Grow up, that is, in that way. Graywolf has been with me since my earliest memories. We have been together for decades now. And it suits me fine.

2   There are two other people who can see him. One is Grady, the old man who lives next to the community garden where I grow herbs and flowers. He can see him as well as I can, and he talks to him. This is reassuring, in a way. It's how I know I'm not insane. I mean, I know I'm not, anyway. But still, it's an added proof. The other person is Bessie, a homeless woman who lives out of a shopping cart and talks about celebrities like they're her friends. "That Tom Cruise, he's a humdinger, we had crew-sants at Dunkin' Donuts," she says. I buy her coffee. She turns and says "thank you" to me and then turns and says "thank you" to Graywolf. He bows and kisses her hand. She giggles like a teenager.

3   Graywolf likes to curl up in the closet or on the bed at my feet. And he vanishes sometimes, when he senses I need some real alone time. But he always comes back. He goes when I need him to, and he comes back when I need him to. It's quite the perfect arrangement. You think I'm lying. But it is the truth.

4   I'm no prude, I've been with men. The one who lasted the longest was Spice, a prep cook at a restaurant, DJ on the side. He was just a kid, with pale vampire skin and a mop of tousled black hair. Friend of a friend. Graywolf didn't approve. Graywolf thought he was a "rotter." He's English, Graywolf.

5   One morning Spice and I were lying there in my bed and he was still asleep—wild coal hair splayed on the pillow next to me, mouth slightly open, like a baby, his scent of tobacco and kitchen and sweat mingling

with the freshly laundered cotton sheets. I was awake, watching a little woodpecker circling the tree trunk outside my window and suddenly it occurred to me Graywolf was right. Spice was a loser who ultimately cared not a whit for me, nor I for him really, though we had our fun.

6   I saw through the whole situation in an instant, like fogged lenses growing clear. I dumped Spice. And it was the right thing to do. After all, I have the extreme privilege of not needing anyone.

7   Graywolf is about six feet tall, give or take. He wears mustard yellow pants and a green shirt. Also a gray velvet cape with a hood that is fastened at the neck with a brass clasp that has an interwoven Celtic design on it. I've asked him a thousand times what it stands for, what it means. "Nothing," he says, but I know that he's lying, that it stands for something important and essential and if I knew what it was I would unlock his secret and perhaps that would be the end. So I don't press it too hard. We all need our secrets.

8   I work in an insurance office, processing claims on a computer. I do research, make phone calls, fill out endless data on endless forms. It's boring but it's a job. While I work, Graywolf prowls around the office or wanders around the city. At night he tells me stories about the curious things he's seen and I write them down in a sketchbook with cream pages and a black cover.

9   I wanted to be an actress. But I didn't have the right look, or so I was always told. Too plain, too unremarkable, too nondescript. I blended in too well. OK, not talented enough, either, I guess. I'm willing to admit it. The closest I ever came to local fame was being an understudy to Carolyn Lonhurst, who played Eleanor of Aquitaine in *The Lion in Winter* at the Rivertown Theater Company. Perhaps you saw it? But it was awful, like being a shadow and I hated it. I was so close to The Stage, it was tantalizing, yet it was just out of reach, anguishing. After that I gave up on my dream. I still help out painting scenery and sewing costumes because I like the color and frenzy of opening night. Graywolf and I stay late sometimes and dress up in the costumes. I like watching the plays and knowing my invisible work is contained in the tiny stitches and the acrylic backdrops.

10   Graywolf has long shaggy fur the color of twilight with all its shades and gradations. His coat is unbelievably soft. He wears his pants long and he walks with a swagger, which is amusing, because he's not aware of it. He has green eyes, the color of jade from a distant time, from deep within a mountain or a story. When the light hits them they are iridescent and supernatural, like a dark place being illuminated. His hearing is acute. He can hear a hawk circling over the bay three miles away.

11   He has his own quirky personality but he rarely gets on my nerves. He is deep and flat, a bottomless well, a picture card that moves. Quiet

as fog, quick as a tongue. Soft spoken. A creature of few words. His form ranges from opaque to transparent. When the sun shines through him he looks like a hologram. Yet he can also achieve full solidity. I stroke his fur, which smells like cardamom.

12   He was born, perhaps, from a fairy tale. As if the wish became so strong it emerged into reality, fully clothed, gentle, fur-clad and unmasked.

13   I love him the way you would love a cat or a dog—simply and wholly, in a way it seems impossible to love another human. Sometimes I wonder what will happen when I meet someone I want to stay with forever. How could I tell him about Graywolf? How could I *not* tell him about Graywolf? It would be a challenge to have a marriage containing three, especially when one of them is invisible. I admit the possibility that Graywolf is the reason I am still "alone." On the other hand, I suppose it keeps me from falling into something that isn't real, as so many people do, out of fear or loneliness or a bizarre sense of purpose.

14   I was not an only child like you might have assumed. I have two younger brothers, Isaac and Michael, athletic types, one in college, one just finished. Our parents are not divorced. My mother is a teacher's aide and my father is an optometrist, which means I own an assortment of glasses in all kinds of fancy frames. I like gauzy skirts, fancy feather pillows, spiderwebs, dark chocolate, warm rainy days, napping during rainstorms, film noir, pasta, the moon, beeswax candles, Loretta Lynn and Jane Austen. I like hanging around with the Goths sometimes, though I wouldn't consider myself one, despite the way I keep one long front streak of my short black hair dyed either bright red or dark purple, depending on my mood. I pin it back when I work in the office and no one seems to care. Half of them have piercings and tattoos anyway. What is unique eventually becomes mainstream.

15   Graywolf and I walk along the quay in a warm autumn drizzle. It is my favorite time of year, soft and vivid, confetti leaves drifting down from the passionate trees. Scarlet and copper. Still, warm, humid. His soft paw clasps my hand. There aren't many people about except for a few indomitable joggers, a couple of bicycles whirring past. The day passes into dusk and the new faux old-fashioned black streetlamps come on and the colored lights sparkle in the black water. The sky clears a bit and Venus peeps out from behind the clouds, white on gray. It is a dream. Even though I am an insurance claims clerk and a failed actress, I have never felt ordinary. Nor have I ever experienced true loneliness. Some sadness and some gaps perhaps, but never the piercing kind of absence I think most everyone in the world feels at some time or another.

16   What is Graywolf? Is he a spirit, a phantom conjured by my own imagination? Yet two other people are able to see him, perhaps more I haven't met yet. Did you ever read the poem "The Tables Turned" by Wordsworth?

17   "Sweet is the lore which Nature brings;
Our meddling intellect
Misshapes the beauteous forms of things—
We murder to dissect.

Enough of Science and of Art,
Close up those barren leaves;
Come forth, and bring with you a heart
That watches and receives."

18   My theory is this: there are portals in this world that connect us to other worlds we know nothing about. Occasionally we glimpse these other worlds, even in science, but because our methods are inherently flawed, because our thoughts are inherently flawed, we dismiss them. We deny. We do not see. Once in a blue moon one of these portals slips open, something passes through, and someone is born with the ability to see it, to feel it, to know it. When we get older, "reason" takes over and the portal closes. I am blessed. For whatever reasons, this particular portal has never yet closed.

19   It is Saturday morning and we go to brunch at Humdingers, the vegetarian restaurant on Temple Street. The irony that I am bringing a wolf to a vegetarian eatery is not lost on me. But of course Graywolf doesn't actually eat. I love this place. It is crowded today but we manage to get a tiny table by the window, a table for two. I slide the other chair out with my foot so Graywolf can sit down.

20   I order coffee and a spinach and mushroom omelet with rye toast and home fries. I wonder why they are called home fries. Humdingers consists of a large room with red booths and tables, potted plants and huge seashells from tropical seas lining the window sills. The walls are bright yellow with pumpkin trim. It is bright and chaotic. There are striking new paintings on display today, a series of small 10" x 10" acrylics in pale birch frames. They are landscapes and cityscapes with one element in common—there is a small red fox in each one.

21   I sip my coffee and scribble in my sketchbook, designs for an opera about Graywolf's imagined childhood and transformation into a "spirit guide," for I've decided spirit guide describes him more accurately than wolf.

22   A flash of orange-red. Baroque. The smell of burning food. The ruddy waitress with a large tattoo of a spider on her upper arm, her blonde hair pinned in a turvy on her head, rhinestone nose ring aglitter, scuttles over, bearing my steaming turquoise plate. "Who did these paintings?" I ask. She nods towards the kitchen. "Dishwasher. Busboy. Jarrod." She vanishes back into the steaming kitchen. I eat my heavenly eggs laced with fresh fungi and spinach doused with ketchup, staring at the small painting over the table of downtown buildings and passersby, including one red fox dressed in an old-fashioned black suit. I am in love with this painting.

23   We start going to Humdingers for brunch on Sundays, though it is an added expense I can scarce afford. We spot Jarrod, the dishwasher/busboy. He is medium-height, thin and lanky with a shock of black hair that flips over his eyes, which are dark, darting and intelligent. Pale skin, rose almost girlish lips, delicate nose, something shy and jittery yet affable in his manner. He glances at me, I glance at him. I guess you could say we are flirting. Graywolf stays mum, stroking his beardish chin fur and humming along with the pop tune on the radio. A flash of red from the kitchen, the smell of burning toast.

24   We've been brunching for about a month and a half and it's winter now, approaching Christmas. The streets are lit with lights in the shape of tangerines, lemons and limes. The store windows are filled with driftwood trees, red-ribboned rocking horses, negligees and calendars. Humdingers is packed. Jarrod is running around bussing tables and helping set them up. His paintings have come down and been replaced by photographs of indigenous Guatemalan children dressed in bright woven clothing. I am sitting at my regular table, my crumb-and-ketchup strewn yellow plate empty, sketching in my sketchbook. There's a line outside the door on this overcast Sunday, but I'm taking my own sweet time. I've earned my spot.

25   Jarrod approaches the table, whisks away my plate.

26   "Wait!" I command and he stops, stands still, waits. I'm at a loss what to say next.

27   "I like your paintings," I say. "Do you have a studio?"

28   He nods.

29   "Can I come visit sometime, see more?"

30   He nods, looks down, looks to the left, toward the clattering kitchen. Then he moves quickly, bearing his heavy plastic bin of plates and silverware. I sit frozen, staring into my empty cup. I don't dare

look up at Graywolf. I can feel the blood in my face. Suddenly Jarrod reappears. He is standing there in his splotched apron, his black sneakers. He hands me a wrinkled card from the restaurant. I turn it over. There is a time, a place. I nod and he is gone.

31   Next Saturday afternoon Graywolf and I walk through a freezing drizzle to a grim brick building behind a faltering white Church of God. The front door is unlocked and we slip inside and go up the wooden stairs to the third floor, a varnished hallway lined with doors. We go to the last one and I pause until my heart slows to a somewhat normal rate, then knock lightly. The door swings opens. A tea kettle whistles on a hot plate. Jarrod walks over, ushers me in. "Hello," he says, his face brighter today, not so pale. "Welcome," he says to Graywolf, shaking his paw and grinning. It dawns on me that he has been able to see Graywolf all along, throughout those many brunches.

32   The room is dim, but in the corner I immediately notice something curled up in an old green armchair—a red fox in an old-fashioned black suit, its piercing black eyes glittering like mica.

Vocabulary in Context

To define the following words, select the option that best defines the word as used in the original context. Then, in the space provided, indicate which definition or synonym you selected.

whit	tantalizing	indomitable	splotched
clasp	gradations	portals	mica
prowls	opaque	inherently	
nondescript	hologram	affable	

_____ 1. Spice was a loser who ultimately cared not a *whit* for me, nor I for him really, though we had our fun. (par. 5)

   a) scrap or bit   b) dollar

_____ 2. He wears mustard yellow pants and a green shirt. Also a gray velvet cape with a hood that is fastened at the neck with a brass *clasp* that has an interwoven Celtic design on it. (par. 7)

   a) jacket   b) hook

_____ 3. While I work, Graywolf *prowls* around the office or wanders around the city. (par. 8)

   a) to hunt   b) to move quietly

____ 4. I wanted to be an actress. But I didn't have the right look, or so I was always told. Too plain, too unremarkable, too *nondescript*. I blended in too well. (par. 9)

    a) ordinary   b) descriptive

____ 5. But it was awful, like being a shadow and I hated it. I was so close to The Stage, it was *tantalizing*, yet it was just out of reach, anguishing. (par. 9)

    a) maddening   b) tempting

____ 6. Graywolf has long shaggy fur the color of twilight with all its shades and *gradations*. (par. 10)

    a) colors   b) ranges

____ 7. His form ranges from *opaque* to transparent. When the sun shines through him he looks like a hologram. (par. 11)

    a) cloudy   b) opal

____ 8. His form ranges from opaque to transparent. When the sun shines through him he looks like a *hologram*. (par. 11)

    a) holy person   b) a three-dimensional image

____ 9. There aren't many people about except for a few *indomitable* joggers, a couple of bicycles whirring past. (par. 15)

    a) unavoidable   b) impossible to subdue

____ 10. My theory is this: there are *portals* in this world that connect us to other worlds we know nothing about. (par. 18)

    a) people   b) passages

____ 11. Occasionally we glimpse these other worlds, even in science, but because our methods are *inherently* flawed, because our thoughts are inherently flawed, we dismiss them. (par. 18)

    a) fatally   b) essentially

____ 12. Pale skin, rose almost girlish lips, delicate nose, something shy and jittery yet *affable* in his manner. He glances at me, I glance at him. (par. 23)

    a) friendly   b) nervous

____ 13. Suddenly Jarrod reappears. He is standing there in his *splotched* apron, his black sneakers. (par. 30)

    a) soiled   b) painted

____ 14. The room is dim, but in the corner I immediately notice something curled up in an old green armchair—a red fox in an old-fashioned black suit, its piercing black eyes glittering like *mica*. (par. 32)

    a) a shiny, hardened mineral   b) a substance used for makeup

Checking In

1. How surprised were you to find out that Graywolf is actually a wolf? How did this fact affect you as you read the story?

2. Did the picture of Graywolf help you visualize him as you read the story? If so, explain why.

Getting the Point

3. In paragraph 2, the narrator discusses the other people who can see Graywolf. One is a homeless woman and the other is an elderly man. Why does the narrator tell the reader about these two people?

4. As discussed in Chapter 6, pivotal scenes are moments when something shifts or changes for the main character. Identify a point in the story when the narrator experiences change. Next, identify what started or caused that change for her.

5. Write a brief summary of the story

Delving Deeper

6. In paragraph 13, the narrator says, "I admit the possibility that Graywolf is the reason I am still 'alone.' On the other hand, I suppose it keeps me from falling into something that isn't real, as so many people do, out of fear or loneliness or a bizarre sense of purpose." What do you think the narrator means when she says people fall "into something that isn't real"?

7. What do you think about the narrator's theory concerning Graywolf's existence? Does it make sense in the story, or did you find it hard to believe? Explain your reasoning.

8. There is a poem within this story by the English poet William Wordsworth called "The Tables Turned." Reread the poem. How is the poem related to what's happening in the story?

9. In paragraphs 22 and 23, the narrator sees a "flash of orange-red" and "a flash of red" from the kitchen. Reread those paragraphs and discuss what you think those "flashes" of red might be.

10. What do you think drew the narrator to the paintings by Jarrod?

11. The narrator says that Graywolf "was born, perhaps, from a fairy tale." What fairy tales do you know of that have featured a wolf as a character? Is Graywolf anything like the wolves in the fairy tales or stories you've heard about? Explain the similarities or differences.

12. Consider the story of Graywolf as a modern-day fairy tale. Now, if it is a fairy tale, it must have an underlying meaning. What do you think that meaning might be?

Evaluating the Author's Strategies

13. In the story, there are times when the author describes Graywolf as having human-like qualities. At other times, he seems very dog- or wolf-like. Discuss the effect these descriptions—see paragraphs 3, 10, 11, and 23 for examples—have upon your idea of who/what Graywolf is.

The Writing Connection

The narrator of this story says, "Lots of children have invisible friends." Did you ever create a friend or a fun place in your mind when you were young? How did this imaginary creation fit into your life?

Using these two questions as a starting point, discuss and describe an invisible friend or place that you imagined when you were young. Keep in mind that when young children are playing with Barbie dolls and action figures, they are involved in imaginative creation. If, however, you never created something imaginary when you were young, discuss why you think some children do create imaginary friends or places.

Accountability and Workplace Relationships

by Lydia E. Anderson and Sandra B. Bolt
from *Professionalism: Real Skills for Workplace Success*

About the Reading

Lydia E. Anderson and Sandra B. Bolt coauthored the textbook *Professionalism: Real Skills for Workplace Success* to help prepare students for the real-world experiences they will encounter upon college graduation. The goal of the textbook is to provide students with realistic expectations and prepare them for everyday situations faced in the workplace. The selection "Accountability and Workplace Relationships" focuses on how to navigate the responsibilities and relationships that come with a position in today's workplace.

Before You Read

Do you think professional behavior is important no matter what type of job you have?

Thematic Links

- Workplace Issues
- Relationships

Part 3 Book Link

- *Listening Is an Act of Love (Work and Dedication)*

Accountability and Workplace Relationships

by Lydia E. Anderson and Sandra B. Bolt

from Professionalism: Real Skills for Workplace Success

Empowerment

In politics, business, and education, everyone should be held account-able for their actions. Unfortunately, too many people do not know what it means to be accountable. This chapter discusses the concepts of accountability and workplace relationships. The concepts of empower-ment, responsibility, and accountability are all about choices. These personal choices not only impact how successful you will be at work but have a tremendous impact on workplace relationships.

In chapter 5, we discussed power bases and how workplace power affects politics and ethical behavior. Everyone in the workplace has power. Unfortunately, everyone in the workplace does not use their power appropriately or at all. As companies put an increased focus on quality, correct decision making by employees becomes more and more important.

Empowerment is pushing power and decision making to the individuals who are closest to the customer in an effort to increase qual-ity, customer satisfaction, and, ultimately, profits. The foundation of this basic management concept means that if employees feel like they are making a direct contribution to the company's activities, they will perform better. This will then increase quality and customer satisfaction.

Consider the case of a manager of a retail customer service coun-ter telling his employee to make the customer happy. The manager feels he has empowered his employee. However, the next day, the manager walks by the employee's counter and notices that the em-ployee has given every customer refunds for their returns, even when the return did not warrant a refund. The boss immediately disciplines the employee for poor performance. But did the employee not do exactly what the manager asked the employee to do? Did the manager truly empower his employee? The answer is no. Telling someone to do something is different than showing someone the correct behavior. The employee interpreted the phrase "make the customer happy" dif-ferently from the manager's intention. The proper way for the manager to have empowered the employee would have been to discuss the com-pany's return policies, role-play various customer scenarios, and then monitor the employee as the employee applied what had been learned. If or when the employee made errors through the training process, the wrong behavior should have been immediately corrected while good performance received positive reinforcement.

When you, as an employee, demonstrate a willingness to learn, you will have accepted responsibility. **Responsibility** means to accept the power that is being given to you. If you are not being responsible, you are not fully utilizing power that has been entrusted to you. Finally, the whole concept of empowerment and responsibility is useless without accountability. **Accountability** means that you accept the responsibility and must report back to whoever gave you the power to carry out that responsibility. Employees at all levels of an organization are accountable to each other, their bosses, their customers, and the company's investors to perform their best. Each employee must take personal responsibility for his or her performance. Each employee must also be accountable for his or her actions and workplace choices.

One of the best ways to gain respect and credibility at work is to begin asking for and assuming new tasks. If you are interested in learning new skills, speak up and ask your boss to teach or provide you opportunities to increase your value to the company. Assume responsibility for these new tasks and report back (become accountable) on your performance. Remember that worthwhile activities support the company's overall mission. Each project for which you assume responsibility must have a measurable goal. If it lacks a goal, it will be difficult to be accountable for your performance.

As you increase your workplace responsibilities, do not ever be afraid to seek assistance. Also, remember that a great amount of learning and success comes from past failure. When you make mistakes, do not blame others. Determine what went wrong and why. Learn from your mistakes, and view them as opportunities to do better in the future.

Cory is rapidly becoming more confident on the job. Cory wanted to be of more value to the company and began studying the concept of personal responsibility and accountability. Cory was excited about the new concepts that were learned and began requesting extra projects at work. Cory gladly kept the boss informed on the status of each project and reported when each project was successfully completed. The boss noticed how Cory took responsibility not only for personal growth but also for the success of the department. As a result, the boss informs Cory that he is impressed with Cory's willingness to improve and is considering Cory for a promotion.

Workplace Relationships

People who are mature and confident behave consistently around others, while those who are not as secure frequently behave differently around the boss or selected colleagues. Some could argue in favor of this behavior, but it is wrong and immature to behave inconsistently around selected audiences. Boss or no boss, you should behave professionally and respectfully at all times, no matter who is around or watching. This section explains the dynamics of workplace relationships and their impact on performance.

Because we spend more time at work than we do with our families, workplace relationships have a profound impact on productivity. The bottom line is that we must treat everyone respectfully and professionally. It is easy to be respectful and professional to those we like; it is much more difficult doing so with those we dislike. Chapter 12, regarding the topic of conflict at work, addresses the sensitive issue of working productively with those whom we do not like. Unfortunately, developing strong friendships at work can be equally as damaging as creating workplace enemies if we fail to keep professional relationships separate from our personal lives. Socializing with our coworkers is both expected and acceptable to a degree, but do not make workplace relationships your only circle of friends. Doing so is dangerous because it becomes difficult to separate personal and work issues. It also has the potential to create distrust among employees who are not included in your circle of workplace friends. Finally, it creates the potential for you to unknowingly or subconsciously show favoritism toward your friends. Even if you are not showing favoritism, those who are not within the circle of friends may perceive favoritism and may become distrustful of you.

As you become more comfortable with your job and company, you will be in various situations that provide opportunities to strengthen workplace relationships with coworkers, executives, investors, vendors, and customers. The following section discusses selected situations and how best to behave in these circumstances.

Executives/Senior Officials

It is often difficult to know how to behave in a room full of executives or senior officials such as members of the board of directors. At work, there are several occasions when you may be in the presence of executives and senior officials. These may include meetings, corporate events, and social functions. While it is tempting to pull a senior official aside and tell him stories about your boss or how perfect you would be for an advanced position, this behavior is both inappropriate and unacceptable. It is important to not draw attention to yourself and always project a positive, professional image. Highlight the successes of your department and not personal accomplishments.

If you are in a meeting that you do not normally attend, do not speak up unless addressed or introduced by the chairman of the meeting. If it is convenient, before or after the meeting, it is acceptable to introduce yourself to senior officials. Remember to not interrupt. Be confident, extend a hand, and state, "Hello, Mrs. Jones, my name is Tim Brandon. I work in the accounting department. It's nice to meet you." Keep your comments brief and positive. Your objective is to create a favorable and memorable impression with the executive. Introduce yourself and make eye contact so that the executive can connect a face, name, and department. Do not speak poorly of anyone or a situation. It is also inappropriate to discuss specific work-related issues, such as wanting to change positions, unless you are in a meeting specifically to discuss that issue. Always let the executive guide the conversation and make sure to read the executive's body language. If the executive's body language includes a nodding head and his or her body is facing you, continue talking. If the executive is glancing away or his or her body is turning away from you, that body language is clearly communicating the executive's desire to be elsewhere. Therefore, tell the executive it was nice meeting him or her, excuse yourself, and leave. Use encounters with executives as opportunities to create favorable impressions for you and your department.

Your Boss

Typically, there is no middle ground when it comes to workers and their feelings for their bosses. We either love them or hate them. There are three common types of bosses: the bad (incompetent) boss, the abusive boss, and the good boss. Before we discuss how to handle each type, it is important to remember that bosses are human. Like us, they too are learning and developing their skills. Although they are not perfect, we should assume they are doing their best.

Let us begin with the bad or **incompetent boss.** An incompetent boss is one who does not know how to do his or her job. As with every work situation, no matter how bad the boss, you must remain professional and respectful. Make it your mission to make your boss look good. That's right; make your bad boss look good! Doing so demonstrates your maturity and diminishes the tension between you and your boss. Do not worry about your boss receiving credit for your hard work. Incompetence rises to the top. If your boss is a poor performer, others in the company will know your boss is not producing the good work being presented. Therefore, if you are doing good work, it will get noticed by others in the company. If your boss really is not incompetent and you and your boss just have a personality conflict, do not allow your personal feelings to affect your performance. Focus on staying positive and being of value to your boss. Even when your coworkers want to bad-mouth the boss, which is a common occurrence at work, do not give in to temptation. You must remain professional and respectful. Moreover, use your bad boss experience as a time to learn what not to do when you become a boss.

Sometime in your career, you may experience an **abusive boss.** The abusive boss is someone who is constantly belittling or intimidating his or her employees. Abusive bosses generally behave that way because they have low self-esteem. Therefore, they utilize their legitimate and coercive power to make themselves feel better by knocking someone else down. There are several ways to deal with an abusive boss. If the abuse is tolerable, do your best to work with the situation. Although common with employees of abusive bosses, do not speak poorly of your boss in public. If the situation becomes intolerable and is beginning to affect your performance, you have several options. The first is to seek confidential advice from someone in the human resource management department. This expert can begin documenting and observing the situation and take corrective action or provide needed management training to your boss. Remember to be factual in reporting inappropriate incidents. Human resource managers only want facts, not emotions. While tempting, do not go to your boss's boss. Doing so implies secrecy and distrust. If your boss's boss does not support you and/or your immediate boss finds out, your plan will backfire. Finally, if it looks as if nothing and no one can improve your boss's behavior, begin quietly looking for another job either in another department within the company or at a new company. Remember that as an employee, you have rights. If your boss ever acts discriminatory or harassing toward you, document and report the behavior immediately. Your boss cannot make you perform functions that do not reasonably support those identified in your job description. Abusive bosses commonly have employees run personal errands. If you are asked to perform unreasonable functions, you should politely decline.

If you have a **good boss,** be thankful but cautious. A good boss is one who is respectful and fair and is grooming you for a promotion. It frequently becomes tempting to develop a personal friendship with a good boss. You must remember to keep the relationship professional. While it is okay to share important activities occurring in your personal life with your boss (e.g., spouse and child issues, vacation plans), you should never divulge too much information. Take advantage of your good boss and use him or her as a professional mentor. Identify what management qualities make your boss valued and begin imitating these qualities in your own workplace behavior. Regardless of what type of boss you have, always give your personal best.

Exercise 1

About Your Boss: *What kind of boss have you worked for—incompetent, abusive, or good? Provide at least two specific examples to support your assessment. If you have never held a job before, ask a friend or family member.*

What kind of boss do you have? Provide examples to support assessment.

_____

_____

_____

_____

COLLEAGUES

Having friends at work is nice. Unfortunately, when workplace friendships go awry, it affects your job. It is for this reason that you should be cautious about friendships developed at work. A friend is someone whom you trust and who knows your strengths and weaknesses. While we should be able to trust all coworkers, they should not know everything about you. It is important to be friendly to everyone at work. There will be some with whom you want to develop a friendship outside of work, but beware. If there is a misunderstanding either at work or away from work, the relationship can go sour and affect both areas. If one of you gets promoted and suddenly becomes the boss of the other, it also creates an awkward situation for both parties. Even if you can both get beyond this issue, others at work may feel like outsiders or feel you are playing favorites with your friend. Finally, if you only socialize with friends developed at work, you risk the danger of getting too absorbed in work issues. The one common thread that binds your friendship is work. Therefore, it is work that you will most likely discuss when you are together. This can be unhealthy and could potentially create a conflict of interest in the decisions you make at work.

OTHERS WITHIN THE ORGANIZATION

The topic of friendships in the workplace should be extended to those throughout the organization. You are, however, encouraged to increase your professional network by meeting others within your company. As discussed in chapter 5, as we build our connection power, we are gaining additional knowledge and contacts to assist us in performing our jobs and perhaps earning future promotions. This is called *networking*. When you interact with others in the organization, remember to keep your conversations positive and respectful of others. Even if the other individual steers the conversation in a negative direction, respond with a positive comment. Do not ever be afraid to defend coworkers when another employee is talking ill about them.

For example, one day, Cory and a friend were sitting in the break room when Vicki, the department's unhappy coworker, walked in. "I just can't stand John!" declared Vicki. "That's too bad. John's a friend of mine," responded Cory's friend. Vicki stood there red-faced, turned around, and left the room. Cory told the friend that Cory never knew he and John were close. "Well," responded the friend, "we're not personal friends, but we work together." The friend went on to explain that it is easy to eliminate negative conversation when you immediately communicate that you will not tolerate bad-mouthing others. Cory thought that was pretty good advice.

Each company should have a **corporate culture (organizational culture)**. Think of corporate culture as the company's personality being reflected through its employees' behavior. The company's culture is its shared values and beliefs. For example, if the company's management team openly communicates and promotes teamwork, the company will most likely have excellent communication and successful teams. In contrast, executives who are always stressed and reacting to crisis situations will create a workplace atmosphere based on stress and crisis management. A company's corporate culture has an enormous impact on **employee morale.** Employee morale is the attitude employees have toward the company. This attitude is a result of the company's corporate culture.

Improving Morale: *What can you do to help improve the employee morale in your workplace?*

Exercise 2

What workplace behavior contributes to poor employee morale?

WHEN RELATIONSHIPS TURN NEGATIVE

Unresolved conflict happens to the best of relationships. Due to a conflict or misunderstanding, a relationship may go bad. Unfortunately, at work, this happens. Sometimes you have no idea what you have done wrong. In other cases, you may be the one that wants to end the relationship. As stated earlier in the text, you do not have to like everyone at work, but no one should know the better. You must show everyone respect and you must behave professionally, even to your adversaries.

If you are the victim of a bad relationship, you need to take the following steps in dealing with the situation:

- If you harmed the other person (intentionally or unintentionally), apologize immediately.
- Tell the other person that you value his or her friendship.
- If the other person accepts your apology, demonstrate your regret by changing your behavior.

- If the other person does not accept your apology and your apology was sincere, you must move on. You must still demonstrate your regret by changing your behavior.
- If you lose the relationship, do not hold a grudge. Continue being polite, respectful, and professional to your lost friend.
- If the lost friend acts rude or inappropriate, do not retaliate by returning the poor behavior. Respond in kindness.
- If the rude and inappropriate behavior impacts your performance or is hostile or harassing, document the situation and inform your boss.

Erin had been one of Cory's favorite coworkers since Cory's first day at work. They took breaks together and at least once a week went out for lunch. One day Cory was working on a project with a short deadline. Erin invited Cory out to lunch and Cory politely declined, explaining why. The next day, Cory asked Erin to lunch and Erin just gave Cory a funny look and turned away. "Erin, what's wrong?" Cory asked. Erin just shook her head and left the room. Cory left Erin alone for a few days, hoping whatever the matter was would boil over and things would be better. After a week of Erin ignoring Cory, things only got worse. Cory decided to try one last time to save the relationship. As Cory approached Erin, Cory said, "Erin, I'm sorry for whatever I've done to upset you and I'd like for us to talk about it." Unfortunately, Erin again gave Cory a hollow look and walked away.

The toughest step when addressing a broken relationship is when the other individual does not accept your apology. We have grown up believing that we must like everyone and that everyone must like us. Because of human nature, this simply is not possible. We cannot be friends with everyone at work. Moreover, people get their feelings hurt and some find it hard to forgive. Your focus at work should be, first and foremost, getting the job done. Any behavior that is not respectful and professional interferes with performance. Remember that the company is paying you to perform. Therefore, if a sour relationship begins to impact your performance, you must respond. First ask yourself if your behavior is contributing to the unresolved conflict. If it is, you must change your behavior immediately. If your wronged coworker is upset or hurt, he or she will most likely begin bad-mouthing you. Do not fuel the fire by retaliating by speaking ill of your coworker. This only makes both of you look petty and immature. Document the facts of the incident and remain a mature adult. If the bad behavior continues for a reasonable period of time and it affects your performance, it is time to seek assistance. This is why documentation is important.

At this point, you must contact your immediate supervisor for an intervention. When you meet with your supervisor, explain the situation in a factual and unemotional manner. Provide specific examples of the offensive behavior and document any witnesses. Do not approach your supervisor to get the other individual in trouble. Your objective is to secure your boss's assistance in creating a mutually respectful and professional working relationship with your coworker. The boss may call you and the coworker into the boss's office to discuss the situation. Do not become emotional during this meeting. Your objective is to come to an agreement on behaving respectfully and professionally at work.

DATING AT WORK

A sticky but common workplace relationship issue is that of dating other employees, vendors, or customers of your place of employment. Because we spend so much time at work, it is natural for coworkers to look for companionship in the workplace. While a company cannot prevent you from dating coworkers who are in your immediate work area, many companies discourage the practice. Some companies go as far as having employees who are romantically involved sign statements releasing the company from any liability should the relationship turn sour. It is highly inappropriate for you to date your boss or if you are a supervisor for you to date your employees. Doing so exposes you, your romantic interest, and your company to potential sexual harassment charges. Your actions will impact your entire department and will most likely make everyone uncomfortable.

If you date customers and vendors/suppliers of your company, use caution. In dating either customers or vendors, you must ask yourself how the changed relationship can potentially impact your job. Remember that you are representing your company 24/7. Therefore, you should never share confidential information or speak poorly of your colleagues or employer. You should be careful to not put yourself in a situation in which you could be accused of a conflict of interest. In short, it is always best to keep your romantic life separate from that of the workplace.

SOCIALIZING

Work-related social activities such as company picnics, potlucks, and birthday celebrations are extremely common. While some individuals enjoy attending these social functions, others clearly do not. You do not have to attend any work-related social function outside of your normal work hours. However, it is often considered rude if you do not attend social functions that occur at the workplace during work hours. If you are working on an important deadline and simply cannot attend, briefly stop by the function and apologize to whoever is hosting the event. If you attend a work-related social function, check to see if guests are being requested to bring items to the party. If you plan on attending, you should bring an item if one is requested. It is considered impolite to show up to a potluck empty-handed. It is also considered rude to take home a plate of leftovers unless offered. Alcohol should not be served on work premises.

Attendance at work-related social events occurring outside the work site is considered optional. As discussed in chapter 6, if the invitation requires an RSVP, be sure to send your reservation or regrets in a timely manner. If you choose not to attend an off-site activity, be sure to thank whoever invited you. This maintains a positive work relationship. If you do attend, do not show up empty-handed and always thank the host for the invitation when arriving and when leaving. If alcohol is being served at a work-related function off of the work site, use caution when consuming alcohol. It is best to not consume at all; but, if you must consume, limit yourself to one drink.

BREAKS AND THE BREAK ROOM

It is a common practice for offices to have a community coffeepot. This means that coffee is available to everyone in the office. Unfortunately, in most cases, the company does not pay for this benefit. The coffee, snacks, and other supplies are typically provided by the boss or someone else in the office. It is common for people to informally contribute to the coffee fund. If you routinely drink coffee or eat the office snacks, you should contribute funds to help pay for this luxury. The same goes for office treats such as doughnuts, cookies, or birthday cakes. If you partake, offer to defer the cost or take your turn bringing treats one day. Many offices have a refrigerator available for employees to store their meals. It is considered stealing to eat someone else's food. Do not help yourself to food being stored in the community refrigerator. If you store your food in this area, remember to throw out any unused or spoiled food at the end of each workweek. Finally, remember to always clean up after yourself. If you use a coffee cup, wash it and put it away when you are finished. Throw away your trash, and leave the break room clean for the next person.

MISCELLANEOUS WORKPLACE ISSUES

While it is tempting to sell fund-raising items at work, the practice is questionable. Some companies have policies prohibiting this practice. If the practice is acceptable, do not pester people nor make them feel guilty if they decline to make a purchase.

It is common and acceptable to give a gift to a friend commemorating special days such as birthdays and holidays. However, you do not have to give gifts to anyone at work. If you are a gift giver, do so discreetly so as to not offend others who do not receive gifts from you. If you advance into a management position, do not give a gift to just one employee. If you choose to give gifts, you must give gifts to all employees and treat everyone equally.

It is also common for employees to pitch in and purchase a group gift for special days such as Boss's Day and Administrative Assistant's Day. While it is not mandatory to contribute to these gifts, it is generally expected that you contribute. If you strongly object or cannot afford to participate, politely decline without attaching a negative comment. If price is the issue, contribute whatever amount you deem reasonable and explain that you are on a budget. If you are the receiver of a gift, verbally thank the gift giver immediately and follow up with a handwritten thank-you note.

SUMMARY OF KEY CONCEPTS

- It is important to take responsibility for the job you perform by being accountable for your actions
- Keep workplace friendships positive, but be cautious that these relationships not be your only friendships away from the workplace
- If a workplace relationship turns negative, remember to remain professional and respectful
- It is best to refrain from dating anyone at work
- Practice good etiquette at social functions that occur within the office

WORKPLACE DO'S AND DON'TS

Do take responsibility for your performance and success at work

Do display consistent, professional behavior

Do always make your boss look good

Do create positive relationships with coworkers

Do practice business etiquette at work-related social functions

Don't wait for someone to tell you what to do

Don't behave appropriately only when the boss is around

Don't speak poorly of your boss

Don't make your workplace friendships your primary friendships away from work

Don't ignore the importance of behaving professionally at work-related social functions

KEY TERMS

abusive boss
accountability
corporate culture
(organizational culture)

employee morale
empowerment
good boss

incompetent boss
responsibility

Getting the Point

IF YOU WERE THE BOSS …

1. How could you get employees excited about assuming additional responsibilities?

2. If you noticed employee morale dropping in your department, how would you respond?

3. How would you handle two employees whose friendship had turned negative?

4. You never give your employees gifts, but one of your employees always gives you gifts for holidays, birthdays, and boss's day. Is it wrong for you to accept these gifts?

For the following items, fill in the blank with information provided in the reading selection.

5. _____ is the attitude employees have toward the company.

6. If you ever harm another, immediately _____.

7. Any behavior that is not _____ or professional interferes with _____.

8. Be cautious in engaging in _____ with coworkers, customers, vendors, or your boss

9. You ____ have to attend any work-related social function outside of your normal work hours.

10. If ____ is being served at a work-related function off of the work site, use caution when consuming, or better yet, do not.

11. If you partake of office treats, it is good manners to _____.

12. Just like at home, you must always _____ in the break room.

13. It is best to not sell _____ items at work.

Delving Deeper

14. You are supposed to attend a meeting tomorrow. Overnight, you have a family emergency. What should you do? Explain your answer.

15. Your boss is always bad-mouthing or belittling your coworkers. You do not like it and you wonder what he says about you when you are not around. What should you do?

16. The company that services your office equipment has hired a new sales-person. This person does not wear a wedding ring and flirts with you. If you go out on a date with this person, what are at least three potential work-related problems that could occur?

Directions: For the chart below, decide whether it is appropriate to discuss the following company information with individuals outside of the company. Why or why not?

INFORMATION	YES OR NO	WHY OR WHY NOT?
17. Key clients/customers		
18. Financial information		
19. Boss's work style		
20. Company mission statement		
21. Names of members of the company's board of directors		

Why Exercise Won't Make You Thin

by John Cloud

About the Reading

John Cloud has been a staff writer for *Time* magazine since 1997. *Time* is a weekly newsmagazine that was first published in 1923; it was the first newsmagazine to be published in the United States. The magazine is known for its original reporting, news analysis, and photojournalism. The article "Why Exercises Won't Make You Thin" was the cover story of the August 17, 2009, U.S. edition of the magazine. The cover headline read: "The Myth About Exercise."

Before You Read

What is your first reaction to the title of this article? Do you believe what it asserts?

Thematic Links

- Health
- Psychology

Why Exercise Won't Make You Thin

By John Cloud

1. Discusses
workout routine

1   As I write this, tomorrow is Tuesday, which is a cardio day. I'll spend five minutes warming up on the VersaClimber, a towering machine that requires you to move your arms and legs simultaneously. Then I'll do 30 minutes on a stair mill. On Wednesday a personal trainer will work me like a farm animal for an hour, sometimes to the point that I am dizzy—an abuse for which I pay as much as I spend on groceries in a week. Thursday is "body wedge" class,  which involves another exercise contraption, this one a large foam wedge from which I will push myself up in various hateful ways for an hour. Friday will bring a 5.5-mile run, the extra half-mile my grueling expiation of any gastronomical indulgences during the week.

2   I have exercised like this—obsessively, a bit grimly—for years, but recently I began to wonder: Why am I doing this? Except for a two-year period at the end of an unhappy relationship—a period when I self-medicated with lots of Italian desserts—I have never been overweight. One of the most widely accepted, commonly repeated assumptions in our culture is that if you exercise, you will lose weight. But I exercise all the time, and since I ended that relationship and cut most of those desserts, my weight has returned to the same 163 lb. it has been most of my adult life. I still have gut fat that hangs over my belt when I sit. Why isn't all the exercise wiping it out?

2. Why isn't exercise helping him lose weight?

3   It's a question many of us could ask. More than 45 million Americans now belong to a health club, up from 23 million in 1993. We spend some $19 billion a year on gym memberships. Of course, some people join and never go. Still, as one major study—the Minnesota Heart Survey—found, more of us at least say we exercise regularly. The survey ran from 1980, when only 47% of respondents said they engaged in regular exercise, to 2000, when the figure had grown to 57%.

4   And yet obesity figures have risen dramatically in the same period: a third of Americans are obese, and another third count as overweight by the Federal Government's definition. Yes, it's entirely possible that those of us who regularly go to the gym would weigh even more if we exercised less. But like many other people, I get hungry after I exercise, so I often eat more on the days I work out than on the days I don't. Could exercise actually be keeping me from losing weight?

5   The conventional wisdom that exercise is essential for shedding pounds is actually fairly new. As recently as the 1960s, doctors routinely advised against rigorous exercise, particularly for older adults who could injure themselves. Today doctors encourage even their oldest patients to exercise, which is sound advice for many reasons: People who regularly exercise are at significantly lower risk for all manner of diseases—those of the heart in particular. They less often develop cancer, diabetes and many other illnesses. But the past few years of obesity research show that the role of exercise in weight loss has been wildly overstated.

6   "In general, for weight loss, exercise is pretty useless," says Eric Ravussin, chair in diabetes and metabolism at Louisiana State University and a prominent exercise researcher. Many recent studies have found that exercise isn't as important in helping people lose weight as you hear so regularly in gym advertisements or on shows like The Biggest Loser—or, for that matter, from magazines like this one.

7   The basic problem is that while it's true that exercise burns calories and that you must burn calories to lose weight, exercise has another effect: it can stimulate hunger. That causes us to eat more, which in turn can negate the weight-loss benefits we just accrued. Exercise, in other words, isn't necessarily helping us lose weight. It may even be making it harder.

The Compensation Problem

8   Earlier this year, the peer-reviewed journal *PLoS ONE*—PLoS is the nonprofit Public Library of Science—published a remarkable study supervised by a colleague of Ravussin's, Dr. Timothy Church, who holds the rather grand title of chair in health wisdom at LSU. Church's team randomly assigned into four groups 464 overweight women who didn't regularly exercise. Women in three of the groups were asked to work out with a personal trainer for 72 min., 136 min., and 194 min. per week, respectively, for six months. Women in the fourth cluster, the control group, were told to maintain their usual physical-activity routines. All the women were asked not to change their dietary habits and to fill out monthly medical-symptom questionnaires.

9   The findings were surprising. On average, the women in all the groups, even the control group, lost weight, but the women who exercised—sweating it out with a trainer several days a week for six months—did not lose significantly more weight than the control subjects did. (The control-group women may have lost weight because they were filling out those regular health forms, which may have prompted them to consume fewer doughnuts.) Some of the women in each of the four groups actually gained weight, some more than 10 lb. each.

10   What's going on here? Church calls it compensation, but you and I might know it as the lip-licking anticipation of perfectly salted, golden-brown French fries after a hard trip to the gym. Whether because exercise made them hungry or because they wanted to reward themselves (or both), most of the women who exercised ate more than they did before they started the experiment. Or they compensated in another way, by moving around a lot less than usual after they got home.

11   The findings are important because the government and various medical organizations routinely prescribe more and more exercise for those who want to lose weight. In 2007 the American College of Sports Medicine and the American Heart Association issued new guidelines stating that "to lose weight… 60 to 90 minutes of physical activity may be necessary." That's 60 to 90 minutes on most days of the week, a level that not only is unrealistic for those of us trying to keep or find a job but also could easily produce, on the basis of Church's data, ravenous compensatory eating.

12   It's true that after six months of working out, most of the exercisers in Church's study were able to trim their waistlines slightly—by about an inch. Even so, they lost no more overall body fat than the control group did. Why not?

13   Church, who is 41 and has lived in Baton Rouge for nearly three years, has a theory. "I see this anecdotally amongst, like, my wife's friends," he says. "They're like, 'Ah, I'm running an hour a day, and I'm not losing any weight.'" He asks them, "What are you doing after you run?" It turns out one group of friends was stopping at Starbucks for muffins afterward. Says Church: "I don't think most people would appreciate that, wow, you only burned 200 or 300 calories, which you're going to neutralize with just half that muffin."

14   You might think half a muffin over an entire day wouldn't matter much, particularly if you exercise regularly. After all, doesn't exercise turn fat to muscle, and doesn't muscle process excess calories more efficiently than fat does?

15   Yes, although the muscle-fat relationship is often misunderstood. According to calculations published in the journal Obesity Research by a Columbia University team in 2001, a pound of muscle burns approximately six calories a day in a resting body, compared with the two calories that a pound of fat burns. Which means that after you work out hard enough to convert, say, 10 lb. of fat to muscle—a major achievement—you would be able to eat only an extra 40 calories per day, about the amount in a teaspoon of butter, before beginning to gain weight. Good luck with that.

16   Fundamentally, humans are not a species that evolved to dispose of many extra calories beyond what we need to live. Rats, among other species, have a far greater capacity to cope with excess calories than we do because they have more of a dark-colored tissue called brown fat. Brown fat helps produce a protein that switches off little cellular units called mitochondria, which are the cells' power plants: they help turn nutrients into energy. When they're switched off, animals don't get an energy boost. Instead, the animals literally get warmer. And as their temperature rises, calories burn effortlessly.

17   Because rodents have a lot of brown fat, it's very difficult to make them obese, even when you force-feed them in labs. But humans—we're pathetic. We have so little brown fat that researchers didn't even report its existence in adults until earlier this year. That's one reason humans can gain weight with just an extra half-muffin a day: we almost instantly store most of the calories we don't need in our regular ("white") fat cells.

18   All this helps explain why our herculean exercise over the past 30 years—all the personal trainers, StairMasters and VersaClimbers; all the Pilates classes and yoga retreats and fat camps—hasn't made us thinner. After we exercise, we often crave sugary calories like those in muffins or in "sports" drinks like Gatorade. A standard 20-oz. bottle of Gatorade contains 130 calories. If you're hot and thirsty after a 20-minute run in summer heat, it's easy to guzzle that bottle in 20 seconds, in which case the caloric expenditure and the caloric intake are probably a wash. From a weight-loss perspective, you would have been better off sitting on the sofa knitting.

Self-Control is Like a Muscle

19   Many people assume that weight is mostly a matter of will-power—that we can learn both to exercise and to avoid muffins and Gatorade. A few of us can, but evolution did not build us to do this for very long. In 2000 the journal Psychological Bulletin published a paper

by psychologists Mark Muraven and Roy Baumeister in which they observed that self-control is like a muscle: it weakens each day after you use it. If you force yourself to jog for an hour, your self-regulatory capacity is proportionately enfeebled. Rather than lunching on a salad, you'll be more likely to opt for pizza.

20   Some of us can will ourselves to overcome our basic psychology, but most of us won't be very successful. "The most powerful determinant of your dietary intake is your energy expenditure," says Steven Gortmaker, who heads Harvard's Prevention Research Center on Nutrition and Physical Activity. "If you're more physically active, you're going to get hungry and eat more." Gortmaker, who has studied childhood obesity, is even suspicious of the playgrounds at fast-food restaurants. "Why would they build those?" he asks. "I know it sounds kind of like conspiracy theory, but you have to think, if a kid plays five minutes and burns 50 calories, he might then go inside and consume 500 calories or even 1,000."

21   Last year the International Journal of Obesity published a paper by Gortmaker and Kendrin Sonneville of Children's Hospital Boston noting that "there is a widespread assumption that increasing activity will result in a net reduction in any energy gap"—energy gap being the term scientists use for the difference between the number of calories you use and the number you consume. But Gortmaker and Sonneville found in their 18-month study of 538 students that when kids start to exercise, they end up eating more—not just a little more, but an average of 100 calories more than they had just burned.

22   If evolution didn't program us to lose weight through exercise, what did it program us to do? Doesn't exercise do anything?

23   Sure. It does plenty. In addition to enhancing heart health and helping prevent disease, exercise improves your mental health and cognitive ability. A study published in June in the journal Neurology found that older people who exercise at least once a week are 30% more likely to maintain cognitive function than those who exercise less. Another study, released by the University of Alberta a few weeks ago, found that people with chronic back pain who exercise four days a week have 36% less disability than those who exercise only two or three days a week.

24   But there's some confusion about whether it is exercise—sweaty, exhausting, hunger-producing bursts of activity done exclusively to benefit our health—that leads to all these benefits or something far simpler: regularly moving during our waking hours. We all need to move more—the Centers for Disease Control and Prevention says our leisure-time physical activity (including things like golfing, gardening and walking) has decreased since the late 1980s, right around the time

the gym boom really exploded. But do we need to stress our bodies at the gym?

25   Look at kids. In May a team of researchers at Peninsula Medical School in the U.K. traveled to Amsterdam to present some surprising findings to the European Congress on Obesity. The Peninsula scientists had studied 206 kids, ages 7 to 11, at three schools in and around Plymouth, a city of 250,000 on the southern coast of England. Kids at the first school, an expensive private academy, got an average of 9.2 hours per week of scheduled, usually rigorous physical education. Kids at the two other schools—one in a village near Plymouth and the other an urban school—got just 2.4 hours and 1.7 hours of PE per week, respectively.

26   To understand just how much physical activity the kids were getting, the Peninsula team had them wear ActiGraphs, light but sophisticated devices that measure not only the amount of physical movement the body engages in but also its intensity. During four one-week periods over consecutive school terms, the kids wore the ActiGraphs nearly every waking moment.

27   And no matter how much PE they got during school hours, when you look at the whole day, the kids from the three schools moved the same amount, at about the same intensity. The kids at the fancy private school underwent significantly more physical activity before 3 p.m., but overall they didn't move more. "Once they get home, if they are very active in school, they are probably staying still a bit more because they've already expended so much energy," says Alissa Frémeaux, a biostatistician who helped conduct the study. "The others are more likely to grab a bike and run around after school."

28   Another British study, this one from the University of Exeter, found that kids who regularly move in short bursts—running to catch a ball, racing up and down stairs to collect toys—are just as healthy as kids who participate in sports that require vigorous, sustained exercise.

29   Could pushing people to exercise more actually be contributing to our obesity problem? In some respects, yes. Because exercise depletes not just the body's muscles but the brain's self-control "muscle" as well, many of us will feel greater entitlement to eat a bag of chips during that lazy time after we get back from the gym. This explains why exercise could make you heavier—or at least why even my wretched four hours of exercise a week aren't eliminating all my fat. It's likely that I am more sedentary during my nonexercise hours than I would be if I didn't exercise with such Puritan fury. If I exercised less, I might feel like walking more instead of hopping into a cab; I might have enough energy to shop for food, cook and then clean instead of ordering a satisfyingly greasy burrito.

Closing the Energy Gap

30   The problem ultimately is about not exercise itself but the way we've come to define it. Many obesity researchers now believe that very frequent, low-level physical activity—the kind humans did for tens of thousands of years before the leaf blower was invented—may actually work better for us than the occasional bouts of exercise you get as a gym rat. "You cannot sit still all day long and then have 30 minutes of exercise without producing stress on the muscles," says Hans-Rudolf Berthoud, a neurobiologist at LSU's Pennington Biomedical Research Center who has studied nutrition for 20 years. "The muscles will ache, and you may not want to move after. But to burn calories, the muscle movements don't have to be extreme. It would be better to distribute the movements throughout the day."

31   For his part, Berthoud rises at 5 a.m. to walk around his neighborhood several times. He also takes the stairs when possible. "Even if people can get out of their offices, out from in front of their computers, they go someplace like the mall and then take the elevator," he says. "This is the real problem, not that we don't go to the gym enough."

32   I was skeptical when Berthoud said this. Don't you need to raise your heart rate and sweat in order to strengthen your cardiovascular system? Don't you need to push your muscles to the max in order to build them?

33   Actually, it's not clear that vigorous exercise like running carries more benefits than a moderately strenuous activity like walking while carrying groceries. You regularly hear about the benefits of exercise in news stories, but if you read the academic papers on which these stories are based, you frequently see that the research subjects who were studied didn't clobber themselves on the elliptical machine. A routine example: in June the Association for Psychological Science issued a news release saying that "physical exercise... may indeed preserve or enhance various aspects of cognitive functioning." But in fact, those who had better cognitive function merely walked more and climbed more stairs. They didn't even walk faster; walking speed wasn't correlated with cognitive ability.

34   There's also growing evidence that when it comes to preventing certain diseases, losing weight may be more important than improving cardiovascular health. In June, Northwestern University researchers released the results of the longest observational study ever to investigate the relationship between aerobic fitness and the development of diabetes. The results? Being aerobically fit was far less important than having a normal body mass index in preventing the disease. And as we have seen, exercise often does little to help heavy people reach a normal weight.

*Bill
Clinton's
Diet
and
Exercise*

35   So why does the belief persist that exercise leads to weight loss, given all the scientific evidence to the contrary? Interestingly, until the 1970s, few obesity researchers promoted exercise as critical for weight reduction. As recently as 1992, when a stout Bill Clinton became famous for his jogging and McDonald's habits, the American Journal of Clinical Nutrition published an article that began, "Recently, the interest in the potential of adding exercise to the treatment of obesity has increased." The article went on to note that incorporating exercise training into obesity treatment had led to "inconsistent" results. "The increased energy expenditure obtained by training may be compensated by a decrease in non-training physical activities," the authors wrote.

36   Then how did the exercise-to-lose-weight mantra become so ingrained? Public-health officials have been reluctant to downplay exercise because those who are more physically active are, overall, healthier. Plus, it's hard even for experts to renounce the notion that exercise is essential for weight loss. For years, psychologist Kelly Brownell ran a lab at Yale that treated obese patients with the standard, drilled-into-your-head combination of more exercise and less food. "What we found was that the treatment of obesity was very frustrating," he says. Only about 5% of participants could keep the weight off, and although those 5% were more likely to exercise than those who got fat again, Brownell says if he were running the program today, "I would probably reorient toward food and away from exercise." In 2005, Brownell co-founded Yale's Rudd Center for Food Policy and Obesity, which focuses on food marketing and public policy—not on encouraging more exercise.

37   Some research has found that the obese already "exercise" more than most of the rest of us. In May, Dr. Arn Eliasson of the Walter Reed Army Medical Center reported the results of a small study that found that overweight people actually expend significantly more calories every day than people of normal weight—3,064 vs. 2,080. He isn't the first researcher to reach this conclusion. As science writer Gary Taubes noted in his 2007 book *Good Calories, Bad Calories: Fats, Carbs, and the Controversial Science of Diet and Health*, "The obese tend to expend more energy than lean people of comparable height, sex, and bone structure, which means their metabolism is typically burning off more calories rather than less."

38   In short, it's what you eat, not how hard you try to work it off, that matters more in losing weight. You should exercise to improve your health, but be warned: fiery spurts of vigorous exercise could lead to weight gain. I love how exercise makes me feel, but tomorrow I might skip the VersaClimber—and skip the blueberry bar that is my usual postexercise reward.

Vocabulary in Context

To define the following words, use the dictionary snapshots to identify the appropriate definition. Then, find a *synonym* for the word, and write the synonym in the space provided.

simultaneously	anecdote	wretched
contraption	dispose	sedentary
expiation	herculean	mantra
rigorous	enfeeble	ingrain
accrue	expend	
compensation	entitlement	

si·mul·ta·ne·ous (sī″məl-ta′nė-əs) *adj.* existing, occurring, or operating at the same time. —**si″mul·ta·ne′i·ty** (-tə-nā′ə-tė), **si″mul·ta′ne·ous·ness**, *n.*

con·trap·tion (kən-trap′shen) *n.* (*Informal*) a contrivance or gadget.

ex′pi·ate″ (eks′pė-at″) *v.t.* atone for; make amends for. —**ex″pi·a′tion**, *n.*

rig·or (rig′ər) *n.* **1,** stiffness; inflexibility. **2,** strictness; austerity; sternness. Also, **rig′our. —rig′or·ous,** *adj.* —**ri″gor mor′tis** (rig″ər môr′tis) (*Lat.*) the stiffening of the body after death.

ac·crue (ə-kroo′) *v.i.* happen in due course; result from natural growth.

com·pen·sa·tion (kom″pən-sā′shən) *n.* **1,** act or result of compensating; offset; pay. **2,** regular payments, in lieu of wages, to a worker injured on the job: *workmen's compensation.*

an·ec·dote (an′ek-dōt″) *n.* a short narrative of an occurrence. —**an″ec·do′tal,** *adj.*

dis·pose (dis′pōz) *v.t.* **1,** place in a particular order; arrange. **2,** regulate; adjust. **3,** incline the mind or heart of. —*v.i.* **1,** (with *of*) part with. **2,** control. —**dis·pos′a·ble,** *adj.* —**dis·pos′al,** *n.*

her·cu′le·an (hēr-kū′-lė-ən) *adj.* endurance, etc. **Herculean** after the Greek demigod *Hercules,* son of Zeus, who possessed superhuman strength.

en·fee′ble (en′fē′bəl) *adj.* **1,** to make feeble. **2,** deprive of strength.

ex·pend (ik-spend′) *v.t.* **1,** use up. **2,** pay out; spend. —**ex·pend′a·ble,** *adj.* dispensable, not too valuable to spare.

en·ti·tle·ment (ən-ti′təl-mənt) *n.* guaranteeing certain benefits to a specific group: *entitlement program.*

wretch·ed (rech′ed) *adj.* **1,** miserable. **2,** mean; lowly. —**wretch′ed·ness,** *n.*

sed·en·tar·y (sed′ən-ter″ė) *adj.* **1,** characterized by a sitting position. **2,** taking little physical exercise. —**sedentary death syndrome,** death caused by inaction and poor diet.

man·tra (man′trə) *n.* a sacred word or formula used in meditation.

in·grain (in-grān′) *v.t.* fix firmly, as in the mind.

1. I'll spend five minutes warming up on the VersaClimber, a towering machine that requires you to move your arms and legs <u>simultaneously</u>.

   What synonym fits this context? _____

2. Thursday is "body wedge" class, which involves another exercise <u>contraption</u>, this one a large foam wedge from which I will push myself up in various hateful ways for an hour.

   What synonym fits this context? _____

3. Friday will bring a 5.5-mile run, the extra half-mile my grueling <u>expiation</u> of any gastronomical indulgences during the week.

   What synonym fits this context? _____

4. As recently as the 1960s, doctors routinely advised against <u>rigorous</u> exercise, particularly for older adults who could injure themselves.

   What synonym fits this context? _____

5. That causes us to eat more, which in turn can negate the weight-loss benefits we just <u>accrued</u>.

   What synonym fits this context? _____

6. Church calls it <u>compensation</u>, but you and I might know it as the lip-licking anticipation of perfectly salted, golden-brown French fries after a hard trip to the gym.

   What synonym fits this context? _____

7. "I see this <u>anecdotally</u> amongst, like, my wife's friends," he says. "They're like, 'Ah, I'm running an hour a day, and I'm not losing any weight.'" He asks them, "What are you doing after you run?"

   What synonym fits this context? _____

8. Fundamentally, humans are not a species that evolved to <u>dispose</u> of many extra calories beyond what we need to live.

   What synonym fits this context? ____

9. All this helps explain why our <u>herculean</u> exercise over the past 30 years—all the personal trainers, StairMasters and VersaClimbers; all the Pilates classes and yoga retreats and fat camps—hasn't made us thinner.

   What synonym fits this context? _____

10. If you force yourself to jog for an hour, your self-regulatory capacity is proportionately <u>enfeebled</u>.

    What synonym fits this context? _____

11. "Once they get home, if they are very active in school, they are probably staying still a bit more because they've already <u>expended</u> so much energy," says Alissa Frémeaux, a biostatistician who helped conduct the study.

    What synonym fits this context? _____

12. Because exercise depletes not just the body's muscles but the brain's self-control "muscle" as well, many of us will feel greater <u>entitlement</u> to eat a bag of chips during that lazy time after we get back from the gym.

    What synonym fits this context? ___

13. This explains why exercise could make you heavier—or at least why even my <u>wretched</u> four hours of exercise a week aren't eliminating all my fat.

    What synonym fits this context? _____

14. It's likely that I am more <u>sedentary</u> during my nonexercise hours than I would be if I didn't exercise with such Puritan fury.

    What synonym fits this context? _____

15. Then how did the exercise-to-lose-weight mantra become so <u>ingrained</u>?

    What synonym fits this context? _____

16. Then how did the exercise-to-lose-weight <u>mantra</u> become so ingrained?

    What synonym fits this context? ____

Checking In

1. What effect does the author's detailing of his exercise routine have on the reader?

2. Do you have any connection to what John Cloud is talking about? Have you ever tried to lose weight by exercising?

Getting the Point

3. According to Cloud, how can exercise make you gain more weight?

4. Why does Cloud spend three paragraphs discussing how humans store and burn calories? What is his point?

5. How does the idea of self-control contribute to Cloud's position that exercising may not lead to weight loss? Be specific in your response and use support from the article.

Delving Deeper

6. What do you find most convincing about Cloud's article? Specifically discuss the supporting details that are persuasive to you.

Evaluating the Author's Strategies

7. How does John Cloud contribute to his credibility in this article?

8. Do you think this article would be considered a reliable source if you were doing research on weight loss? Why or why not?

The Writing Connection

As a consumer in today's world, it is hard to avoid seeing advertisements for weight loss products, weight loss programs, and weight loss equipment. And that's just the weight loss advertising. There is also an abundance of information bombarding the average consumer with other ways to change how he/she looks—shinier hair, longer eyelashes, brighter smiles, and smoother skin, to name a few.

Do you think American society focuses too much on appearance and looking good? Are other personal qualities, like generosity, kindness, and integrity, dwindling or becoming deemphasized as a result of America's obsession with looks?

When Journalists Get It Wrong

by Sal Fichera

About the Author

Sal Fichera is a professional speaker, exercise physiologist, author, and wellness consultant. On the lecture circuit, he has earned a reputation for motivating audiences to take action by giving them the knowledge and skills they need to lead healthier, more youthful lifestyles.

From his television appearances on *CNN, Dateline NBC, NY1 News* and New York City's *WB11 Morning News*, Fichera has provided concise, articulate and insightful commentary on a variety of topics. He is the author of the book *Stop Aging, Start Training*, a valuable resource on how we can stop the effects of aging through proper lifestyle choices. He has also written for *Cosmopolitan, NY Daily News, Good Housekeeping*, and *Fitness Management*.

Fichera attained a master's of science degree in exercise physiology from the City University of New York and went on to found FicheraWellness, a company that blends holistic philosophy with cutting-edge scientific research. Fichera resides in New York City with his wife and son.

In the article "When Journalists Get It Wrong," Fichera challenges the claims made by John Cloud in the previous reading.

Before You Read

This article responds to ideas presented in "Why Exercise Won't Make You Thin." Does the background of the author and title of this article give you an idea of what it will be about?

Thematic Links

■ Health

When Journalists Get It Wrong

By Sal Fichera

1   Journalists are bright, educated people. Most research and verify the information they include in articles they write about before submitting a piece for publication. Unfortunately, however, cursory research cannot overcome the lack of knowledge that occurs when journalists cover topics for which they have no expertise. Consequently, while they may be skilled at writing stories, their stories may not always be accurate.

2   This is precisely what happened when a *Time* magazine cover story declared, "Why Exercise Won't Make You Thin." This article was about how exercise doesn't help with weight loss. Considering the facts that most Americans hate and/or avoid exercise and most Americans (70%) are overweight, this may appear to be news for celebration.

3   But don't start eating the icing on that cake just yet; there are major misconceptions that make this news more sour than sweet.

4   In the August 17, 2009 issue of *Time*, John Cloud wrote the article, "Why Exercise Won't Make You Thin." His view is that exercise will make you fatter; he states that when you exercise, your appetite increases, thereby causing you to consume more calories than you'll burn. Although this may be true in rare circumstances, this is generally the opposite from what commonly occurs.

5   Naturally, if you burn 300 calories in one hour of exercise, you will need to eat more than usual. The key, and the natural tendency, is to eat fewer calories than you burned, thereby creating a "calorie deficit"—even if that calorie deficit is only 50 calories. Two things will begin to happen over time: you'll start to feel better about yourself and more easily become mindful of the quality (as well as quantity) of calories you eat, and your metabolism will rise, helping your body to burn fat tissue around-the-clock—something you can't do through diet alone.

6   There are three other contentious points in Cloud's article. In the first, Cloud states correctly that there are 45 million Americans who belong to gyms and that obesity has been rising. However, it's incorrect to make an association between the two. Just because the two exist within the same span of time, asserting that health clubs and exercise are therefore ineffective at halting the obesity epidemic is faulty reasoning. One factor simply has nothing to do with the other. The total number of gym members makes up only 15% of USA's population. Of the 45 million gym members, perhaps 30–40% of them work out regularly,

bringing the total to 6% of our population. It's virtually impossible for such a small portion of Americans to have enough of an impact on the 35+% of Americans who are obese—or the 70+% who are overweight.

7　The bitter truth of this situation is that the reason obesity keeps rising is partly because of the fact that more people don't belong to gyms. Also, one overlooked factor is that diets have exploded in popularity over the past 20 years, concurrent to the rapid rise in obesity; recognizing that 90% of all diets fail, perhaps it's time to get dieters to join gyms and start moving their glutes!

8　Cloud also claims that a pound of muscle burns only 6 calories per day and that you can convert fat to muscle—two mistakes in one paragraph. First of all, each pound of muscle burns between 30 and 50 calories per day. By adding 10 pounds of muscle tissue, your metabolism would rise by 300 to 500 calories per day, whether you are standing, sitting, or lying down. Secondly, fat and muscle are two discrete tissues; one doesn't convert to the other. Muscles do, however, burn fat.

9　Finally, the biggest error is when Cloud states, "pushing people to exercise more actually could be contributing to our obesity problem." He reasons that "exercise depletes not just the body's muscles, but the brain's self-control muscle as well." In reality, exercise increases energy flow, improves mood and mental function, and encourages people to eat more healthfully. It's when we don't exercise that our hormones become unbalanced, blood flow to the brain slows down, blood sugar becomes unbalanced, and cravings for unwholesome foods rise.

10　The moral to this story is, don't believe everything you read—even if it is in a national magazine like *Time*. Even scientific studies can be poorly designed. As we all know, if something sounds too good to be true, that's because it is. To assist you with navigating through the plethora of health articles that promise you the next best idea, always remember the two basic principles of human design:

> The human body was designed to absorb proper (healthful) nutrients; and
> The human body was designed to be in motion.

11　By following both principles, you will be healthier, more energized... and leaner.

12　It's difficult to know what to believe when gathering information through the media. There is no shortage of myths, misperceptions, and misinterpretations in the health field, and, unfortunately, editors don't leave the writing on health topics to health experts. There are journalists who write about health, even though they don't specialize in health sciences, and this is dangerous because we are, after all, talking about people's health.

Vocabulary in Context

Use the vocabulary strategies covered in Chapter 3 to *define* these words from the article. The paragraph in which the word is used is given in parentheses. Use the vocabulary strategies as much as possible before you refer to a dictionary. Once you feel confident about your definitions, use the words to complete the sentences that follow.

cursory (par. 1)   epidemic (par. 6)
misconception (par. 3)   concurrent (par. 7)
metabolism (par. 5)   discrete (par. 8)
contentious (par. 6)   plethora (par. 10)

1. I've known many women who used to eat whatever they wanted and had no weight gain; but now these same, formerly thin women point to their body's slowing _____ as the reason they are gaining weight.

2. The initial search was _____ , so the detectives returned to the crime scene to conduct a thorough investigation.

3. The findings are likely to fuel the debate over what's driving America's obesity _____ (Jerry Hirsch).

4. I heard a _____ of reasonable excuses, including in-depth descriptions of the big break around the corner (Stephanie Ericsson).

5. A graduate student in the clinical psychology program said the situation in Haiti is complicated because the children's trauma appears to be more chronic rather than isolated to the _____ experience of a natural disaster (Shanda Bradshaw).

6. After a few _____ conversations with Jay, I stopped trying to talk to him about his awful behavior at the restaurant.

7. Many students fail their first semester of college because they enter the classroom with the _____ that college will be just like high school.

8. The university's growth, _____ with a shrinking budget, has pushed some classes near triple-digits in attendance, putting a large burden on instructors who may know little about a student they are evaluating (Megha Satyanarayana).

Checking In

1. What expertise does the author, Sal Fichera, bring to this topic?

2. Do you think the author has the right to evaluate what another writer has published? Explain your reasoning.

Getting the Point

3. What does the author offer to contradict the idea that exercise makes you "fatter"? Restate his explanation in your own words.

4. What does Fichera feel is John Cloud's biggest mistake? Why does he feel that way?

Delving Deeper

5. Why would the idea that exercise doesn't help you lose weight make some people happy or want to "celebrate"? Support your response with information from this article.

6. How can the two principles Fichera offers help readers judge the information they read, hear, and see about health and fitness?

Evaluating the Author's Strategies

7. Do you feel that Fichera presents an objective response to John Cloud's article? Explain your reasoning.

Technology Tip

In his article, Sal Fichera does what many readers sometimes want to do: tell an author what they feel about his/her point of view. Using Fichera's example, select an article from a media source—a newspaper, online blog, or a magazine—and write a response that clarifies or disputes something the author says. Be sure to summarize the original article in your response.

Global Wealth:
Three Worlds

by James Henslin

from *Sociology: A Down-to-Earth Approach*

About the Reading

James Henslin is a professor of sociology at Southern Illinois University. In a letter to students who use his textbook *Sociology: A Down-to-Earth Approach*, he says that he has been hooked on sociology since he was a teen. The goal of his book, Henslin says, is to foster a love of discovery and investigation—central concepts in sociology—within those who read his textbook.

The textbook *Sociology: A Down-to-Earth Approach* is arranged thematically in five parts: The Sociological Perspective, Social Groups and Social Control, Social Inequality, Social Institutions, and Social Change. The excerpt included here is from Part III: Social Inequality. In this excerpt, the roots and effects of the worldwide distribution of wealth are explored.

Before You Read

Have you ever wondered how your life would be different if you had been born in a different country?

Thematic Links

- Sociology
- World Views

Part 3 Book Links

- *The Kite Runner*
- *Three Cups of Tea*

Global Wealth: Three Worlds

by James Henslin

from *Sociology: A Down-to-Earth Approach*

Let's contrast three "average" families from around the world:

For Getu Mulleta, 33, and his Zenebu, 28, of rural Ethiopia, life is a constant struggle to avoid starvation. They and their seven children live in a 320-square-foot manure-plastered hut with no electricity, gas, or running water. They have a radio, but the battery is dead. The family farms teff, a grain, and survives on $130 a year.

The Mulletas' poverty is not due to a lack of hard work. Getu works about eighty hours a week, while Zenebu puts in even more hours. "Housework" for Zenebu includes fetching water, cleaning animal stables, and making fuel pellets out of cow dung for the open fire over which she cooks the fam-

ily's food. Like other Ethiopian women, she eats after the men.

In Ethiopia, the average male can expect to live to age 48, the average female to 50.

The Mulletas' most valuable possession is their oxen. Their wishes for the future: more animals, better seed, and a second set of clothing.

****

In Guadalajara, Mexico, Ambrosio and Carmen Castillo Baldera and their five children, ages 2–10, live in a four-room house. They also have a walled courtyard, where the family spends a good deal of time. They even have a washing machine, which is hooked up to a garden hose that runs to a public water main several hundred yards away. Like most Mexicans, they do not have a telephone, nor do they own a car.

Unlike many, however, they own a refrigerator, a stereo, and a recent purchase that makes them the envy of their neighbors: a television.

Ambrosio, 29, works full-time as a wholesale distributor of produce. He also does welding on the side. The family's total annual income is $3,600. They spend 57 percent of their income on food. Carmen

The average life expectancy for males in Mexico is 70. For females, it is 76.

The Castillo Balderas' most valued possessions are the refrigerator and television. Their wish for the future: a truck.

****

Springfield, Illinois, is home to the Kellys—Rick, 36, Patti, 34, Julie, 10, and Michael, 7.

The Kellys live in a three-bedroom, 2 ½-bath, 2,524-square-foot, carpeted ranch-style house, with a fireplace, central heating and air conditioning, a basement, and a two-car garage. Their home is equipped with a refrigerator, washing machine, clothes dryer, dishwasher, garbage disposal, vacuum cleaner, food processor, microwave, and convection

works about 60 hours a week taking care of their children and keeping their home spotless. The neatness of their home stands in stark contrast to the squalor of their neighborhood, whose dirt roads are covered in litter. As in many other Mexican neighborhoods, public utilities and roadwork do not keep pace with people's needs.

stovetop and oven. They also own six telephones (three cellular), four color televisions (two high-definition), two CD players, two digital cameras, digital camcorder, two DVD players, iPod, Wii, a computer, and a printer-scanner-fax machine, not to mention two blow dryers, an answering machine, a juicer, and an espresso coffee maker. This count doesn't include such items as electric can openers, battery-powered toothbrushes, or the stereo-radio-CD/DVD players in their pickup truck and SUV.

Rick works forty hours a week as a cable splicer for a telephone company. Patti teaches school part-time. Together they make $58,407, plus benefits. The Kellys can choose from among dozens of superstocked supermarkets. They spend $4,883 for food they eat at home, and another $3,710 eating out, a total of 15 percent of their annual income.

In the United States, the average life expectancy is 75 for males, 80 for females.

On the Kellys' wish list are a new hybrid car with satellite radio, a 200-gigabyte laptop with Bluetooth Wi-Fi, a 50-inch plasma TV with surround sound, a DVD camcorder, a boat, a motor home, an ATV; and, oh, yes, farther down the road, an in-ground heated swimming pool. They also have an eye on a cabin at a nearby lake.[1]

Social & Global Stratification

Some of the world's nations are wealthy, others poor, and some in between. This division of nations, as well as the layering of groups of people within a nation, is called *social stratification*. Social stratification is one of the most significant topics we shall discuss in this book, for, as you saw in the opening vignette, it profoundly affects our life chances—from our access to material possessions to the age at which we die.

Social stratification is a system in which groups of people are divided into layers according to their relative property, power, and

---

[1]Sources: Menzel 1994; Statistical Abstract 2009: Tables 98, 666, 673, 929.

prestige. It is important to emphasize that social stratification does not refer to individuals. It is a way of ranking large groups of people into a hierarchy according to their relative privileges.

Just as the people within a nation are stratified by property, power, and prestige, so are the world's nations. Until recently, a simple model consisting of First, Second, and Third Worlds was used to depict global stratification. First World referred to the industrialized capitalist nations, Second World to the communist (or socialist) countries, and Third World to any nation that did not fit into the first two categories. The breakup of the Soviet Union in 1989 made these terms outdated. In addition, although first, second, and third did not mean "best," "better," and "worst," they implied it. An alternative classification that some now use—developed, developing, and undeveloped nations—has the same drawback. By calling ourselves "developed," it sounds as though we are mature and the "undeveloped" nations are somehow retarded.

To resolve this problem, I use more neutral, descriptive terms: *Most Industrialized, Industrializing,* and *Least Industrialized* nations. We can measure industrialization with no judgment implied as to whether a nation's industrialization represents "development," ranks it "first," or is even desirable at all. The intention is to depict on a global level the three primary dimensions of social stratification: property, power, and prestige. The Most Industrialized Nations have much greater property (wealth), power (they usually get their way in international relations), and prestige (they are looked up to as world leaders). The three families sketched in the opening vignette illustrate the far-reaching effects of global stratification.

The Most Industrialized Nations

The Most Industrialized Nations are the United States and Canada in North America; Great Britain, France, Germany, Switzerland, and the other industrialized countries of western Europe; Japan in Asia; and Australia and New Zealand in the area of the world known as Oceania. Although there are variations in their economic systems, these nations are capitalistic. As Table 9.2 shows, although these nations have only 16 percent of the world's people, they possess 31 percent of the earth's land. Their wealth is so enormous that even their poor live better and longer lives than do the average citizens of the Least Industrialized Nations.

The Industrializing Nations

The Industrializing Nations include most of the nations of the former Soviet Union and its former satellites in eastern Europe. As Table 9.2 shows, these nations account for 20

Table 9.2   Distribution of the World's Land and Population

	Land	Population
Most Industrialized Nations	31%	16%
Industrializing Nations	20%	16%
Least Industrializing Nations	49%	68%

percent of the earth's land and 16 percent of its people.

The dividing points between the three "worlds" are soft, making it difficult to know how to classify some nations. This is especially the case with the Industrializing Nations. Exactly how much industrialization must a nation have to be in this category? Although soft, these categories do pinpoint essential differences among nations. Most people who live in the Industrializing Nations have much lower incomes and standards of living than do those who live in the Most Industrialized Nations. The majority, however, are better off than those who live in the Least Industrialized Nations. For example, on such measures as access to electricity, indoor plumbing, automobiles, telephones, and even food, most citizens of the Industrializing Nations rank lower than those in the Most Industrialized Nations, but higher than those in the Least Industrialized Nations. As you saw in the opening vignette, stratification affects even life expectancy.

The benefits of industrialization are uneven. Large numbers of people in the Industrializing Nations remain illiterate and desperately poor. Conditions can be gruesome, as we explore in the following *Thinking Critically* section.

Thinking Critically

Open Season: Children as Prey

What is childhood like in the Industrializing Nations? The answer depends on who your parents are. If you are the son or daughter of rich parents, childhood can be pleasant—a world filled with luxuries and even servants. If you are born into poverty, but live in a rural area where there is plenty to eat, life can still be good—although there may be no books, television, and little education. If you live in a slum, however, life can be horrible—worse even than in the slums of the Most Industrialized Nations. Let's take a glance at a notorious slum in Brazil.

Not enough food—this you can take for granted—along with wife abuse, broken homes, alcoholism, drug abuse, and a lot of crime. From your knowledge of slums in the Most Industrialized Nations, you would expect these things. What you may not expect, however, are the brutal conditions in which Brazilian slum (*favela*) children live.

Sociologist Martha Huggins (Huggins et al. 2002) reports that poverty is so deep that children and adults swarm through garbage dumps to try to find enough decaying food to keep them alive. You might also be surprised to discover that the owners of some of these dumps hire armed guards to keep the poor out—so that they can sell the garbage for pig food. And you might be shocked to learn that some shop owners have hired hit men, auctioning designated victims to the lowest bidder!

Life is cheap in the poor nations—but death squads for children? To understand this, we must first note that Brazil has a long history of violence. Brazil also has a high rate of poverty, has only a tiny middle class, and is controlled by a small group of families who, under a veneer of democracy, make the country's major decisions. Hordes of homeless children, with no schools or jobs, roam the streets. To survive, they wash windshields, shine shoes, beg, and steal (Huggins and Rodrigues 2004).

The "respectable" classes see these children as nothing but trouble. They hurt business, for customers feel intimidated when they see begging children—especially teenaged males—clustered in front of stores. Some shoplift; others dare to sell items that place them in competition with the stores. With no effective social institutions to care for these children, one solution is to kill them. As Huggins notes, murder sends a clear message—especially if it is accompanied by ritual torture: gouging out the eyes, ripping open the chest, cutting off the genitals, raping the girls, and burning the victim's body.

Not all life is bad in the Industrializing Nations, but this is about as bad as it gets.

For Your Consideration

Death squads for children also operate in the slums of the Philippines ("Death Squads..." 2008). Do you think there is anything the Most Industrialized Nations can do about this situation? Or is it, though unfortunate, just an "internal" affair that is up to the particular nation to handle as it wishes?

The Least Industrialized Nations

In the Least Industrialized Nations, most people live on small farms or in villages, have large families, and barely survive. These nations account for 68 percent of the world's people but only 49 percent of the earth's land.

Poverty plagues these nations to such an extent that some families actually live in city dumps... Although wealthy nations have their pockets of poverty, most people in the Least Industrialized nations are poor. Most of them have no running water, indoor plumbing, or access to trained teachers or

Table 9.3   An Alternative Model of Global Stratification

Four Worlds of Development

1. Most Industrialized Nations
2. Industrializing Nations
3. Least Industrializing Nations
4. Oil-rich, nonindustrializing nations

physicians. As we will review in Chapter 20, most of the world's population growth is occurring in these nations, placing even greater burdens on their limited resources and causing them to fall farther behind each year.

Modifying the Model

To classify countries into Most Industrialized, Industrializing, and Least Industrialized is helpful in that it pinpoints significant differences among them. But then there are the oil-rich nations of the Middle East, the ones that provide much of the gasoline that fuels the machinery of the Most Industrialized Nations. Although these nations are not industrialized, some have become immensely wealthy. To classify them simply as Least Industrialized would gloss over significant distinctions, such as their modern hospitals, extensive prenatal care, desalinization plants, abundant food and shelter, high literacy, and computerized banking...

Kuwait is an excellent example. Kuwait is so wealthy that almost none of its citizens work for a living. The government simply pays them an annual salary just for being citizens. Everyday life in Kuwait still has its share of onerous chores, of course, but migrant workers from the poor nations do most of them. To run the specialized systems that keep Kuwait's economy going, Kuwait imports trained workers from the Most Industrialized Nations.

How Did The World's Nations Become Stratified?

How did the globe become stratified into such distinct worlds? The commonsense answer is that the poorer nations have fewer resources than the richer nations. As with many commonsense answers, however, this one, too, falls short. Many of the Industrializing and Least Industrialized Nations are rich in natural resources, while one Most Industrialized Nation, Japan, has few. Three theories explain how global stratification came about.

Colonialism

The first theory, **colonialism,** stresses that the countries that industrialized first got the jump on the rest of the world. Beginning in Great Britain about 1750, industrialization spread throughout western Europe. Plowing some of their profits into powerful armaments and fast ships, these countries invaded weaker nations, making colonies out of them (Harrison 1993). After subduing these weaker nations, the more powerful countries left behind a controlling force in order to exploit the nations' labor and natural resources. At one point, there was even a free-for-all among the industrialized European countries as they rushed to divide up an entire continent. As they sliced Africa into pieces, even tiny Belgium got into the act and acquired the Congo, which was *seventy-five* times larger than itself.

The purpose of colonialism was to establish *economic colonies*—to exploit the

> Colonialism: the process by which one nation takes over another nation, usually for the purpose of exploiting its labor and natural resources.

nation's people and resources for the benefit of the "mother" country. The more powerful European countries would plant their national flags in a colony and send their representatives to run the government, but the United States usually chose to plant corporate flags in a colony and let these corporations dominate the territory's government. Central and South America are prime examples. There were exceptions, such as the conquest of the Philippines, which President McKinley said was motivated by the desire "to educate the Filipinos, and uplift and civilize and Christianize them" (Krugman 2002).

Colonialism, then, shaped many of the Least Industrialized Nations. In some instances, the Most Industrialized Nations were so powerful that when dividing their spoils, they drew lines across a map, creating new states without regard for tribal or cultural considerations (Kifner 1999). Britain and France did just this as they divided up North Africa and parts of the Middle East—which is why the national boundaries of Libya, Saudi Arabia, Kuwait, and other countries are so straight. This legacy of European conquests is a background factor in much of today's racial-ethnic and tribal violence: Groups with no history of national identity were incorporated arbitrarily into the same political boundaries.

World System Theory

The second explanation of how global stratification came about was proposed by Immanuel Wallerstein (1974, 1979, 1990). According to **world system theory,** industrialization led to four groups of nations. The first group

> **World system theory:** economic and political connections that tie the world's countries together.

consists of the *core nations*, the countries that industrialized first (Britain, France, Holland, and later Germany), which grew rich and powerful. The second group is the *semiperiphery*. The economies of these nations, located around the Mediterranean, stagnated because they grew dependent on trade with the core nations. The economies of the third group, the *periphery*, or fringe nations, developed even less. These are the eastern European countries, which sold cash crops to the core nations. The fourth group of nations includes most of Africa and Asia. Called the *external area,* these nations were left out of the development of capitalism altogether. The current expansion of capitalism has changed the relationships among these groups. Most notably, eastern Europe and Asia are no longer left out of capitalism.

The **globalization of capitalism**—the adoption of capitalism around the world—has created extensive ties among the world's nations. Production and trade are now so interconnected that events around the globe affect us all. Sometimes this is immediate, as happens when a

> **Globalization of capitalism:** capitalism (investing to make profits within a rational system) becoming the globe's dominant economic system.

civil war disrupts the flow of oil, or—perish the thought—as would be the case if terrorists managed to get their hands on nuclear or biological weapons. At other times, the effects are like a slow ripple, as when a government adopts some policy that gradually impedes its ability to compete in world markets. All of today's societies, then, no matter where they are located, are part of a *world system*.

The interconnections are most evident among nations that do extensive trading with one another.

Culture of Poverty

The third explanation of global stratification is quite unlike the other two. Economist John Kenneth Galbraith (1979) claimed that the cultures of the Least Industrialized Nations hold them back. Building on the ideas of anthropologist Oscar Lewis (1966a, 1966b), Galbraith argued that some nations are crippled by a **culture of poverty,** a way of life that perpetuates poverty from one generation to the next. He explained it this way: Most of the world's poor people are farmers who live on little plots of land. They barely produce enough food to survive. Living so close to the edge of starvation, they have little room for risk—so they stick closely to tried-and-true, traditional ways. To experiment with new farming techniques is to court disaster, for failure would lead to hunger and death.

> **Culture of poverty:** the assumption that the values and behaviors of the poor make them fundamentally different from other people, that these factors are largely responsible for their poverty, and that parents perpetuate poverty across generations by passing these characteristics to their children.

Their religion also encourages them to accept their situation, for it teaches fatalism: the belief that an individual's position in life is God's will. For example, in India, the Dalits (untouchables) are taught that they must have done very bad things in a previous life to suffer so. They are supposed to submit to their situation—and in the next life maybe they'll come back in a more desirable state.

Evaluating the Theories

Most sociologists prefer colonialism and world system theory. To them, an explanation based on a culture of poverty places blame on the victim—the poor nations themselves. It points to characteristics of the poor nations, rather than to international political arrangements that benefit the Most Industrialized Nations at the expense of the poor nations. But even taken together, these theories yield only part of the picture. None of these theories, for example, would have led anyone to expect that after World War II, Japan would become an economic powerhouse: Japan had a religion that stressed fatalism, two of its major cities had been destroyed by atomic bombs, and it had been stripped of its colonies. Each theory, then, yields but a partial explanation, and the grand theorist who will put the many pieces of this puzzle together has yet to appear.

Maintaining Global Stratification

Regardless of how the world's nations became stratified, why do the same countries remain rich year after year, while the rest stay poor? Let's look at two explanations of how global stratification is maintained.

Neocolonialism

Sociologist Michael Harrington (1977) argued that when colonialism fell out of style it was replaced by **neocolonialism.** When World War II changed public sentiment about sending soldiers and colonists to exploit weaker countries, the Most Industrialized Nations turned to the international markets as a way of controlling the Least Industrialized Nations. By selling them goods on credit—especially weapons that their elite desire so they can keep themselves in power—the Most Industrialized Nations entrap the poor nations with a circle of debt.

> **Neocolonialism:** the economic and political dominance of the Least Industrialized Nations by the Most Industrialized Nations.

As many of us learn the hard way, owing a large debt and falling behind on payments puts us at the mercy of our creditors. So it is with neocolonialism. The *policy* of selling weapons and other manufactured goods to the Least Industrialized Nations on credit turns those countries into eternal debtors. The capital they need to develop their own industries goes instead as payments toward the debt, which becomes bloated with mounting interest. Keeping these nations in debt forces them to submit to trading terms dictated by the neocolonialists (Carrington 1993; S. Smith 2001).

Relevance Today. Neocolonialism might seem remote from our own lives, but its heritage affects us directly. Consider the oil-rich Middle Eastern countries, our two wars in the Persian Gulf, and the terrorism that emanates from this region (*Strategic Energy Policy* 2001; Mouawad 2007). Although this is an area of ancient civilizations, the countries themselves are recent. Great Britain created Saudi Arabia, drawing its boundaries and even naming the country after the man (Ibn Saud) whom British officials picked to lead it. This created a debt for the Saudi family, which for decades it repaid by providing low-cost oil, which the Most Industrialized Nations need to maintain their way of life. When other nations pumped less oil—no matter the cause, whether revolution or an attempt to raise prices—the Saudis helped keep prices low by making up the shortfall. In return, the United States (and other nations) overlooked the human rights violations of the Saudi royal family, keeping them in power by selling them the latest weapons. This mutually sycophantic arrangement continues, but fluctuations in oil supplies have disrupted its effectiveness.

Multinational Corporations

Multinational corporations, companies that operate across many national boundaries, also help to maintain the global dominance of the Most Industrialized Nations. In some cases, multinational corporations exploit the Least Industrialized Nations directly. A prime example is the United Fruit Company, which used to control national and local politics in Central America. This U.S. corporation ran Central American nations as fiefdoms for the company's own profit while the U.S. Marines waited in the wings. An occasional invasion to put down dissidents reminded regional politicians of the military power that backed U.S. corporations.

Most commonly, however, it is simply by doing business that multinational corporations help to maintain international stratification. A single multinational corporation may manage mining operations in several countries, manufacture goods in others, and market its products around the globe. No matter where the profits are made, or where they are reinvested, the primary beneficiaries are the Most Industrialized Nations, especially the one in which the multinational corporation has its world headquarters.

Buying Political Stability. In their pursuit of profits, the multinational corporations need cooperative power elites in the Least Industrialized Nations (Sklair 2001; Wise and Cypher 2007). In return for funneling money to the elites and selling them modern weapons, the corporations get a "favorable business climate"—that is, low taxes and cheap labor. The corporations politely call the money they pay to the elites "subsidies" and "offsets"—which are much prettier to the ear than "bribes." Able also to siphon money from their country's tax system and government spending, these elites live a sophisticated upper-class life in the major cities of their home country. Although most of the citizens of these countries live a hard-scrabble life, the elites are able to send their children to prestigious Western universities, such as Oxford, the Sorbonne, and Harvard.

You can see how this cozy arrangement helps to maintain global stratification. The significance of these payoffs is not so much the genteel lifestyles that they allow the elites to maintain, but the translation of the payoffs into power. They allow the elites to purchase high-tech weapons with which they oppress their people and preserve their positions of dominance. The result is a political stability that keeps alive the diabolical partnership between the multinational corporations and the national elites.

Unanticipating Consequences. This, however, is not the full story. An unintentional by-product of the multinationals' global search for cheap resources and labor is to modify global stratification. When these corporations move manufacturing from the Most Industrialized Nations to the Least Industrialized Nations, they not only exploit cheap labor but they also bring jobs and money to these nations. Although workers in the Least Industrialized Nations are paid a pittance, it is more than they can earn elsewhere. With new factories come opportunities to develop skills and accumulate a capital base from which local elites can launch their own factories.

The Pacific Rim nations provide a remarkable example. In return for providing the "favorable business climate" just mentioned, multinational corporations invested billions of dollars in the "Asian tigers" (Hong Kong, Singapore, South Korea, and Taiwan). These nations have developed such a strong capital base that they have begun to rival the older capitalist countries. This has also made them subject to capitalism's "boom and bust" cycles, and workers and investors in these nations are having their dreams smashed as capitalism suffers its current downturn.

Technology and Global Domination

The race between the Most and Least Industrialized Nations to develop and apply the new technologies might seem like a race between a marathon runner and someone with a broken leg. Can the outcome be in doubt? As the multinational corporations amass profits, they are able to invest huge sums in the latest technology while the Least Industrialized Nations are struggling to put scraps on the table. So it would appear, but the race is not this simple. Although the Most Industrialized Nations have a seemingly insurmountable head start, some of the other nations are shortening the distance between themselves and the front-runners. With cheap labor making their manufactured goods inexpensive, China and India are exporting goods on a massive scale. They are using the capital from these exports to adopt high technology to modernize their infrastructure (transportation, communication, electrical, and banking systems), with the goal of advancing their industry. Although global domination remains in the hands of the West, it could be on the verge of a major shift from West to East.

Unintended Public Relations. Bono and others have used the media in a campaign to get G8 to forgive the debts of some of the poorest of the world's nations. (G8 is the Group of Eight, an association of wealthy and powerful nations—Canada, France, Germany, Italy, Japan, Russia, the

United Kingdom, and the United States—that meet annually to discuss global issues.) Their efforts made a good story, which the mass media loved to promote. G8, however, knows how to milk the media, too. To cancel the debts of poor nations amidst television reporters and global drum rolls projects an image of goodhearted capitalists having mercy on the poor. Although G8 had written these debts off as uncollectible in the first place, the publicity that accompanied their pronouncements helps to soften opposition to the global dominance of capitalism.

Vocabulary in Context

To define the following words, use the dictionary snapshots to identify the appropriate definition. Then, find a *synonym* for the word and write the synonym in the space provided.

squalor	spoils	siphon
vignette	arbitrarily	genteel
stratify	entrap	diabolical
variation	sycophant	pittance
plague	fluctuation	insurmountable
desalinization	fiefdom	
onerous	dissident	

squal´or (skwol´er; skwä´ler) *n.* filthy and depressed condition.

vi·gnette´ (vin-yet´) *n.* **1,** a photograph shaded at the edges so as to have no clear border. **2,** a descriptive literary sketch. **3,** a decorative illustration in a book. —*v.t.* **1,** outline; describe. **2,** make a (photographic) vignette of.

strat´i·fy" (strat´ə-fīl) *v.t.* form in layers. —**strati·f"i·ca´tion**, *n.*

var"i·a´tion (vărllė-ā´shən) *n.* **1,** the act or process of varying; change; modification. **2,** a point or aspect of difference. **3,** the amount of change; variance. **4,** a different form. **5,** (*Music*) a theme repeated with changes or elaborations.

plague (plāg) *n.* **1,** a pestilential epidemic disease. **2,** severe trouble; scourge. **3,** (*Informal*) a nuisance. —*v.t.* **1,** harass; annoy. **2,** afflict with the plague. — **pla´guy**, *adj.*

de·sal´i·nate" (dė-sal´ə-nātl) *v.t.* remove the salt from. Also, **de·sal´i·nize"** (-nīz), **de·salt´.**

on´er·ous (on´ər-əs) *adj.* burdensome. —**on´er·ous·ness**, *n.*

spoil *v.t.* **1,** seriously impair. **2,** overindulge, as a child. **3,** plunder; despoil. —*v.i.* decay; become tainted. —*n.* (*pl.*) plunder. —**spoil´age**, *n.*

ar´bi·trar"y (är´bə-trärllė) *adj.* **1,** not regulated by fixed rule or law. **2,** despotic. **3,** capricious; unreasonable. —**ar´bi·trar"i·ness**, *n.*

en·trap′ *v.t.* [**-trapped′, -trap′ping**] catch in a trap; snare. — **en·trap′ment,** *n.*

syc′o·phant (sīk′ə-fənt) *n.* a servile flatterer. —**syc′o·phan·cy** (-fən-sē) *n.*

fluc′tu·ate″ (fluk′chû-ātl) *v.i.* change continually; vary irregularly; rise and fall, like waves. —**fluc″tu·a′tion,** *n.*

fief (fēf) *n.* an estate held under feudal law.

dis′si·dence (dis′ə-dəns) *n.* difference in opinion; disagreement. —**dis′si·dent,** *adj.* & *n.*

si′phon (sī′fən) *n.* **1,** a bent tube used to draw a liquid over an elevation. **2,** a bottle for aerated water. —*v.t.* draw off with a siphon.

gen·teel′ (jen-tēl′) *adj.* affectedly refined. —**gen·teel′ness,** *n.*

di″a·bol′ic (dīlə-bol′ik) *adj.* devilish; infernal. Also, **di″a·bol′i·cal.**

pit′tance (pit′əns) *n.* a very small and inadequate quantity, esp. of money.

sur·mount′ (sēr-mownt′) *v.t.* **1,** pass over. **2,** overcome; prevail over. — **surmountable,** *adj.*

1. The neatness of their home stands in stark contrast to the <u>squalor</u> of their neighborhood, whose dirt roads are covered in litter.

   What synonym fits this context? _____

2. Social stratification is one of the most significant topics we shall discuss in this book, for, as you saw in the opening <u>vignette</u>, it profoundly affects our life chances—from our access to material possessions to the age at which we die.

   What synonym fits this context? _____

3. Just as the people within a nation are <u>stratified</u> by property, power, and prestige, so are the world's nations.

   What synonym fits this context? ____

4. Although there are <u>variations</u> in their economic systems, these nations are capitalistic.

   What synonym fits this context? _____

5. Poverty <u>plagues</u> these nations to such an extent that some families actually live in city dumps.

   What synonym fits this context? _____

6. To classify them simply as Least Industrialized would gloss over significant distinctions, such as their modern hospitals, extensive prenatal care, <u>desalinization</u> plants, abundant food and shelter, high literacy, and computerized banking.

   What synonym fits this context? _____

7. Everyday life in Kuwait still has its share of <u>onerous</u> chores, of course, but migrant workers from the poor nations do most of them.

   What synonym fits this context? _____

8. In some instances, the Most Industrialized Nations were so powerful that when dividing their <u>spoils</u>, they drew lines across a map, creating new states without regard for tribal or cultural considerations (Kifner 1999).

   What synonym fits this context? _____

9. This legacy of European conquests is a background factor in much of today's racial-ethnic and tribal violence: Groups with no history of national identity were incorporated <u>arbitrarily</u> into the same political boundaries.

   What synonym fits this context? _____

10. By selling them goods on credit—especially weapons that their elite desire so they can keep themselves in power—the Most Industrialized Nations <u>entrap</u> the poor nations with a circle of debt.

    What synonym fits this context? ____

11. This mutually <u>sycophantic</u> arrangement continues, but fluctuations in oil supplies have disrupted its effectiveness.

    Which synonym fits this context? _____

12. This mutually sycophantic arrangement continues, but <u>fluctuations</u> in oil supplies have disrupted its effectiveness.

    What synonym fits this context? _____

13. This U.S. corporation ran Central American nations as <u>fiefdoms</u> for the company's own profit while the U.S. Marines waited in the wings.

    What synonym fits this context? _____

14. An occasional invasion to put down <u>dissidents</u> reminded regional politicians of the military power that backed U.S. corporations.

    What synonym fits this context? ___

15. Able also to <u>siphon</u> money from their country's tax system and government spending, these elites live a sophisticated upper-class life in the major cities of their home country.

    What synonym fits this context? ___

16. The significance of these payoffs is not so much the <u>genteel</u> lifestyles that they allow the elites to maintain, but the translation of the payoffs into power.

    What synonym fits this context? ____

17. The result is a political stability that keeps alive the <u>diabolical</u> partnership between the multinational corporations and the national elites.

    What synonym fits this context? __

18. Although workers in the Least Industrialized Nations are paid a <u>pittance</u>, it is more than they can earn elsewhere.

    What synonym fits this context? _____

19. Although the Most Industrialized Nations have a seemingly <u>insurmountable</u> head start, some of the other nations are shortening the distance between themselves and the front-runners.

    What synonym fits this context? _____

Checking In

1. What is the most shocking or interesting fact you learned while reading the opening family sketches? Why was that fact noteworthy to you?

2. After you read the sketches, what did you understand about global stratification, or the way the world's wealth is distributed?

Getting the Point

3. What is the author's goal when he renames the three levels of global stratification—developed, developing, and undeveloped nations—as Most Industrialized, Industrializing, and Least Industrialized?

4. Describe how each family in the opening sketch represents one of the three levels of stratification in terms of property, power, and prestige. Be specific in your description.

Delving Deeper

5. The author discusses the way Least Industrializing nations have been shaped by the more powerful, Most Industrialized nations. Do you think the author is suggesting that Least Industrializing nations' only option is to accept their fate? Or is he suggesting that some other state of affairs may be possible? Explain your response.

The Writing Connection

Consider the section on colonialism, especially where the author discusses the effects of colonialism as seen in today's world. For example, Henslin says, "This legacy of European conquests is a background factor in much of today's racial-ethnic and tribal violence: Groups with no history of national identity were incorporated arbitrarily into the same political boundaries."

Investigate an international conflict between people from the same country or between neighboring countries. Try to determine if the effects of past colonialism contributed to the conflict. As a place to begin, consider some of the countries on the African continent: Rwanda, Zimbabwe, South Africa, or Nigeria, to name a few. Also, you may look at countries in the Middle East like Israel, Kuwait, Iraq, and Iran. Other countries like Pakistan and India might also be of interest. Discuss the historical roots you find in your research and how this reading on global stratification has helped you understand your findings.

The Lesson

by Toni Cade Bambara

About the Author

Toni Cade Bambara (1939–1995) was born and raised in New York City. She attended a number of colleges including the University of Florence, the City University of New York, and The New School for Social Research.

Her writings have appeared in a diversity of magazines, and she published several collections of short fiction and one novel. This story, "The Lesson," was published in her first short story collection, *Gorilla, My Love* (1972). Her other books include *The Sea Birds Are Still Alive* (1977), *The Salt Eaters* (1980), and the novel *If Blessing Comes* (1987).

In the story "The Lesson," a girl recounts an incident that occurred in her youth. The narrator's experience begins like any other summer day, but takes on added significance as the story progresses. The brash, foul-mouthed voice of the narrator is one of the more distinctive personalities one might encounter in a short story and tells a tale all its own.

Before You Read

Research the toy store F.A.O. Schwarz. What type of customers do you think shop in F.A.O. Schwarz?

Thematic Links

- Sociology
- Coming of Age
- Relationships
- Community

Part 3 Book Link

- *Listening Is an Act of Love*
- *The Color of Water*

The Lesson

by Toni Cade Bambara

B ack in the days when everyone was old and stupid or young and foolish and me and Sugar were the only ones just right, this lady moved on our block with nappy hair and proper speech and no makeup. And quite naturally we laughed at her, laughed the way we did at the junk man who went about his business like he was some big-time president and his sorry-ass horse his secretary. And we kinda hated her too, hated the way we did the winos who cluttered up our parks and pissed on our handball walls and stank up our hallways and stairs so you couldn't halfway play hide-and-seek without a goddamn gas mask. Miss Moore was her name. The only woman on the block with no first name. And she was black as hell, cept for her feet, which were fish-white and spooky. And she was always planning these boring-ass things for us to do, us being my cousin, mostly, who lived on the block cause we all moved North the same time and to the same apartment then spread out gradual to breathe. And our parents would yank our heads into some kinda shape and crisp up our clothes so we'd be presentable for travel with Miss Moore, who always looked like she was going to church, though she never did. Which is just one of the things the grownups talked about when they talked behind her back like a dog. But when she came calling with some sachet she'd sewed up or some gingerbread she'd made or some book, why then they'd all be too embarrassed to turn her down and we'd get handed over all spruced up. She'd been to college and said it was only right that she should take responsibility for the young ones' education, and she not even related by marriage or blood. So they'd go for it. Specially Aunt Gretchen. She was the main gofer in the family. You got some ole dumb shit foolishness you want somebody to go for, you send for Aunt Gretchen. She been screwed into the go-along for so long, it's a blood-deep natural thing with her. Which is how she got saddled with me and Sugar and Junior in the first place while our mothers were in a la-de-da apartment up the block having a good ole time.

So this one day, Miss Moore rounds us all up at the mailbox and it's puredee hot and she's knockin herself out about arithmetic. And school suppose to let up in summer I heard, but she don't never let up. And the starch in my pinafore scratching the shit outta me and I'm really hating this nappy-head bitch and her goddamn college degree. I'd much rather go to the pool or to the show where it's cool. So me and Sugar leaning on the mailbox being surly, which is a Miss Moore word. And Flyboy checking out what everybody brought for lunch. And Fat Butt already wasting his peanut-butter-and-jelly sandwich like the pig he is. And Junebug punchin on Q.T.'s arm for potato chips. And Rosie Giraffe shifting from one hip to the other waiting for somebody to step on her foot or ask her if she from Georgia so she can kick ass, preferably Mercedes'. And Miss Moore asking us do we know what money is, like we a bunch of retards. I mean real money, she say, like it's only poker chips or monopoly papers we lay on the grocer. So right away I'm tired of this and say so. And would much rather snatch Sugar and go to the Sunset and terrorize the West Indian kids and take their hair ribbons and their money too. And Miss Moore files that remark away for next week's lesson on brotherhood, I can tell. And finally I say we oughta get to the subway cause it's cooler and besides we might meet some cute boys. Sugar done swiped her mama's lipstick, so we ready.

So we heading down the street and she's boring us silly about what things cost and what our parents make and how much goes for rent and how money ain't divided up right in this country. And then she gets to the part about we all poor and live in the slums, which I don't feature. And I'm ready to speak on that, but she steps out in the street and hails two cabs just like that. Then she hustles half the crew in with her and hands me a five-dollar bill and tells me to calculate 10 percent tip for the driver. And we're off. Me and Sugar and Junebug and Flyboy hangin out the window and hollering to everybody, putting lipstick on each other cause Flyboy a faggot anyway, and making farts with our sweaty armpits. But I'm mostly trying to figure how to spend this money. But they all fascinated with the meter ticking and Junebug starts laying bets as to how much it'll read when Flyboy can't hold his breath no more. Then Sugar lays bets as to how much it'll be when we get there. So I'm stuck. Don't nobody want to go for my plan, which is to jump out at the next light and run off to the first bar-b-que we can find. Then the driver tells us to get the hell out cause we there already. And the meter reads eighty-five cents. And I'm stalling to figure out the tip and Sugar say give him a dime. And I decide he don't need it bad as I do, so later for him. But then he tries to take off with Junebug foot still in the door so we talk about his mama something ferocious. Then we check out that we on Fifth Avenue and everybody dressed up in stockings. One lady in a fur coat, hot as it is. White folks crazy.

"This is the place," Miss Moore say, presenting it to us in the voice she uses at the museum. "Let's look in the windows before we go in."

"Can we steal?" Sugar asks very serious like she's getting the ground rules squared away before she plays. "I beg your pardon," say Miss Moore, and we fall out. So she leads us around the windows of the toy store and me and Sugar screamin, "This is mine, that's mine, I gotta have that, that was made for me, I was born for that," till Big Butt drowns us out.

"Hey, I'm going to buy that there."

"That there? You don't even know what it is, stupid."

"I do so," he say punchin on Rosie Giraffe. "It's a microscope."

"Whatcha gonna do with a microscope, fool?"

"Look at things."

"Like what, Ronald?" ask Miss Moore. And Big Butt ain't got the first notion. So here go Miss Moore gabbing about the thousands of bacteria in a drop of water and the somethinorother in a speck of blood and the million and one living things in the air around us is invisible to the naked eye. And what she say that for? Junebug go to town on that "naked" and we rolling. Then Miss Moore ask what it cost. So we all jam into the window smudgin it up and the price tag say $300. So then she ask how long'd take for Big Butt and Junebug to save up their allowances. "Too long," I say. "Yeh," adds Sugar, "outgrown it by that time." And Miss Moore say no, you never outgrow learning instruments. "Why, even medical students and interns and," blah, blah, blah. And we ready to choke Big Butt for bringing it up in the first damn place.

"This here costs four hundred eighty dollars," say Rosie Giraffe. So we pile up all over her to see what she pointin out. My eyes tell me it's a chunk of glass cracked with something heavy, and different-color inks dripped into the splits, then the whole thing put into a oven or something. But for $480 it don't make sense.

"That's a paperweight made of semi-precious stones fused together under tremendous pressure," she explains slowly, with her hands doing the mining and all the factory work.

"So what's a paperweight?" ask Rosie Giraffe.

"To weigh paper with, dumbbell," say Flyboy, the wise man from the East.

"Not exactly," say Miss Moore, which is what she say when you warm or way off too. "It's to weigh paper down so it won't scatter and make your desk untidy." So right away me and Sugar curtsy to each other and then to Mercedes who is more the tidy type.

"We don't keep paper on top of the desk in my class," say Junebug, figuring Miss Moore crazy or lyin one.

"At home, then," she say. "Don't you have a calendar and a pencil case and a blotter and a letter-opener on your desk at home where you do your homework?" And she know damn well what our homes look like cause she nosys around in them every chance she gets.

"I don't even have a desk," say Junebug. "Do we?"

"No. And I don't get no homework neither," say Big Butt.

"And I don't even have a home," say Flyboy like he do at school to keep the white folks off his back and sorry for him. Send this poor kid to camp posters, is his specialty.

"I do," says Mercedes. "I have a box of stationery on my desk and a picture of my cat. My godmother bought the stationery and the desk. There's a big rose on each sheet and the envelopes smell like roses."

"Who wants to know about your smelly-ass stationery," say Rosie Giraffe fore I can get my two cents in.

"It's important to have a work area all your own so that..."

"Will you look at this sailboat, please," say Flyboy, cutting her off and pointin to the thing like it was his. So once again we tumble all over each other to gaze at this magnificent thing in the toy store which is just big enough to maybe sail two kittens across the pond if you strap them to the posts tight. We all start reciting the price tag like we in assembly. "Handcrafted sailboat of fiberglass at one thousand one hundred ninety-five dollars."

"Unbelievable," I hear myself say and am really stunned. I read it again for myself just in case the group recitation put me in a trance. Same thing. For some reason this pisses me off. We look at Miss Moore and she lookin at us, waiting for I dunno what.

"Who'd pay all that when you can buy a sailboat set for a quarter at Pop's, a tube of glue for a dime, and a ball of string for eight cents? It must have a motor and a whole lot else besides," I say. "My sailboat cost me about fifty cents."

"But will it take water?" say Mercedes with her smart ass.

"Took mine to Alley Pond Park once," say Flyboy. "String broke. Lost it. Pity."

"Sailed mine in Central Park and it keeled over and sank. Had to ask my father for another dollar."

"And you got the strap," laugh Big Butt. "The jerk didn't even have a string on it. My old man wailed on his behind."

Little Q.T. was staring hard at the sailboat and you could see he wanted it bad. But he too little and somebody'd just take it from him. So what the hell. "This boat for kids, Miss Moore?"

"Parents silly to buy something like that just to get all broke up," say Rosie Giraffe.

"That much money it should last forever," I figure.

"My father'd buy it for me if I wanted it."

"Your father, my ass," say Rosie Giraffe getting a chance to finally push Mercedes.

"Must be rich people shop here," say Q.T.

"You are a very bright boy," say Flyboy. "What was your first clue?" And he rap him on the head with the back of his knuckles, since Q.T. the only one he could get away with. Though Q.T. liable to come up behind you years later and get his licks in when you half expect it.

"What I want to know is," I says to Miss Moore though I never talk to her, I wouldn't give the bitch that satisfaction, "is how much a real boat costs? I figure a thousand'd get you a yacht any day."

"Why don't you check that out," she says, "and report back to the group?" Which really pains my ass. If you gonna mess up a perfectly good swim day least you could do is have some answers. "Let's go in," she say like she got something up her sleeve. Only she don't lead the way. So me and Sugar turn the corner to where the entrance is, but when we get there I kinda hang back. Not that I'm scared, what's there to be afraid of, just a toy store. But I feel funny, shame. But what I got to be shamed about? Got as much right to go in as anybody. But somehow I can't seem to get hold of the door, so I step away from Sugar to lead. But she hangs back too. And I look at her and she looks at me and this is ridiculous. I mean, damn, I have never been shy about doing nothing or going nowhere. But then Mercedes steps up and then Rosie Giraffe and Big Butt crowd in behind and shove, and next thing we all stuffed into the doorway with only Mercedes squeezing past us, smoothing out her jumper and walking right down the aisle. Then the rest of us tumble in like a glued-together jigsaw done all wrong. And people lookin at us. And it's like the time me and Sugar crashed into the Catholic church on a dare. But once we got in there and everything so hushed and holy and the candles and the bowin and the handkerchiefs on all the drooping heads, I just couldn't go through with the plan. Which was for me to run up to the altar and do a tap dance while Sugar played the nose flute and messed around in the holy water. And Sugar kept given me the elbow. Then later teased me so bad I tied her up in the shower and turned it on and locked her in. And she'd be there till this day if Aunt Gretchen hadn't finally figured I was lying about the boarder takin a shower.

Same thing in the store. We all walkin on tiptoe and hardly touchin the games and puzzles and things. And I watched Miss Moore who is steady watchin us like she waitin for a sign. Like Mama Drewery watches the sky and sniffs the air and takes note of just how much slant is in the bird formation. Then me and Sugar bump smack into each other, so busy gazing at the toys, 'specially the sailboat. But we don't laugh and go into our fat-lady bump-stomach routine. We just stare at that price tag. Then Sugar run a finger over the whole boat. And I'm jealous and want to hit her. Maybe not her, but I sure want to punch somebody in the mouth.

"Watcha bring us here for, Miss Moore?"

"You sound angry, Sylvia. Are you mad about something?" Givin me one of them grins like she tellin a grown-up joke that never turns out to be funny. And she's lookin very closely at me like maybe she plannin to do my portrait from memory. I'm mad, but I won't give her that satisfaction. So I slouch around the store being very bored and say, "Let's go."

Me and Sugar at the back of the train watchin the tracks whizzin by large then small then getting gobbled up in the dark. I'm thinkin about this tricky toy I saw in the store. A clown that somersaults on a bar then does chin-ups just cause you yank lightly at his leg. Cost $35. I could see me askin my mother for a $35 birthday clown. "You wanna who that costs what?" she'd say, cocking her head to the side to get a better view of the hole in my head. Thirty-five dollars could buy new bunk beds for Junior and Gretchen's boy. Thirty-five dollars and the whole household could go visit Grand-daddy Nelson in the country. Thirty-five dollars would pay for the rent and the piano bill too. Who are these people that spend that much for performing clowns and $1000 for toy sailboats? What kinda work they do and how they live and how come we ain't in on it? Where we are is who we are, Miss Moore always pointin out. But it don't necessarily have to be that way, she always adds then waits for somebody to say that poor people have to wake up and demand their share of the pie and don't none of us know what kind of pie she talking about in the first damn place. But she ain't so smart cause I still got her four dollars from the taxi and she sure ain't gettin it. Messin up my day with this shit. Sugar nudges me in my pocket and winks.

Miss Moore lines us up in front of the mailbox where we started from, seem like years ago, and I got a headache for thinkin so hard. And we lean all over each other so we can hold up under the draggy-ass lecture she always finishes us off with at the end before we thank her for borin us to tears. But she just looks at us like she readin tea leaves. Finally she say, "Well, what did you think of F.A.O. Schwarz?"

Rosie Giraffe mumbles, "White folks crazy."

"I'd like to go there again when I get my birthday money," says Mercedes, and we shove her out the pack so she has to lean on the mailbox by herself.

"I'd like a shower. Tiring day," say Flyboy.

Then Sugar surprises me by sayin, "You know, Miss Moore, I don't think all of us here put together eat in a year what that sailboat costs." And Miss Moore lights up like somebody goosed her. "And?" she say, urging Sugar on. Only I'm standin on her foot so she don't continue.

"Imagine for a minute what kind of society it is in which some people can spend on a toy what it would cost to feed a family of six or seven. What do you think?"

"I think," say Sugar pushing me off her feet like she never done before, cause I whip her ass in a minute, "that this is not much of a democracy if you ask me. Equal chance to pursue happiness means an equal crack at the dough, don't it?" Miss Moore is besides herself and I am disgusted with Sugar's treachery. So I stand on her foot one more time to see if she'll shove me. She shuts up, and Miss Moore looks at me, sorrowfully I'm thinkin. And somethin weird is goin on, I can feel it in my chest.

"Anybody else learn anything today?" lookin dead at me. I walk away and Sugar has to run to catch up and don't even seem to notice when I shrug her arm off my shoulder.

"Well, we got four dollars anyway," she says.

"Uh, hunh."

"We could go to Hascombs and get half a chocolate layer and then go to the Sunset and still have plenty money for potato chips and ice cream sodas."

"Uh, hunh."

"Race you to Hascombs," she say.

We start down the block and she gets ahead which is O.K. by me cause I'm going to the West End and then over to the Drive to think this day through. She can run if she want to and even run faster. But ain't nobody gonna beat me at nuthin.

Cost of Living in 1962	F.A.O. Schwarz Prices in 1962
• Average wages per year: $5,556	• Sailboat: $1,195
• Average cost of rent per month: $110	• Paperweight: $480
• Factory worker's pay per week: $94.87	• Clown: $35

Vocabulary in Context

Use the vocabulary strategies covered in Chapter 3 to decipher the meaning of the following words. After you have defined the word, indicate which strategy you used.

WORD IN CONTEXT	DEFINITION	STRATEGY USED
sachet, par. 1		
pinafore, par. 2		
surly, par. 2		

Checking In

1. Describe the narrator of this story. Where does she live, how old is she, and what is her ethnic background? How would you describe her personality and view of life? Offer a few details that support your description.

Getting the Point

2. In paragraph 2, when Miss Moore asks the kids about money, what do you think Miss Moore is really asking them?

3. In paragraph 3, what does Miss Moore say that the narrator, Sylvia, feels isn't true? Why do you think Sylvia disagrees with Miss Moore?

4. What becomes clear about the group of kids as they stand outside the toy store and talk to Miss Moore about what they see in the store window? What does this show about their previous experience/exposure?

5. When Sylvia and Sugar decide to enter the store, what happens and why?

Delving Deeper

6. After being in the store for a while, Sylvia asks, "Watcha bring us here for, Miss Moore?" Why does Miss Moore take the kids to the toy store? Do you think Sylvia realizes why Miss Moore brought them there?

7. On the train ride home, Sylvia is thinking about a clown she saw in the store. What does the price of the clown help her realize?

8. Later, after they leave the store and are talking about the experience, something changes between the girls, Sugar and Sylvia. What is it, and do you think it is an important moment?

9. What can you predict about Sylvia given her last line: "But ain't nobody gonna beat me at nuthin"?

Evaluating the Author's Strategies

10. The author, Toni Cade Bambara, could have written this story in many ways. Why might she have chosen to use the childish but foul-mouthed language of Sylvia to tell this story?

The Writing Connection

"The Lesson" is partly about the startling differences in how people live. Can you recall a time when you became aware of a disparity or difference in the way your family lived and how others lived? Write about what you recall of the experience.

The Peculiar Institution

by R. Jackson Wilson, James Gilbert, Karen Ordahl
Kupperman, Stephen Nissenbaum, and Donald M. Scott
from *The Pursuit of Liberty: A History of the American
People, Vol. 1*

About the Reading

The textbook *The Pursuit of Liberty: A History of the American People* seeks to
present history through the eyes of the people who made it happen. Rather than
recounting the various facts, this textbook seeks to offer
an understanding of the people, places, and events that
made history—and all the connections among them.

In the selection that follows, the authors begin with
a discussion of the United States in 1830–1860 and
the particular concerns and issues being faced by the
American people at that time. This selection focuses on
the southern United States and the "peculiar institution"
known as slavery.

> **Before You Read**
>
> *Have you ever heard of something
> described as "peculiar"? What
> "peculiar institution" do you think
> the title refers to?*

Thematic Links

- *Sociology*
- *History*

Part 3 Book Link

- *Narrative of the Life of Frederick Douglass*

The Peculiar Institution

by R. Jackson Wilson, James Gilbert, Karen Ordahl Kupperman, Stephen Nissenbaum, and Donald M. Scott

from *The Pursuit of Liberty: A History of the American People*

The Historical Setting (1830–1860)

1   The labor of millions of African-American slaves enabled some white people to live lives of a comfort that shaded into luxury with a confidence that shaded into arrogance. But behind the comfort and the confidence, the luxury and the arrogance, there was always a haunting fear that the slaves might rise up and wrathfully strike for their freedom.

2   This white nightmare came true on an August morning in 1831 in Southampton County, Virginia. A slave who became known as Nat Turner led a band of rebels into bloody insurrection. Panic-stricken and enraged white people struck back, brutally murdering African Americans without knowing whether they had taken part in the revolt. Nat Turner himself was able to hide out for two months, but then he was captured, tried, and put to death—asking, poignantly, "Was not Christ crucified?"

3   Nat Turner's rebellion was not the first slave revolt in North America, but it was the largest and bloodiest. It came at a key moment in the history of American slavery. In the three decades following the American Revolution more and more southern slaves had been able to gain their freedom by purchasing it or through voluntary manumission by their masters. In fact, by 1810, there were almost 135,000 free blacks in the South (8.5 percent of the black population). But by the early 1820s, this pattern had reversed itself: in 1830, the percentage of free blacks in the South was actually less than it had been in 1810.

4   As they saw the opportunity for emancipation diminish, some blacks became more vehement in their opposition to slavery. In 1822, Denmark Vesey, a former slave who had purchased his freedom, organized a slave revolt in South Carolina that was thwarted only at the last minute when authorities got wind of his plot. And in 1829, David Walker, a North Carolina free black who had moved to Boston, published a passionate appeal to blacks to rise up against slavery.

5   The retreat from manumission as well as the angry response of blacks to it was a symptom of changes taking place not only in slavery itself but in the place of slavery in Southern life and society. In almost every way—economically, socially, politically, and ideologically—slavery deepened its hold on the South after 1830. By 1850, slavery was no longer a "peculiar institution" that happened to exist in the South; the South itself had become a slave society. Its economy revolved around forms of large-scale agriculture that depended on slave labor; its society was organized around a system of caste and class in which the divide between slave and master, black and white, was fixed and immutable; its politics centered on the defense of its "peculiar institution" against any and all perceived threats; its ideology extolled slavery, not as a necessary evil, but as a "positive good," the foundation of a noble civilization.

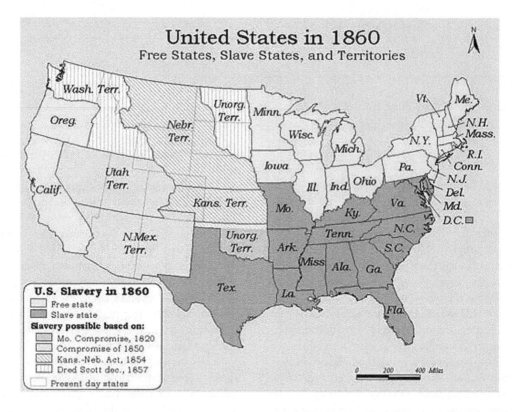

United States in 1860
Free States, Slave States, and Territories

U.S. Slavery in 1860
- Free state
- Slave state

Slavery possible based on:
- Mo. Compromise, 1820
- Compromise of 1850
- Kans.-Neb. Act, 1854
- Dred Scott dec., 1857
- Present day states

Slavery as a Social System

6   Slavery was not just a labor system, it was a social system that involved the legal status of the slave and the master; the organization of labor; patterns of landholding and land use; and religion, both white and black.

7   This complex and all-inclusive character is what has caused so much dispute about slavery—dispute that has lasted for more than a century since the emancipation of blacks during the Civil War. In particular, historians have argued vehemently about how masters treated their slaves.

8   Some have argued that slavery was a cruel and brutal system—though admitting the existence of some humane masters. They point to the meager cotton dresses, shirts, and pants, the crude huts and furnishings, and the protein-poor diets masters gave their slaves. Most of all, they point to the often sadistic and brutal forms of punishment—whipping, chaining, branding, maiming, and killing—to which some masters subjected their slaves.

9   Other historians have argued that in actual practice slavery was relatively mild—though admitting that there were plenty of abuses. They suggest that whippings were relatively infrequent, and that many masters did not resort to whipping at all. They argue that many slaves were better off than many southern poor whites, and better off than much of the working class of industrial Europe and the North.

They point out that slave housing was at least as good as that of most poor whites, and that the slave diet, especially when it was supplemented by produce from the slaves' garden plots and by game and fish, was considerably better. They argue that on many plantations, children, the sick, and the elderly were better taken care of than were the children, sick, and aged in the working classes of free society.

Varieties of Slave Experience

10   In practice, slavery differed considerably according to the size of the plantation or farm, the nature of the crop work, and the place the slave lived. Slavery in the older, eastern states of Virginia, North Carolina, and South Carolina, and in border states like Maryland, Kentucky, and Tennessee often had a milder character than slavery on the generally larger, more efficient, and more productive cotton and sugar plantations of Alabama, Mississippi, and Texas. There, work was often harder, and both the heat and the treatment more brutal. In fact, masters in the eastern and border states used "sell down the river" as both a threat and a punishment for slaves they considered disobedient or unruly.

11   On small farms where there were only a few slaves, they might do a wide variety of jobs—much like hired hands in the free states. Like Nat Turner, they might move from farm to farm and belong to a series of owners. But a majority of slaves belonged to large, essentially self-contained black communities on a single plantation, to which their families might be attached for generations. Many of the slaves on the Cameron family's plantations in North Carolina in the 1850s, for example, were descended from slaves who had been in the family since the 1770s.

12   But in spite of the numerous guises slavery could take, all slaves had one thing in common.

They were chattel—property. Like horses or land, they could be bought and sold, claimed for payment of a debt, transferred, and inherited. The law, at least in theory, offered slaves some protection. It was a crime for a master wantonly to maim or kill a slave. Still, slaves had no legal standing as persons. They had no access to the courts. They could not charge whites with a crime, bring a suit, or testify in court against whites. Slave marriages and families had no legal standing or protection. Like Nat Turner's marriage, they could be broken up simply by a master's decision to sell one of his slaves.

13   In formal, legal ways, slavery in the American South was harsher and more complete than anywhere else in the Western Hemisphere. But in actual practice, it could often be considerably milder. Many of the prohibitions were loosely or only sporadically enforced. Some slaves were taught to read and write, and some, like Nat Turner, continued to teach themselves. Slaves were sometimes able to gather in their own religious, familial, and festive ceremonies. Many had a small garden plot and a few animals to tend. Most probably had some personal possessions beyond the clothes, shelter, and rations provided by masters. Still, they had no rights in any of these things. A master could always confiscate their possessions, and slaves who were sold usually had to leave everything behind. The only rights, finally, were the masters' rights in their slave property.

14   Slaves engaged in a number of different kinds of labor and worked under all sorts of conditions. They served as valets and personal maids, wet nurses and nannies, cooks and butlers, grooms and coachmen. Some slaves were artisans—seamstresses, shoemakers, blacksmiths, carpenters, bricklayers. Slaves worked in mills and occasionally even in factories and were often "hired out" as skilled craftsmen. The vast majority of slaves, however, were field

hands, who did the hardest and most menial forms of farm labor.

15 Their work was organized in various ways. On farms with only a few slaves, masters might work alongside slaves. On small plantations, owners might directly supervise the slaves' work. But on large plantations, owners hired overseers (usually whites from a lower social class) to manage the day-to-day work of the plantation. The overseers used "drivers," trusted slaves, to supervise work in the fields. The most common arrangement of labor on large tobacco, sugar, and cotton plantations was the gang system, in which the field hands were divided into groups, each of which was directed by a driver.

16 The day-to-day relations between slaves and masters varied enormously. On the larger plantations, field hands and masters lived in separate worlds; the master was a remote figure with whom few field hands had much direct contact. These slaves worked in the fields all day, under the supervision of black drivers, and spent the rest of the time in the quarters, where the master rarely came. Drivers and "mammies" (who were the household equivalents of the drivers) lived in both the black and the white worlds. They were the master's agents, responsible for getting the other slaves to do the work the master wanted done. At the same time, however, they were also agents of the slave community. They could provide their fellow slaves with information about the master and his family, and they could give advice on how to deal with masters and overseers. Other slaves often relied on them to use their influence with mistress or master to modify treatment or improve conditions, or to convey complaints against the overseer—often the most hated figure on the plantation.

17 The personal servants of the master's family had the most complicated relationship of all. A personal servant was often attached to a member of the planter's family when both were children and stayed with him or her for the rest of their lives. Personal servants lived in the "big house" and were in close, constant attendance on their masters and mistresses, at their immediate beck and call. Within the social system of the plantation itself, personal servants held a privileged position. They ate better, dressed better, and were treated better than most of the other slaves on the plantation. A personal servant often ranked higher in his or her master's esteem than did the white overseer. Many personal servants and their masters or mistresses established enduring bonds of trust, loyalty, and affection. It was partly this kind of loyalty that saved the lives of a few white people during Nat Turner's rebellion.

18 But privilege often had its price. The personal servants inhabited their master's world and had little physical or psychological space of their own. They were expected to cater at once to their owner's whims and desires. They were subject to his or her changing moods and absolute authority, within easy range of verbal, psychological, and even physical abuse. It is no wonder that they often developed a complex set of poses —"puttin' on ole massa"—to mask their own feelings and cushion themselves against the arbitrariness of their master's changing humor.

The Master's Power

19 Trying to figure out what slavery was really like by drawing up a balance sheet between cruelty and humaneness—as historians sometimes do—misses an essential point. The common thread that ran through slavery in all its variety and complexity was the absolute and arbitrary power of the master over the slave. It could be exerted for reasons, in ways,

and at times that lay totally within the master's whimsy. Most masters, most of the time, probably did not abuse, mistreat, or (one of the cruelest things a master could do to a slave) sell most of their slaves. But many masters at some time did punish or sell at least some of their slaves. Even more to the point, master and slave alike knew that the power was there and available, and that little could or would prevent masters from exerting it if they wanted to. Even "good" masters came down hard on anything—especially running away—that seemed to defy their authority or undermine the spirit of submission they expected of their slaves.

20   Neither the law nor the planter's white neighbors were likely to interfere with a master's "right" to punish or instill obedience and subordination in his slaves. The master's sovereignty was nearly complete on his own plantation. In 1829 Justice Thomas Ruffin of the North Carolina Supreme Court spelled out the ultimate logic, which seemed to dictate that "the power of the master must be absolute to render the submission of the slave perfect." He recognized the "harshness of the proposition" and agreed that as a private "moral principle" a good man "must repudiate it." Still, he argued, so long as slavery existed there was no getting around it. "Absolute power and perfect submission belong to the state of slavery. They cannot be disunited without abrogating at once the rights of the master and absolving the slave from his subjection. It constitutes the curse of slavery to both the bond and the free portion of our population. But it is inherent in the relation of master and slave."

Slave Responses To Servitude

21   The slaves themselves responded to their servitude in a number of ways. Bondage often exacted a heavy toll. Many were scarred physically and psychologically. It was humiliating to be whipped publicly, or to be forced to stand by helplessly when fellow slaves or family members were whipped or sold. Bondage was also demeaning even in its milder forms. When in the presence of masters or whites, slaves were expected to pay continual homage to their master's authority and to the whites' "superiority."

Resistance

22   But slaves were not simply passive victims of bondage. They resisted slavery in various ways. Some stole. Others committed sabotage. Punishment itself can be seen as a partial index of resistance: slaves who defied their masters and seemed to refuse to submit to authority were probably the ones most often whipped or sold. Running away, of course, was the most common form of overt resistance to slavery—and the act slaveholders were most anxious to prevent and quick to punish.

23   The slaves shielded themselves against the effects of bondage in other ways as well. Some were able to use special skills or hard work to earn the praise and esteem of their masters and partially immunize themselves against harsh treatment. (Many plantations contained slaves whom their masters thought of as "exceptional.") There was also a good bit of dissembling, playing dumb to avoid punishment or excessive work. By conforming to stereotyped notions that they were inherently lazy, slaves could exert at least some control over the rhythm of work.

24   The notion of slave contentedness could also be used to advantage. Some planters used fear and punishment to extract as much

work as possible from their slaves. But by the 1840s it had become a widely held maxim that contented slaves worked best. And there were a number of ways discontented slaves could disrupt the smooth operation of the plantation. Masters often noted the disarray that followed when they or their overseers whipped or sold a slave, imposed unusually heavy work schedules, or took away festival and holiday times.

The Slave Family

25   One of the most important buffers against the effects of bondage was the slave family. Slave and master both attached great importance to the families the slaves created—though for very different reasons. Many planters and defenders of slavery argued that such families were a testament to how well slavery had civilized the slaves and elevated them out of the supposed degradation of their African past. In addition, they considered the family as a way to control slaves: in a family state, slaves seemed to be less "wild," more content, and better workers. Besides, it was believed, firm family ties made them less likely to run away.

26   This was not the way the slaves saw it. Masters might extol the slave family as a mechanism for domesticating the former Africans to bondage. But slaves cherished their families for just the opposite reason—as a barrier against the incursions and influences of the master's world. The slaves' families connected them to their past, helped them forge personal identity and esteem, and brought them into a community of mutual support and protection. Here slave children picked up the skills they needed for adulthood and to cope with their lot as slaves. Here they were taught the

special values and sense of mutual identity and obligation by which the slave community sheltered itself against the harshest features of bondage. Because of this, not because their masters wanted it, slaves created their own families and clung to them so tenaciously.

27   Slave families could never escape the reach of the master's power and were never free of the threat of disruption through sale, migration, or inheritance. Slave wives and husbands often belonged to different owners and lived apart, meeting in secret or only when the husband had a "pass" to visit his wife. But in spite of such obstacles, the slaves created a remarkably durable familial order. They often managed to keep ties between husbands and wives and parents and children alive even under the most difficult circumstances. They tried desperately to keep track of distant spouses, children, parents, and siblings and, whenever an opportunity seemed to arise, tried to unite with them. (Masters, in fact, first looked for runaways in the neighborhoods of the family members from which they had been separated.) And when emancipation finally did come after the Civil War, tens of thousands of slave couples, many of whom had been separated for years, came forward to have their informal slave marriages finally sanctified by law.

The Social Structure of The South

28   More than two-thirds of the white families in the slaveholding states were not slaveholders at all. Moreover, all white southerners had many things in common with white northerners: They had a common history, voted in the same political parties, worshiped in the same denominations, read many of the

same things in their books and newspapers, and did many of the same kinds of work. They also shared the same social and political values. Still, the South in the 1840s and 1850s was increasingly a slave society—"the peculiar institution" touched all other institutions and all people. So powerful, in fact, was the presence of the institution that by the 1850s most white southerners, whether they owned slaves or not, had begun to think of themselves as belonging to a society that was very different from that of the free states.

29   The antebellum South was a hierarchical society. At the top were the few thousand great planters who cultivated 1,000 or more acres and owned at least fifty slaves. Below them were the middling planters who farmed at least 350 acres and possessed ten or more slaves. Closely allied to these planters were merchants, manufacturers, and professionals, many of whom were sons of planters and some of whom owned plantations of their own. In 1850 there were about 6,000 great planters. There were another 35,000 planters with between twenty and fifty slaves, and approximately 75,000 more who owned between ten and twenty slaves. On the next social rung were the 275,000 whites who owned fewer than ten slaves; they were not really planters at all, but farmers. The overwhelming majority of southern whites owned no slaves and had little direct contact with the institution of slavery. Small-scale, independent farmers, they lived lives very similar to those of their counterparts in the North.

30   Beneath these property-owning classes were three other groups. The slaves, permanently fixed in bondage, were at the bottom of the social hierarchy. But there was also a second underclass, the poor whites.

Contemptuously referred to as "white trash," "crackers," or "sand-hillers," these people lived degraded, disease-ridden lives, surviving largely by hunting and fishing, and often living as squatters on poor lands in the hills or pine barrens.

31   Finally, there were about 250,000 free blacks. A few had purchased their freedom; but most were descended from slaves who had been freed before southerners came to view slavery as a positive good. Though not slaves, the free blacks were only minimally free. They were confined to segregated neighborhoods, restricted in employment, denied most civil rights, and curtailed in their freedom to move about or assemble. White southerners feared and distrusted the free blacks; their very presence seemed to be a threat to the institution of slavery. By the 1840s many states had passed laws that either prohibited manumission altogether or required all newly freed slaves to leave the state. There were even attempts to reenslave some of the freed blacks.

32   The class system of the antebellum South was more fixed than the class system in the rest of the country. Some great planters were descended from the "older" gentry of colonial Virginia and South Carolina and thought of themselves as almost a hereditary aristocracy. (One element in the myth of the Old South was that the planters, unlike the New England Puritans, were descended from the nobles of seventeenth-century England.) In fact, the planter class was open to rapid invasion from below, especially in the cotton states of the Mississippi Valley. Most of the cotton lords of that region, in fact, were nouveaux riches who had risen from more obscure and ordinary ranks. They built grand manor houses and quickly adopted the manners and style of life of the "southern gentleman."

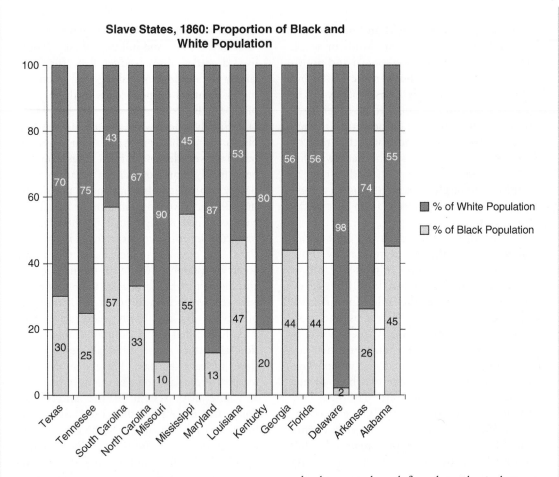

Slave States, 1860: Proportion of Black and White Population

■ % of White Population
□ % of Black Population

Planter Rule

33 Although the planter class constituted little more than 1 percent of the population of the South, it dominated southern politics and society far more than the merchant or manufacturing elites dominated northern society. An overwhelming majority of nonslaveholding whites readily accepted planter rule. There were several reasons for this. The planter class and its allies had the wealth and leisure to pursue politics. Southern culture still retained some of the older styles of deference, in which people of the lower orders deferred to the judgment and rule of their social "betters." Moreover, few nonslaveholding whites saw themselves as exploited or harmed by planter rule. In fact, there was little in planter rule that seemed to them to go against the interests of the small-scale independent farmer. Many actually looked to the planters to protect their interests for them. In addition, many small farmers aspired to the planter class: Like the "common man" in the rest of the country, they wanted to rise above their circumstances and often hoped to become slaveholders themselves.

34   Most nonslaveholding whites in the South were also firm supporters of the institution of slavery. To them, slavery was less a labor system than a system of race relations that gave them status and guaranteed them a sort of freedom. Slavery gave all whites, even the most lowly, social standing above the black slave. White racial solidarity seemed to cut across the social and economic gulf dividing planters and ordinary whites. All whites considered blacks to be an inferior race. As long as blacks were strictly tied to the lowliest forms of labor, even the poorest whites could believe themselves "free" and "independent," people whose lives and labor belonged to themselves. It was this belief, as much as anything else, that unleashed the fear and rage with which slaveholding and nonslaveholding whites alike had wrought their bloody revenge for Nat Turner's rebellion. The same belief, in 1861, would lead them to fight for southern "independence" and the preservation of the South's way of life, its slave society.

Vocabulary in Context

Use the vocabulary strategies covered in Chapter 3 to decipher the meaning of the following words. After you have defined the word, indicate which strategy you used.

WORD IN CONTEXT	DEFINITION	STRATEGY USED
chattel, par. 12		
wantonly, par. 12		
sporadically, par. 13		
confiscate, par. 13		
valets, par. 14		
drivers, par. 15		
agents, par. 16		
cater, par. 18		
humor, par. 18		
arbitrary, par. 19		
sovereignty, par. 20		
repudiate, par. 20		
abrogating, par. 20		
absolving, par. 20		
homage, par. 21		
dissembling, par. 23		
maxim, par. 24		
extol, par. 26		

WORD IN CONTEXT	DEFINITION	STRATEGY USED
incursions, par. 26		
curtailed, par. 31		
manumission, par. 31		

Checking In

1. Based on what you've read about slavery as it existed in the southern United States, why do you think it was called a "peculiar institution"? Offer details from the reading to support your response.

2. Did you learn anything in this selection that you had not known previously? If so, briefly explain what you learned.

3. Do you know something about slavery that you did not see discussed in this selection? If so, briefly explain what you didn't see discussed. Why do you think the authors of this selection excluded or did not mention that information?

Getting the Point

4. According to this reading, what specific issue about slavery have historians debated since the Civil War?

5. In paragraph 13, what do the authors indicate made slavery milder "in actual practice" than it was legally? Be specific and refer to the reading to support your answer.

6. Of the types of work a slave might do on a plantation, what was the most complicated job? Why was it the most complicated?

7. What roles did family play in a slave's life? Be specific and refer to the reading.

Delving Deeper

8. In paragraph 20, the authors discuss the power that a master held over his slaves. What can you conclude might be a problem arising from this absolute power?

9. Paragraph 23 says, "By conforming to stereotyped notions that they were inherently lazy, slaves could exert at least some control over the rhythm of work." How do you think conforming to stereotypes helped some slaves deal with slavery?

The Writing Connection

The history of slavery in the United States may bring up uncomfortable feelings for modern citizens. Although it is almost 150 years in the past, the terrible legacy that slavery has left us with in today's race relations is still discussed. However, there are other legacies or lessons that we can take from this period of American history. Consider, for example, how the authors of this selection discuss the triumph of the human spirit. Specifically, the authors of "The Peculiar Institution" discuss how enslaved men and women endeavored to bring happiness and meaning into their lives—meaning that was separate from their position as slaves.

For your writing connection, consider how some modern people—those who live and struggle during our time—have made the best from less-than-ideal circumstances. You may consider your own experience, your family's experience, or experiences of those you've read about or seen on television. Be sure to describe what the challenge is for the individual(s) you discuss and how he/she/they overcome(s) or struggle(s) against the situation.

The Icing on the Cake

by **Blanca and Connie Alvarez**
from *Listening is an Act of Love,* Dave Isay, Editor

About the Authors

In this selection, Blanca Alvarez tells her daughter, Connie, about crossing the border from Mexico to the United States. Blanca and Connie recorded their conversation in a StoryCorps booth in Santa Monica, California. StoryCorps is an oral history project that spans the breadth of the United States and records the stories of everyday people from every walk of life.

This conversation is from *Listening Is an Act of Love,* a collection of voices from across the United States. Once you begin reading, you will have the sense that the United States is not just a country, but a united state of being human. Indeed, a sense of the universal human experience is exactly what these interviews and conversations evoke.

> ### Before You Read
>
> *Have you ever asked your parents about the challenges they faced in their younger lives?*

Thematic Links

- *Family, ,*
- *Education*
- *Relationships*

Part 3 Book Link

- *Listening Is an Act of Love (Home & Family, Journeys)*

The Icing on the Cake
by Blanca and Connie Alvarez

BLANCA ALVAREZ, 55, interviewed by her daughter, CONNIE ALVAREZ, 33 RECORDED IN SANTA MONICA, CALIFORNIA, January 9, 2006

Connie Alvarez: When I was little and I heard pieces of the story of how you crossed from Mexico, I used to hear you guys talk about a coyote, and I didn't understand that that's what you call the people who crossed you. For the longest time when I was growing up I thought you were running with real coyotes in the desert, and they somehow were able to bring you over and carry me safely into the United States. So I thought that I had a special connection with coyotes. But now I know what a coyote means. What was the journey like?

Blanca Alvarez: We were walking and walking. For me it was an eternity. I don't know how long. I didn't have a watch with me or anything. He told us to take our shoes off. He said, "I don't want no noise because the dogs are very, very good to detect every noise." And he said, "I'm going to whistle when the border patrol change shifts." He told us two different kind of whistles that he was going to make. He said, "When I whistle like this, you're going to duck, and when I whistle like this, you're going to run."

He whistled, so we went on our stomachs and we stayed there. Oh my God, I could see big ants crawling, and I was so scared. Because I was very scared and I wanted to go back, my cousin told me, "Don't worry. It's not going to take us that long." So when he whistled again, we stood up and we ran. He told us, "Run right now! Run!" I remember it was torture on those rocks without shoes. So we ran as fast as we could, and then he said, "Put your shoes on right here."

We were at kind of like a bridge, and he said, "You're going to walk over that bridge. I'm going to walk behind you, and you're going to put your hand behind and give me the money there. There's a post office. You go in the post office, and if you have money, buy stamps. And then from there you're on your own."

Connie: Why do you think he wanted you to buy stamps?

Blanca: I don't know. Probably because he didn't want them to think we were crossing the border. I don't know. There was a telephone booth, and I called a taxi to get to your aunt's house. I wasn't sure if I had enough money to pay for the taxi, but my cousin did. And, besides, I couldn't walk anymore because of the rocks.

We went through a lot of things—like, for example, not eating. For six months your father lost his job, and we never told you that. I guess because we never want to worry you.

Connie: I do remember a lot of beans, bean tacos. And I had to wear boys hand-me-downs. What kinds of jobs did you have?

Blanca: We were gardeners. And we were cleaning offices.

Connie: I remember the offices. I remember being with my brother in our pajamas with the little plastic feet, and I have memories of running into everyone's office and eating candy from their candy dishes. You used to put us to bed on people's office couches while you worked all night.

Blanca: You remember that?

Connie: And I also remember you would always buy us a Cup o' Noodle from the vending machine, like a snack, a soup snack, and then put us to bed, and then you'd carry us to the car when you guys were done cleaning the offices. I remember that. How old was I when you decided to go back to school here in the U.S.?

Blanca: I guess you were nine years old when I went to high school and then went to college, and then went to university. I was so busy going to school that I guess I neglected you a little bit.

Connie: No. Because for me, watching you go to school with two kids and trying to make ends meet—that was the biggest inspiration for me to finish college. I felt there was no way that I couldn't finish if you could do it with all of that. Even when I wanted to drop out, I thought there's nothing that could stand in my way that didn't stand in yours more. So there was no neglect there. You don't have to worry about that.

Blanca: You never told me you felt like that.

Connie: It's the most important thing for me, having gone to college. And I feel like anything I do from here on out is okay, because I have already achieved my dream of getting a college degree. Everything else is icing on the cake.

Checking In

1. What are some of the ways that the young Connie Alvarez may have felt about her "special connection" with real coyotes? Do you think her special connection might have helped her as a young girl? Why or why not?

Getting the Point

2. Reread Blanca Alvarez's description of crossing the border. What are some emotions Blanca likely felt during that experience? List the emotions and indicate which details from the conversation suggest those emotions.

Delving Deeper

3. Describe the type of mother Blanca was to her children. Base your description on the details provided in the conversation.

4. Why do you think Connie wanted to interview her mother and record this conversation? Use details from the conversation to support your response.

Technology Tip

"The Icing on the Cake" is one of thousands of conversations recorded by the StoryCorps Project, which has an online site where you can listen to the conversations people across America have recorded. Go to this site and listen to Blanca and Connie's recorded conversation.

Recording Link: http://storycorps.org/listen/stories/blanca-and-connie-alvarez/

On the StoryCorps site are also a few conversations that have been made into animated short films. Blanca and Connie Alvarez's conversation is one of them. View the animated short of their conversation, and then answer the brief questions below.

Animation Link: http://storycorps.org/animation/the-icing-on-the-cake/

1. How do the transcribed conversation, the voice recording of the conversation, and the animated short differ from one another?

2. Which of the three versions do you prefer?

3. Using details, indicate why you prefer this version.

What's in It for Me?
Why Friendship Matters

by Barbara Hansen Lemme

from *Development in Adulthood*

About the Reading

Barbara Hansen Lemme is a psychology professor at the College of DuPage and has taught psychology for over twenty-five years. Her textbook *Development in Adulthood,* from which the following reading on friendship is excerpted, is considered the most current, comprehensive, scholarly, and readable text on adult development and aging available. *Development in Adulthood* is a multidisciplinary text that presents an empowering view of adulthood through its examination of the influences of age, gender, cohort, race/ethnicity, socioeconomic status, and culture.

In the selection that follows, the role of friendship in adulthood is explored. Why do we make friends? What makes a friendship last throughout a lifetime? Are the relationships of men and women the same? These questions and more are explored in this reading.

Before You Read

Why do you think we make friends? What do friends add to our lives?

Thematic Links

- Friendship
- Psychology
- Relationship

Part 3 Book Link

- *Listening Is an Act of Love*
- *The Kite Runner*

What's in It for Me? Why Friendship Matters

by Barbara Hansen Lemme

from *Development in Adulthood*

Friendship

Friendship is one of two major social domains, the other being the family. As Ainsworth (1989) points out, the term friendship can connote many different kinds of associations, from casual acquaintanceships to more intimate and enduring bonds. Our interest here is primarily in the latter.

Research Problems

Though there is growing research interest in the nature and development of friendship, studies of the development of friendship in adulthood are rare (Tesch, 1983). Many of the studies that do exist are based on adolescent or college samples (Sapadin, 1988) and so may tell us little about friendship among young, middle-aged, or older adults. Definitions of key terms such as *friendship* and *intimacy* vary widely among studies, making it difficult to compare findings and leading to inconsistent conclusions (Caldwell & Peplau, 1982; Roberto & Kimboko, 1989; Sapadin, 1988). As in almost every other aspect of adult development research, few longitudinal studies exist that could illuminate cohort differences as well as patterns of friendship maintenance and change over time (Griffin & Sparks, 1990; Roberto & Kimboko, 1989; Tesch, 1983). Instead, we get a "snapshot picture" of these relationships (Roberto & Kimboko, 1989, p. 11). Finally, Caldwell and Peplau (1982) warn against overgeneralizing the results of friendship studies, given evidence that friendship patterns vary by sex, age, marital status, employment, and other variables.

Nature of Friendship

Why Do We Make Friends?

Many theorists speculate that a basic behavioral system has evolved in human beings—Marvin (1977) calls it the **sociable system**—which motivates them to seek and maintain relationships with peers because there is survival value in doing so (Ainsworth, 1989). Group membership offers protection as well as assistance with tasks that have traditionally required cooperation (such as hunting). The operation of this system may explain why infants seldom show any fear or wariness around unfamiliar age peers, though they may show distinct signs of fear of strange adults (Ainsworth, 1989). So, we may be driven to seek proximity with peers, and some of these relationships may become sufficiently close and satisfying to be called friendships. As in other significant social relationships, the partner in the friendship dyad is viewed as important, unique, and irreplaceable in the relationship (Wright, 1982).

Unique Qualities of Friendship

Friendship is a voluntary association between equals who are high in similarity and whose primary orientation in the relationship is toward enjoyment and personal satisfaction. Let's examine these relationships more closely.

Friendship is distinct from other social relationships in a number of ways. First, the role of friend is present from early childhood to old age, in contrast to many more structured social roles, which are limited to certain portions of the life span—such as those of spouse, parent, worker (Tesch, 1983).

Second, unlike family ties, friendships are voluntary and are less regulated by societal and legal rules (Sapadin, 1988; Wiseman, 1986). Friendships have "broad and ambiguous boundaries" (Wright, 1982, p. 3). This may also mean that individuals have highly subjective definitions of what friendship is and what it means to be a friend.

Third, friendship is based in similarity. Friends are usually chosen from those of the same age, sex, and background (Aizenberg & Treas, 1985; Botwinick, 1984). This contributes to commonality of needs, interests, experiences, and perspectives. Morgan's (1986) concept of a shared knowledge structure and Stephen's (1986) notion of a web of shared meaning stress the importance of friends "speaking the same language" and "seeing things through the same eyes." "Congeniality of interests and activities" is important, both in the initiation and in the maintenance of a friendship (Ainsworth, 1989, p. 714).

Fourth, friendships are primarily oriented toward enjoyment and personal satisfaction, as opposed to the accomplishment of a particular task or goal (Wiseman, 1986). In fact, negative affect is a predictor of termination of a friendship, especially in the early stages of its development, while mutually positive feelings are associated with its continuation (Hays, 1985). Hays (1989, p. 35) suggests that "fun, enjoyable interactions may be the requisite base upon which all friendships must be built."

Fifth, though trust is an important element of most close relationships, it may be especially so in friendship because of its voluntary nature (Jones, Bloys, & Wood, 1990).

Blau (1973, p. 67) offers an effective summary: "Friendship rests on mutual choice and mutual need and involves a voluntary exchange of sociability between equals." Friends are often defined in terms of intimacy, dependability, sharing, acceptance, caring, closeness, and enjoyment (Sapadin, 1988).

Casual versus Close Friends

Like other relationships, friendship is dynamic and evolving (Hays, 1989). A number of studies have examined differences between casual friendships and those that have developed into closer, more intimate associations. Here are a few key findings. First, in its early stages, a friendship may have a sort of amorphous, unstructured quality. However, as the relationship progresses, the partners may develop expectations about how the relationship should function (Wiseman, 1986).

Second, close friendships are also characterized by greater interdependence, contact, and support than casual friendships (Hays, 1989; Kelley, 1979). Subjects in a study by Roberto and Kimboko (1989) indicated that the difference between a friend and a close friend was mostly a matter of degree.

Third, while close friendships offer greater benefits, they also entail higher costs, such as conflict, dissatisfaction, inconvenience, and the expenditure of emotional and tangible resources. The cost-benefit ratio seems to be more closely monitored in the early stages of a friendship (Hays, 1989). As the relationship progresses, the relationship orientation may shift from an exchange to a communal type, in which the mutual wellbeing of both partners is of greater concern than "keeping score" (Jones & Vaughan, 1990; Kelley, 1979). Friendship, particularly close friendship, is a challenge, requiring the individual to balance "freedom with commitment, intimacy with distance" (Sapadin, 1988, p. 401).

Functions of Friendship

Friendship serves many purposes. These purposes may vary by life stage or particular circumstances. In addition, different friends may play different roles. Regardless of age, having friends is beneficial (Reis, Collins, & Berscheid, 2000). Because friendships involve voluntary, mutually satisfying relationships between people with many commonalities, friends contribute to self-esteem (Blau, 1973; Wright, 1982). They also serve as confidants, models of coping, and, by offering support during difficult times, serve as buffers against stressful life experiences (Aizenberg & Treas, 1985). Cramer (1990b, p. 290) found that one particularly potent form of emotional support provided by friends is acceptance: "being available, listening attentively, enabling you to say what you want and being understanding." Hightower (1990) found evidence that harmonious peer relationships in adolescence were correlated with positive mental health in middle adulthood. A number of studies have found friendship to have a significant positive effect on morale, happiness, and life satisfaction among older adults (Aizenberg & Treas, 1985; Fisher, Reid, & Melendez, 1989; Roberto & Kimboko, 1989). Some studies have found morale in the elderly to be more strongly related to interaction with friends than with adult children (Wood & Robertson, 1978). Friends may have stimulation value, adding interest and opportunities for socializing to life, expanding the individual's knowledge, ideas, or perspectives (Rook, 1987; Wright, 1982). Friends are a major source of enjoyment, generating greater positive affect than interactions with family (Larson, Mannell, & Zuzanek, 1986). They may also have utility value, contributing assistance and resources to help the individual meet needs or reach goals (Wright, 1982). Hartup and Stevens (1999) describe friendship with socially well-adjusted individuals as being like money in the bank, "social capital" that can be drawn on when needed. On the other hand, poorly adjusted friends can drain resources, increasing one's own risks.

Friendship versus Kinship

Researchers disagree about whether friends supplement (and can substitute for) family relationships or are functionally different and independent of them (Aizenberg & Treas, 1985). According to the functional-specificity-of-relationships model, different types of relationships serve different purposes, so that they are not interchangeable components of the social network.

A number of researchers have compared the nature of friend versus family relationships. Regardless of age, friends offer enjoyment, respect, trust, affection, acceptance, and spontaneity. Friends are most often named as those with whom adults of all ages enjoy spending time and engaging in leisure activities and who have the most positive impact on psychological well-being (Antonucci & Akiyama, 1995). Because friendship is voluntary, being chosen as a friend seems to contribute significantly to positive feelings about the self. As stated earlier, friends are typically highly similar to one another. This contributes to the positive qualities of these relationships.

Family members, on the other hand, are relied on to provide more significant and long-term assistance when necessary, offering reciprocal support within and across generations. These relationships are not voluntary, but rather obligatory. Hochschild (1973) feels that family ties are so dominant that their strength and nature may, in fact, dictate friendship patterns. Aizenberg and Treas (1985) describe Cantor's hierarchical model of social support in which family members are preferred regardless of the task, with children preferred over more distant relatives, and friends and neighbors preferred over governmental agencies. Those with no or poor relationships with family have lower levels of well-being, perhaps because the absence of ties that should be present leads to shame or embarrassment. Unlike friends, family members are often very different in terms of personality, interests, age, and cohort; they may not have a lot in common except kinship. People of all ages report that family members "get on their nerves" more than friends do. Destructive family ties are also difficult to sever.

Others point out that friendship and kinship relations often overlap (doesn't everyone have an "aunt" or "uncle" who is not really a family member, for example?), and that friends and family members can and do substitute for one another (Adams, 1967; Ballweg, 1969). For example, a friend might step in to augment the social support system in times of need. The answer may be that though relationships tend to specialize, and family ties may be stronger and more dominant, some crossover and substitution are possible when needed, as in times of crisis and when kin either do not exist or are not available. Both types of relationships are important. The marital relationship may be unique, representing a blending of family and friendship characteristics. This may explain its significant impact on life satisfaction and well-being (Antonucci & Akiyama, 1995).

Gender Differences

There is a lot of interest in determining whether and how friendship differs among men and women (Reis, Collins, & Berscheid, 2000). Gender role seems to have a pervasive effect on patterns of casual friendship, while studies of especially close and long-lasting friendships have found no significant differences among men and women (Aizenberg & Treas, 1985; Wright, 1982). Further, even when differences are found, they are not so substantial as to be able to predict the quality of any one friendship between males or females (Wright, 1982). In addition, like other relationships, a friendship exists in a larger social context. For example, marital status may influence friendship patterns in significant ways, and these may vary for men and women (Sapadin, 1988; Tschann, 1988). Failure to take such influences into account may have confounded some of the research on gender differences in friendship, leading to conflicting findings.

Are Male or Female Friendships Superior?

Attempts are often made to build a case that either men's or women's relationships are superior. Tiger (1969) proposed that men had a stronger tendency to form intense, enduring same-sex bonds as a survival of their evolutionary past and the hazards of hunting and warfare. Wright (1982) cites evidence that historical and literary sources seldom represent female friendship, at least not positively.

Sapadin (1988, p. 401) suggests the existence of a "friendship myth," an idealized image of what a friend is, which serves as a standard against which friendships are compared:

> For most of recorded history, this friendship myth has been modeled on the characteristics of men's friendships—bravery, loyalty, duty and heroism. Indeed, women were considered incapable of true friendship because it was thought that they did not possess these qualities. More recently, a new "friendship myth" has developed in our culture that emphasizes deep bonds of trust, caring, and intimacy, qualities more characteristic of women's relationships. Now it is questioned in some circles whether men can ever be intimate or nurturing enough to be "real" friends with each other.

The current consensus is that the male gender role mitigates against the development of close friendship in males (Levinson, 1978; Lewis, 1978), leading to emotional inexpressiveness (Dosser, Balswick, & Halverson, 1986). Studies on gender differences in friendship have yielded remarkably similar findings (Sapadin, 1988). Women's relationships are generally described as closer, deeper, and more intimate than men's. Taylor (2002) argues that women's more social nature evolved to enhance female survival and is thus biologically based and evident from birth.

Females report offering more support in their relationships (Hays, 1989) and also being more satisfied than males with their same-sex friendships (Wheeler, Reis, & Nezlek, 1983). Male friendship tends to be more group and activity oriented and more guarded, less self-disclosing, and less intimate (Caldwell & Peplau, 1982; Sapadin, 1988). Female friendship has a more communal, or helping, orientation, as compared to the exchange orientation more typical of male friendship (Jones, Bloys, & Wood, 1990). While women's friendships may provide greater nurturance and intimacy, more commitment and involvement in the relationship are also expected (Sapadin, 1990). Men may expect and get less and may be more tolerant of conflict in the relationship. Finally, Roberto and Kimboko (1989) found greater levels of continuity in close friendships over time among women. Throughout life, women have more close friends than men do and see them more often than men see theirs.

In a summary of research on gender differences in close relationships, Hinde (1984) concludes that male friendships are based on shared activities, while female friendships are based on emotional support. When asked what they would prefer to do with a friend, 84 percent of the male subjects in Caldwell and Peplau's (1982) study chose "doing some activity;" while 57 percent of the females chose "just talking." When men do talk with friends, it is generally about some activity. This characterization is in keeping with the male instrumental and female expressive gender roles (see Chapter 3). Wright (1982) summarizes the research by describing male friendship as "side-by-side" and female friendship as "face-to-face." However, deep and long-lasting friendships of men and women are both side-by-side and face-to-face. He cautions that there are more similarities than differences in male and female friendship and that there is no basis for assuming the superiority of either. Despite all the reports of gender differences, both sexes experience benefits like trust, acceptance, sharing, and enjoyment in their friendships (Sapadin, 1988; Wright, 1982).

Friendship Development Over The Life Span

Weiss and Lowenthal (1975) studied various aspects of friendship in four generations of subjects: seniors in high school, newlyweds, middle-aged adults, and preretirement adults. Rate of interaction declined after high school and rose again in the oldest group. Similarly, Hartup and Stevens (1999) found that middle-aged adults spend less than 10 percent of their time with friends; newlyweds have the largest friendship network. About 7 percent of adults report having no friends; this number increases to 12 percent for women and 24 percent for men among those over 65 (Dykstra, 1995).

Descriptions of the qualities of friends and friendships were essentially similar across the four age groups in the Weiss and Lowenthal study. Likewise, Candy, Troll, and Levy (1981) found that the functions of friendship remained constant in a group of women between the ages of 14 and 60. Regardless of age, people consistently cite mutuality and reciprocity (both offering and receiving support) as a key element of friendship (Hartup & Stevens, 1999). Several studies suggest that friendships may become less oriented toward the self and more oriented toward others in adulthood; friendships also become less focused on similarity, with a corresponding increase in the appreciation of the uniqueness of the friend (Candy, Troll, & Levy, 1981; Tesch, 1983; Weiss & Lowenthal, 1975). Unfortunately, all of these studies were cross-sectional.

Friendships are often durable, lasting over many years. In a study of 115 males and females age 60 and over, 68 percent reported having a close friend throughout their lives, 17 percent since they were teenagers (Roberto & Kimboko, 1989). Only 4 percent indicated that they did not have a close friend until later in life. Similarly, 72 percent of respondents in a study by Field and Minkler (1988) reported that most of their friends were people they had known for years. Interestingly, women's friendships were more likely to be continuous from childhood and adolescence, while males who maintained friends were more likely to have done so since midlife. Fifty-three percent of subjects in the same study indicated that friends had become more important to them as they got older. Women indicated that this was primarily because of an increase in available time; women (but not men) also attributed the growing importance of friends to greater need. Men most frequently said that friends had taken the place of family members. Among older adults, friends may fill the gap in support left by loss of a spouse. Dykstra (1995) describes the emotional support and assistance of friends as a major protection against loneliness for those without partners.

Older adults risk losing friends through death, illness, or geographic mobility. Given the importance of friendship for health and well-being, these losses could be significant (Hogg & Heller, 1990). Is it easy to make friends late in life? Roberto and Kimboko (1989) report that 68 percent of their sample had not made any new close friends within the last year, though 94 percent indicated that they currently had at least one close friend. All of Kaufman's (1986) subjects (age 70 to 97) mentioned that they had outlived many of their friends. The sadness caused by these losses was aggravated by their perception that they would not be able to make a close friend in old age. "In old age, most friends are old friends," according to Carstensen (1991, p. 198). As one woman said, "The friends I've made recently I consider very much on the surface. When you're older you don't go deep into friendship.... You have no place to grow together" (Kaufman, 1986, p. 110). In addition, as the columnist Russell Baker (1991) pointed out, the older you get, the fewer the people who share your culture, your experience of the world, and your history. As we lose those with whom we share knowledge and meanings, we experience a different kind of loneliness. Perhaps we feel more comfortable with people who have shared "memories of the same ball players, movie actors, automobiles, politicians, dances...slang...clothing styles" (Kalish, 1975, p. 87). Remember that similarity of experiences and perspectives is an important basis of friendship. Bernice Neugarten (1995–1996, p. 1) speaks eloquently of the "costs of survivorship":

> As I grow older, I am more than ever struck by the psychological costs of growing very old. As a young or middle-aged person, I stood in a landscape populated by friends and rivals, by seniors, peers, and juniors, by mentors, colleagues, and students. But as I have aged past the median life expectancy, my landscape has begun to thin out. As those who occupied my social environment die, the psychological environment is also impoverished.... In my observation, and for people of my generation, the experience of the thinned landscape is significant. Really old friends cannot be replaced.

She goes on to say that the experience is different for women, who have a more complex and extensive social network than men. The result is that women have "a less acute sense of being alone in the world."

Hogg and Heller (1990) suggest that social isolation among older adults may be due in part to deficiencies in social skills such as assertiveness, empathy, and role taking, which are necessary to initiate and maintain new friendships. The need to replenish components of the social network may require older adults to brush up on or learn relevant social skills.

The Future of Friendship

Several observers speculate that friendship may assume even greater importance to future generations of elderly. For example, baby boomers will have fewer children in their support network, and their daughters, who have traditionally been the primary kinkeepers and caregivers, will be employed and therefore less available (Fisher, Reid, & Melendez, 1989). Friends may be increasingly relied on to fill this gap.

Vocabulary in Context

To define the following words, use the list of word parts provided in Chapter 3 to parse, or break up, the words into parts that you can define. Then create a definition that fits the context of the original sentence.

amorphous, par. 11   correlated, par. 14   interchangeable, par. 15   interdependence, par. 12

EXAMPLE

	Prefix	Root/Base Word	Suffix	Definition
audiophile	audio-	-phile		= one that loves sound
Definition	hear-ing	one that loves		

1	Prefix	Root/Base Word	Suffix	Definition
amorphous				
Definition				

2	Prefix	Root/Base Word	Suffix	Definition
correlate				
Definition				

3	Prefix	Root/Base Word	Suffix	Definition
interchangeable				
Definition				

4	Prefix	Root/Base Word	Suffix	Definition
interdependence				
Definition				

To define the following words, use the dictionary snapshots to identify the appropriate definition. Then, find a *synonym* for the word and write the synonym in the space provided.

domain	initiation	tangible	augment
connote	requisite	confidant	confound
dyad	evolve	buffers	mitigate
subjective	entail	reciprocal	durable
ambiguous	expenditure		deficient

---

do·main´ (dō-mān´) *n.* **1,** territory owned or governed. **2,** sphere of action or knowledge. **3,** an address of a computer network.

con·note´ (kənôt´) *v.t.* imply; suggest; denote secondarily. —**con"no·ta'tion,** *n.*

dy´ad (dī'ad) *n.* **1,** two units treated as one. **2,** (*Chem.*) an element with a valence of two, as oxygen in H_2O. **3,** (*Biol.*) a secondary unit of organization; one of a pair of chromosomes.

sub·jec´tive (sub-jek'tiv) *adj.* **1,** pertaining to the thinking subject; not objective. **2,** introspective. —**sub"jec·tiv'i·ty,** *n.*

am·big´u·ous (am-big´û-əs) *adj.* of doubtful purport; open to various interpretations; having a double meaning.

in·i′ti·ate″ (i-nish′ė-āt″) *v.t.* **1,** set going; begin; originate. **2,** give instruction to. **3,** induct to membership in a club, etc. —**in-i″ti·a′tion,** *n.*

req′ui·site (rekwə-zit) *adj.* required; indispensable. —*n.* something essential or indispensable.

e·volve′ (i-volv′) *v.t.* **1,** form gradually, as though by unfolding; develop. **2,** emit. —*v.i.* come into being, or change, gradually.

en·tail′ (en-tāl) *v.t.* **1,** limit the inheritance of (property) to a specified line of heirs. **2,** bring about; cause to ensue; involve as a consequence. **3,** impose as a burden. —**en·tail′ment,** *n.*

ex·pend′i·ture (ik-sped′di-chər) *n.* **1,** consumption; disbursement. **2,** something expended; outlay.

tan′gi·ble (tan′jə-bəl) *adj.* **1,** capable of being touched; having corporeal existence. **2,** definite or concrete; capable of being realized. —**tan″gi·bil′i·ty,** *n.*

con″fi·dant′ (kon″fi-dänt′) *n.* one trusted with secrets. Also, **con″fi·dante′,** *n.* (*usu. fem*)

buff′er (buf′ər) *n.* **1,** a polisher. **2,** anything that serves to deaden the shock of striking forces. **3,** (*Computers*) a temporary holding area in memory for data.

re·cip′ro·cal (ri-sip′rə-kəl) *adj.* in mutual relation; concerning, giving, or owned by each with regard to the other. —*n.* (*Math.*) **1,** the quotient resulting from the division of unity by a quantity, as the reciprocal of 4 is ¼. **2,** a complement.

aug·ment′ (âg-ment′) *v.t.* cause to increase; add to. —*v.i.* increase. —**aug″men·ta′tion,** *n.*

con·found′ (kon-fownd′) *v.t.* **1,** throw into confusion; perplex; astound. **2,** mistake for another. —**con·found′ed,** *adj.* (*Informal*) damnable.

mit′i·gate″ (mit′ə-gât″) *v.t. & i.* lessen or moderate in severity. —**mit″i·ga′tion,** *n.*

du′ra·ble (dyû′rə-bəl) *adj.* lasting; long wearing; not perishable or changeable. —**du″ra·bil′i·ty,** *n.*

de·fi′cient (di-fish′ənt) *n.* inadequate; imperfect. —**de·fi′cien·cy,** *n.*

---

1. Friendship is one of two major social <u>domains</u>, the other being the family.

   What synonym fits this context? ____

2. As Ainsworth (1989) points out, the term friendship can <u>connote</u> many different kinds of associations, from casual acquaintanceships to more intimate and enduring bonds.

   What synonym fits this context? ____

3. As in other significant social relationships, the partner in the friendship <u>dyad</u> is viewed as important, unique, and irreplaceable in the relationship (Wright, 1982).

   What synonym fits this context? __

4. Second, unlike family ties, friendships are voluntary and are less regulated by societal and legal rules (Sapadin, 1988; Wiseman, 1986). Friendships have "broad and <u>ambiguous</u> boundaries" (Wright, 1982, p. 3).

   What synonym fits this context? ____

5. This may also mean that individuals have highly <u>subjective</u> definitions of what friendship is and what it means to be a friend.

   What synonym fits this context? _____

6. "Congeniality of interests and activities" is important, both in the <u>initiation</u> and in the maintenance of a friendship (Ainsworth, 1989, p. 714).

   What synonym fits this context? _____

7. Hays (1989, p. 35) suggests that "fun, enjoyable interactions may be the <u>requisite</u> base upon which all friendships must be built."

   What synonym fits this context? _____

8. Like other relationships, friendship is dynamic and <u>evolving</u> (Hays, 1989).

   What synonym fits this context? _____

9. Third, while close friendships offer greater benefits, they also <u>entail</u> higher costs, such as conflict, dissatisfaction, inconvenience, and the expenditure of emotional and tangible resources.

   What synonym fits this context? ____

10. Third, while close friendships offer greater benefits, they also entail higher costs, such as conflict, dissatisfaction, inconvenience, and the <u>expenditure</u> of emotional and tangible resources.

    What synonym fits this context? _____

11. Third, while close friendships offer greater benefits, they also entail higher costs, such as conflict, dissatisfaction, inconvenience, and the expenditure of emotional and <u>tangible</u> resources.

    What synonym fits this context? __

12. They also serve as <u>confidants</u>, models of coping, and, by offering support during difficult times, serve as buffers against stressful life experiences (Aizenberg & Treas, 1985).

    What synonym fits this context? _____

13. They also serve as confidants, models of coping, and, by offering support during difficult times, serve as <u>buffers</u> against stressful life experiences (Aizenberg & Treas, 1985).

    What synonym fits this context? _____

14. Family members, on the other hand, are relied on to provide more significant and long-term assistance when necessary, offering <u>reciprocal</u> support within and across generations.

    What synonym fits this context? _____

15. For example, a friend might step in to <u>augment</u> the social support system in times of need.

    What synonym fits this context? _____

16. Failure to take such influences into account may have <u>confounded</u> some of the research on gender differences in friendship, leading to conflicting findings.

    What synonym fits this context? _____

17. The current consensus is that the male gender role <u>mitigates</u> against the development of close friendship in males (Levinson, 1978; Lewis, 1978), leading to emotional inexpressiveness (Dosser, Balswick, & Halverson, 1986).

    What synonym fits this context? _____

18. Friendships are often <u>durable</u>, lasting over many years.

    What synonym fits this context? _____

19. Hogg and Heller (1990) suggest that social isolation among older adults may be due in part to <u>deficiencies</u> in social skills such as assertiveness, empathy, and role taking, which are necessary to initiate and maintain new friendships.

    What synonym fits this context? _____

Checking In

1. What does the author warn readers about in the section called "Research Problems"? Why do you think she makes this warning?

2. What are the areas that the author discusses in the section the "Nature of Friendship"?

Getting the Point

3. What is the definition of friendship as provided by this reading?

4. How is friendship distinct from other social roles? List the ways that friendship is different.

5. Does the author believe that friendships generally replace family relationships? Refer to the reading to support your answer.

6. Describe one of the key differences between same-sex friendships of men and those of women.

Delving Deeper

7. In paragraph 14, the author states, "Cramer (1990b, p. 290) found that one particularly potent form of emotional support provided by friends is acceptance: 'being available, listening attentively, enabling you to say what you want and being understanding.' Hightower (1990) found evidence that harmonious peer relationships in adolescence were correlated with positive mental health in middle adulthood." Explain what these statements mean.

8. After considering the information presented in this textbook chapter on friendship, do you think friendships are an important part of adult lives? Explain your reasoning.

The Writing Connection

When studying a subject like adult development—which is the subject area from which this reading was selected—there is hardly a person who doesn't see some connection to his or her own life.

Think about the friendships you have had in your life. Which stage of adulthood are you in right now? What role do your friendships play in your life? What other characteristics discussed in this reading are reflected in your friendships?

Write a short essay discussing and describing your friendships and the role they play in your life now and the role they played in the past.

Hurricane Katrina: A Man-Made Disaster

by Charise Hayman

About the Reading

Charise Hayman is a freelance writer with a special interest in the environment. She was a student attorney at the Environmental Law Clinic at Rutgers University School of Law in Newark, New Jersey, from which she received a Juris Doctor degree in 2001. She now practices law in Orlando, Florida.

Hurricane Katrina hit the city of New Orleans on August 29, 2005, and left behind massive damage, hundreds of deaths, and a failing levee system. Over 80 percent of New Orleans was submerged after the levees failed in the wake of the hurricane. The storm's damage was experienced primarily in Louisiana, Mississippi, and Florida. The death toll stands at 1,836, with over 700 people declared missing. The essay "Hurricane Katrina: A Man-Made Disaster" explores some of the issues that have emerged in the aftermath of the historic storm.

Before You Read

What do you know about Hurricane Katrina? Jot down the facts that you can recall regarding the disaster.

Thematic Links

- Sociology

- Journalism

- Community

Part 3 Book Link

- *Listening Is an Act of Love (Fire and Water)*

Hurricane Katrina: A Man-Made Disaster

By Charise Hayman

1   Five years after Hurricane Katrina slammed into the Gulf coast of the United States, some people still disagree about how to discuss the ensuing catastrophe. For example, recently, the *New York Times* rejected a petition to mandate use of the phrase "man-made disaster" in place of "natural disaster" in articles about the devastation that followed Katrina's landfall in New Orleans. Though denied, the petition, which was organized by the non-partisan advocacy group Levees.org, is about more than just words.

2   Sandy Rosenthal, co-founder of Levees.org, argues that it is important to acknowledge the man-made aspects of the disaster so that the responsible parties are held accountable for their failures. And there is no reasonable question that Katrina's catastrophic impact on the city of New Orleans was largely due to human failure in three major respects: 1) incompetent preparation and response by government officials; 2) the failure of the Army Corps of Engineers in constructing and maintaining the regional flood control system and navigation projects; and 3) prevailing, negative social attitudes toward the residents of New Orleans, which appear to have played a crucial role in responses by media, law enforcement, government officials, and ordinary citizens.

3   Since 2005 much has been made of the failures in disaster preparation and response by government officials, with the debate often divided along partisan lines. But there has been less meaningful, mainstream discussion about two other significant factors: the negligence of the Army Corps of Engineers and general social attitudes toward the residents of New Orleans. These two factors, in turn, point to vital questions at the heart of all great societal conversations: what value does our society place on individual human lives, and how is this value reflected in our public institutions and interactions?

The Case Against the Army Corps of Engineers

4   The Army Corps of Engineers has been a permanent institution of the U.S. government since 1802. It is responsible for many public engineering projects, but perhaps its most import duty is its duty to protect the American people from floods. Long before the Corps adopted this role, the New Orleans metropolitan area was protected from hurricane flooding by a natural barrier made up of miles of wetlands and natural forests. But in a remarkable violation of its responsibility to the people of the region, the Corps severely damaged this natural flood protection by dredging miles of canals in service to powerful corporate and political interests. The Mississippi River Gulf Outlet (MRGO) is the most infamous of these water projects. It was built between 1958 and 1968 as a $65 million, 76-mile shortcut—basically a water highway—for ships traveling between the Port of New Orleans and the Gulf of Mexico. So, when Congress passed the Flood Control Act of 1965 making the Corps responsible for building a system to shield the city of New Orleans from hurricane flooding, it was simply instructing the Corps to repair

A dredging crew digs a portion of the Mississippi River-Gulf Outlet through wet-lands in New Orleans on March 12, 1958.

what it had destroyed. But the Corps did not make the proper repairs; instead, it replaced the natural barrier with a woefully inadequate man-made barrier that failed to protect the people of New Orleans from Katrina's deadly floodwaters.

5   In "Progmation: Why Hurricane Katrina was a manmade disaster," Michael Grunwald, writing for *The New Republic*, explains that the Corps built the flood-control system in a way that prioritized corporate and po-litical interests over the safety of New Orleans

The I-510 bridge goes over the Intracoastal Waterway with the Mississippi River-Gulf Outlet splitting off to the right.

residents. For instance, instead of prioritizing levee[1] building around already populated areas, the Corps emphasized building levees to protect then unpopulated areas on the edges of the city in order to hasten development in those areas thereby lining the pockets of influential landowners and developers. According to Grunwald, these scrambled priorities are part of a larger pattern: the Corps also has a history of manipulating its own studies to justify projects encouraged by politicians and "lobbyists for ports, shipping firms, energy companies, and other corporate interests." This corporate influence has generally resulted in increased profits and savings for corporations, increased corporate campaign money for members of Congress, and increased costs for tax payers: a seamless redistribution of wealth upwards. Former staff economist and top lobbyist for the Corps, Larry Prather, recorded his thoughts about the agency in private emails that he was forced to disclose in a legal proceeding. According to Grunwald, Prather "described his agency's politically inspired projects as 'swine' and economic duds with huge environmental consequences." The money and energy diverted to these projects could have been spent on optimizing flood-control protections for the most vulnerable parts of New Orleans. But, as Grunwald demonstrates, Louisiana congressional delegations, their corporate supporters, and the Army Corps of Engineers had other priorities.[2]

6   In 2009, the United States District Court of the Eastern District of Louisiana added its voice to the Corps' list of critics.

The court found that the Corps was grossly negligent for the failure of the levees, which led to the flooding that consumed eighty percent of the city. The American Society of Civil Engineers had come to the same conclusion in a 2007 report, and Raymond B. Seed, Professor of Geo Engineering at the University of California-Berkley, put the catastrophe in stark, dramatic terms: "The failure of the New Orleans regional flood protection system was one of the two most costly failures of engineered systems in history (rivaled only by the Chernobyl reactor meltdown)."

7   Unfortunately, the court ruled that the Flood Control Act gives the Corps immunity from lawsuits over its negligent construction and maintenance of the levees. So, thousands of New Orleans residents will be unable to obtain justice against the Corps for the devastating dereliction of its duty to provide effective flood control protection. However, legal claims against levee districts for the failure of the levees have been allowed to proceed. Also, the court said that the Flood Control Act does not give the Corps immunity for destroying the region's natural flood barrier through its construction of navigation projects like the MRGO, and so far, it has ordered the Corps to pay damages to five New Orleans area residents. According to Grunwald, opponents had long warned that the MRGO, which replaced miles of protective wetlands, was "a storm-surge shotgun pointed at New Orleans" and "a hydrological Trojan horse that would transport the Gulf into the city." At one point, the Corps itself even admitted

---

[1]A levee is a structure designed to prevent a body of water from flooding.

[2]In fact, flood-protection was not a sufficient focus of the Orleans Levee District, which was responsible for overseeing the levees that the Corps was responsible for installing. Grunwald says that in 1982, the districts encouraged the Corps to lower its design standards in order to lessen the district's financial responsibility for maintaining the levees, preferring instead to spend this money encouraging business-friendly projects like riverboat gambling.

that the MRGO's costs were shown to be "high and the benefits…speculative." Also, a 1957 report informed the Corps that in the event of a hurricane, "…the existence of the [MRGO] will be an enormous danger." But despite the warnings, the Corps claimed that the MRGO was justified and Congress approved it, after pressure from powerful shipping interests and their Congressional allies. Ultimately, experts say that the critics were right: the canal functioned as a "hurricane highway" for Katrina by creating a funnel effect that intensified the strength of the storm surge, which overwhelmed the levees and drowned the city of New Orleans.

8   So, why would an agency that exists to protect citizens from hurricane flooding use taxpayer money to destroy natural flood protections, and then replace these natural protections with insufficient man-made protections? And why isn't this wasteful, flagrant, and ultimately deadly dereliction of public duty by the Army Corps of Engineers the focus of nationwide public outrage?

9   Well, the reasons behind the Corps' destruction of wetlands is clear: as the Corps busied itself with satisfying powerful corporate and political interests, it failed to serve the interests of the far less powerful residents of the area, and as a result, many of those residents drowned. Those who survived suffered enormous, heartbreaking losses. As for the lack of nationwide attention and outrage: In a country whose highest court says that money is "speech" and that a corporation is a "person" entitled to constitutional rights, perhaps the answer is that many Americans have simply grown accustomed to the fact that corporate money 'speaks' louder than the voices that rise to defend the interests of individual citizens—like the voices that warned that construction of the Mississippi River

Gulf Outlet would have tragic consequences for the wetlands and the people who depend on them, and, more recently, the voices that warned of the consequences of deep-sea oil drilling long before the April 2010 BP oil spill that furthered the industrial assault on the already fragile wetlands of Louisiana.

10   In short, the story of the Corps' negligence is proof that Hurricane Katrina's impact on the city of New Orleans was, in many respects, a man-made disaster. Equally important: the circumstances surrounding this negligence show that overvaluing corporate interests often involves devaluing the interests of individual human beings.

The Case Against Classism

11   Another cause of tragedy in the aftermath of Hurricane Katrina that did not derive directly from hurricane winds was the criminalization of hurricane survivors by media, law enforcement, and individual citizens. As many residents struggled with the loss of relatives, friends, and homes, tales of looting, rape, and murder dominated media coverage. In her essay, "The Criminalization of New Orleanians in Katrina's Wake," Sarah Kaufman highlighted national headlines like "The Looting Instinct" and "Thugs Reign of Terror." As later reporting revealed, many tales of violence were greatly exaggerated, if not flat-out manufactured. For example, Lieutenant Colonel Jacques Thibodeaux of the Louisiana National Guard, who was head of security at the Superdome, said that widespread reports of "complete lawlessness" at the Superdome and the convention center were "just false." Of the 25,000 survivors trapped in the Superdome for several days without proper food, clothes, supplies, or even plumbing, he said, "For the amount of the people

in the situation, it was a very stable environment." Kaufman attributes the widespread media focus on false, exaggerated, or unattributed tales of mayhem to two primary factors: 1) American media's instinctive fixation on violence; and 2) problematic class and race-based assumptions.

12   As to the media's general fascination with crime and violence, Kaufman notes that during the 1990s, national homicide rates declined 33 percent, a statistic that would probably shock the average American because national news coverage of homicide actually quadrupled during this same time. Kaufman also points out that the murder rate for prime-time television characters is roughly eleven times the actual murder rate. In other words, violence is a major commercial media product. Since mainstream media is a vital means for Americans to learn about one another and the world around them, the media's tendency to sensationalize violence predictably has an enormous impact on American attitudes toward one another.

13   This impact is further complicated by ideas about social status, especially with respect to class and race. For instance, Kaufman points to the case of two images posted to *Yahoo!* in September 2005, which show people wading through floodwaters in New Orleans carrying food and drinks. In one photo featuring a young black man, the caption characterizes the man's actions as "looting"; the other photo, featuring a white man and a light-skinned woman, characterizes the couple's behavior as "finding" items. In response to criticism surrounding the contrasting depictions, defenders of *Yahoo!* and the photographers have pointed out that the pictures were taken and captioned by two different photographers, and that the photographer who

captured the young black man claims to have seen the young man coming out of a grocery store, whereas the photographer who captured the couple claims not to have seen where they got the items. Whatever the defenses advanced for these contrasting representations, the controversy symbolizes the importance of perception.

14   Unfortunately, the perception that violence is responsible for hollowing out many lives in New Orleans, before and after Katrina, is a reality. There are very few economic options for young New Orleanians beyond the generally low-wage tourism industry or the deadly, illegal drug trade. In 2003, the city's murder rate—a by-product of the drug trade—was almost eight times the national average, and even before Katrina, Mayor Ray Nagin sought to bolster the resources of the New Orleans Police Department. But according to observers, such efforts have been typically hampered by the NOPD's reputation as the most decayed branch of a perennially rotting criminal justice system. Officers have been investigated for every form of abuse and corruption—from selling drugs to torturing, raping, and murdering citizens belonging mostly to the city's black lower- and working-classes.

15   But for the people of New Orleans, contending with the popular perception of their home as merely a poor, black, crime-ridden, and corrupt city has been an additional cross to bear. Not much attention is paid to the city's prominent black middle- and upper middle-classes, which date back to slavery and French ownership of the city, when many white slaveowners provided foreign education and inheritances to their children by black women. The typical narrative of New Orleans does not include recognition of how its black

residents struggled against the brutal forces of Jim Crow[3] to achieve semblances of security and success, including the creation of four of the area's colleges, which continue to graduate young people who swell the ranks of the black middle-class across the region and the nation. Ignoring such large swaths of the population and the many layers of their lives creates a poverty of perception that distorts popular understanding of the city and its residents.

16 In the aftermath of Hurricane Katrina, the media's focus on reporting often-exaggerated stories of violence, affected the public's perceptions of those New Orleans residents who were simply trying to survive. In some cases, the perception that hurricane survivors were merely a bunch of violent criminals led to acts of unthinkable violence against them.

17 On September 1, 2005, Donnell Herrington and two other New Orleans residents were walking through the Algiers Point neighborhood on their way to an evacuation site set up by the U.S. Coast Guard at a ferry terminal. But before they could reach safety, a man approached the group with a shotgun and opened fire. The first shot tore into Donnell Herrington's throat, chest, and arms; the second blast, which came after the assailant was joined by two other men, hit Herrington in the back. Amazingly, though Herrington lost a baseball cap in the attack, he was spared his life, and his two companions received only minor injuries. More than four years after the shooting, and after much pressure from a few passionate reporters with public interest news organizations *PBS* and *ProPublica*, the New Orleans Police Department (NOPD) finally got around to launching an investigation. Terry Benjamin,

a former Algiers Point resident so traumatized by the incident that she left the state, returned in 2010 to submit grand jury testimony against one of her former neighbors. She has said that on the day of the shooting, Roland Bourgeois was "hooting and hollerin' like he was big game hunting" in front of a crowd of cheering friends, who continued to cheer when he brandished a bloody baseball cap and bragged that he'd claimed a target. Benjamin says that Bourgeois later told her: "Darlin', anything coming up that street darker than a brown paper bag is getting shot." Reporting about the incident suggests that Bourgeois was part of a gang of neighborhood vigilantes who targeted black hurricane survivors fleeing the floodwaters on the premise that any such survivors must be looters. Though Bourgeois was arrested for drug possession in 1992, he has no criminal record in New Orleans; however, on July 15, 2010, the federal government indicted him on charges of conspiracy, the commission of hate crimes, firearms violations, and obstruction of justice in relation to the shooting of Donnell Herrington. Bourgeois's trial is scheduled to start some time in 2011.

18 On September 2, 2005, David Warren, an officer with the NOPD, shot 31-year-old Henry Glover in the chest near a strip mall in Algiers Point. According to reporting by Brendan McCarthy and Laura Maggi of the *Times-Picayune* and A.C. Thompson of *ProPublica*, Warren, an expert marksman who earned a precision shooting award as an NOPD recruit, fired a high-powered rifle from his perch on a second-story balcony in the strip mall because he saw Glover heading toward a store below him and assumed that

---

[3]Jim Crow refers to the pervasive system of racial discrimination against black Americans enforced by state governments and by brutal acts of mob violence throughout the southern United States from the late 1800s to the 1960s.

he was a looter. Later news reports indicate that Glover's friend, who was with him at the time of the shooting, ran for Glover's brother, who then waved down a passing car for help. The driver, William Tanner, a lawnmower repairman who was searching for gasoline, stopped his car and helped hoist Glover inside. Believing that Glover would die before they could make it to a hospital, Tanner drove the men to an elementary school where he'd heard that police had set up camp. He'd hoped that the officers would be able to get help for Glover. However, Tanner said that when they arrived at the elementary school, the police accused the men of being looters, then handcuffed, interrogated, and beat them as Glover lay bleeding in Tanner's Chevy Malibu. Eventually, officers seized the Malibu and drove off with it. Several weeks later, Tanner's car was found abandoned and scorched on a levee along an isolated part of the Mississippi River with Glover's charred remains inside. A.C. Thompson, initially, the only member of the media to cover the story or view photos of Glover's remains, described what was left of the father of four: "…black ashes and bones…A charred skull, shards of rib, an arm bone, clumps of roasted flesh." On December 10, 2010, a federal jury convicted three men—current and former NOPD officers—in connection with Glover's killing and the subsequent cover-up, including the desecration of his corpse.[4] Evidence surrounding the incident indicates that as many as a dozen more NOPD officers may have known about Henry Glover's murder and the cover-up by their fellow officers.

19   On September 4, 2010, a group of four hurricane survivors was heading to a supermarket for supplies on the east side of Danziger Bridge in New Orleans when they were approached by a group of seven plain clothes police officers in a rental truck who were responding to reports of gunfire in the area. The officers opened fire on the unarmed citizens, fatally shooting James Brissette, 17. According to the *Times-Picayune*, the teenager "was shot numerous times, from the heel of his foot to his head." The officers also struck Susan Bartholomew, who lost part of her arm to a large-caliber round, and her husband, Leonard Bartholomew III, who took a bullet to the head. The *Times-Picayune* also reported that the Bartholomews' teenage daughter's legs "were torn apart by bullets," and their nephew "was struck multiple times, from his face to his abdomen, and [he later] had to wear a colostomy bag for years after the incident." After killing Brissette and wounding the Bartholomew family, officers then traveled to the west side of the bridge where they encountered two brothers, Ronald and Lance Madison, who had begun running at the sound of gunfire from the officers' attack on Brissette and the Bartholomews. Lance was a FedEx worker and Ronald was a severely mentally disabled 40-year-old who lived with his mother. Lance says he and Ronald were on their way to their brother's dentistry office when NOPD officers intercepted them, and killed Ronald by firing their guns into his back seven times. In both cases, the officers claimed that the shootings were justified. A year later, when the Orleans Parish District Attorney filed murder and attempted murder charges against the officers, supporters anointed them "the Danziger 7" and greeted them in cheering crowds, repeatedly chanting

---

[4]On May 4, 2011, a judge overturned the conviction of former NOPD officer Travis McCabe who was accused of participating in the cover-up. The judge granted McCabe a new trial.

"heroes" and showering them with hugs and kisses. Since then, although a New Orleans state judge threw out the case, five other officers came forward to admit that they had manufactured evidence to make the shootings appear justified. The cover-up involved false reports, phony witnesses, and a planted gun, and included the filing of false attempted murder charges against Lance Madison. In at least one case, police testimony has offered additional horrifying details: Officer Michael Hunter has said that after the officers had already shot a round of bullets at the hurricane survivors on Danziger Bridge, one officer "leaned over the concrete barrier, held out his assault rifle, and, in a sweeping motion, fired repeatedly at the civilians lying on the ground." According to Officer Hunter, this same officer approached Ronald Martin as he lay dying on the pavement and began "kicking or stomping [him] repeatedly with his foot." In July 2010, six current or former NOPD officers were indicted in federal court in connection with the Danziger Bridge shootings and the subsequent cover-up. On August 5, 2011, a jury handed down convictions for five of the officers; a sixth is scheduled to go to trial in September 2011.[5]

20   The foregoing assaults all occurred in an atmosphere ignited by exaggerated reports of mayhem, and in some cases, the excuse used by the accused was that the attacks were justified because the victims were looters. While there were instances of 'criminal' looting—including looting by police officers—journalist Dan Baum's reporting adds some perspective to the tales of looting in the immediate aftermath of Katrina:

Looters smashed their way along Canal Street... St. Claude... [and]...the suburbs...Yet what was striking was not how many stores were ransacked but how few. Television crews, their trailers parked on Canal Street, saw the worst. In the French Quarter and the commercial districts along St. Charles Avenue and Magazine Street, storefronts stayed largely intact. Antiques and fine art rested behind unshielded plate-glass windows. People pried open pharmacies and grocery stores, taking diapers, aspirin, food, water, and soft drinks, but left wine and liquor on the shelves, intact.

21   Also, Kaufman points to the first-hand account of two middle-aged, white paramedics who were trapped in New Orleans with thousands of other survivors:

Two days after Hurricane Katrina struck New Orleans, the Walgreens store at the corner of Royal and Iberville Streets in the city's historic French Quarter remained locked. The dairy display case was clearly visible through the windows. It was now 48 hours without electricity, running water, plumbing, and the milk, yogurt, and cheeses were beginning to spoil in the 90-degree heat. The owners and managers had locked up the food, water, pampers and prescriptions, and fled the city. Outside Walgreens' windows, residents and tourists grew increasingly thirsty and hungry. The much-promised federal, state, and local aid never materialized, and the windows at Walgreens gave way to the looters. There was an alternative. The cops could have broken one small window and

---

[5] *ProPublica* has chronicled this case and several others in a compelling series on police and vigilante violence in the aftermath of Hurricane Katrina.

distributed the nuts, fruit juices and bottled water in an organized and systematic manner. But they did not. Instead, they spent hours playing cat and mouse, temporarily chasing away the looters.

22　The paramedics go on to tell of their experiences as part of a group of two hundred tired, traumatized, but ultimately optimistic people, including senior citizens and babies, who sought to survive the drowning of New Orleans together. After walking for miles, and arriving at a bridge leading out of the city, their optimism was deflated by a group of armed Jefferson Parish sheriffs who blocked their route to evacuation, firing warning shots above their heads in an effort to keep them out of the suburbs.

23　Presently, the Department of Justice is conducting several other investigations into civil rights violations against New Orleans residents by law enforcement in the aftermath of Hurricane Katrina. But even before these investigations are resolved, one fact is already apparent: just as New Orleans residents lived in daily fear of violent street criminals before Katrina, in the harrowing days immediately after the hurricane, many residents had reason to fear that stereotypes associated with black New Orleans residents would be used as a premise to disregard their individual humanity, even by those who were sworn to protect them.

The Case Against the People

24　Many social commentators have placed the bulk of the blame for the Katrina catastrophe on hurricane survivors. Commonly made accusations against these survivors are: 1) they are at fault for living in a city that is below sea level; 2) they are at fault for not evacuating the city when warned of the approaching storm; and 3) their inability to evacuate was due to poverty, and this poverty is the result of their own poor character.

25　The argument that survivors invited tragedy by choosing to live in a city perilously placed below sea level is based on common fallacies and misinformation. According to Levees.org, half of New Orleans, including the severely flooded Ninth Ward, is actually above sea level. What's more, the city has been a center of trade since it was founded in 1718, thus, the city's supposedly doomed geography has not prevented it from serving as one of the most important ports in the United States for centuries. As noted earlier, nature provided New Orleans with a natural protective barrier that the Army Corps of Engineers fatally weakened by dredging miles of canals. While this recklessness did leave the city especially vulnerable to hurricane flooding, modern technology, properly deployed, is quite capable of solving this problem. Many cities around the country and the world are below sea level. For instance, according to Levees.org, twenty-four percent of Holland is below sea level, including several vital urban centers. These areas are protected by "a well-connected, well-built and maintained levee system." The American people should demand from American public institutions a similar level of competence and devotion to the common good.

26　Not surprisingly, there is a similarly misguided corollary to the above argument: Immediately after the disaster, many observers began attacking New Orleans residents for not carrying flood insurance. In fact, Cato Institute chairman William Niskanen gave this testimony before Congress in September 2005: "Although flood insurance is heavily subsidized, many—even most—property owners in New Orleans do not buy this insurance, expecting the federal government to bail them out whether or not they are insured." Mr. Niskanen's testimony exemplifies the uninformed contempt directed at New Orleans residents by many observers—casting them as irresponsible, and characterizing them as constantly in search of government handouts. But Mr. Niskanen is wrong. Citing data compiled by Donald Powell, the Bush Administration liaison to the disaster zone, the *Times-Picayune* newspaper reported the following: "Of the 113,053 singe-family homes that sustained hurricane-related damage in 2005, at least 72,787—64.4 percent—were covered by flood insurance. By comparison, just 30 percent of the 28,800 flooded homes in Mississippi had flood insurance." The *Times-Picayune* further points out that two out of three, or 67 percent of, New Orleans residents carried flood insurance—much higher than the national rate of about 5 percent. Evidently, like many of the attacks leveled against New Orleans residents in the wake of Hurricane Katrina, Mr. Niskanen's testimony was influenced more by bias than facts.

27 The argument chastising New Orleanians for refusing to evacuate the city is similarly flawed and biased. Television personality Bill O'Reilly offered an especially inaccurate and degenerate view when he opined about those who failed to evacuate ahead of Hurricane Katrina: "They weren't going to leave no matter what...They were drug addicted...They were thugs, whatever." A fact-based analysis by contrast would have included an acknowledgement that the eighty-percent evacuation rate for the New Orleans metropolitan area was "an impressive public response to an approaching threat..." and "about double the usual [hurricane evacuation] rate" according to the National Oceanic and Atmospheric Administration.

Furthermore, a review of the literature on evacuation behavior reveals that the decision to stay put in the face of an approaching hurricane is not uncommon, and is certainly not limited to "thugs." In fact, actual experts on hurricane evacuation behavior agree that there are many variables that influence a decision to stay in one's home in defiance of a hurricane evacuation notice. These variables range from the presence of an elderly or disabled relative to lack of transportation and lack of money to provide for alternative shelter at a moment's notice. Also, Earl. J. Baker, a researcher with the Department of Geography at Florida State University points out that a "belief that one's own home is subject to flooding," rather than mere knowledge of an approaching hurricane, is strongly associated with an occupant's evacuation decision-making. This factor is essential in assessing Hurricane Katrina evacuation behavior, considering that the hurricane winds did not cause the bulk of the damage; rather, the vast majority of the devastation resulted from the flooding caused by the Army Corps of Engineer's destruction of the natural flood barrier and installation of faulty levees. It is reasonable to assume that if there had been popular understanding of the danger posed by the city's inadequate flood protection system, still more people may have found a way to leave. In fact, Lieutenant General Carl A. Strock, former Commanding General of the Army Corps of Engineers, admitted "better communication from the Corps of the risk associated with the existing levee system might have spurred more people to evacuate in advance of Katrina."

28 But in the aftermath of Katrina, many commentators steadfastly refused to allow their ignorance of the multifarious factors surrounding the catastrophe to prevent them from piling blame onto hurricane survivors. Citing

sensationalized reports of violence in the mainstream media, commentator Robert Tracinski blamed the chaos following Katrina's landfall in New Orleans entirely on the city's poorest residents and the "psychological consequences of the welfare state." Mr. Tracinski said that he came to this conclusion after watching four days of disaster coverage on the Fox News Channel. One among scores of context-free and fact-free analyses, Mr. Tracinski's article made no mention of the fact that in 2002, three years before Hurricane Katrina made landfall, only 3.6 percent of the city's families were receiving cash welfare, and that in the preceding six years, Louisiana's welfare rolls had plunged by sixty-six percent. In response to the abundance of armchair welfare dependency theorists like Tracinski, Rush Limbaugh, Sean Hannit, Bill O'Reilly, and others, Timothy Brezina of Georgia State University conducted a study of the most vulnerable occupants of New Orleans, who remained behind during the storm. Brezina concludes that "contrary to the expectations of welfare dependency theorists, more than half of the New Orleanians in question were employed full time before the storm and most displayed initiative after the disaster." But actual research and fact-based analysis take time and deliberation, and an appreciation of the complexity of human nature and society. Unfortunately, lazy, convulsive, stereotype-driven commentary like Tracinski's is much easier and more popular.

29   Blissfully unaware of the Army Corps of Engineers' complicity in the failed levee system and destruction of natural flood-protection, popular columnist George F. Will's contribution to Katrina commentary was a stern admonition of New Orleans residents for violating the three rules that supposedly ensure a poverty-free life: "Graduate from high school, don't have a baby until you are married, don't marry while you are a teenager." While offering indisputably good advice, Will is clearly oblivious to the fact that thirteen million American children live in poverty, a statistic which proves that poverty is not always a consequence of violating one of Will's life rules, since most of these young Americans are not old enough to break, or even be bound by these rules. In fact, history demonstrates that poverty, like wealth, is often the result of both choice and circumstance. Many Americans harbor the fantasy that middle-class status is the natural condition of the American people, and that people who do not enjoy this status are pathological exceptions, (i.e., Will's rule-breakers). But the facts demonstrate that poverty is as American as concentrated wealth. In 1724, Hugh Jones, an early chronicler of the country, described early Americans as "the poorest, idlest and worst of mankind, the refuse of England and Ireland." Admittedly, this is a harsh description which undoubtedly reflects class prejudice, but it is true that as many as seventy-five percent of immigrants in the English Colonies were indentured servants.[6] In other words, most early Americans did not belong to the middle-class—they belonged to the ranks of the poor (and were evidently

---

[6]In colonial days, indentured servants were people who agreed to work for an employer in exchange for passage to the American colonies, room and board, and "freedom dues." Indentured servitude agreements typically lasted for four to seven years, but could be extended as punishment for bad behavior. Although they generally had harsh lives, indentured servants had rights that were protected by law, and once free, their freedom dues could include land, food, clothes, and money. As labor demands grew, indentured servitude proved costly for landowners, so it was soon phased out and replaced with racial slavery.

viewed by the economic and cultural elite of their time with the same type of contempt with which the likes of Tracinski and Will view today's poor). Immediately after the Revolutionary War, Americans on the brink of poverty took up arms against the government and big business of the day over fiscal policies favoring the economic elite.[7] Perhaps social commentators like Will would have admonished these early Americans for blaming their economic plight on others and for petitioning government for help, but the truth is that throughout history most Americans have occupied the lower classes, in part, because of a confluence of circumstances often beyond their control.

30 Most recently, in the aftermath of the stock market crash of 2008 and the ensuing Great Recession, the numbers of Americans who relied exclusively on food stamps for their income soared by approximately fifty percent. Whatever their personal choices or personal character, it is clear that the economic fortunes of these Americans were impacted by factors other than their level of adherence to George F. Will's life rules. And despite attempts by Will and others to place blame for the devastation following Hurricane Katrina squarely on the shoulders of New Orleans residents, the proven culpability of the Army Corps of Engineers, the New Orleans area levee districts, the New Orleans Police Department, and other powerful actors entrusted with the duty to secure public wellbeing makes it clear that the catastrophe following Hurricane Katrina's landfall shouldn't be reduced to a simple morality play in which hurricane survivors are portrayed as villains.

31 Fortunately, when Katrina collided with the Gulf Coast, flooding the public imagination with images of American citizens in despair, many Americans responded with more empathy. Foundations, corporations, and individuals donated record amounts of money to relief efforts. But to truly correct the man-made failures exemplified by this disaster, Americans must work hard to ensure that our appreciation for human life is always reflected in our interactions with and observations of one another, our participation in the political process, and our insistence that public figures and institutions work for the public good rather than against it.

Bibliography

Applebaum, L. D. (2001). The influence of perceived deservingness on policy decisions regarding aid to the poor. *22* (3), 419–442.

Baden, MD, Michael M. (2006 29-June). Re-Autopsy Report of Ronald Martin.

Baker, E. J. (1991). Hurricane evacuation behavior. *9* (2), 287–310.

Deparle, J., & Gebeloff, R. M. (2010 2-January). Living on nothing but food stamps. *New York Times*.

Dwyer, J., & Drew, C. (2005 29-September). Fear exceeded crime's reality in New Orleans. *New York Times*.

Fogel, R. W. (2000). *The Fourth Great Awakening and the Future of Egalitarianism*. Chicago: University of Chicago Press.

Gelinas, N. (2005). *Who's killing New Orleans?* Retrieved 2010 29-May from City Journal: http://city-journal.org/printable.php?id=1879

---

[7]The most famous of these disturbances was Shays Rebellion.

H. Boushey, C. B. (2001). *Hardships in America: The real story of working families.* Economic Policy Institute.

Hoyt, C. (2010 14-May). Semantic Minefields. *New York Times.*

In re: Katrina Canal Breaches Consolidated Litigation, 2:05-cv-04182-SRD-JCW Doc.19255 (United States District Court Eastern District of Louisiana 2009 8-September).

Kaufman, S. (2006 11-June). *The criminalization of New Orleanians in Katrina's wake.* Retrieved 2010 24-May from Social Science Research Council: http://understandingkatrina.ssrc.org/kaufman/

Knutson, R. (2010 17-April). *Fourth New Orleans police officer charged in post-Katrina shootings at Danziger bridge.* Retrieved 2011 22-March from ProPublica: http://www.propublica.org/nola/story/fourth-new-orleans-police-officer-charged-in-post-katrina-shooting-at-danzi

McCarthy, B., & Maggi, L. (2010 7-April). *Judge in Danziger case sickened by raw brutality of the shooting and the craven lawlessness of the cover-up.* Retrieved 2011 16-April from nola.com: http://www.nola.com/crime/index.ssf/2010/04/judge_sickened_by_raw_brutalit.html#incart_mrt

McCarthy, B., Maggi, L., & Thompson, A. (2010 13-March). *Algiers police shooting report altered, sources say.* Retrieved 2011 13-March from ProPublica: http://www.propublica.org/nola/story/algiers-police-shooting-report-altered-sources-say-313

Media Matters. (2005 15-September). *O'Reilly: "Many, many, many" hurricane victims who failed to evacuate New Orleans are "drug-addicted...thugs."* Retrieved 2010 29-May from Media Matters: http://mediamatters.org/mmtv/200509150001

Meitrodt, J., & Mowbray, R. (2006 19-March). *After Katrina pundits criticized New Orleans claiming too many residents had no flood insurance. In fact, few communities were better covered.* From Times-Picayune.

National Oceanic and Atmospherice Administration (NOAA). (2006 12-December). *Hurricane Katrina.* Retrieved 2010 31-May from NOAA: http://celebrating200years.noaa.gov/events/katrina/welcome.html#forecast

Peacock, W. G., Morrow, B. H., & Gladwin, H. (1997). *Hurricane Andrew: ethnicity, gender, and the sociology of disasters.* Routledge.

Rank, M. (2004). *One nation underpriviledged.* Oxford: Oxford University Press.

Schlereth, T. (1991). *Victorian America: transformations in everyday life, 1876–1915.* New York: HarperCollins.

Shankman, S. (2010 29-December). *Post-Katrina shootings by police: where things stand.* Retrieved 2011 18-April from ProPublica: http://www.propublica.org/nola/story/post-katrina-shootings-by-police-where-things-stand/

Thevenot, B. (2006 December/January). Myth-making in New Orleans. *American Journalism Review.*

Thevenot, B., & Russell, G. (2005 26-September). Reports of anarchy in the superdome overstated. *Seattle Times.*

Thompson, A. (2008 19-December). *Body of Evidence.* Retrieved 2011 22-March from ProPublica: http://www.propublica.org/article/body-of-evidence

Thompson, A. (2009 28-March). *FBI opens inquiry into the death of Henry Glover.* Retrieved 2011 22-March from ProPublica: http://www.propublica.org/article/fbi-open-inquiry-into-death-of-henry-glover-090328

Thompson, A. (2010 10-December). *In wake of glover verdicts what's next for New Orleans' troubled police force?* Retrieved 2011 22-March from ProPublica: http://www.propublica.org/nola/story/in-wake-of-glover-verdicts-what-next-for-new-orleans-troubled-police-force

Thompson, A. (2008 19-December). *Post-Katrina white vigilantes shot african-americans with impunity.* Retrieved 2011 23-March from ProPublica: http://www.propublica.org/article/post-katrina-white-vigilantes-shot-african-americans-with-impunity

Times-Picayune Staff (2011 13-July). *Teenage Danziger victim was struck by projectiles from at least three different guns.* Retrieved September 13, 2011 from http://www.nola.com/crime/index.ssf/2011/07/teenage_danziger_victim_was_st.html

Times-Picayune Staff. (2011 5-August). *5 NOPD officers guilty in post-Katrina Danziger Bridge shootings, cover-up*. Retrieved September 13, 2011 from http://www.nola.com/crime/index.ssf/2011/08/danziger_bridge_verdict_do_not.html

Tracinski, R. (2005 11-September). *Hurricane Katrina exposed: the man-made disaster of the welfare state*. Retrieved 2010 10-May from Pittsburgh Tribune-Review: http://www.pittsburghlive.com/x/pittsburghtrib/s_372587.html

U.S. Census Bureau. (2009). *Current Population Survey, Annual Social and Economic Supplements*.

United States v. Michael Hunter, Factual Basis (United States District Court Eastern District of Louisiana 2010 1-April).

Walton, G. M. (2001). *A History of the American Economy* (9th ed.). South-Western College Pub.

Whitehead, J. C., Edwards, B., Van Willigen, M., Mariolo, J. R., Wilson, K., & Smith, K. T. (2000). *Factors affecting real and hypothetical hurricane evacuation behavior*. Study.

Will, G. F. (2005 September 13). A poverty of thought. *Washington Post*.

Wise, T. (2005 27-October). *Katrina, Conservative Myth-Making and the Media*. From Counterpunch: http://www.counterpunch.org

Zinn, H. (2010). *A People's History* (Dix Rep edition ed.). Harper Perennial Modern Classics.

Zinn, H. (2003). *The Twentieth Century*. Harper Perennial.

Vocabulary in Context

Use the vocabulary strategies covered in Chapter 3 to decipher the meaning of the following words. After you have defined the word, indicate which strategy you used.

WORD IN CONTEXT	DEFINITION	STRATEGY USED
partisan, par. 3		
stark, par. 6		
immunity, par. 7		
negligent, par. 7		
flagrant, par. 8		
devaluing, par. 10		
manufactured, par. 11		
depictions, par. 13		
bolster, par. 14		
hampered, par. 14		
perennially, par. 14		
brandished, par. 17		
anointed, par. 19		
oblivious, par. 29		
plight, par. 29		
adherence, par. 30		

Checking In

1. After reading the first few paragraphs of this essay, describe what you consider to be the difference between a natural disaster and a man-made disaster. Is understanding the difference between the two necessary to understand this essay? Explain your response.

Getting the Point

2. Review paragraphs 1–3. Which statement(s) most clearly express(es) the author's central point? Is there anywhere else in the essay where this central point is stated?

3. In what way, according to the author, is the Army Corps of Engineers responsible for the disaster resulting from Hurricane Katrina?

4. Examine paragraphs 17–19 once again. What do you think the author wants the reader to understand from these incidents?

Delving Deeper

5. According to the author, why did Louisiana politicians, who should have been working for the citizens of New Orleans, seem not to have taxpayers' best interests in mind? Be specific and refer to the essay.

6. The author is making two points in paragraphs 12 and 13. She makes the first point using statistics and the second point using an example. Explain what points she is making in those two paragraphs.

7. In paragraph 20 and elsewhere, the author discusses the "atmosphere ignited by exaggerated reports of mayhem." Based on the evidence presented in this essay, who or what is at least partially to blame for the "atmosphere" that led to the acts of violence described in this essay? Support your response with details from the essay.

Evaluating the Author's Strategies

8. How would you describe the author's tone?

9. Describe the intended audience for this essay.

10. Does the author provide a balanced view of the events? Provide an example from the essay that supports your response.

The Writing Connection

The author of this essay brings to the forefront a topic rarely covered in American discussions: class. One reason for this lack of discussion stems from what we Americans believe about our country: specifically, that anyone can pull himself or herself up from the bottom if he/she works hard enough. This idea is even suggested in a few of the readings included in this textbook— "Superman and Me," "Learning to Read and Write," and "The Men We Carry in Our Minds," to name a few. So, the belief that anyone can make it with hard work is, indeed, central to the self-concept of Americans.

However, tied to the belief that anyone can make it if he/she works hard enough is the flipside: if you don't make it, it is your fault because you didn't work hard enough. James Henslin talks about this idea on a global scale when he discusses the culture of poverty in the reading "Global Wealth: Three Worlds." Charise Hayman also talks about this idea in her discussion of how some people blamed the victims of Hurricane Katrina for the troubles they suffered. The flipside of the American dream is, oddly enough, the nightmare—a nightmare in which you are chased and eaten by monsters, but you are both the chased and the chaser.

Write about experiences you've had, heard about, or witnessed that highlight the flipside of the "dream"—the nightmare. The experience(s) you write about can cover any topic, but the general idea should be that someone suffers some hardship and instead of being helped or supported, is accused of causing the problem.

The Pied Piper of Brooklyn

by David Winner

About the Author

David Winner (1964–) grew up in Charlottesville, Virginia. He received an MFA from the University of Arizona and a PhD from New York University. He teaches developmental English at Hudson County Community College in Jersey City, New Jersey, and is the fiction editor of *The American*, an international magazine based in Rome.

Winner's novel, *The Cannibal of Guadalajara*, which won the 2009 Gival Press Novel, was a finalist for the 2010 *USA Best Book Award*. A short film based on a story of his played at Cannes in 2007, and other writing has won the *Ledge Magazine* fiction contest and has been nominated for two Pushcarts and an AWP Intro Contest. His work has appeared in *The Village Voice, Fiction, Confrontation, Bookforum, Cortland Review, Berkeley Fiction Review, Dream Catcher, Staple,* and several other publications in the United States and the United Kingdom. He is the fiction editor of *The American*, www.theamericanmag.com, a monthly magazine based in Rome.

In "The Pied Piper of Brooklyn," Winner examines what it's like to interact with cultures that are very different from our own. A young secular Jewish man tries to "rescue" an adolescent girl from what he feels to be the oppressive strictures of Orthodox Judaism.

Before You Read

Have you ever heard of a pied piper? To what old story does this story's title refer?

Thematic Links

- Relationships
- Sociology
- Friendship
- Community

Part 3 Book Link

- *The Color of Water*

The Pied Piper of Brooklyn

by David Winner

1   "You wouldn't believe the yearning," is how Feldman describes them on the day I let him back into my apartment. On the little Hasid[1] faces, means Feldman, the innocent denizens of Bedford Street across from us in Brooklyn. They always gaze, he tells me, down to the river and across the bridge at our opulence, at our freedom. Away from arranged marriages, dour black clothes and girlish sideburns towards exotic tasting foods, unusual sexual positions, the late twentieth century in all its glory.

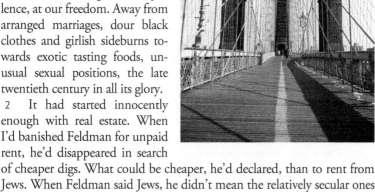

2   It had started innocently enough with real estate. When I'd banished Feldman for unpaid rent, he'd disappeared in search of cheaper digs. What could be cheaper, he'd declared, than to rent from Jews. When Feldman said Jews, he didn't mean the relatively secular ones like us, he meant the "real ones." Nineteenth century life-style, he figured, nineteenth century prices.

3   Yes, I have questions, doubts about the logic, the likelihood of all Feldman's stories, this one included. But such objections are cavalierly cast aside. Was I there, his open-handed gestures invariably imply, what did I know? This is to explain why I didn't suggest to him that those famous Brooklyn separatists would hardly rent to the likes of us, practically goyim.[2] I didn't dare suggest he should rent from the Poles a neighborhood away.

***

---

[1]Hasid—a person who follows the strict, Orthodox Jewish faith.
[2]Goyim—Jewish name for a non-Jew; informal, often has offensive connotation.

4   No, I didn't exactly expel him. I didn't say he couldn't stay with me while he searched for a place he could afford: our 400 a month Avenue B apartment apparently too much for him despite his father's assistance. It wasn't really necessary for him to dramatically throw some but not all of his possessions (I found a large pile remaining in his room) into his lime green suitcase and walk, in order to save carfare, over the Williamsburg bridge to where the Jews were.

5   He explained how the bridge turned out to be eerily deserted as if he was already transitioning into some emptier Jewish past. Bedford Street, though, was packed. It may have been their ineffable foreign-ness—the male Jews in their big beards and the female Jews in their helmet wigs and housedresses—that got him actually thinking that it might not be so easy to arrange a rental.

6   Across the street, a yeshiva[3] teemed with school life, a "just let out" anarchy that Feldman hadn't expected from the ordered lives of the Jews. Boys in sideburns, hair vulnerably short on top, girls in dark parochial skirts, ran in and out of the main doors. An old yellow school bus arrived to pick up some of them, but several of the older ones, approaching the double digits of their lives, made their way across the street towards Feldman. Their destination was the old-fashioned candy store in front of which he had been standing. Kids were easier to talk to, Feldman figured. Adult conversations could follow, which could lead, in turn, to the broaching of the topic of real estate.

***

7   On a late summer day in a middle-western university town a few years before, the middle of the eighties, I stared at my cinder block dorm room wondering what the "Peter Elias Feldman" who was due to enter, would be like. His bags came first, boatloads of them including the lime green suitcase that appeared to date from the sixties, two American Touristers, which housed his soon to be signature dusty, three-piece suits, and a bona fide trunk of the type you saw carried aboard ships by servants in old movies.

8   Finally, in Florida old man polyester pants worn *with* a button-down shirt but *without* traceable irony, and a misshapen hat pushed up from his skull by overflowing corkscrew locks: Feldman. From his slightly blistered lips, came his first story, an entrancing but not altogether believable hitchhiking tale from New York to the Midwest, involving domestic animals and a farm girl in a corn silo.

---

[3]Yeshiva—an Orthodox Jewish elementary or secondary school.

9   "How did you?"

10 "Parents drove," I told Feldman. I've yet to match him.

***

11 A little rougher for wear, those little lines around the eyes that we're already getting in our twenties, Feldman buys the little Jews candy and asks them predictable questions. He wants to know their favorite food, their grades in school, their career ambitions. They are not like other American children. They provide more than the sullen monosyllables we've come to expect. Their darling, high-pitched German accents respond with thought and enthusiasm. They are seven, eight; one is twelve. They, the boys at least, can't decide if they want to be truck drivers, cantors,[4] appliance salesmen or doctors. Eagerly, they stick the gooey Kosher candies into their mouths and politely ask for more.

12 Slick as a politician, he promises them infinite sweets and constant conversation if they help him.

13 Help him how, they wonder?

14 (Recall this is Feldman's version, nothing witnessed, nothing corroborated.)

15 Help him find housing, a bed to lay his weary head. It all went together too, for how could he make good on his promises to them without a place to stay nearby.

16 Wait, says a future doctor, the boarder in the Levi house across the street is marrying and moving to a town of Jews upstate.

17 So our Feldman bids his little children adieu to receive the steely Levi stares that we might consider a more believable response to this oddly-dressed, almost non-Jew.

18 "No room," the long gray beard tells Feldman, "no room for *goyim*." (Our story, as it turns out, hinges on this oddly explicit rejection.)

19 Pop Feldman, an ordinary man, Westchester lawyer unextraordinaire, told me the one time we met, how shocked he'd been by the inexplicable creature that had emerged from his wife's loins. Lawyer, though, still a lawyer's son.

20 The Human Right's Commission of the City of New York, says Feldman, will not take kindly to discrimination against gentiles.[5] Hardly legal. One might think that heavily accented old Levi would not have heard of such an institution, but any Jew knows the dangers of the wrong side of the law, the oily graves of the losers of law suits.

---

[4]Cantor—an official who sings liturgical music and leads prayer in a synagogue.
[5]Gentile—a person who is not Jewish.

21   "Ridiculous, absurd," he says before breaking into the harsh, nasal world of yid.[6] There's a hesitance in his tone, though, the beginning of a question.

22   "Full name?" demands Feldman, "Identification?" Gestapo, Swazi, New York City Human Right's Commission. In the little room in back of the Levi kitchen for little money indeed, did Feldman find a home for himself and his lime-green suitcase. The rent was so undemanding that Feldman could entirely cease and desist with that most unappetizing of activities, the search for work. Lawyer Feldman's monthly support, intended as merely supplemental, was suddenly enough, when added to the array of credit cards that Feldman somehow managed to procure without ever paying off.

23   How did Feldman spend his days among the Jews? Yes, he had considered the possibility of incognito, fake beard, sideburns and the like, but the word was probably out about the *goyim* in their midst. So, in the crumpled old suits that had only gotten more threadbare since undergraduate days, he promenaded up and down Bedford: coffee at the diner in what looked like a trailer home, Kosher Chinese from around the corner, and, when the Levis were not about, the furtive consumption of rice and beans and even Kielbasa from the neighborhoods surrounding the *shtetl*.[7] And, more to the point of our story, he fulfilled his promise to the little ones.

24   Every afternoon after school, he brought them candy and tried to free them from the Jews.

***

25   Feldman at the large Midwestern university took unpopular classes on liberations and complained about the unfathomable uncommunism of his own family. All the other children and grandchildren of depression-era Jews had such different stories to tell, even myself: the common man, the better woman, a socialist Brooklyn, a utopian Bronx. But from Great-grandfather Feldman in Latvia on down, there was no such tomfoolery. Your duty was to family and business. You were not even supposed to consider biting the hand that fed you.

26   Obvious dime store psychology provides our best explanation for Feldman's love of liberation: the family communism that wasn't. While I ineffectually tried to adopt the fratboy conservatism of my peers, Khakis and Izods in the dusking days of preppy, Bush, Reagan, "don't tread on

---

[6]Yid—shortened form of the word Yiddish, which is a language spoken by Jews in the United States, Russia, and Israel mainly.
[7]Shtetl—a small Jewish town or village.

me," Feldman worried about the abandoned peoples of our earth: Kurds, Gypsies, Palestinians. Of this, we seldom spoke. We understood each other and kept our distance: two sides of a classically Jewish coin. You'd hear his oddly compelling, nasal voice in dorm hallways and cafeteria tables painting surprisingly articulate word pictures of the deluded, the mislaid, those who failed to question the regimes and religions that erased them. He seemed to get away with even that most ubiquitous of cave analogies: why couldn't you just look outside and see the light, what was being done to you, what was being done in your name.

27   This was the root of the revolution he preached on Bedford Street, which began, as it always should with the young, the impressionable little Jews. Subtle, careful not to play his hand too fast, he began by asking questions about the lives they expected for themselves. From the boys, he heard tales of commerce, of wives, of study, of being catered to once this messy business of childhood were over. The little female Jews, though, were the real objects of his scrutiny. From them, he heard contented but dreary stories of marriage, of children, of servitude.

28   Liberation, apparently, could easily be adapted to the circumstances of the oppressed. No, he didn't want to create some socialist utopia in Williamsburg. He didn't want little Lenins, diminutive Emma Goldmans. All he wanted for his charges was the freedom of the secular life. It didn't matter how low his opinion of our more capitalist side of the river—he could only concentrate on one set of chains at a time.

29   "Won't you miss your hair," he asked one girl, who was older and closer to marriage, "won't you miss it." The thought of the wigs of married women, the remaining hair for a husband's private consumption, was almost the worst of our Feldman's burdens.

30 "Yes," she said, no need for his seeds of discontent, "of course."

31 She, and all the other little girl Jews, were the target audience of the hairy tales that soon followed of life across the river, the exotic colors, (blond and black, red and orange, blue and green) the vast array of styles: curls, waves, spikes.

***

32 Feldman chain-smokes his hand-rolled cigarettes as he talks to me, sipping cold black coffee left over from that morning. His face looks eager but a little impatient. It's crucial information but a little hard to explain.

33 When he finally pauses, I repeat it back to him, the basic gist at least. It sounds ridiculous from my mouth.

34 "So you rented an apartment over there and talked to these pre-teen girls about what they could do with their hair if they moved to the city." Such shallow fashion should reek, in Feldman's mind, of capitalist excess. Even I feel offended when hairdressers suggested feathery styles, short in front, long in back or visa versa. To pay money on haircuts at all was shameful for Feldman. Somehow he managed to never look like he's had one without his hair looking ostentatiously long.

35 "Well," he hesitates, not sure if he likes it so baldly put.

36 "Yes, that's right," he finally concludes.

***

37 The older girl who spoke about missing her hair was rather odd-looking. She and Feldman must have made a good pair. Fourteen or fifteen, her nose tilted slightly to one side as if it had been broken. One leg was longer than the other too, so there was a hint of a limp. The way her coal black eyes started so deep inside of their sockets, said Feldman, made her seem oddly wise.

38 What she was doing there wasn't clear, as she was much too old for the Yeshiva across the street.

39 One morning, he found her waiting for him outside the Levi house. She scampered away after she was discovered but was back that afternoon with the smaller children at the candy store.

40 The distribution of sweets, Feldman interrupted himself to explain, had found its way into ritual. The children who lacked buses to board or mothers to pick them up would charge across the street towards Feldman and his gooey candy the minute after the school bell rang. He insisted on passing out his treasures with insufferable slowness, one at a time, for fear of quickly running out. Solemnly, he placed his candies into their hands like communion wafers on tongues as he told his tales.

41   On that afternoon, the week anniversary of his arrival among the Jews, his lesson for his charges involved the food available across the river. And what a steaming, gleaming picture he painted, so far from Bedford Street's dreary dumplings and boiled meats: noodles in twisted shapes and fluorescent colors, vibrant sauces and piercing flavors, the Chinese, the Malay, the Italian. The bits of fish uncooked with rice were intriguing even as they were disgusting for the little Jews as well as the curries and chilies, the creams and cheeses. Feldman avoided, or so he told me, the obvious trope; the issue of pork was left well enough alone. While the younger children learned of the food across the gentile river, distaste tinted with desire, the old girl, the young woman, stood a bit apart at the nearest doorway, pretending to be reading some sort of schoolbook. While the others dispersed to their homes, their bellies filled with sweets, their imaginations crammed with more exotic fare, Feldman approached for the second time that day.

42   This time she did not flee.

***

43   Taking a long sip of the cold coffee and pulling a sensual drag from his cigarette, Feldman paused. My occasional fumblings led to little luck with girls. However far from stereotypically attractive, Feldman did quite a bit better. In college days, here in the city too, he was the object of impetuous crushes. Sometimes he obliged.

44   "What they think is this," he once told me by way of explanation, "it's dull to spend your life with who you were supposed to be with." The straight, the boring, the handsome, the kind. Feldman was "unanticipated," "out of character." How could they not give him at least one night?

45   But is that what our fourteen or fifteen year old little maideleh[8] has in mind as she let Feldman approach her? Sexual liberation? I want to suggest to him that she probably had very little idea of what sex even was. Her parents floundered through punctured sheets, if the old story is true, during the non-Mikvah times of the month. But Feldman, to give him credit when credit was due, wasn't suggesting those sorts of motives.

***

46   She just asks questions. They, Feldman explained, wonder what goes on inside our doors and behind our windows.

47   "What's it like inside?" she wants to know, her nose twitching like she's trying to smell it.

---

[8]Maideleh—affectionate Yiddish name for a girl.

48   "Newer," says Feldman, trying to recall Manhattan interiors, the relatively rich ones about which the little maideleh has no doubt dreamed.

49   "More room," he goes on, thinking of the large families crammed into small spaces on Bedford Street, "more light."

50   The maideleh wants more specifics: bedrooms, kitchens, delicatessens, restaurants.

51   It's hard to answer, though. There are too many exceptions to figure out the rules.

52   He doesn't seem fazed, however, by being asked to describe what he so disapproves of. I've never confessed to Feldman that his admiration for my dingy flat kind of misses the point. My reasons for staying put are not based on ideals. An old family stinginess, inertia too, has prevented me from moving into the pleasanter world that my computer job could probably afford me. (Besides, I can't abandon Feldman, who can barely make half the rent on poor old avenue B.)

53   But apparently Feldman would have rhapsodized about wealthy Manhattan as much as he could if he had known what to say. Yes, he's got some images in his head, but he can't put them into words. The best he can do is show her.

54   It is in this spirit that Feldman makes his boldest step thus far. With the slyest, slightest, most subtle of "come hither" hand gestures, he takes off down Bedford Street in the direction of the Williamsburg Bridge. With something like Orpheus in mind, he doesn't look back for nearly half a block. When he does, though, he sees her in the distance staring at him but not moving. That makes him impatient. (And Feldman, for all his Zennish mysteries, is an impatient man.)

55   "Come on then," he barks.

56   And she does.

57   They silently take the streets towards the bridge over gentile waters: him in front, her a hesitant step behind. They stare straight ahead, tunnel vision. But no one pays them any mind as they cross over the highway, past the used goods market, and climb the stairs to the footpath over the bridge, nearly empty this mid-afternoon. Every few steps or so, one or the other of them looks back at Brooklyn growing farther and farther away.

58   The train, clanking by on its way to Manhattan, is about the only living thing they see, that and an empty barge being pulled slowly northward. By the middle of the bridge, Feldman is tired of how timidly she lurks behind. Taking her by the hand, protector but also accelerator, he pulls her forward.

59   On the other side of the river, the path continues ever more desolately for what seems like forever, just huge Soviet-style housing projects in every direction. In other words, it's Brooklynesque, terribly far from the magical Manhattan Feldman had been spending so much time trying to conjure. Does she wonder if he's made it up? Does Brooklyn just continue on the other side of the river?

***

60   As Feldman is done with his coffee, he gestures with his cup. More and this time fresh. I won't do it. He has this quiet, insidious way of asking for things, and, before you know it, you are waiting on him hand and foot. It seems unlikely that the girl had never crossed the bridge that lay so close to her house. It wasn't like you didn't see them all over Manhattan. The whole story is as unlikely as any Feldman has told, but if I question him too much, he will look wanly away and drift into silence.

61   When a cab drives past after they've descended from the path, Feldman hails it. He's got to get to the real Manhattan as soon as possible before his peculiar little charge is swallowed up by uncertainty. Besides, he figures, he also has to get her home before Bedford Street rises up in alarm at her absence and casts him out of his cheap rental.

62   "Where to?" asks the driver. Stumped, Feldman just deflects the question.

63   "Where to?" asks Feldman of the little maideleh.

64   She doesn't appear surprised or particularly put on the spot.

65   "One of the hotels," she says.

66   The hotels of which he had spoken were palatial, floor upon floor of marble and gold, restaurants with waiters in ethereal white suits, stores with jewelry and luxury tourist items.

67   "The Plaza," he directs. His father put his grandfather up there once as a way to impress him. It had to be at least sort of grand. It was definitely all he could think of.

68   The streets grow larger as they head uptown, wider and grander as they get farther from the ghetto across the river. The driver has the wonderful good sense to take them right up to the entrance of the grand hotel in order for the door to be opened by a formally dressed footman.

69   The little maideleh's exuberant skip, past the doorman to charge inside, reminds him of her years or lack thereof. Thirteen or fourteen, only ten or eleven in gentile years once you took her outside the neighborhood.

70   A more serious issue has arisen. But when our Feldman manages, after a thorough scouring of coat, pants and wallet to approximate the

carfare, the driver meditates upon it for a moment, ninety-five cents shy not to mention the tip, rumbles something in his native tongue and drives slowly away.

71   Inside the Plaza, Feldman sees that the girl has lost some momentum. Wide-eyed and tentative, she gazes at the commotion, tourists dashing in and out wearing such non-Jewish clothes. A little further inside, the tea room is right from Feldman's descriptions: lavishly table-clothed, waiters in glimmering white and gold, a string quartet playing on a raised platform in front of a Greco-Roman fountain. Before they know it, they are being led to a table near the music and handed enormous, elaborately printed menus.

72   I wait for Feldman's inevitable crack about how phony it all is, those anachronisms about the rich he used to love: "fat cats" "stuffed coats." But there is something almost like reverence in his tone.

73   I reach for my wallet instinctually, but there is no way I have been conned into paying for an afternoon tea that took place days ago. Somehow, though, I am making Feldman more coffee as he pauses, once again, mid tale. In the old days of my grandfather's stories when the rich looked like the rich and only the poor wore disreputable clothes, they wouldn't have been served at the Plaza in the first place.

74   Of course, she has no idea what to order. The foods were uniformly incomprehensible: petit fours, scones, crème fraiche.

75   Our usually savvy Feldman did not know to refuse when the waiter arrived to ask if they wanted "the tea," did not know that that was a lavish and extremely expensive ensemble.

76   Which proceeds to arrive almost immediately. The little maideleh looks up at the waiter and at Feldman with really quite stereotypical city bumpkin wonder as the enormous pots of tea and chocolate arrive, quickly proceeded by a multi-storied platter of treats. At first, they are tentative consumers. A sly nervous sip, a disconcerted chew. But they pick up energy as they go along. A few bits or every last bite, Feldman figures, will cost the same money they do not have. By the middle of their meal, they are crudely tearing the scones and delicately crusted pastries and slurping the chocolate and tea.

77   The little maideleh can't quite articulate in words the message she's receiving from her bladder.

78   A bashful smile, and she flees the table. Once outside the tea room area, she dashes first to the right and then to the left. When she returns after a longer gap of time, it is with a look of relief.

79   As he sees her approach, Feldman knows he needs to act. (He does not confess to the thought that I know must have crossed his mind, ditching her to deal with the check and taking off to end up—where

else?—at my apartment.) All the surly Eastern European waiters are in the far quadrants of the tearoom.

80   "I'll show you where the facilities are located," says Feldman loudly in case anyone was listening. Then he grabs the little maideleh by the hand, and off they go out the front door of the Plaza in an ostensible, if maladroit search for the bathroom.

81   On neither their way to the subway, nor on the subway itself, does she question their unusual exit. Perhaps she understands that those of their ilk cannot behave conventionally. You may go to the Plaza for tea, but you have to slip away afterwards in a make-believe bathroom search. The basic issue could not be such an unusual one. There were checks after meals on the other side of the river.

82   Chronic taletellers such as Feldman had explanations up their sleeves to fill their more gaping holes and glaring inconsistencies. The reason no alarm had been raised on Bedford Street, no accusations of kidnapping or white slave trading, was that she was "practically an orphan," mother dead, father a drunk. It was, I thought, a rather Victorian plot twist.

***

83   But a serious problem did await Feldman when he made his way to the candy store the following afternoon. The little maideleh had spread the word. He had not expected someone so retiring in appearance to have risked a father's drunken ire to boast about her afternoon away. Now, they all wanted to go. They were bubbling with it.

84   "Take me, take me," they begged. Some even refused his candy in hopes of future treats. They planted a wonderful idea in our Feldman's mind.

85   Yes, he would take them, all of them. They would follow behind him, the Pied Piper of the little Jews, down Bedford just like the day before. Ten, fifteen, maybe thirty of them would clank over the Williamsburg Bridge to be met by a fleet of cabs, maybe a prearranged bus. The whole tearoom would be taken over by an unusual form of liberation: Che Feldman. Yes, the post-tea future could not be predicted. Who could guess what lay ahead? But a seed of resistance would be planted. The little girl Jews would no longer be content to serve their husband/masters. No more dreary clothes. No more dreary lives. An absolute moratorium on wigs. The little boy Jews would yearn for the richer more vibrant life over the river, the shtetl life no longer good enough for them.

86   The look I give Feldman, now sipping the beer I'd found for him in the refrigerator, is one of aggravated doubt. Was he really going to

try to have me believe that he had brought all this to fruition? At this moment, were little Jews waiting politely outside to be brought into my apartment for safekeeping until better plans could be laid. Besides, Feldman had always so bitterly complained about the dangers of life on *our* side of the river: the fat cats everywhere, the poor folks like us. He would be dumping the little Jews from the frying pan into the fire.

87   Strands of realism get breathed occasionally into the tales of Feldman. He couldn't really take them anywhere, not all of them. That was why he had to flee Bedford Street. They were pressuring and pressuring, bullying and cajoling, making life generally unbearable. He had to return to live across the river, however cheap the rent he had paid, however charmed the life he had led.

***

88   It goes without saying that Feldman believed enough resistance had been planted anyway, just by the stories, just by his presence among the Jews. But what did he really do—I have cause enough to wonder—sow depression, frustration, early suicide? Would the little boys and girls be ineffably dissatisfied from then on? Those glimpses across the river, that ever told story.

89   But even as these doubts circle my mind, I know I have fallen yet again for one of Feldman's stories. Maybe, just maybe—I can't help but wonder—some of it may have been true?

90   It won't leave my mind. The days pass, the weeks, a month almost. Feldman and I have fallen into our usual routines. He wanders the streets drinking coffee in cafes and diners, writing down lunatic schemes and enigmatic diagrams on napkins and shoplifted post-it notes. I go to my job, flow charts and html codes. For the first month, at least, Feldman pays me his share of the rent. Nothing more is said of the Jews across the river. Whatever plans have replaced them in Feldman's mind are in their silent, hatching phase.

91   Was it Costello who got the hypnosis intended for Abbot or Lucy for Ricky in those old routines? Whatever the little Jews across the river may or may not have been feeling, the seeds of Feldman's story grow in me until I am pregnant with them. But it is not until a slightly hung-over Sunday, a warm, late spring morning that I embark on a fact-checking mission over the gentile river.

92   Feldman had not returned the evening before from wherever it was he had been. Not entirely unusual but a little lonely-making. The little Jews, it occurs to me, have also been abandoned.

93   It is only fitting that the journey should be made on foot. But it is rather a painful day to be outside: the sky brilliantly blue, the

few flowers and plants on the walk in that fierce early bloom, the kind of day to be spent if not in the arms of a lover at least in a park or playing field.

94   Near the foot of the bridge on the other side indeed lies Bedford Street. The Jews, as is their wont, are out on a Sunday. They stroll in family packs: tall, bearded patres familias followed by wives and little ones.

95   Can it really be true that they have so few glimpses of the world across the river? Can an afternoon at the Plaza really alter the course of their lives? Feldman exaggerates, extenuates, incorporates but does not, to my knowledge, hallucinate. Somewhere, there are shards of truth. But the yeshiva with the candy store across the street doesn't verify Feldman's tale; it could be just the fact woven into the fiction.

96   The store itself is open. The old man with the long gray beard looks up at me with a nod of faint recognition. There are those who have felt I look like Feldman despite my taller height, my shorter nose, my straighter, calmer hair. I don't hunch that badly either.

97   "Yes," I ask the old man as if he'd said something.

98   "I thought you were someone else," grumbles the predictably Yiddish basso.

99   "Feldman?" I ask.

100   *I don't know* he shrugs. It's not as if Feldman would have introduced himself by name.

101   The old man looks at me expectantly, and I oblige, buying some sticky looking candy.

102   When I leave the store, there is indeed a little Jew outside, just one. Not the older girl with the deep, dark eyes, not a girl at all.

103   The little boy sticks out his hand in search of candy. Feldmanesque, I hand him a piece.

104   "When's he coming back?" asks the boy.

105   Before I can think what to say, he's run up the street to where his family is still strolling by.

106   This is where the little Jews run wild, parents not seeming to notice or particularly care. Pigeons around crumbs, flies around honey, little Jews around candy: suddenly, there are three more. A boy and two little girls, eight or nine maybe. They don't seem satisfied with just the candy.

107   "I don't know where he is," I beat them to their question, "I don't know when he's coming back."

108   They look up at me a little puzzled, not a hundred percent sure what I'm talking about. I don't have any stories for them, if that's what they want. I won't take them to tea across the river.

109 Finally, an opportunity to find the truth behind a tale of Feldman, but the sources run off without giving me a chance to ask. No one else appears outside the candy store for the several more minutes that I wait there.

110 The cardboard "for rent" sign a few blocks further up Bedford is really too weathered to have only been up for the month or so since Feldman had left.

111 It is enough that Feldman could have been there, that it can't be proved false, reasonable undoubt: a street called Bedford, a yeshiva in front of a candy store, a room for rent down the street.

112 My shaky index finger approaches the buzzer. Through the wardrobe into Feldman's tale. I can threaten the Human Right's Commission if the old man won't rent.

Vocabulary in Context

To define the following words, select the option that best defines the word as used in the reading.

denizens	unextraordinaire	inertia
cavalierly	procure	rhapsodized
invariably	incognito	incomprehensible
ineffable	promenaded	ostensible
anarchy	ubiquitous	maladroit
parochial	ostentatiously	wont
broaching	trope	extenuates
corroborated		

____ 1. On the little Hasid faces, means Feldman, the innocent *denizens* of Bedford Street across from us in Brooklyn. (par. 1)

    a) defenders   b) occupants

____ 2. Yes, I have questions, doubts about the logic, the likelihood of all Feldman's stories, this one included. But such objections are *cavalierly* cast aside. (par. 3)

    a) carelessly   b) angrily.

____ 3. But such objections are cavalierly cast aside. Was I there, his openhanded gestures *invariably* imply, what did I know? (par. 3)

    a) always   b) carefully

____ 4. It may have been their *ineffable* foreignness—the male Jews in their big beards and the female Jews in their helmet wigs and housedresses—that got him actually thinking that it might not be so easy to arrange a rental. (par. 5)

    a) sudden   b) indescribable

_____ 5. Across the street, a yeshiva teemed with school life, a "just let out" *anarchy* that Feldman hadn't expected from the ordered lives of the Jews. (par. 6)

a) disorder   b) situation

_____ 6. Across the street, a yeshiva teemed with school life, a "just let out" anarchy that Feldman hadn't expected from the ordered lives of the Jews. Boys in sideburns, hair vulnerably short on top, girls in dark *parochial* skirts, ran in and out of the main doors. (par. 6)

a) decorated   b) church-like

_____ 7. Adult conversations could follow, which could lead, in turn, to the *broaching* of the topic of real estate. (par. 6)

a) bring up   b) understand

_____ 8. Recall this is Feldman's version, nothing witnessed, nothing *corroborated.* (par. 14)

a) confirm   b) seen

_____ 9. Pop Feldman, an ordinary man, Westchester lawyer *unextraordinaire,* told me the one time we met, how shocked he'd been by the inexplicable creature that had emerged from his wife's loins. (par. 19)

a) not extraordinary   b) very special

_____ 10. Pop Feldman, an ordinary man, Westchester lawyer unextraordinaire, told me the one time we met, how shocked he'd been by the *inexplicable* creature that had emerged from his wife's loins. (par. 19)

a) unexplained   b) quickly

_____ 11. Lawyer Feldman's monthly support, intended as merely supplemental, was suddenly enough, when added to the array of credit cards that Feldman somehow managed to *procure* without ever paying off. (par. 22)

a) extend   b) obtain

_____ 12. Yes, he had considered the possibility of *incognito,* fake beard, sideburns and the like, but the word was probably out about the goyim in their midst. (par. 23)

a) disguise   b) changing religions

_____ 13. So, in the crumpled old suits that had only gotten more threadbare since undergraduate days, he *promenaded* up and down Bedford.... (par. 23)

a) leisurely walk   b) careful search

_____ 14. He seemed to get away with even that most *ubiquitous* of cave analogies: why couldn't you just look outside and see the light, what was being done to you, what was being done in your name. (par. 26)

a) outlandish   b) found everywhere

_____ 15. Somehow he managed to never look like he's had one without his hair looking *ostentatiously* long. (par. 34)

a) obviously   b) girlishly

_____ 16. Feldman avoided, or so he told me, the obvious *trope*; the issue of pork was left well enough alone. (par. 41)

a) conventional idea   b) a group

_____ 17. An old family stinginess, *inertia* too, has prevented me from moving into the pleasanter world that my computer job could probably afford me. (par. 52)

a) still, unmoving   b) ghost

_____ 18. But apparently Feldman would have *rhapsodized* about wealthy Manhattan as much as he could if he had known what to say. (par. 53)

a) speak eloquently   b) rant about

_____ 19. He has this quiet, *insidious* way of asking for things, and, before you know it, you are waiting on him hand and foot. (par. 60)

a) nice   b) sneaky

_____ 20. The foods were uniformly *incomprehensible*: petit fours, scones, crème fraiche. (par. 74)

a) very expensive   b) not understandable

_____ 21. Then he grabs the little maideleh by the hand, and off they go out the front door of the Plaza in an *ostensible*, if maladroit search for the bathroom. (par. 80)

a) desperate   b) seemingly, but not really, true

_____ 22. Then he grabs the little maideleh by the hand, and off they go out the front door of the Plaza in an ostensible, if *maladroit* search for the bathroom. (par. 80)

a) evil   b) clumsy

_____ 23. The Jews, as is their *wont*, are out on a Sunday. (par. 94)

a) custom   b) plan

_____ 24. Feldman exaggerates, *extenuates*, incorporates but does not, to my knowledge, hallucinate. (par. 95)

a) extends   b) exterminates

Checking In

1. Where does the narrator live? Is that important to the story? Why or why not?

2. How does the narrator feel about Feldman's stories? What details support your response?

Getting the Point

3. According to Feldman, why does the man, Levi, agree to let Feldman rent the room?

4. Reread paragraph 26. What does that paragraph tell the reader about Feldman? Is it important to the story? Why or why not?

5. There are a few pivotal scenes in this story. One is when Feldman rents the room from Levi. What is another pivotal scene? Describe the moment and why it is important to the development of the story.

Delving Deeper

·6. Why is the narrator so surprised that Feldman "would have rhapsodized about wealthy Manhattan as much as he could" (par. 53)?

7. When Feldman realizes that the other children have heard about his trip across the bridge and want to go too, is it a surprise that Feldman decides to leave and head back to his old life? Why or why not?

8. The story ends with the narrator taking his own trip across the bridge. What do you think he wants from this experience? Why does he retrace Feldman's steps? Explain your response.

9. As discussed in Chapter 6, fiction writers often use recurring images and ideas to convey meaning. Identify and discuss one image or idea that recurs in this story.

10. Consider all of the ideas you've explored in these questions. What is an overall idea conveyed by Feldman's experience with the young people he met? Point to supporting details as evidence of that idea.

Evaluating the Author's Strategies

11. Within this story, the author references quite a few culturally specific customs that Hasidic Jews practice. Why do you think the author chose to make those references? Does it help clarify some aspects of the story?

The Writing Connection

One of the most obvious aspects of this story is the idea of being among people who live differently than you do. The narrator of the story is part of the culture in some ways—he is Jewish although not Hasidic—but the families across the bridge still seem very different to him.

Have you ever had the experience of being a part of something but yet not a part of it? Was your experience based on culture, religion, ethnicity, race, or something else? Discuss and describe your experience in a short essay.

The Reading Guide

These reading guides are intended to be used in conjunction with the books to which they refer.

BOOK 1

Listening Is an Act of Love, edited by Dave Isay
(nonfiction)

BOOK 2

*Narrative of the Life of Frederick Douglass,
an American Slave*, by Frederick Douglass
(autobiography)

BOOK 5

Three Cups of Tea, by Greg Mortenson
and David Oliver Relin (nonfiction)

BOOK 3

The Kite Runner, by Khaled Hosseini
(fiction)

BOOK 4

The Color of Water, by James McBride
(memoir)

Listening Is an Act of Love

edited by Dave Isay

Synopsis

Dave Isay, the founder of StoryCorps and the editor of *Listening Is an Act of Love*, shares the experiences that led him to begin the StoryCorps project in his essay "The Story of StoryCorps." One of the experiences involved his showing homeless and near-homeless men who live on the lower East Side of New York City some pages of a soon-to-be-published book that feature photographs of them and the text of their oral histories. Isay writes:

> One of the men looked at his story, took it in his hands, and literally danced through the halls of the hotel shouting, "I exist! I exist!" I was stunned. I realized as never before how many people among us feel completely invisible, believe their lives don't matter, and fear they'll someday be forgotten.

Isay's experience with this man, who had never before felt that he existed in the larger world, who felt that he could live or die with no impact, speaks to the undertaking that is StoryCorps. StoryCorps is an oral history project that spans the breadth of the United States and records the stories of everyday people, from every walk of life. These oral histories are preserved in the Library of Congress to stand as testimonies to the people who lived and loved, dreamed and died, suffered and recovered during the twentieth and twenty-first centuries in America. The stories are real, the people are real, and the connection the reader feels is also real.

Listening Is an Act of Love is a collection of these voices from across the United States. Once you begin reading, you will have the sense that the United States is not just a country, but a united state of being human. Indeed, a sense of the universal human experience is exactly what these interviews and conversations—conversations that reveal stories—evoke in this collection.

The book is divided into five sections that group the StoryCorps interviews by theme: Home and Family, Work and Dedication, Journeys, History and Struggle, and Fire and Water. Each of these thematic groupings reveals a cross section of the American experience as told by the people who have lived and are living that experience.

READING CONNECTIONS

"Hurricane Katrina: A Man-Made Disaster"   Hurricane Katrina hit the city of New Orleans on August 29, 2005, and left behind massive damage, hundreds of deaths, and a failing levee system. Over 80 percent of New Orleans was submerged after the levees failed in the wake of the hurricane. The storm's damage was experienced primarily in Louisiana, Mississippi, and Florida. The death toll stands at 1,836, with over 700 people declared missing. The essay "Hurricane Katrina: A Man-Made Disaster" explores some of the issues that have emerged in the aftermath of the historic storm.

"The Icing on the Cake"   Blanca Alvarez tells her daughter, Connie, about crossing the border from Mexico to the United States. Blanca and Connie recorded their conversation in a StoryCorps booth in Santa Monica, California.

UNDERSTANDING CONTEXT

As mentioned in the synopsis of *Listening Is an Act of Love*, editor and famous radio producer Dave Isay shares, in an essay titled "The Story of StoryCorps," the experiences that led him to begin the StoryCorps project. Before reading the interviews, consider reading "The Story of StoryCorps," which is located near the end of the book. It truly lays out the map for the journey upon which this collection will send you.

TECHNOLOGY TIP

To better understand the StoryCorps project, please visit the website www.storycorps.net. On the website, you can read about the founding of StoryCorps, listen to the actual recordings of the interviews in this book and others, find out how to record your own interview, and much more.

FOCUS ON STRATEGY

Dave Isay, the editor of this collection, has chosen to include these particular interviews with one underlying goal: to share incredible stories. With that in mind, a major focus for the reader is to understand the experience being shared. To aid the reader's understanding, the primary function of the questions in this reading guide is to promote a deeper and more reflective understanding of the conversations featured in this collection.

Home and Family (11 conversations)

Conversation	Subject/Focus	Themes
Cynthia Rahn is interviewed by her friend Adrienne Lea.	*The creativity of mothers*	*sacrifice, fitting in, and appreciation*
Dr. Richard Collins is interviewed by his grandson Sean Collins.		
Seth Fleischauer interviews his grandfather William Jacobs.		
Joyce Kim Lee interviews her mother, Hee-Sook Lee.		
Sulochana Konur is interviewed by her daughter-in-law Melissa Konur.		
Victoria Keller Fraser speaks with her grandson Christopher James Fraser.		
Brad Skow interviews his birth mother, Mary Lou Maher.		
Cherie Johnson shares memories with her cousin James Ransom.		
Karen Washabau shares memories with her husband, Dave Washabau.		
Anthony D'Andrea is interviewed by his daughters Monica Mcinerney and Mary D'Andrea.		
Rebecca Katechis speaks with her sister Carolyn Schlam.		

HOME AND FAMILY

Checking In

1. Review the eleven conversations shared in this section. Which one was most memorable to you? Briefly explain why it stood out for you.

Getting the Point

2. Select three of the conversations in Home and Family and discuss the similarities you found in either the experiences shared or the themes evoked by the conversations.

3. In many of the conversations, a sense of belonging emerges from the story. Locate and discuss two examples of what you consider a sense of belonging.

Delving Deeper

4. Discuss a recurring theme that you found in this section. Go beyond the idea of Home and Family to discuss other recurring themes in these conversations.

5. There are three conversations between a grandparent and a grandchild in this section. Based on the nature of those three conversations, what can you conclude about the role that some grandparents play in a family? Refer to the conversations to support your response.

> ### Collaboration Challenge
>
> *Working in small groups, students should read three or four StoryCorps conversations and then select the two they want to share with the rest of the class. Alternatively, students may select two conversations to share and answer one of the questions in this section.*

The Writing Connection

If you were able to select any person in your family to have a conversation with in the StoryCorps booth, who would it be? What would you like to say to that person?

If possible, have the conversation with the person you selected and record what is shared. When it is over, transcribe the conversation from the recording.

If it is not possible to speak with the person you selected, imagine how you think the conversation would go. Or record yourself speaking to that person as if he/she were present with you. Or share your thoughts about that person with a friend or family member and record the conversation. However you conduct your conversation, write it down afterward.

Near the end of the book is a checklist for recording great conversations. Be sure to look it over as you prepare for your own amazing conversation.

Work and Dedication (13 conversations)

Conversation	Subject/Focus	Theme
Dr. Monica Mayer is interviewed by her cousin and patient Spencer Wilkinson Jr.		
Ken Kobus shares with his friend Ron Baraff.		
Samuel W. Black is interviewed by his wife, Edda Fields-Black.		
Joyce Butler is interviewed by her daughter Stephanie Butler.		
Sharon St. Aubin is interviewed by her nephew Jerrold Arneson.		
Lori Fitzgerald interviews her father, Lendal Hill.		
Barb Fuller-Curry is interviewed by her son Craig Curry.		
Rick Kincaid is interviewed by his friend Danny Terry.		
Phyllis Johnson is interviewed by Danny Perasa.		
Ronald Ruiz is interviewed by facilitator Brett Myers.		
Barney Feldman is interviewed by his daughter Susan Beckman.		
Scott Kohanek and his wife, Catherine Kohanek, share memories.		
Janet Lutz is interviewed by her friend Lori Armstrong.		

WORK AND DEDICATION

Checking In

1. What do you think "dedication" in this section's title refers to? Did you see evidence of "dedication" in these conversations? Explain your response.

Getting the Point

2. In the first conversation of this section, Dr. Monica Mayer discusses the lesson her father taught her and her two sisters when they were young. A quick summary of that lesson could be: *work hard in school or work hard in life*. Discuss another conversation from this section in which a person reveals a lasting lesson or idea that a parent passed on to him/her.

3. In a few of the conversations, the speaker expresses an undeniable pride or love for his/her work. Discuss two instances of this prideful employment, and refer specifically to details that show this pride or love.

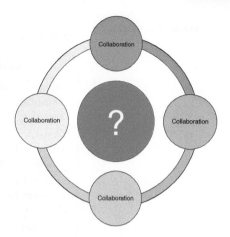

Delving Deeper

4. While quite a few of the conversations reveal a passion for a particular type of work, other conversations touch on how the love of life actually convinced the person to leave or avoid a particular type of work. Review the conversations and discuss two instances where you see a person reach a turning point in regard to work—a turning point that is actually a turning away from some specific type of work.

> **Many Minds Review**
>
> *Student teams should respond to the same question. Which team will compose the most inventive but relevant response? Take the challenge!*

5. The last conversation in this section involves a hospital chaplain, Janet Lutz, who talks about how each year she will "bless the hands of all the people who work in the hospital." She describes this blessing of hands as a way of saying thank you for all the hard work—the thank-less, anonymous, and the behind-the-scenes work—that hospital employees undertake.

    Using the idea of blessing the hands of those who work hard, describe how another person in one of the other interviews "blesses the hands" of someone he/she loves with the words in the conversation.

The Writing Connection

Whether or not a person has ever worked a day in his/her life, by the time most people reach adulthood, they have absorbed a few lessons about the workplace and working. Consider what you have learned about working—either from your own experience or from the experiences of those around you. Share the lesson as a story you would tell someone.

Journeys (11 conversations)

Conversation	Subject/Focus	Theme
Brittany Conant interviews her mother-in-law, Martha Conant.		
Blanca Alvarez is interviewed by her daughter Connie Alvarez.		
Eddie S. Lanier Jr. is interviewed by his friend David Wright.		
Paul Mortimer and Shawn Fox interview each other.		
John Brown is interviewed by his brother Paul Corbit Brown.		
Kim Schumer is interviewed by her sister Amy Schumer.		
Curtis Cates is interviewed by his wife, Cindy Connolly Cates.		
George Caywood is interviewed by his daughter Gina Caywood.		
Shasti O'Leary-Soudant is interviewed by her husband, Jethro Soudant.		
Gregg Korbon speaks to his wife, Kathryn Korbon.		
Katherine Meers interviews her father, Sam Meers.		

JOURNEYS

Checking In

1. This section honors the journeys of men, women, and children from all walks of life. Certain experiences speak to us in very special ways. Which of these eleven journeys truly spoke to you? Explain what aspect of the interview resonated with you most.

Getting the Point

2. In the first conversation included in this section, Martha Conant describes how she flew away from the Denver airport and when she landed, her life had changed dramatically. In what ways did Martha Conant actively behave and think differently after the plane crash? Be specific and refer to the text.

3. In the experiences of Blanca Alvarez and Eddie Lanier is the similarity that a parent paved the way for a child's journey. Discuss how Blanca's lesson to her daughter and Eddie's lesson from his father differ in the impact they had.

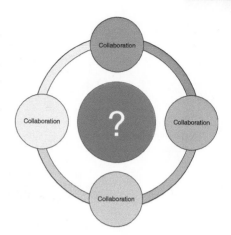

Delving Deeper

4. Consider the interviews in this section. What is a theme, or recurring idea, that you identified as you read? Where do you see evidence of that theme?

5. In a number of the stories told in this section, the speakers reveal a harrowing journey through great suffering. What seemed to be the one thing that helped guide these individuals through their experiences? Provide evidence from the text to support your answer.

6. The loss that Gregg Korbon and his wife, Kathryn Korbon, share is devastating yet, strangely, also a thing of wonder. Discuss, with references to the details of the interview, how the loss of their son could be both devastating and wondrous.

> ### Collaboration Challenge
> *Working in small groups, students should read three or four StoryCorps conversations and then select the two they want to share with the rest of the class. Alternatively, students may select two conversations to share and answer one of the questions in this section.*

The Writing Connection

In "The Road Not Taken," one of Robert Frost's most famous poems, the American poet compares life's journey to a road taken and another road not taken. Upon choosing to take the second of the two roads—one path in life—Frost writes:

> Oh, I marked the first for another day!
> Yet knowing how way leads on to way
> I doubted if I should ever come back.

This section, Journeys, reveals moments in a person's life when two paths were presented and the person's choice led him/her onward—sometimes to great joy, sometimes to devastating consequence, but always irrevocably.

Consider your life's journeys. Can you identify a point when you realized "that way leads on to way" and that a major journey had begun or, as sometimes happens, that a major journey had just ended? Describe and discuss your experience.

The Reader's Notebook

History and Struggle (10 conversations)

Conversation	Subject/Focus	Theme
Virginia Hill Fairbrother is interviewed by her daughter Laurel Kaae.		
Manny Diaz Jr. is interviewed by his friend Blanca Vasquez.		
Debra A. Fisher is interviewed by facilitator Karen Dimattia.		
Joseph L. Robertson is interviewed by his son-in-law John H. Fish Jr.		
Marie Desantis is interviewed by her daughter Mary-Lu Hayes and her grandson Mark Hayes.		
Sam Harmon is interviewed by his grandson Ezra Awumey.		
Theresa Burroughs is interviewed by her daughter Toni Love.		
Taylor Rogers speaks with his wife, Bessie Rogers.		
Tom Geerdes talks with his daughter Hannah Campbell.		
Mary Caplan is interviewed by her friend Emily Collazo.		

HISTORY AND STRUGGLE

Checking In

1. The first two interviews in History and Struggle reference a defining moment for anyone who lived through it: the Great Depression. Besides not having money, what similarity can you identify in these stories about life during the Great Depression?

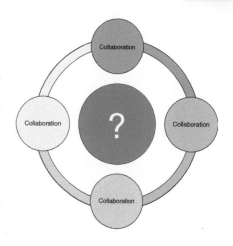

Getting the Point

2. Debra A. Fisher says, "The images that he painted for me in that room, what happened to him and his brothers and others around him, they were so horrific. I felt a part of me die." She is talking about her father's experience in the Nazi concentration camp, Auschwitz. In the very next interview, Joseph L. Robertson remembers a young man whom he had to shoot while fighting in World War II. Robertson says, "And to this day I wake up many nights crying over this kid."

    Both Fisher and Robertson are touching on one of the unspoken tragedies of war. What do you think that unspoken tragedy is? Refer to details in their stories to support your response.

> **Many Minds Review**
> *Student teams should respond to the same question. Which team will compose the most inventive but relevant response? Take the challenge!*

Delving Deeper

3. Sam Harmon and Theresa Burroughs share memories of the discrimination they faced as African Americans. Harmon and Burroughs both believed in the sanctity of an ideal while pursuing their goals. Discuss what that ideal was for Harmon and what it was for Burroughs. *Keep in mind that the ideal, or principle, is not the same for both of them.* Refer to the interviews to support your response.

4. The history of the United States is taught every year in schools across the nation. However, the place where individual lives intersect with history is rarely revealed outside of family circles. Consider the interviews of retired sanitation worker Taylor Rogers and his wife and of Vietnam veteran Tom Geerdes. What insight about historical events do they offer?

5. The final interview in History and Struggle brings us to 1986, when the AIDS epidemic had taken hold in communities across the country. Mary Caplan's description is vivid and heart-wrenching. Discuss what insight you gained from Caplan's narrative about caring for her brother and his friends.

The Writing Connection

The last lines of the conversation between Taylor and Bessie Rogers reflect Bessie's thoughts about the legacy of struggle passed on to a new generation: "They're just blessed things have really worked out good for them. A man had to come in and give his life for them." While her statement speaks directly about the struggle of the sanitation workers in Memphis, Tennessee, and the assassination of Martin Luther King Jr., it also speaks about the experiences of many of the individuals who are featured in the section History and Struggle.

Reflect on the struggles of the family members who have come before you. What sacrifices did they make so that your life might be easier? For some, the answer to this question will come easily; for others, it may not be something that you've considered. In either case, have conversations with the people in your family to find out what their history and struggles have been. As the title of this book indicates, listening is an act of love, and your asking a simple question may be the hug someone needs.

UNDERSTANDING CONTEXT: *FIRE AND WATER*

The final section of *Listening Is an Act of Love* honors the lives of those with firsthand knowledge of the events of September 11, 2001, and Hurricane Katrina in August 2005. Explore the factual record to understand these two disasters more fully. A very brief overview of the two events is provided here.

Fire

On September 11, 2001, at approximately 8:46 a.m., American Airlines Flight 11 crashed into the North Tower of the World Trade Center in New York City at a speed of 490 mph, entering the building between the 94th and 98th floors. At approximately 10:28 a.m., the North Tower collapsed.

At 9:03 a.m. United Airlines Flight 175 crashed into the South Tower of the World Trade Center at a speed of 590 mph, entering the building between the 78th and 84th floors. The South Tower collapsed at 10:58 a.m.

The loss of life from those attacks on the World Trade Center—2,759 lives—was devastating. The two interviews in the section Fire and Water cast a glimmer of light on that dark experience.

Water

Hurricane Katrina formed on August 23, 2005, and grew into one of the deadliest hurricanes to ever strike the United States. On August 29,

Hurricane Katrina hit New Orleans and left behind massive damage, hundreds of deaths, and a failing levee system. The failure of the New Orleans levees ultimately proved to be a catastrophe. Over 80 percent of New Orleans was submerged after the levees failed in the wake of the hurricane. The storm's damage was experienced primarily in Louisiana, Mississippi, and Florida. The death toll is 1,836, with over 700 people declared missing.

The essay "Hurricane Katrina: A Man-Made Disaster" offers one view of the events that led to and occurred during and after the hurricane. This reading may shed light on the events discussed in the three interviews in Fire and Water. Each interview offers a different perspective of Hurricane Katrina from the most important vantage point—that of the residents who lived through it.

Fire and Water (5 conversations)

Conversation	Subject/Focus	Theme
Richard Pecorella talks about his fiancée, Karen Juday, with facilitator Jackie Goodrich.		
Joseph Dittmar is interviewed by facilitator Rani Shankar.		
Rufus Burkhalter and Bobby Brown talk about their work.		
Douglas Paul deSilvey is interviewed by facilitator Nick Yulman.		
Kiersta Kurtz-Burke is interviewed by her husband, Justin Lundgren.		

FIRE AND WATER

Checking In

1. When you realized that this section would feature interviews related to the events of September 11, 2001, did you have any particular reaction? Prior to reading, did you feel that you already knew and understood what happened from the perspectives of the people who were there?

2. How much did you know about Hurricane Katrina before reading these interviews? What is the most surprising thing you learned about the events surrounding Hurricane Katrina?

Getting the Point

3. Richard Pecorella begins his interview by stating, "Karen Juday is my fiancée's name." How does this simple statement capture the essence of the message Pecorella wants to share? Refer to details from his interview to support your response.

Delving Deeper

4. Joseph Dittmar is a survivor of the World Trade Center's South Tower. While narrating his flight from the tower, Dittmar touches on a few ideas that have been expressed throughout the interviews in this book. Discuss one of the ideas Dittmar expresses in his interview and connect it to another interview in the book. Be specific in your explanation of the connection between the two interviews.

5. Rufus Burkhalter and Bobby Brown survived Hurricane Katrina together. Kiersta Kurtz-Burke also survived the hurricane and the floods. Beyond this feat, the three interview subjects share another bond—one that emerges only after reading about their experiences. What do you think that bond is? Offer support from the interviews to clarify and develop your answer.

6. Undeniably, Douglas Paul deSilvey suffered a terrific loss in August 2005. What message do you think he wants to share with those who read or listen to his experience? What does he say that supports your response?

The Writing Connection

Tragedies of the magnitude that occurred in New York City in 2001 and in New Orleans in 2005 do not happen often; however, tragedies of the heart know no bounds, and for the individual experiencing such pain, the tragedy is always colossal. Reflect on the experiences you have read about in Fire and Water and discuss what these individuals have shown you about the human heart. Include observations from your own life if you have additional insight into these matters.

Narrative of the Life of Frederick Douglass, an American Slave

1818–1895 Frederick Douglass

Synopsis

In 1845, when Frederick Douglass penned this autobiography, the landscape of the United States could not have been more different from today's. What links our time with the world Douglass inhabited is a yearning for the truth—the truth of the human experience as lived by someone of blood and flesh like us but of birth and circumstance so very different from ours. Frederick Douglass's narrative takes us to the core of such an experience.

Beginning with his birth in 1818 and concluding after his escape in 1838, Frederick Douglass's autobiography is a testament to the human spirit—its resilience and its weaknesses. This narrative was written during a time when Northerners and others who had not experienced or witnessed American slavery for themselves did not believe the tales of abuse and violence that contradicted the propaganda produced by slaveholders, who were active in fighting for their right to a continue a system that sustained their lifestyle. False accounts of happy slaves who worked only until noon, who received ample food and clothing, and who were treated like favored children were broadcast to those who had no idea of the truth. Douglass's autobiography, indeed his life, was a response to these misleading pictures of slavery.

Today, Frederick Douglass's narrative lives on as a tribute to the desire for freedom and the power of the written word to help achieve that freedom.

READING CONNECTIONS

"The Peculiar Institution"   This textbook selection, included in Part 2, provides an overview of the institution of slavery as a social system. The selection focuses on the time period during which Frederick Douglass reached adulthood, 1830–1860.

"Learning to Read and Write"   Chapter 3 of this textbook includes this excerpt from Douglass's autobiography. Students can become acquainted with his writing style and the themes of his narrative. In addition, Chapter 3 provides many strategies for understanding the vocabulary that Douglass uses throughout his narrative.

TECHNOLOGY TIP

Much can be found online about Frederick Douglass. A good place to begin to explore his life and times is http://www.nps.gov/archive/frdo/freddoug.html. Here you will find a link to the National Park Service's online exhibit. That link discusses his life and shares artifacts from his home. Another link provided through the site gives biographical information and historically relevant information. You are encouraged to spend some time reviewing one or both of these sites as you read the autobiography.

UNDERSTANDING CONTEXT

Frederick Douglass was born in 1818 in Maryland as Frederick Bailey. Douglass published his autobiography in 1845, about seven years after he'd escaped the grip of slavery. At the time his autobiography was published, he lived in Massachusetts with his wife and children.

In order to establish the truthfulness of his account, Douglass had to reveal his true identity and that of his former master. By doing this, Douglass risked being re-enslaved should his old master seek him out. Consequently, Douglass sailed to England when the book was published. Two supporters of Douglass raised the seven hundred dollars needed to purchase his freedom in 1846, and he returned to the United States a free man in 1847. He moved to New York shortly thereafter and began publishing his own abolitionist newspaper, *North Star.*

Frederick Douglass was neither the first nor the last former slave to publish an account of his life in slavery. His autobiography is, however, one of the most famous. During his lifetime, the book's success was a reflection of the success Douglass had as an orator. Before the abolition of slavery in 1865 by the Thirteenth Amendment to the U.S. Constitution and less formally by the Emancipation Proclamation in 1863, the abolition movement was publicized through speeches. Speeches by prominent anti-slavery speakers like Harriet Beecher Stowe (author of *Uncle Tom's Cabin*); William Lloyd Garrison, who wrote the Preface to Douglass's autobiography; and former slaves brought the message of the abolitionists to thousands of people. The former slaves who spoke at these events had to be outstanding storytellers to capture the hearts and minds of a skeptical Northern audience because many citizens found it hard to believe that slavery was as horrid and dehumanizing as former slaves and abolitionists claimed. Moreover, as Douglass lectured more frequently and his skill as an orator grew, some people began to doubt that such an eloquent speaker could have been a self-taught slave just a few years prior. It was for these reasons that Douglass risked his freedom to publish his story: he wanted to reach more people than his voice alone could. He wanted to reveal the horrors of slavery in vivid detail—and with little room for doubt as to the truthfulness of his account.

FOCUS ON STRATEGY

This autobiography is known as much for the story Douglass tells as it is for its eloquence. As you read, it may seem astounding that a man who was self-taught wrote with such precision and beauty. Indeed, Douglass uses language to paint the heart's emotions in striking detail. Note the passages where you find his language especially descriptive, for it is in those moments that the thematic power of images is evident (see Chapter 7 for a discussion of images and themes).

Character List: Keep an ongoing list of characters as you encounter them. As you read further, note which characters are major and which are minor.

Character's Name	Notes

Key Terms: Keep a list of key terms or phrases that you come across in the reading. You may also define the terms or phrases here. **Vocabulary:** Here is also a great place to note unfamiliar vocabulary that you encounter in the book.

Term/Phrase	Meaning

Term/Phrase	Meaning

Conflicts: For help in identifying the key issues of Douglass's narrative, keep track, as you read each chapter, of what appear to be conflicts or possible conflicts.

Person(s) Involved	Conflict or Problem

PREFACE AND LETTER OF SUPPORT

Checking In

Teaching a slave to read and write was prohibited, so it was no small feat for an enslaved individual to find the means to gain literacy. Even more so was it a feat to convince a skeptical Northern populace that what the formerly enslaved described in their writing was the true nature of the institution. For this reason, each narrative that was written by a former slave needed to make a case not only for abolition but also for its own authenticity. As in so many other matters during the nineteenth century, the word of a black person was not proof enough, even in establishing his/her own identity; consequently, a white person needed to vouch for the would-be author of a slave narrative. In Frederick Douglass's case, his vouchers were William Lloyd Garrison and Wendell Phillips.

Read the Preface by these two supporters of Frederick Douglass and consider their contribution to Douglass's story.

1. Do you feel that William Lloyd Garrison's telling of Douglass's growth as a speaker adds to the *Narrative*?

2. Did Wendell Phillips's letter answer any questions you had about Douglass's *Narrative*? Did it make you eager to read the *Narrative*?

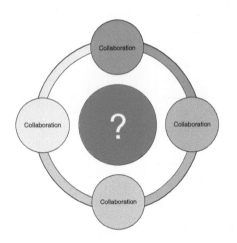

CHAPTERS 1–4

Checking In

1. The first chapter of Douglass's autobiography establishes his identity and his earliest memories. For many people, their first memories are of discovery and love, and, generally, these memories are about one's closest family members. How does Douglass's description of his earliest discoveries and memories contrast with most people's first memories?

Getting the Point

2. In each of these four chapters, Douglass touches on a common occurrence in a slave's life. What do you see as a common occurrence in these chapters? Why do you think Douglass mentions it so often?

> **Many Minds Review**
>
> *Student teams should respond to the same question for these chapters. Which team will develop the most inventive but relevant response? Take the challenge!*

3. In Chapters 2 and 3, Douglass writes about a sort of pride that slaves held. What "prides" does he mention, and how does he explain their function in slave life?

Delving Deeper

4. In the course of these first four chapters, Douglass discusses the characteristics of the overseers and masters he had known in his early years. What appear to be common characteristics of the men he describes? Be specific and refer to the text for support.

Evaluating the Author's Strategies

5. Consider the episodes that Douglass has chosen to describe in greatest detail. Select one such descriptive episode and discuss what Douglass's intent might have been when he included it in his narrative.

The Writing Connection

Consider the information Douglass has provided about the overseers and masters he knew. Also, think about people you've known or learned about who have had great power over other people. Do you think it is possible for someone to be given absolute power over other people, or even one other person, and still remain a *good* person? Whatever your response, discuss the reasons that support your view. Use examples from Douglass or elsewhere to help make your point.

CHAPTERS 5–7

Checking In

1. Chapter 5 opens with a description of the manner in which Douglass was treated while he lived on Colonel Lloyd's plantation. What detail about his life as a young slave do you find most disturbing/interesting? Explain why that detail stands out for you.

Getting the Point

2. Douglass describes his new mistress as "a woman of the kindest heart and the finest feelings" when he initially arrives in Baltimore. What changes her attitude toward him? Be specific and refer to the text.

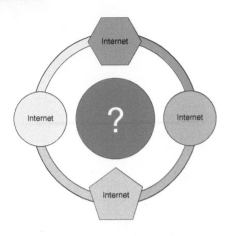

3. In Chapter 6, Douglass says, "What he most dreaded, that I most desired. What he most loved, that I most hated. That which to him was a great evil, to be carefully shunned, was to me a great good, to be diligently sought…." What is Douglass talking about in this passage, and why do he and Mr. Auld feel so differently about it? Explain your answer fully.

Delving Deeper

4. During the course of these three chapters, Douglass describes a great change in his new mistress, Mrs. Auld. He says, "slavery proved as injurious to her as it did to me." What do you think he means by this? Use details from Chapters 5–7 to support your explanation.

5. In Chapter 7, Douglass describes a deepening sadness that would sometimes overcome him. He says, "I would at times feel that learning to read had been a curse rather than a blessing." Based on his experience, do you think he would agree that slaves should not be taught to read? Use details from the text to support your response.

The Writing Connection

At the end of Chapter 5, Douglass talks about the fortunate fact of his having been sent to Baltimore. He acknowledges that had he remained at the plantation, his life would have followed a wholly different path. He also admits that he had long held "a deep conviction that slavery would not always be able to hold me within its foul embrace; and in the darkest hours of my career in slavery, this living word of faith and spirit of hope departed not from me…."

While your life has likely not mirrored Douglass's, the sentiment that he expresses—that longing and hope for a more promising future—is familiar to many. Describe a time when your journey in life seemed to be blocked at every angle, but some inner strength or hidden conviction helped pull you through.

CHAPTERS 8–9

Checking In

1. Chapter 8 reveals one of the most troubling aspects of slavery: that of enslaved men and women being treated like livestock or chattel. What impression does this scene have upon you as you imagine Frederick Douglass among those being surveyed to determine their value?

Getting the Point

2. While Douglass escapes from living under the wrath of Master Andrew, Chapter 8 reveals the types of situations most other slaves had to endure. What does Chapter 8 reveal about the fates and circumstances of most slaves? Select a specific detail or incident from the text to support your view.

Delving Deeper

3. Chapter 9 introduces the reader to another characteristic of some slaveholders: piousness. How does religion influence most of the slaveholders whom Douglass speaks about? What point do you think Douglass wants to make by focusing on this aspect?

> **Many Minds Review**
>
> *Student teams should respond to the same question for these chapters. Which team will develop the most inventive but relevant response? Take the challenge!*

Evaluating the Author's Strategies

4. While this is an autobiography, Douglass employs storytelling strategies to share his narrative. For example, the use of foreshadowing in the final pages of Chapter 9 helps to prepare the reader for what is to come next. What details are being used to foreshadow future events? What do you predict is being foreshadowed by these details?

CHAPTER 10

Checking In

1. In the early pages of Chapter 10, Douglass mentions a woman, Caroline, who is owned by Mr. Covey. How is her situation different from that of male slaves?

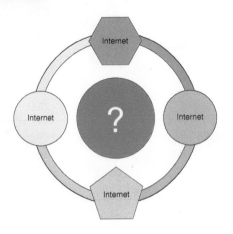

Internet Challenge

Working in small groups, select one of the questions for these chapters and search for supporting evidence or information on the Internet. Pictures, audio, maps, letters, and text are all possible Internet finds.

Getting the Point

2. What happens to Douglass during his first six months with Mr. Covey? Do you see a change in Douglass? Support your responses with details from the text.

3. When Douglass declares, "You have seen how a man was made a slave; you shall see how a slave was made a man," what did you think was about to happen? Were you surprised by what does occur later in the chapter? Why or why not?

4. Why do the other slaves join Douglass at the Sabbath day school he conducts? Do you think their masters approve of them being taught to read and write? How do you know?

Delving Deeper

5. Consider the scene where Sandy gives Douglass the root that will protect him from further whippings. Do you think Douglass believes in the root? Why or why not? Use support from the text to back up your answer.

6. According to Douglass, why do slaveholders encourage their slaves to drink excessively during the post-Christmas holiday break the slaves are given?

7. Douglass takes time in this chapter to write about the longing he feels for freedom. What images does he evoke to represent freedom? Refer to specific places in the chapter to support your answer.

8. Who do you believe revealed the plan that Douglass and the others had to escape? What details from the text support your view? Why didn't Douglass say who he and the others determined the "informant" to be?

Evaluating the Author's Strategies

9. Frederick Douglass's goal in writing his narrative was to expose slavery for the inhumane and unjustified institution that it was. After he returns to Baltimore, his attention moves from the abuse of the slaveholders to something else that he finds problematic. What is that issue, and how does Douglass tie it into his narrative?

CHAPTER 11 AND APPENDIX

Checking In

1. Reading this narrative from the vantage point of the twenty-first century, it is easy to forget that when the narrative was published, the threat of slavery was still very real to Frederick Douglass. Chapter 11 opens with a reminder of this ever-present threat. What was your reaction to Douglass's comments in the opening pages of Chapter 11?

Getting the Point

2. What happens, early in Chapter 11, that makes it clear to Douglass that a life of slavery is suitable to him no longer? Why do you think this incident bothers him so deeply?

3. If the first incident makes it clear that slavery is a chain Douglass has to break, what later incident regarding money absolutely confirms his resolve to escape? What details of this second incident tell Douglass that he must gain freedom or die from the lack of it?

Delving Deeper

4. Once Douglass is free and has made it to New Bedford, he is astonished to see how richly Northerners live. Explain the misconception that had Douglass believing that Northern whites lived as poor, nonslaveholding Southern whites lived.

Evaluating the Author's Strategies

5. Douglass devotes the Appendix of this narrative to explaining his views about religion as some slaveholders practice it. Discuss and refer to places in the narrative where Douglass highlights what he sees as the hypocrisy of religious slaveholders. Be specific and refer to the text for support.

The Writing Connection

In the Preface to this autobiography, Wendell Phillips mentions the fable "The Man and the Lion." Below is that fable. Read it and respond to the question that follows.

The Man and the Lion

Translated by George Flyer Townsend

A man and a Lion travelled together through the forest. They soon began to boast of their respective superiority to each other in strength and prowess. As they were disputing, they passed a statue, carved in stone, which represented "a Lion strangled by a Man."

The traveler pointed to it and said: "See there! How strong we are, and how we prevail over even the king of beasts."

The Lion replied: "This statue was made by one of you men. If we Lions knew how to erect statues, you would see the man placed under the paw of the Lion."

One story is good, till another is told.

What do you interpret this fable to mean? How does the Narrative of the Life of Frederick Douglass, an American Slave illustrate the theme of "The Man and the Lion"? As you respond to the question, consider the broader aims and goals Douglass had in writing his narrative. Discuss, as well, the themes that emerge in his narrative and how those themes refer to the fable, if they do.

The Kite Runner

by Khaled Hosseini

Synopsis

Two boys born a year apart, Amir and Hassan, grow up inseparable. And yet the culturally rich, tradition-bound world of Afghanistan in 1975 never allows them to truly forget the differences that set them apart.

The Kite Runner follows the lives of the boys from their childhood in Afghanistan to their adulthood in California in 2001. Amir, a poetic boy who never knew his mother, is the only son of a successful businessman. He craves his father's love and respect, but manages to get only his father's disdain. Hassan, a confident boy who is also motherless, is Amir's servant and lives in a small hut with his father when he is not serving Amir and Amir's father. The complexity of the friendship between Amir and Hassan explodes tragically in the winter of 1975 and shapes the lives of the two boys ever after.

The novel moves the reader through the secrets hidden in shadows to the very public national struggle that Afghanistan becomes embroiled in when the Russian army invades the country. Against the backdrop of a nation pulled apart by war, Amir and Hassan's story is a tale of loyalty and friendship, love and loss, acceptance and rejection, and, finally, redemption and forgiveness. The Kite

Runner is the story of a country destroyed by the passions of war, and a friendship devastated by a desire for acceptance.

READING CONNECTIONS

"What's in It for Me? Why Friendship Matters"   In this textbook reading, the role of friendship is explored. Why do we make friends? What makes a friendship last throughout a lifetime? Are the relationships of men and women different? These questions and more are explored in this reading.

"Graywolf: A Romance"   In this short story, a modern-day fairy tale is presented as a young woman reveals the relationship she has with her friend, Graywolf, who has been by her side since childhood. The idea of a friend who can see you truly, and whom you can truly see, has an unexpected twist in this delightful tale.

"Global Wealth: Three Worlds"   This textbook excerpt in Part 2 provides an overview of how the wealth of nations trickles down to the people within each nation. The reading is helpful in understanding life outside of the United States.

TECHNOLOGY TIP

To see the author's biography and other information related to his novel *The Kite Runner*, visit Khaled Hosseini's website at www.khaledhosseini.com

UNDERSTANDING CONTEXT

Khaled Hosseini's *The Kite Runner* centers on events that occur in Afghanistan. To begin to understand the events of the story, it is helpful to gather information about Afghanistan first.

To begin, research and locate one interesting fact about Afghanistan as it was prior to 2001. The events of September 11, 2001, changed the way many people think about Afghanistan and, indeed, changed the course of history in the country itself. Consequently, for the purposes of reading and understanding the events in the novel, look for information regarding Afghanistan that occurred *before* September 2001.

Share the results of your research with your instructor and other students.

Another source of contextual understanding for the pre-2001 situation in Afghanistan is the movie *Charlie Wilson's War*. This 2007 movie starring

Tom Hanks and Julia Roberts sheds light on America's covert operations in support of the Afghani's fight against the Soviet Union in the 1980s.

FOCUS ON STRATEGY

Authors have in their arsenal of writing techniques many choices for crafting the masterful tales that readers love. Khaled Hosseini uses many such techniques in *The Kite Runner*. Of particular importance is his use of foreshadowing, the technique when a writer gives hints or clues about events that may take place later in the story. For the careful reader, these inconspicuous markers sprinkled throughout the story serve as guideposts to accurate predictions.

As an active reader, look for foreshadowing as you read *The Kite Runner*. Use the active reading strategy of prediction to foresee where the story is leading. In other words, grab a hold of the kite's string and see where the wind leads you!

Character List: Keep an ongoing list of characters as you encounter them. As you read further, note which characters are major and which are minor.

Reader's Notebook

Character's Name	Notes

Key Terms: Keep a list of key terms or phrases that you come across in the reading. You may also define the terms or phrases here. **Vocabulary:** Here is also a great place to note unfamiliar vocabulary that you encounter in the novel.

Term/Phrase	Meaning

Conflicts: For help in identifying the key issues of the novel, keep track, as you read each chapter, of what appear to be conflicts or possible conflicts.

Person(s) Involved	Conflict or Problem

Person(s) Involved	Conflict or Problem

CHAPTERS 1–3

Checking In

1. Based on Chapter 1, what can you predict about the setting of *The Kite Runner*?

2. Based on Chapters 1 and 2, what can you determine about the narrative structure of *The Kite Runner*?

Getting the Point

3. The reader is introduced to Amir, the narrator, in the first chapter. What is the dominant emotion that he seems to feel in this chapter? What details support your response? Do you think this emotion will be important to what happens later? Explain your reasoning.

4. Summarize the major events of Chapters 1–3.

5. Describe three pivotal scenes that occur in these chapters. For each scene you select, be sure to discuss what happens, who is involved, and why the scene is important to the story.

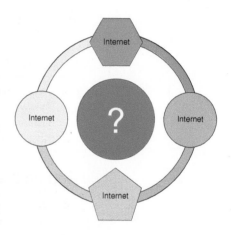

Internet Challenge

Working in small groups, select one of the questions for these chapters and search for supporting evidence or information on the Internet. Pictures, audio, maps, letters, and text are all possible Internet finds.

Delving Deeper

6. After having read Chapters 1–3, what do you know for sure about the narrative structure and setting of *The Kite Runner*? Do you think these elements are important to the novel's plot?

7. Based on all that has happened in these chapters, what do you think is a primary motivation for the young Amir? What is a primary motivation for Hassan? Explain your reasoning.

8. What do you see as an emerging theme in the novel? Discuss what statements or incidents influence your reasons for selecting this theme.

9. The last line in Chapter 3 reads, "Rahim Khan had been wrong about the mean streak thing." What do you think Amir means by this?

Evaluating the Author's Strategies

10. Why do you think the author, Khaled Hosseini, chose to end the chapter with the aforementioned statement? Explain your reasoning.

CHAPTERS 4–6

Checking In

1. Chapter 4 details the story of how Ali came to live in Baba's household. The two, Baba and Ali, grew up together. How is the relationship between Baba and Ali and that of their sons, Amir and Hassan, similar? Do you think those similarities are important to the story? Why or why not?

Getting the Point

2. Summarize the major events of Chapters 4–6.

3. Describe three pivotal scenes that occur in these chapters. For each scene you select, be sure to discuss what happens, who is involved, and why the scene is important to the story.

Delving Deeper

4. These three chapters offer further insights into the friendship of Amir and Hassan. Using details from the chapters, describe at least three of the attributes, or characteristics, of their friendship. Be specific and explain why those attributes may be important to the story.

5. Analyze the scene where Assef confronts Amir and Hassan. Discuss what the young bully represents to Amir and Hassan, and what he may represent on a larger scale.

6. What do you see as an emerging or continuing theme in the novel? Discuss what statements or incidents influence your reason(s) for selecting this theme.

Evaluating the Author's Strategies

7. At the end of Chapter 5, the reader learns that the next winter will be the one where "Hassan stopped smiling." Consequently, when Chapter 6 begins with the word "winter," the reader begins looking for what will cause Hassan's smile to disappear. However, Chapter 6 does not reveal the tragedy at the heart of this novel. What does the author choose to focus upon in Chapter 6? Why do you think that choice is made?

CHAPTERS 7–9

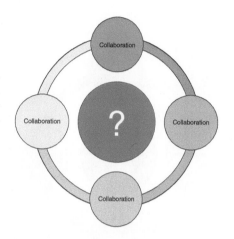

Checking In

1. In Chapter 7 the event that has seared itself upon Amir's mind is revealed. What about the incident in the alley and Amir's response surprised you most? Explain your reasoning.

2. For the first three chapters, you were asked to consider one of Amir's primary motivations. Do you see further evidence of one of those motivations in Chapter 7? What details support your view?

Getting the Point

3. Summarize the major events of Chapters 7–9.

4. Describe three pivotal scenes that occur in these chapters. For each scene you select, be sure to discuss what happens, who is involved, and why the scene is important to the story.

> **Many Minds Review**
>
> *Student teams should respond to the same question for these chapters. Which team will develop the most inventive but relevant response? Take the challenge!*

Delving Deeper

5. In what ways has Amir's betrayal of Hassan been foreshadowed? (See Focus on Strategy for a review of foreshadowing.)

6. Hassan's loyalty to Amir is pushed beyond measure. What incidents in earlier chapters hinted that this might come to pass?

7. You have been charting in your Reader's Notebook the various conflicts that arise. What conflict is resolved in these chapters? What new conflict replaces it or takes center stage? Refer to incidents or statements from Chapter 7, 8, or 9 that support your response.

Evaluating the Author's Strategies

8. The narrative of Chapter 7 is interrupted four times with memories or dreams that Amir retells. Analyze one of those episodes and discuss why the author may have chosen to include the memory or dream at that point in the narrative.

9. Chapter 8 ends with a scene from Amir's thirteenth birthday celebration. The scene has Amir watching Hassan. Review that closing scene and discuss what the scene may foreshadow.

CHAPTERS 10–12

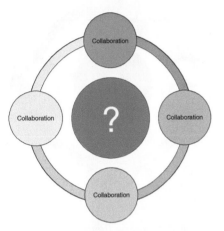

Checking In

1. Chapter 10 opens with Baba and Amir in a "tarpaulin covered cab of an old Russian truck" traveling with strangers in the middle of the night. This sudden change of setting and circumstance may be disorienting. How does reading about Amir's carsickness reacquaint the reader to the characters?

Getting the Point

2. Summarize the major events of Chapters 10–12.

3. Describe three pivotal scenes that occur in these chapters. For each scene you select, be sure to discuss what happens, who is involved, and why the scene is important to the story.

Delving Deeper

4. The majority of Chapter 10 focuses upon Baba and Amir's escape from Afghanistan. The chapter is, in a sense, a bridge from their old world to the new one awaiting them. What incidents on their journey recall their past life? What incidents give hints of what is yet to come?

5. In Chapter 11 we join Amir nearly two years since he and Baba left Afghanistan. How is Amir adjusting to his American life? How is Baba adjusting? How has their relationship shifted?

Many Minds Review

Student teams should respond to the same question. Which team will develop the most inventive but relevant response? Take the challenge!

6. Review the scenes in Chapter 12 where Amir and Soraya begin to learn about one another. What are some things that Soraya says that remind Amir of his past? Discuss something particular that Soraya says and link it to the memory it evokes for Amir.

7. Despite Baba's growing illness, why do you think Amir wants to follow tradition and have Baba ask General Taheri for Soraya's hand in marriage? Support your response with details from the chapter.

Evaluating the Author's Strategies

8. These three chapters bring about a series of life-altering circumstances for Baba and Amir. At each of these junctures, Amir is reminded of his past, try as he might to forget it. Select one of the scenes in these chapters that reflects this idea, and discuss why the author might have chosen to have Amir pulled back to his past in this way.

CHAPTERS 13–15

Checking In

1. Chapter 13 opens with a scene between Amir and Baba. What do you think is notable about this first scene?

Getting the Point

2. Summarize the major events of Chapters 13–15.

3. Describe three pivotal scenes that occur in these chapters. For each scene you select, be sure to discuss what happens, who is involved, and why the scene is important to the story.

Delving Deeper

4. Chapter 13 marks several important transitions. In doing so, it also resolves at least two conflicts. Discuss what conflicts you think are resolved in this chapter, and explain your reasoning.

5. What new conflict emerges in Chapter 13?

6. Chapter 14 opens in June 2001, and Amir has just received a call from Rahim Khan. Rahim asks Amir to come to Pakistan because he is dying. What do you think motivates Amir to go to Pakistan after all? Provide details to support your view.

7. What do you see as an emerging or continuing theme in these chapters? Discuss what statements or incidents influence your reason(s) for selecting this theme.

8. At the end of Chapter 14, Amir is thinking about something Rahim Khan said to him on the phone: "Come. There is a way to be good again." This same phrase appears in Chapter 1. What do you think Rahim means when he says that? What do you think Amir will need to do to become "good again"?

Evaluating the Author's Strategies

9. The author could have chosen many different ways of drawing Amir back to Afghanistan. Why do you think he chose to have Rahim Khan deliver the message that "there is a way to be good again"?

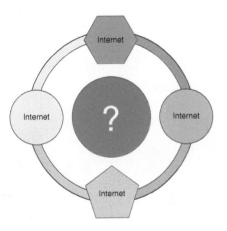

Internet Challenge

Working in small groups, select one of the questions for these chapters and search for supporting evidence or information on the Internet. Pictures, audio, maps, letters, and text are all possible Internet finds.

CHAPTERS 16–19

Checking In

1. In Chapter 16, the reader is finally told what has happened to Hassan since he left Amir and Baba's home. What do you find most surprising or unexpected in what Rahim Khan tells Amir? Why?

Getting the Point

2. Summarize the major events of Chapters 16–19.

3. Describe four pivotal scenes that occur in these chapters. For each scene you select, be sure to discuss what happens, who is involved, and why the scene is important to the story.

Delving Deeper

4. Rahim Khan makes his real request to Amir in Chapter 17. Is Amir's response to Rahim's request to bring Sohrab to Pakistan surprising? Do you think Rahim expects Amir to respond as he does? Why or why not?

5. What major conflict does Amir confront in Chapter 18? Analyze Chapter 18 and discuss whether or not the conflict is resolved.

6. Rahim Khan gives Amir an envelope that contains a photograph and a letter. The letter is from Hassan. Is there anything important about Hassan writing a letter to Amir? Discuss briefly. Use details from the novel to support your view.

7. During his journey to Afghanistan, Amir meets two brothers, Farid and Wahid. Initially, Farid believes Amir is a coward for deserting Afghanistan. Wahid, upon hearing that Amir is returning to save Sohrab, thinks Amir is a "true Afghani." Farid changes his opinion of Amir, too. Of the two views of himself, which does Amir believe is the truth about who he is? Support your response with details from the novel.

Evaluating the Author's Strategies

8. The author makes a unique choice in Chapter 16. This is the only time that the narration comes from someone other than Amir. What effect does the shift in perspective have on the way you understand the events Rahim relates? Do you think it makes a difference to have Rahim tell this story? Why or why not?

CHAPTERS 20–22

Checking In

1. "Rubble and beggars." That is how Amir describes Kabul upon returning with Farid. One of the beggars that Amir meets turns out to have known his mother, and the beggar shares information about her with Amir. Do you think this incident is important? Why or why not?

Getting the Point

2. Summarize the major events of Chapters 20–22.

3. Describe three pivotal scenes that occur in these chapters. For each scene you select, be sure to discuss what happens, who is involved, and why the scene is important to the story.

Delving Deeper

4. Amir and Farid find the orphanage where Sohrab was taken, but the boy is no longer there. A Talib official who often gives the orphanage director cash for a child has taken Sohrab. What happens to the children, like Sohrab, who are taken? Use details from the novel to support your response.

Internet Challenge

Working in small groups, select one of the questions for these chapters and search for supporting evidence or information on the Internet. Pictures, audio, maps, letters, and text are all possible Internet finds.

5. In Chapter 21 the brutality and poverty in Kabul becomes apparent to Amir. At the stadium, Amir witnesses two accused adulterers being stoned to death by the very official he seeks to meet. What does this tell Amir about the man he will soon meet?

6. During their conversation, Assef tells Amir about the beating that helped him see his true mission in life. The guard beat a kidney stone out of Assef, and Assef saw that as a sign from God that he should live. How is that idea of redemption, or being saved, later repeated in Chapter 22?

Evaluating the Author's Strategies

7. Khaled Hosseini uses the technique of circling or repetition in *The Kite Runner*. Events, situations, and behaviors repeat again and again in the characters' lives. This circling is made horrifyingly apparent in Chapter 22. Discuss what cycle you see repeating in this chapter, and analyze its significance.

CHAPTERS 23–25

Checking In

1. In Chapter 23 the reader finds Amir recovering from the brutal beating at the hands of Assef that he once escaped as a child. Throughout the novel, each completion brings with it a new beginning. What do you think will grow from Amir's encounter with violence?

Getting the Point

2. Summarize the major events of Chapters 23–25.

3. Describe three pivotal scenes that occur in these chapters. For each scene you select, be sure to discuss what happens, who is involved, and why the scene is important to the story.

Delving Deeper

4. Amir asks Farid to find Betty and Thomas Caldwell, but Farid discovers that they never existed. "Not here in Peshawar, anyhow," he says. Why do you think Rahim Khan told Amir that these nonexistent Americans would take care of Sohrab?

5. In Chapter 6, Amir asks Hassan if he would "eat dirt if I told you to." Hassan says he would, but counters by asking Amir if he would ever ask him to do such a thing. Amir says he would not. Hassan, Amir says, means everything that he says. "And that's the thing about people who mean everything

they say. They think everyone else does too," Amir acknowledges to him-self. That Amir does not always mean what he says hurts Hassan terribly. How does this same issue repeat in Chapters 23–25?

6. There is a major moment in Chapter 25 that shows a transformation has occurred within Amir regarding his cowardice. What is that transforma-tion, and how does it show a change in Amir?

Evaluating the Author's Strategies

7. Sohrab comes home with Amir and is welcomed by the family. However, neither the healing nor their journey is complete. That does not happen until March 2002, as Amir tells the reader. Analyze the final scene that takes place at Lake Elizabeth Park between Amir and Sohrab. Discuss what is important about this scene and why the author has chosen to end the book at this point.

THE WRITING CONNECTION: ESSAY TOPICS

Theme One

Throughout the novel are instances of betrayal and forgiveness. Consider these instances. What are the ways that betrayal takes place? What motivates forgiveness? Using specific incidents that supported your responses to the pre-vious questions, discuss the themes of betrayal and forgiveness as they occur in *The Kite Runner*.

Theme Two

Beginning with Baba's birth in 1933 and ending with Sohrab's rescue in 2001, the personal and political are interconnected in *The Kite Runner*. At several moments in the novel, the events of the characters' lives coincide with political and social upheavals in Afghanistan. Discuss these incidents and analyze their importance.

The Color of Water

A Black Man's Tribute to His White Mother

by James McBride

Synopsis

James McBride's memoir is a celebration of family—of mothers and fathers, brothers and sisters, and those far-flung relatives who dip into his life from time to time just when he needs them. McBride shares both his mother's and his own journey from childhood uncertainty to adult understanding. With a zigzagging narrative that begins with his mother's early life in the 1920s and 1930s and jumps to his childhood in the 1950s and 1960s, McBride carefully weaves a familial history that stretches across the Atlantic to Eastern Europe. The effects of his mother's choices show up in the day-to-day activities of McBride's own life and impact his search for answers and meaning in the face of life's challenges. McBride does not step over the more difficult aspects of his mother's life, but lets the reader share in the emotional upheavals and pitfalls that his mother recounts.

Through the frank voice of Ruth McBride Jordan, the reader learns of the regimented and lonely life she led as the eldest daughter of a traveling rabbi who settled in Virginia and opened a ramshackle store. After watching her mother wither inside a loveless marriage, Ruth left her family behind to forge ahead and build a life that encompassed two love-filled marriages. Within her two marriages, Ruth raised twelve children, all of whom cherish and love her dearly. One of those children, James, shares his memories of growing up in their large, robust family and his own search for identity as the mixed-race child of a woman who refused to be limited by social prescriptions about race or religion. *The Color of Water* is the joining of two voices, two narratives that reveal the contours of a family bursting at the seams and the woman who held it all together.

READING CONNECTIONS

"The Pied Piper of Brooklyn"   In "The Pied Piper of Brooklyn," the author examines what it's like to interact with a culture that is very different from one's own. In this story, a young secular Jewish man tries to "rescue" an adolescent girl from what he feels to be the oppressive strictures of Orthodox Judaism. The resulting escapade leaves the young man with more questions than he knows how to answer.

"The Lesson"   In "The Lesson" a tough group of city kids realizes that the world beyond their neighborhood offers more than they've ever imagined.

TECHNOLOGY TIP

James McBride, the author of *The Color of Water*, is both an acclaimed writer and an accomplished musician. To learn more about his work, visit his website, www.jamesmcbride.com, where you will find a biography, reviews of his books, information on his music, and much more. There is also a special section devoted to his mother, Ruth McBride Jordan.

Another very interesting online resource is the PBS website http://www.pbs.org/itvs/fromswastikatojimcrow/story.html. A significant portion of Ruth McBride Jordan's narrative takes place in the Virginia of the 1920s and 1930s. The social rules and restrictions Ruth discusses may be unfamiliar to some students, so the contextual history provided by PBS in *From Swastika to Jim Crow* may be very informative. *From Swastika to Jim Crow* tells the story of Jewish intellectuals who escaped persecution by Nazis in Europe and found homes and employment in the southern United States at black colleges. The connection between southern African Americans and Jewish scholars highlights both groups' struggle for freedom and equality.

UNDERSTANDING CONTEXT

A Brief History of the Jewish People
By Donald Held

Early Jewish history is shrouded in mystery. Sometime in the second millennium B.C.E. a people known later as the Israelites formed in the Middle East. They are credited for having the first monotheistic religion (belief in one God) known as Judaism and for the creation of the old testament of the bible. After the reign of King David and his son Solomon, the Israelite kingdom divided into two separate entities: Israel and Judah. Israel was destroyed in 720 B.C.E. and Judah in 586 B.C.E. when the ruling classes were carried off to Babylon. After regaining a period of independence, Judea as it was then known, was absorbed by the Roman Republic. Following a disastrous revolt in the year 69, the Romans destroyed the holy temple and dispersed the Jews throughout the known world, hence the term *Diaspora* to describe the Jewish community in its long history of wandering amongst the nations.

The European Jews have a long and storied history in Europe. Many settled in Russia and especially in Poland. In the 18th century, the ruler of Russia decreed that Jews could live only in a certain area away from the Russian heartland known as the "pale of settlement." Several million Jews were crammed in the Pale, many living in poverty in small villages known as *shtetls*. Some areas of the pale included what would later become the independent nation of Poland in 1918. Because of the poverty and oppression they experienced, Jews migrated in record numbers to the United States in the 19th and 20th centuries.

Daily life in Judaism is regulated in its every facet by the Torah, (the first five books of the bible), the written law, and its interpretation by qualified religious authorities known as rabbis. Every aspect of daily life is regulated: dietary, relations between the sexes, worship, and personal ethical behavior. Though many Rabbis garnered tremendous prestige in the community because of their learning and piety, there were some who found it difficult to make a living and whose learning might not have been up to standards.

Judaism, in the words of Mordechai Kaplan, is an "evolving religious civilization," meaning that the varied history of the Jewish people is expressed through its religion. The traditional Jewish orthodox culture described in *The Color of Water* is just one of many cultures of the evolving civilization known as Judaism. There are many other communities with their own distinct cultures in Arab countries, the Mediterranean lands and even in far away Central Asia. Today there are many forms of the religion, some of which are particularly well represented in the United States. Reform, Reconstructionist and Conservative Judaism vie with the more traditional varieties for the allegiance of American Jews.

A few definitions:

Shiva is the traditional period of mourning after the death of a loved one. To "sit Shiva" refers to the first 7 days after death when one sits on a low stool or box to show one's bereaved state. Mourning is divided into 7, thirty-day and one-year periods with severity of observance decreasing with time. It is appropriate for the loved one's family members to say the *Kadish* prayer for the deceased. Curiously, the text of the *Kadish* prayer does not mention death or the afterlife.

Kosher is the system of dietary laws also known as Kashrus. It calls for a separation of meat and dairy and necessitates separate dishes, tableware, and cooking utensils. It also requires humane slaughtering of animals as prescribed by traditional religious law known as *Halakah*. The blood must be drained away from the carcass and the meat salted. Jewish dietary laws and the Torah forbid eating pork, shellfish, and carrion of any kind.

The *Holy Sabbath* or *Shabbat* in Hebrew enjoins Jews to refrain from work on the 7th day, the day according to the Torah (see Genesis chapters 1 and 2) in which God rested from his creation. As practiced by the strictly observant, it forbids any kind of work, automobile driving, handling of money, and kindling fire. Under certain conditions the laws of the Sabbath are set aside, as for example when saving a life.

Jewish tradition requires a strict separation of men and women with sharply defined roles in the Synagogue and home. Rules under the term "modesty" circumscribe dress and require a married woman's hair to be covered with a scarf or a wig, as is often the case with many Hasidim or Hasidic Jews.

According to Jewish tradition, God speaks Hebrew with the angels and wrote the Torah himself in Hebrew, although the Torah nowhere explicitly states this. Thus, Hebrew, the ancient language of the Israelites is the "holy tongue" for prayer and Torah study. Yiddish is a Germanic language developed by the European Jews and spoken by them in their daily life. The primary language of many Jewish immigrants to the United States in the 19th and 20th centuries, it is rarely spoken now. The Holocaust, which saw the demise of 6 million Jews in Nazi occupied Europe, effectively ended Yiddish as a living, spoken language in Europe.

Svartzer is the Yiddish noun for "black." Though in itself it is not an offensive word, when it is used to describe African-Americans it has become so and can be considered derogatory. Like many Yiddish words (chutzpah, nosh, schlep) it has made its way into the American lexicon.

In summation, Judaism has continued to enrich American cultural life going forward. In the words of Steven L. Pease:

> The huge premium Jews have placed on education, on rearing strong families, their push for innovation and entrepreneurship, tolerance for differing opinions, accountability for one's performance in this life, and their sense of duty to help make the world better (tikkun olam) are but a tiny sample of cultural values that they have added to our melting pot.[1]

Donald Held is a history professor, freelance typesetter, and marathon runner. He lives in Long Beach, New York with his wife, Angela, and their two cats, Gina and Hank.

FOCUS ON STRATEGY

As the writer of a memoir, James McBride has carefully selected which aspects of his life to share. Not only must he present the events that he does share in a way that typifies his life, but he must also create connections from one event to another. This is one challenge of a writer—weaving a complete story from various parts. One of the ways that McBride con-

---

[1] Steven L. Pease, a venture capitalist and community activist, is the author of *The Golden Age of Jewish Achievement: The Compendium of a Culture, a People, and Their Stunning Performance.*

nects the various parts of both his life and his mother's is through use of symbols. For example, commonplace objects that one might encounter in everyday life take on greater significance within McBride's narrative. These commonplace objects symbolize an emotional truth or struggle with which McBride or his mother is dealing.

As you read *The Color of Water*, pay special attention to everyday objects that seem to represent more than is at first apparent. Often these objects will be mentioned more than once in the memoir.

Name List: Keep an ongoing list of family and friends as you encounter them in the book. As you read, note which people are important to the main characters and which are not.

Reader's Notebook

Name	Notes

Key Terms: Keep a list of key terms or phrases that you come across in the reading. You may also define the terms or phrases here. **Vocabulary:** Here is also a great place to note unfamiliar vocabulary and culturally specific terms that you encounter in the book.

Term/Phrase	Meaning

Symbols: For help in identifying the key issues of McBride's memoir, keep track of what appear to be symbols of a theme or emotional conflict.

Symbol	Thematic Meaning or Emotional Conflict

Symbol	Thematic Meaning or Emotional Conflict

CHAPTERS 1–4

Checking In

1. Ruth McBride Jordan's narrative begins with her saying that she is dead. The reader soon learns that her first family considers her dead. What mistake or failure do you think is great enough that a family might treat someone as if he or she were dead?

Getting the Point

2. In Chapter 1, the reader learns the basics of Ruth's family, and Chapter 3 goes further into her life. Discuss one aspect of Ruth's family life that you found interesting and explain why it stood out for you.

3. The author of the memoir, James McBride, is Ruth's son. In Chapter 2, the reader begins to learn about his life with her in New York. Which aspect(s) of James's family do you find unique?

Delving Deeper

4. Ruth discusses the way her family lived in Europe. What is a recurring issue in her memories of life in the old country? Refer to the book to explain your response.

5. At the end of Chapter 3, Ruth talks about her fears of being buried alive and of being in tight spaces. Analyze this fear in relation to what she has described about her family life in Virginia and suggest possible interpretations.

6. In Chapter 4, James says, "Conflict was a part of our lives, written into our very faces, hands and arms, and to see how contradiction lived and survived in its essence, we had to look no farther than our own mother."

Internet Challenge

Working in small groups, select one of the questions for these chapters and search for supporting evidence or information on the Internet. Pictures, audio, maps, letters, and text are all possible Internet finds.

What do you think James is talking about here? How is conflict written on his skin?

Evaluating the Author's Strategies

7. The author alternates between his narrative and his mother's narrative. What effect does this have on you as a reader? Is one narrative more interesting or powerful than the other, in your view?

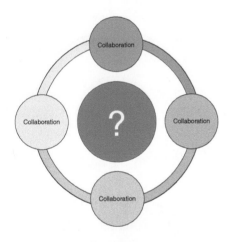

Many Minds Review

Student teams should respond to the same question. Which team will develop the most inventive but relevant response? Take the challenge!

CHAPTERS 5–8

Checking In

1. What is your first impression of the title of Chapter 5? Why do you think the author chose that title for this chapter?

Getting the Point

2. What is the feeling that most characterizes Ruth's childhood once her family settles in Suffolk? Explain your choice.

3. What is a behavior or practice that carries over from Ruth's childhood to her method of raising her children?

Delving Deeper

4. In Chapters 7 and 8, Ruth and James, respectively, talk about their siblings. In both recollections, a similar theme emerges. Discuss a theme you've identified in these chapters and refer to the text to support your interpretation.

Evaluating the Author's Strategies

5. The difference between an autobiography and a memoir lies in the focus of the book. An autobiography recounts a person's entire life generally. A memoir is focused on a select period in time during which something memorable occurred for the author. *The Color of Water* is a memoir. What or who is the focus of this memoir and how can you be sure? Consider the titles of the chapters and their organization to help you think about and answer this question.

CHAPTERS 9–12

Checking In

1. Chapter 9 opens with Ruth's memories of school. Do you find the poor treatment she experienced in school surprising? Why or why not?

Getting the Point

2. Why does James struggle so hard to understand who he is? What makes his identity so confusing to him?

3. In Chapter 10, what point does the author make by sharing the memory about the storeowner and the spoiled milk?

Delving Deeper

4. What circumstances made it likely that Ruth would fall in love with Peter? Be specific and refer to the text to support your analysis.

5. In Chapter 12, James recounts the life and death of his step-father, Hunter Jordan. What theme links this chapter to the previous one (Chapter 11), in which his mother falls in love for the first time?

The Writer's Connection

The Color of Water is a celebration of James McBride's mother. However, it is also a tribute to fathers. Consider the role Hunter Jordan plays in Ruth's family, and then write about the role that fathers, in general, hold in family life. Has it changed over the last few decades? Has it grown more important or less important?

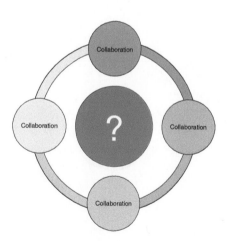

CHAPTERS 13–16

Checking In

1. Ruth's mother sends her to New York City to stay with her sisters and grandmother. Is Ruth's view of New York similar to your perception of the famous city?

> ### Many Minds Review
> *Student teams should respond to the same question for these chapters. Which team will compose the most inventive but relevant response? Take the challenge!*

Getting the Point

2. How are the lives of Ruth's aunts different from Ruth's and her mother's lives?

Delving Deeper

3. What lesson do you think James learns from Chicken Man and the other men from the corner? Be specific and refer to the text.

4. What is the primary theme or issue of Chapter 16? What details support your view?

The Writer's Connection

Within Chapters 13–16, both James and his mother travel away from home, James to the country and his mother to the city. Have you ever spent a significant amount of time, such as a few months or years, in a place that differs from your permanent home? Write about the impact that living elsewhere had upon your life.

If you have not traveled, think about a time when someone traveled to your home and whether or not that person or visit had an impact on you and your family.

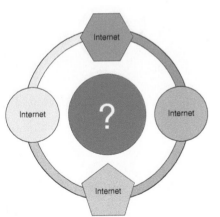

CHAPTERS 17–20

Checking In

1. In Chapter 17, Ruth leaves her aunt's factory in search of something new in Harlem. Why do people react so oddly to Ruth's requests for a job?

Getting the Point

2. Why do Ruth and her children move to Delaware?

3. What challenges does the family face once they are in Delaware? Be specific and refer to the text.

Delving Deeper

4. If Ruth had kept her promise to her sister Dee-Dee in Chapter 19, what might her life have been like? Why didn't Ruth keep her promise to Dee-Dee? Use details from the text to support your response.

Internet Challenge

Working in small groups, select one of the questions for these chapters and search for supporting evidence or information on the Internet. Pictures, audio, maps, letters, and text are all possible Internet finds.

5. Given all the information in the previous chapters and in Chapter 20, what can you say about Ruth's father and how he treated his family? Use details from the text to support your interpretation.

Evaluating the Author's Strategies

6. In Chapter 20, James learns that his mother had been called "Rachel" in her youth. What other names has his mother had? Discuss how his mother's various names reflect on her personal journey as it is recounted here in this memoir.

CHAPTERS 21–23

Checking In

1. Chapter 21 is titled "A Bird Who Flies." If you could add a word or words to the end of that title, what would you add? Base your addition on what occurs in Chapter 21.

Getting the Point

2. James has returned to his mother's town of Suffolk for the second time in 1992. He speaks of the clues he found to his mother's old life. What stopped him from attempting to find his aunt, his mother's sister Dee-Dee?

Delving Deeper

3. Why does James become so emotional at the end of Chapter 22?

4. In Chapter 23, Ruth finally shares her memories about life with James's father, Andrew Dennis McBride. Using evidence from this chapter, explain how Ruth's relationship with Dennis changed her life. Be specific and refer to the text.

Evaluating the Author's Strategies

5. *The Color of Water* is nearly at its end before the reader hears the story of Ruth's first marriage. What reason(s) might the author have for telling this story so late in the book?

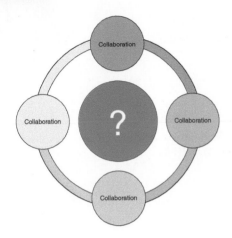

CHAPTERS 24 & 25

Checking In

1. Consider the title of Chapter 24. What is the title referring to? What else could the title mean?

Getting the Point

2. In Chapter 24, James explains why his mother rarely spoke about his father, Dennis. What is the reason?

3. Why was Ruth displeased with the new minister of New Brown?

Many Minds Review

Student teams should respond to the same question for these chapters. Which team will develop the most inventive but relevant response? Take the challenge!

Delving Deeper

4. Chapter 25 is titled "Finding Ruthie," but could just as well be titled "Finding James." Explain why this chapter could also be titled "Finding James."

5. Discuss how James's search for his own identity is linked to his mother's identity.

The Writer's Connection

Many themes emerge in *The Color of Water*. Discuss two themes and show how they are reflected in the experiences of James McBride and his mother, Ruth.

Three Cups of Tea

One Man's Mission to Promote Peace…One School at a Time

by Greg Mortenson and David Oliver Relin

The Korphe School

Synopsis

Greg Mortenson traveled to the most dangerous mountain in the world with one goal in mind: to conquer it. Mortenson spent months scaling the rocks of Pakistan's K2 only to find himself depleted and unable to make the final push to the top of the world's second-highest mountain. As he made his way down from the high altitudes of K2, he lost his way and stumbled into a small village called Korphe. The kindness and care that the village chief and his family showed to Mortenson left a deep impression on him. In fact, Mortenson pledged to return and give back to the village by building a school for the village's children.

Mortenson's promise turned into the most important commitment he had ever made. Over the ensuing ten years, Mortenson would not only build a school for Korphe's children, but would also build schools for thousands of children in the impoverished but culturally rich villages of northern Pakistan. Greg Mortenson had lost his chance to scale one mountain, but had found a way to climb a much higher summit—that of compassion. Mortenson's efforts to build schools in the complicated and increasingly dangerous outer ranges of Pakistan reveal the tenacity and depth of one man's desire to combat poverty and ignorance with the lasting hope of education. *Three Cups of Tea* is an adventure tale, a story of redemption, and a lesson of love. It is also a testament to the power of compassion and love when championed by a gentle man who knows how to keep a promise.

READING CONNECTIONS

"Building Safe Schools for Girls in War Zones"   This article, included in Chapter 2, offers a post-2006 view of the work that Greg Mortenson has produced. The article discusses the publication of the book *Three Cups of Tea* and a few of Mortenson's and his organization's successes and achievements for the children of Pakistan and Afghanistan.

"Global Wealth: Three Worlds"   This textbook excerpt from Part 2 provides an overview of how the wealth of nations impacts the lives of the people within each nation. The reading is helpful in understanding some of the issues faced by those living outside the United States and other economically wealthy nations.

TECHNOLOGY TIP

Greg Mortenson's book *Three Cups of Tea* has received worldwide acclaim. The website for this book, www.threecupsoftea.com, has a number of valuable resources for the curious reader. In addition to interviews with Mortenson are descriptions of his other books and ways to get involved in his organization.

More information about his organization, the Central Asia Institute, can be found on the website www.ikat.org

UNDERSTANDING CONTEXT

Much of the action in *Three Cups of Tea* takes place in northern Pakistan. The authors provide a map of the area of Pakistan under discussion, but it would be helpful for students to investigate the region on their own. In particular, students may want to research the Karakoram Range, where the world's second-highest and most dangerous mountain, K2, rises into the sky. The images of the Karakoram Range, and other locations in Pakistan that are featured in the book, reveal much more than words and maps can convey.

FOCUS ON STRATEGY

Greg Mortenson and journalist David Oliver Relin wrote *Three Cups of Tea*. The story told within the book's pages is Mortenson's, but Relin molded Mortenson's narrative so that he could share it with the world. Consequently, the book has the features of a memoir, a nonfiction narrative, and a biography. As you read, pay particular attention to the ways that Relin uses narrative techniques to create suspense, journalistic exposition to discuss historical and future events, and direct quotations and dialogue to convey voice and emotion. These elements and others are highlighted in the study questions titled "Evaluating the Author's Strategies."

Reader's Notebook

Character List: Keep an ongoing list of the people Mortenson meets in his travels. As you read further, note which people are major players and which are not.

Person's Name	Notes

Key Terms: Keep a list of key terms or phrases that you come across in the reading. You may also define the terms or phrases here. **Vocabulary:** Here is also a great place to note unfamiliar vocabulary and foreign words that you encounter in the book.

Term/Phrase	Meaning

Conflicts: For help in identifying the key issues of the book, keep track, as you read each chapter, of what appear to be conflicts or challenges.

Person(s) Involved	Conflict or Challenge

Person(s) Involved	Conflict or Challenge

CHAPTERS 1–4

Checking In

1. Before you began reading this book, did you know anything about mountain climbing? If not, what is the most surprising aspect of mountain climbing you discovered?

Getting the Point

2. In the first chapter Mortenson is lost. How does he get so lost and in such a weakened physical state?

3. Who is Mouzafer and why is he so able to handle the rigors of mountain climbing?

Delving Deeper

4. In Chapter 3, Mortenson realizes that he wants to give back to Haji Ali and the village of Korphe. What else drives him to dedicate himself to building a school for the children? Use details from the text to support your response.

5. How did Mortenson's family history prepare him for the undertaking he will attempt in Korphe?

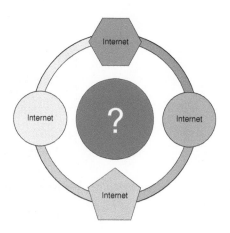

Internet Challenge

Working in small groups, select one of the questions for these chapters and search for supporting evidence or information on the Internet. Pictures, audio, maps, letters, and text are all possible Internet finds.

Evaluating the Author's Strategies

6. In these first few chapters, the author uses a narrative technique called flashback, the technique in which the narration is interrupted by a memory that is often influential to the present circumstance—although its relevance may not be initially obvious.

   Locate a flashback in these chapters and discuss how the flashback enhances or is relevant to Mortenson's situation in the story's present.

CHAPTERS 5–8

Checking In

1. The opening of Chapter 5 has Mortenson planning to write five hundred letters asking for money to build the Korphe school. What did you initially think about his plan to raise the money? Did you think he would be successful? Why or why not?

Getting the Point

2. How long does it take Mortenson to compose the first three hundred letters? What type of issues does he encounter while typing and writing those first three hundred letters?

3. Discuss two of the lucky breaks Mortenson receives during Chapter 5. Explain what Mortenson did to have these opportunities arrive in his life.

Delving Deeper

4. Mortenson is not the first mountain climber to dedicate himself to building schools for children. What other famous mountain climber did so as well, and how does that man's experience building schools compare to Mortenson's?

5. Chapters 6, 7, and 8 show Mortenson immersed in Pakistani culture as he gathers materials to build the Korphe school. What incidents in these chapters demonstrate important aspects of Mortenson's character? Discuss why you identify those aspects as important.

The Writing Connection

Within the book as a whole, and these chapters in particular, children play a significant role in Mortenson's life. Discuss the ways that children impact Mortenson as he works to build the school. Also discuss the way in which children are important to this story overall.

CHAPTERS 9–12

Checking In

1. After Mortenson leaves Korphe knowing that he has to raise money to build a bridge, did you think he would be angry at all he had to do?

Getting the Point

2. In Chapter 9 Mortenson hits a very low point in his journey. What saddens him and how does he recover?

3. Even though Mortenson knows that building a bridge will help the village of Korphe, why does he worry that it may harm them in the long run?

Delving Deeper

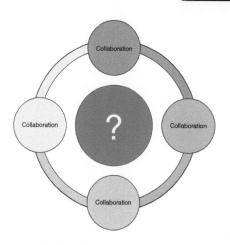

4. As the reader learns about the progress Mortenson makes in building the Korphe school, the reader also learns the characteristics of the Balti culture. Discuss a cultural lesson that Mortenson learns and how it impacts his efforts to build the school.

5. Throughout these chapters are several instances where a person shows his or her commitment to an idea or cause greater than his or her own needs or desires. Discuss one example of someone (other than Mortenson) who expresses a commitment to a principle or idea.

Evaluating the Author's Strategies

6. While narrating Mortenson's efforts to build the Korphe school and keep his life together, Relin occasionally includes the voices of people who have met Greg Mortenson. Locate an instance where a third party offers commentary on Mortenson's mission, and discuss what this third-party input offers to the account.

CHAPTERS 13–16

Checking In

1. Chapter 13 opens with a description of the Waziri people of northern Pakistan. The chapter then goes on to describe the rise of the Taliban in

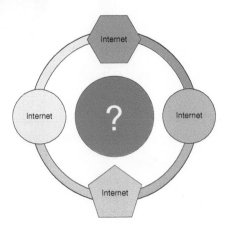

Internet Challenge

Working in small groups, select one of the questions for these chapters and search for supporting evidence or information on the Internet. Pictures, audio, maps, letters, and text are all possible Internet finds.

Afghanistan and the arrival of Osama Bin Laden, also in Afghanistan. What purpose does this information serve? How did this information affect you as a reader?

Getting the Point

2. What happens to Mortenson in Chapter 13 that changes the way he does business in Pakistan? Support your response with details from the text.

3. Discuss the two major turning points that occur in Chapter 14 and explain their importance to Greg Mortenson's life and mission.

4. Two terms are used repeatedly in Chapter 15: *fatwa* and *infidel*. Define these terms in the context of this book. Also, explain how the two terms relate to Mortenson.

Delving Deeper

5. In the later chapters of this section, the breadth of the work Mortenson undertakes in Pakistan grows. Explain what ambition or idea seems to motivate Mortenson and the Central Asia Institute (CAI) to take on a project. Provide details or an example from the text to support your view.

The Writing Connection

As noted near the end of Chapter 16, Greg Mortenson makes changes in the CAI schools after attending a conference on development. Mortenson says that unlike boys, who leave home after being educated, girls "… stay home, become leaders in the community, and pass on what they've learned. If you really want to change a culture, to empower women, improve basic hygiene and health care, and fight high rates of infant mortality, the answer is to educate the girls."

Using the quotation as a starting point, write about the impact that an education can have in the lives, families, and communities of impoverished women. Consider researching organizations, like the CAI, that have made a commitment to educate women in undeveloped areas to support your discussion.

CHAPTERS 17–20

Checking In

1. Chapter 17 opens with Fatima Batool's experience during the fighting between Pakistan and India in 1999. Why do you think the chapter begins this way?

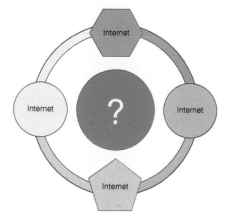

Getting the Point

2. According to Chapter 18, what are some of the challenges that Mortenson faces when he is home in the United States? How does he handle those challenges?

3. What details in Chapter 19 prove to be crucial indicators of the coming trouble that erupts with the September 11 terrorist attacks?

Delving Deeper

4. After Mortenson finds out that his dear friend Haji Ali has died, he takes a moment to "listen to the wind." What Mortenson hears are the children at the Korphe school. He tells himself to always "think of them." What do you think that means? How is that thought—to "think of them"—important for Mortenson as he navigates the post-9/11 world of Pakistan?

> ### Internet Challenge
> *Working in small groups, select one of the questions for these chapters and search for supporting evidence or information on the Internet. Pictures, audio, maps, letters, and text are all possible Internet finds.*

Evaluating the Author's Strategies

5. Throughout the chapters of *Three Cups of Tea*, the authors create moments that reflect back on earlier moments. This is accomplished through recurring descriptions, repeated situations, and narrative techniques. Consider, for example, Chapter 20, which ends with Mortenson being introduced to a packed crowd of supporters. What scene in Chapters 17–19 does this moment reflect upon? Explain how the moment at the end of Chapter 20 revisits that earlier scene, and discuss what has changed since the earlier scene.

CHAPTERS 21–23

Checking In

1. In your view, how do the 9/11 attacks and the war in Afghanistan affect the way people view the work Mortenson has accomplished in Pakistan? Do you think Mortenson handles people's opinions appropriately?

Getting the Point

2. When Mortenson travels to Kabul, Afghanistan, he meets a female teacher who has a strong impact upon him. What does this teacher say and do that makes an impression on Mortenson?

3. After returning to the United States and having a chance encounter with Mary Bono, a congressional representative, Mortenson has the opportunity to speak about his mission on Capitol Hill. When he is offered millions from the U.S. military to build schools, why doesn't he accept it?

Delving Deeper

4. At the end of Chapter 22, Jahan, the first woman to be educated in Korphe, says, "I want to be a ... Superlady." What is significant about this statement? What do you think Jahan means by "superlady"? Refer to details from the text to support your response.

The Writing Connection

In the final pages of Chapter 23, Mortenson discusses the prospect of building schools with *Commandhan* Sadhar Khan. Mortenson's experience on Sadhar Khan's rooftop is described as follows:

> This rooftop, surrounded by these harsh, stony hills, was a fork where he had to choose his way. And if he turned in the direction of this man, and these stones, he could see the path ahead painted more vividly than the decade-long detour he'd begun one distant day in Korphe.

Considering this paragraph and the other closing passages of the book, discuss what you believe to be the path that Mortenson sees ahead of him. Discuss, as well, how you feel this path may be different from or similar to his previous experiences.

Text Credits

Chapter 1

page 9: Sherman Alexie, "Superman and Me". Copyright (c) 1998 Sherman Alexie. All rights reserved; **page 22:** CICCARELLI, SAUNDRA; WHITE, J. NOLAND, PSYCHOLOGY: AN EXPLORATION, 1st,©2010. Printed and Electronically reproduced by permission of Pearson Education, Inc., Upper Saddle River, New Jersey.

Chapter 2

page 24: Jean Folkerts, Stephen Lacy, Ann Larabee, The Media in Your Life: An Introduction to Mass Communication, 2008. Used by permission of Pearson Education; **page 36:** Jacqueline Vogtman, "A Story I'll Tell You When You're Big," Vestal Review, 2010. Used by permission of the author.

Chapter 3

page 71, 72: From NEW AMERICAN WEBSTER'S HANDY COLLEGE DICTIONARY by Philip D. Morehead and Andrew T. Morehead, copyright 1951 (renewed), (c) 1955, 1956, 1957, 1961 by Albert H. Morehead, 1972, 1981, 1985, 1995 by Philip D. Morehead and Andrew T. Morehead. Used by permission of Dutton Signet, a division of Penguin Grop (USA) Inc.; **page 86:** Copyright (c) 1992 by Stephanie Ericsson. Reprinted by the permission of Dunham Literary as agents for the author. Originally published by The Utne Reader.

Chapter 4

page 98: GOSHGARIAN, GARY J; KRUEGER, KATHLEEN, DIALOGUES: AN ARGUMENT RHETORIC AND READER, 7th,©2011. Printed and Electronically reproduced by permission of Pearson Education, Inc., Upper Saddle River, New Jersey; **page 100:** Jean Folkerts, Stephen Lacy, Ann Larabee, The Media in Your Life: An Introduction to Mass Communication, 2008. Used by permission of Pearson Education; **page 107:** HEWITT, PAUL G.; LYONS, SUZANNE A; SUCHOCKI, JOHN A.; YEH, JENNIFER, CONCEPTUAL INTEGRATED SCIENCE, 1st,©2007. Printed and Electronically reproduced by permission of Pearson Education, Inc., Upper Saddle River, New Jersey; **page 109:** HEWITT, PAUL G.; LYONS,

Chapter 5

Chapter 6

Chapter 7

MYTHOLOGY by Edith Hamilton. Copyright (c) 1942 by Edith Hamilton; Copyright (c) renewed 1969 by Dorian Fielding Reid and Doris Fielding Reid. By permission of Little, Brown and Company; **page 210:** Andrew Lam, "The Palmist," Manoa, 16:2, 2004. Used by permission of Andrew Lam. Andrew Lam is author of "Perfume Dreams" Reflections on the Vietnamese Diaspora" and "East Eats West: Writing in Two Hemispheres."; **page 217:** Used by permission of the author; **page 222:** CROSS, GARY; SZOSTAK, RICK, TECHNOLOGY AND AMERICAN SOCIETY, 2nd,©2005. Printed and Electronically reproduced by permission of Pearson Education, Inc., Upper Saddle River, New Jersey.

Chapter 8

page 235: Reprinted with permission from the Natural Resources Defense Council; **page 242:** Maia Szalavitz, Excerpt from "The Trouble With Troubled Teen Programs," Reason, January 2007. Used by permission; **page 245:** Used by permission of the author; **page 252:** Used by permission of Red and Black; **page 256:** Mike Rose, Why School? Reclaiming Education For All of Us, New Press, 2009. Used by permission.

Part 2

page 287: John Cloud, "Why Exercise Won't Make You Thin," Copyright TIME INC. Reprinted by permission. TIME is a registered trademark of Time Inc. All rights reserved; **page 295:** From NEW AMERICAN WEBSTER'S HANDY COLLEGE DICTIONARY by Philip D. Morehead and Andrew T. Morehead, copyright 1951 (renewed), (c) 1955, 1956, 1957, 1961 by Albert H. Morehead, 1972, 1981, 1985, 1995 by Philip D. Morehead and Andrew T. Morehead. Used by permission of Dutton Signet, a division of Penguin Grop (USA) Inc.; **page 300:** Used by permission of Salvatore Fichera; **page 305:** HENSLIN, JAMES M., SOCIOLOGY: A DOWN-TO-EARTH APPROACH, 10th,©2010. Printed and Electronically reproduced by permission of Pearson Education, Inc., Upper Saddle River, New Jersey; **Page 315–316:** From NEW AMERICAN WEBSTER'S HANDY COLLEGE DICTIONARY by Philip D. Morehead and Andrew T. Morehead, copyright 1951 (renewed), (c) 1955, 1956, 1957, 1961 by Albert H. Morehead, 1972, 1981, 1985, 1995 by Philip D. Morehead and Andrew T. Morehead. Used by permission of Dutton Signet, a division of Penguin Grop (USA) Inc.; **page 321:** "The Lesson", copyright © 1972 by Toni Cade Bambara, from GORILLA, MY LOVE by Toni Cade Bambara. Used by permission of Random House, Inc.; **page 331:** WILSON, R. JACKSON; GILBERT, JAMES; KUPPERMAN, KAREN ORDAHL; NISSENBAUM, STEPHEN; SCOTT, DONALD M., PURSUIT OF LIBERTY, VOLUME I, THE, 3rd,©1996. Printed and Electronically reproduced by permission of Pearson Education, Inc., Upper Saddle River, New Jersey; **page 379:** David Winner, "The Pied Piper of Brooklyn." Used by permission of the author; **page 347:** LEMME, BARBARA HANSEN,

Photo Credits

Index